NEW ENGLAND STRIPERS

W9-BWD-964

A FISHING ANTHOLOGY

Printed in the U.S.A.

ISBN# 0-9706538-3-2

10 9 8 7 6 5 4 3 2 1

Chris Megan, Publisher
Neal Larsson, General Manager
Gene Bourque, Editor
Elizabeth Scanland, Copy Editor
Bill Hough, Contributing Publisher
Book and cover design by Andy Nabreski

Cover Photograph by Ethan Gordon
www.ethangordon.com

The photo on the back cover is of Neil Cordeiro, circa 1968.
-photo courtesy of Riverview Bait & Tackle, South Yarmouth, MA

Contributing Writers:

LARRY BACKMAN • DAVE BEAUMONT • LEO BEDARD • GENE BOURQUE • BILL BRETT

CHARLES E. CINTO • ALAN CORDTS • CAPTAIN DAVID DECASTRO • AL DELDOTTO

CAPTAIN MIKE HOGAN • CARL A. JOHANSEN • JEFFREY JOINER • FRED KHEDOURI • DAVE LAPORTE

JOE LYONS • DAVE MANZI • JANET MESSINEO • DAVE PEROS • DAVID PICKERING • THOM PELLETIER

RON POWERS • AL RAYCHARD • BOB SAMPSON JR. • STEVE SHIRAKA • JOHN D. SILVA

ROBERT SIROIS • JOHN SKINNER • CAPTAIN CHARLEY SOARES • CAPTAIN BEN TRIBKEN

An **On The Water** Publication

INTRODUCTION

The wind had dropped off to less than three knots, allowing the ebb tide to take hold of the 17-foot Montauk, pushing us in and out of trouble along a minefield of boulders. The sun had set hours before, giving way to a glorious but stark hunter's moon, a welcome companion at that point in the season. We had set out from Woods Hole with a bucket of eels, a couple of light-tackle rods, a half-dozen pre-tied leaders and a small, beat-up cooler with some essentials to fish the night tide. The ride out along the Elizabeth Islands brought back memories of my childhood, bombing down narrow country roads on our bikes at midnight, with nothing but the moon to guide us. The cool pockets of air that hung in the night reminded me that autumn was creeping in with each passing sunset. Swept in with the crisp air swam opportunity in the form of big fish migrating south.

The end of our run came just past Henry Frank's rock off Pasque Island, when my good friend Bill Hough cut back on the engine, slipping the boat into neutral. Bill had introduced me to most of these waters, and over the years I had worked hard to learn how to fish them. I immediately sprang to the bow as we glided softly into the shallows. It was my responsibility to spot the big rocks, the hull eaters, the ones that might have a huge bass lurking behind them. The signs were there if you read the water. We would follow the current and it would lead us to fish. Bill cut the engine completely and proceeded to lift the engine to about a 45-degree angle. The engine would still act as a rudder but was now free from most of the trouble we could encounter from below.

We had fished together enough that few words were spoken as we went about rigging up with live eels, a favorite offering for stripers. By the time Bill turned to the eel bucket, I was out of his way, moving back to the bow, about to launch the first cast toward the cobble beach. With the running lights off, it wasn't long before our night vision took over. If you have never fished at night under a clear, moonlit sky, you haven't lived. Stars fill the sky in all directions while the moon highlights waves cresting and breaking, giving indications of tide, current and wind direction. The fish had to be nearby; we just had to find them.

It wasn't long before Bill gave the slightest of gestures that both of us had been waiting for. The dropping of his rod tip from 11 o'clock to 8 said it all. I continued to slowly retrieve my eel while fixated on Bill's line, which was peeling off.

"Good fish?" I asked quietly. "I think so. . . ." he answered in the same soft voice, as though the fish were listening to our conversation and might drop the eel if it didn't like what it heard. The circle hook Bill was fishing allowed the fish to run with the eel with little chance of a gut hook. We had fished big bass in skinny water many times, and experience taught us that letting the fish run a bit with an open bail ensured more hookups. No sooner had I silently counted to three than Bill had taken up the slack and tightened on the fish.

The next sound we heard was the one that keeps you up at night and coming back for more. It's the 280-yard drive down the middle of the fairway, the pop of a baseball hit so perfectly off a wooden bat that you never imagined a ball could go so far. When monster bass realize they have been hooked in shallow water, there is no place to go but up. The explosion a big bass creates in thin water is a sound that lives only with striper fishermen who have heard it. Bill's fish didn't disappoint us, but it did surprise us. When fishing at night, visual perception takes a back seat to feel, and you can only guess where your fish is going to erupt. Sometimes they surprise you, which only adds to the story when you relate it to your friends. Bill's fish crashed the surface almost 20 feet from where I guessed it would.

"Holy *%@#! That sounds like someone just dropped a refrigerator in the water. You still got him?" I asked, with a bit of envy.

"Oh yeah, but she's running for the rocks," Bill replied.

"I'll start the boat while you turn her," I said.

After any big bass shoots through the surface and can't throw the hook, they are off and running. Hooked bass seek deep water and structure, which offer them the best chances of escape. In the middle of a minefield of boulders, these fish have more than a fighting chance if they can get into the rocks. Seventeen-pound test is no match for a 35-pound bass that has wrapped the line around a jagged rock. Those first few seconds are critical, and as I watched, Bill put the hammer down. There is a fine line between turning a fish and breaking him off, and I watched anxiously as Bill cupped the spool of his reel and walked the fish from the stern to the bow, slowly working it into deep water. The fish ripped off line and the drag sang for a good 20 seconds before the fish tired and came to a halt. The line remained taut as Bill started reclaiming some of the 200 feet of monofilament that disappeared into Vineyard Sound. Our hope was that the line would hold and the fish would tow the boat around and out of the rocks into deeper water. By then the bow was pointed straight at the fish, and I had stopped fishing and was getting into position to help when the fish made its second run, which was sure to come. Bill had collected enough line that the boat was clearly visible to the fish, and although we could not see her, she wanted no part of it. This run was half of the first, but it was suddenly interrupted with a heavy pull on Bill's line, and it wasn't the fish.

Trouble comes in many different forms when fishing at night. Other boats drift into your water with the lights off. Rocks seem to appear out of nowhere. Lobster buoys that would normally sit on the surface disappear during that glorious but hard-running full-moon tide. The real contest had begun.

Some stripers live in our memories more than others, fish that were brought to the side of the boat or dragged onto a sandy beach, or never even seen after an epic battle. For most anglers, though, it is the experience over the long term that gives deeper satisfaction. And with that satisfaction comes confidence and a deeper understanding of both the magnificent striped bass and what motivates us to try to catch them.

Throughout this book you will learn from some of the finest fishermen in the Northeast as they share their insights on how to locate and catch the most popular fish targeted by recreational anglers in our near-shore waters. You will find tales of big fish and big-fish techniques, and be taken along by expert anglers to striper fishing destinations that will have you packing your surf gear or loading up your boat. Striper fishing is more than a pastime for many, and its mystique, culture and history are essential parts of the story.

The night I have described fishing with Bill Hough was one of the last trips we took in the fall of 1995 and one of many that proved to be the inspiration for starting *On The Water* magazine. We launched *On The Water* the following spring in May of 1996 as a unique format in which others could candidly share their experiences. We sought out fishermen first and wrestled pens into their hands, many kicking and screaming, with the simple goal of capturing where, what, when, how and why they fish. Many of these original voices like Dave Peros, Steve Shiraka and Dave LaPorte (a true kicker and screamer!) cut their publishing teeth with *On The Water*, and we are proud to have them included in this book. I thank all of the contributing writers and the staff who have worked at OTW over the years; without them there would be no magazine and no book, which brings me back to Bill Hough. I thank him for letting me start *On The Water* with him as a partner and allowing me to realize the dream of owning the magazine.

Bill is a good man and a great friend, and those are the very reasons why I maneuvered his 17-foot Montauk through the dark and around the lobster buoy his fish had found. I keep reminding him that without me on that cool autumn night, over 10 years ago, he never would have seen that broom of a tail next to the buoy. Of course, he sees things a little differently! I guess I'm over the fact that it was not my fish . . . but what a fish it was!

-Chris Megan
Publisher, On The Water

Chapter One: Striper Destinations

Chapter Two: Tackle & Techniques

Chapter Three: Striper Tales

Chapter One

Striper Locations Throughout New England

———◆———

From the craggy coast of Maine to Massachusetts' North and South shores to the legendary waters of Cape Cod and the Islands; to the rocky ledges and sandy beaches of Rhode Island, and south to the reefs of Connecticut and through Long Island Sound. Striped bass fill all these waters at certain times each season, and while their movements can be predicted with a fair degree of accuracy, understanding where and why they stay in each area requires knowledge that can only be gained by spending time searching them out. Here are some, but by no means all, of the justifiably famous areas to begin your search.

Lesser-Known Reefs That Hold Fish
– Inshore Reefs Of Eastern Long Island Sound

By Bob Sampson Jr.

My first boat was a 14-foot Lund, a beamy, seaworthy little craft that took me all over eastern Long Island Sound, with obvious wave and weather limitations. Places like The Race were out of the question. Occasionally seas were flat enough to allow a poke out to Catumb Rocks or Sugar Reef and Fishers Island, but most of my saltwater fishing was limited to the more protected bays and inshore reefs along the Connecticut coast. This was not a serious limitation because many of these less heavily fished spots hold fish and, at times, are very productive. Due to the loads of structure and the advantage of being able to lie on the leeward side of land under many wind conditions, many hours were spent fishing the 14-footer in and around the Mystic River and nearby reefs.

On one of the more memorable trips to Ram Island Reef, a favorite spot of mine in this area, Pete Minta, a long-time hunting and fishing partner, and I had gone out with the intention of catching a big striper to test a new smokehouse recipe. In those days the legal size was 36 inches, and typically the catches seemed to drop off at around 35 inches, but a nighttime eel trip could usually do the trick.

Ram Island Reef has a shallow, flat shelf with 15 to 19 feet of water, rising up to 8 to 11 feet. It then drops off on the east edge to 25 or 30 feet and to over 40 feet way out towards the reef marker that sits on a rock that reaches the surface at low tide. It's a beautiful piece of structure. Unfortunately, it does not always hold fish on the shallow end, but there are usually some honkers off the deep side and around the edge of the outer, deep-water portion of this reef.

I prefer to drift or cast eels with no or very little weight on spinning gear with 16- to 20-pound-test Fireline. In those days it was all mono and we were running 16-pound-test Trilene XT or Big Game.

To the west of Ram Island is a large, rock-studded shoal that is dangerous to run through at any tide, and after dark at low tide you don't want to be there. At night during high water, bass feeding in this area are forced out and around the front side of the island with the ebb tide, often creating a few hours of great big bass action when the ebb tide is at dusk or during the night.

Pete and I arrived just at dusk on the turn of the tide. Our first three drifts were fishless, and, to my dismay, we weren't marking either fish or bait on the fishfinder. On the fourth pass, the one we said we would quit on if there were no signs of life, an upside-down check mark appeared on the screen. I started a mission control type of countdown, and right on cue, Pete had a pickup and set back into a good fish. After a short battle he had a very nice bass by the jaw. I picked up the yardstick I had tossed into the boat and held it next to the bass. It came up short and we released the fish.

On the next drift it was the same scenario, only there were a half-dozen good-sized marks on the screen, plus some bait. When the countdown reached about three, I was into a better bass that put up a hard fight. I lipped it, held the stick up to its side in the dark and again it came up a short, this time by about an inch.

On the third pass we each caught bluefish that weighed over 10 pounds, one of which we kept for the smoker. Things slowed for a while before another slug of fish moved through. This time Pete hooked into a good one, the best of the evening. Once in the boat he had a tough time holding it up for the stick, again it was short, but only by a fraction of an inch. He placed the fish back in the water, sat down and said, "Geeze, that seemed like a pretty big fish to me." I agreed.

One of us turned on a flashlight to tie a knot. The beam struck the ruler on the bottom of the boat and we had a realization. I had grabbed a meter stick, which is 39 inches, not a yardstick. Neither of us had bothered turning on a light to get an exact measurement when checking our fish in the darkness. All three bass had been 37 to just under 39 inches, and the big one was a fat fish that probably weighed nearly 30 pounds, but we never doubted our yardstick. We had a good laugh and didn't catch a fish for the rest of the tide.

That's the way fishing often is on the smaller, inshore reefs. There are usually fish around at some point in the tide. It's a matter of learning the quirks of each spot and being there at the right time. As a rule of thumb, most of the big bass are caught under low light conditions after the spring blitzes fade. Most of the big bass are caught on the ebb tide, pretty much all season long, and the preferred baits are live eels, live herring, live hickory shad or chunked fish. An increasing number of jumbos are caught each year on those foolish-looking, but very effective,

The Spindle at Groton Long Point is always a great spot to cast a plug. It nearly always holds schoolies like this one and occasionally surprises you with a big bass, especially if the offering is an eel at dusk.

tube-and-worm rigs so many anglers are employing.

When fish are scarce, if they are not at one reef, they may be at the next spot down-tide from there, so don't be afraid to move around and hunt the fish out. Smaller fish may be present and even on the surface during the day, especially when it's overcast, but the big guys tend to stay deep and move into shallow water under low light conditions. Many anglers, myself included, are often satisfied to hit a reef with flies or light spinning tackle and catch the available schoolies and bluefish. False albacore and bonito will be present in some areas by the end of this month.

I often like to take a run over the deep water before dark to see if fish are holding near a particular reef. Because I don't like using the clunky gear required to get down 60 to 100 feet, I prefer to find out if fish are present by using my fishfinder and then waiting for them to move into shallower water where they can be effectively reached with lighter spinning or bait-casting gear. This tactic isn't foolproof. Sometimes the fish stay deep and do not show in the shallows as scheduled, but it is effective enough to be a normal part of my battle plans when fishing places that do not always hold fish. It is also a good tactic to employ when fishing in new, unfamiliar areas.

Moving west there are three great rocky reefs and shorelines to fish, each about a mile from the last. First is Groton Long Point. The rocky spindle at the outer tip is a great striper spot that usually holds fish on the ebb tide. Be careful inside the spire unless you know the area, because there are many rocks within the range of a spinning propeller. To the west is Crowell's Point, a second rocky outcrop that marks a steep drop-off into 25 feet of water, a lightly fished spot that holds potential to produce some big bass due to its great structure and tide-swept rocks.

Across Mumford Cove is the rocky, bass-holding shoreline of Bluff Point State Park. These rocks usually hold some good bass (and blackfish for anyone interested in dropping a crab down beside any of the large boulders). In the fall bluefish and small tunas often feed their way into this area and adjacent beaches where they corner bait. Bluff Point is one of the largest shore-based access points in the eastern part of Connecticut. The drawback is a mile-long walk from the parking lot to the rocks, which filters out all but the most avid anglers. When fish are around, this walk is well worth the effort because anglers have a great rocky shoreline, beach and salt pond in which to search out some fish.

Offshore and about halfway between Groton Long Point and Bluff Point is Horseshoe Reef. This is a shallow, dangerous little rock pile that juts off the bottom far enough to bust a lower unit. It is a spot with good potential that is generally skipped by most anglers as they motor out to The Race or larger reefs in the area. It's one of those places I keep telling myself to fish, but I've never fished for bass over this little reef, though many fluke have been caught from the smooth bottom nearby.

Another mile to the west is Pine Island and Bushy Point, two more rocky structures that provide great bass fishing. Inside here is the Poquonnock River, which provides good striper action, particularly in the spring and fall. However, bass do move into this shallow cove after dark all season long to feed on worms, eels and small fish.

The mouth of the Thames River is guarded by Eastern Point, another rocky, lobster-pot-strewn piece of fish-holding structure. This spot is a good one at the bottom of a dropping tide, because many of the fish that work their way down and out of the Thames hold in this area to pick off bait as it is pulled out of the river and out into the Sound.

The best boat access to these spots is Bayberry State Launch in Groton, or the launches under the I-95 bridge in Groton and New London.

The mouth of any big river should never be overlooked. The lower Thames always holds some bass and bluefish. Look up the east shore from the bridge to the Nautilus exhibit at the submarine base, and don't overlook Junk Island and the rocky shores near

Millstone Point Outflow is a great fish attractor with a warm, strong flowing river of water pouring out into the Sound it seems to draw the earliest inshore bluefish action in the area and the bass are always present as well. It is always a hot spot for small tunas and will attract such rare visitors as Spanish mackerel and even an occasional tarpon.

Osprey Beach and the lighthouse.

Farther to the west, the best landmark is Ocean Beach, unmistakable with its large tower. Fish from the western edge of this beach from Alewife Cove and all along the rocky shore that runs past Harkness State Park. Harkness is certainly one of the best shore access points to the Sound for fishermen. There is no swimming allowed, so the entire beach and rocky shore is accessible to surf-fishermen. It is a very productive spot that has a number of regulars who take fish at it throughout the season. Night striper fishing from shore at Harkness Park is excellent.

Offshore from the park is Little Goshen Reef, another largely overlooked but excellent striper, bluefish and small tuna spot. This is another fairly shallow spot, with some rocks less than 11 feet from the surface and a quick drop from 25 to 40 or 50 feet on the seaward edge.

Less than a mile west of here, marked by a bell buoy, is Bartlett Reef, one of the area's more popular and productive reefs. Twotree Channel is a deep channel that runs north between Bartlett Reef and Little Goshen Reef. In the trough between Bartlett Reef and Little Goshen Reef there is a second shallow spot where the bottom rises from 50 to 26 feet. This is a fabulous spot during the ebb tide. Again, there are rocks and high spots on this reef that need to be identified, especially when fishing from larger craft. Twotree Channel is also an excellent and productive fluke drift, heavily utilized by anglers fishing out of the Niantic area.

Twotree Channel runs north of Bartlett Reef all the way to Millstone Point where the warmwater discharge also draws and holds fish throughout the season. This discharge is always a great spot to fish at and seems to draw in some of the earliest bluefish of the year. Later on when the bonito and false albies show up, many anglers head for Millstone first. During warm summers, the warm-water discharge will attract and hold occasional Spanish mackerel and, more rarely, tarpon and even cobia. Be sure to heed signs regard-

Never ignore a river mouth. This is "betweem the bridges" in Niantic River. Boat traffic during the day makes fishing tough. But after things calm down after dark, this rocky entrance to Niantic River is notorious for producing huge stripers.

ing how close you can approach the power plant.

Across Niantic Bay from Bartlett Reef is Black Point, another premier striper destination. Swept with strong tides and with a 96-foot hole off its southern tip, this is another spot that always has big fish hanging around in it. The deep hole is legendary for producing huge bass to bait fishermen who drop jigs, eels and live baits to the bottom. It is also a spot that has the potential to give up some doormat fluke.

These spots are most easily reached either from the Niantic Bay State Launch north of the drawbridge in Niantic, or from Dock Road State Launch near the Pleasure Beach section of Waterford. Both are excellent launch facilities.

A short distance west of Black Point is Rocky Neck State Park, another state-owned, shore-fishing access point that is not quite as productive as either Harkness Park or Bluff Point. Anglers take fluke, bass and blackfish off the long breakwall, but most of the best action in this shallow area occurs after dark.

To the east of the Connecticut River mouth by a few miles lies another prime big bass spot, Hatchett Reef, located roughly a mile off Hatchett Point, the first noticeable rocky point along the shore heading east from the Connecticut River mouth. This reef rises from 40 feet to 5 feet from the surface. Anglers drift live eels, bounce jigs, use hook baits or troll deep around this reef and the waters between there and Hatchett Point for big bass throughout the season. It's one of those spots that the local big bass specialists concentrate on during the season. There are almost always some jumbo bass hanging in the deep waters off the reef's outer edge. They often move right up to the point and beaches after the sun sets.

Lying at a right angle to the flow of the Connecticut River is Long Sand Shoal, a shallow sandbar that creates terrific striper holding rips a mile or so off the mouth of the river. This is a prime spot to drift eels or troll tube-and-worms or wire-line with bucktails for bass and bluefish. The shoal itself is over two miles long, running from Griswold Point well past Crane Reef to the west of the Connecticut River. It is a great spot to drift baits for fluke, and as the sun sets, the bass move in to feed. The best section is the eastern third of this reef, which is marked with numerous humps and bumps that attract and hold bass, particularly after the sun goes down.

There is a 1,000-foot-long angler access dock at the DEP Marine Fisheries Headquarters at the end of Rope Ferry Road in Lyme. Down Route 1 at Great Island is a state launch, and a second, deeper-water facility is across the river under the I-95 bridge in Saybrook. The Great Island Launch is O.K. for small boats, but it may be too shallow at low tide for larger craft.

West of the river mouth are two more great bass reefs. Cornfield Point is a shore spot that has limited access. Strung out from this fishy, tide-swept point are a series of rock piles, reefs and humps called Halftide Rock, the Hen and Chickens and Crane Reef, all great striper and bluefish spots. These are treacherous places with a couple of dangerous rocks, especially just off the corner at Cornfield Point. At dusk a live eel or well-placed lure around any of these fishy looking hazards to navigation is likely to take a few bass of considerable size.

Crane Reef also has a reputation for producing some huge bluefish. During the late 1980s I took an 18-pounder there that netted me $1,000 in a bluefish tournament, and it was only the fifth largest fish. In just about any other year that fish would have been worth ten to twenty grand!

Any and all of these reefs will produce big bass after dark to anyone sinking or drifting a live eel around their edges. If menhaden should move into the area, live-lining one into the depths of any of these places on a three-way rig is the closest thing to a guaranteed huge bass during the summer months. Best spots for live eels and menhaden are Black Point, Bartlett Reef or Hatchett Reef. Light-line anglers will have consistent fun casting Slug-Gos, swimming diving plugs, jigheads with shad bodies or Lunker City's new thin-profile Salt Shaker shad body. Of course, a classic bucktail, tipped with squid or a Mario's Scented Squid Strip will always take some bass in the deeper waters around the edges of any reef or rock pile.

These are all classic, highly productive fishing spots that don't get the press and attention of The Race, Plum Gut or Watch Hill. However, for the anglers who take the time to learn these areas, the catch rate and numbers of big bass produced can be very impressive without the long ride and bumpy fishing of the more popular offshore areas.

Winter Stripers
On The Thames River

By Bob Sampson Jr.

If you put your time in on the water, Mother Nature will come up with a gift from time to time. Just about every winter, around Christmas, she is usually quite generous when it comes to giving out striped bass. No, this is not a typo: Some of the best striper action of the year can be found in southeastern Connecticut's Thames River, between mid-December and early February. On average the fish are small schoolies, but if you enjoy racking up catch totals, or simply putting a bend in a light rod when others are pulling their fish through a six-inch hole in the ice, then you might want to give this unique fishery a try.

One of my more memorable "Christmas presents" occurred during a fishing trip to the Thames River a few winters ago. It was around the time when the striped bass population was first beginning its return from near oblivion. It was the holiday season, about three or four years after the production of the record-setting 1993 year-class in Chesapeake Bay, and the waters were dominated by stripers that were from 16 to about 22 inches. These fish were just about everywhere in the river. Being a nursery area of sorts, the Thames

Jigs are very productive at times for taking school stripers in this size range. When jigs fail, try trolling with small deep divers or spreader rigs with short tubes.

River was overflowing with these small stripers during the winter of 1996 or 1997. Ten to twelve years and 20 to 30 pounds later, these little fish have grown up; today they are the quality 36- to 40-inchers that everyone is catching up and down the striper coast.

Two of my good fishing buddies are teachers so we have the week between Christmas and New Years off, which is a great time to get down to the Thames River for some often (but not always) fast and furious winter striped bass fishing. At this time of the year, water temperatures have not yet bottomed out for the winter, so the stripers are still fairly active. Try to fish a dropping tide, under low-light conditions, after dark or on an overcast day, and the fishing can be phenomenal. Add a dropping barometer with the approach of a storm front and it may be even better than that.

On this particular day, I called my buddy Eric Covino to see if he wanted to make a "temporary withdrawal" of striped bass from Norwich Harbor. I hadn't made a river fishing trip since deer season started and was anxious to put a few bends in the rod. The previous winter Eric and I were averaging 50-plus fish per trip on the

Thames around Christmastime, and we knew the fishing would be great on this particular day because a storm system was rapidly approaching from the southwest.

We joined a mutual friend, Al Lazuk, to make a midday, midweek, midwinter fishing trip. With an excellent launch ramp right in Norwich, the run to the fishing grounds, which are out in the middle of the harbor, is a short one of about 200 yards. On that day we immediately found what we call a "building" or "the wall" on the depthfinder screen, as the boat moved into the 42- to 44-foot-deep main channel.

The term "wall" is a reference to the often steep sides of the tremendous schools of stripers that winter over in the Thames River every year. These very densely packed wintering schools have a much different "fingerprint" than the diffuse, schools that show up like groups of upside-down check marks during the spring-through-fall fishing period. During the warmwater season, anglers normally expect to see individual fish or clusters of upside-down check marks near structure. By comparison, the huge schools of bass in the Thames are packed so tightly together down in the river's murky depths that the school may have a nearly flat top and right-angled sides, and be so dense that it produces gray lines like a soft mud or sand bottom. This unusual image can occasionally fool the uninitiated into thinking they are marking bottom, not a mammoth school of fish. Newcomers to this fishery have been known to drive over these densely packed schools, run around the river, never find a conventional mark on the screen and give up. I've seen guys pulling their boats out of the harbor, telling us, "The fish have moved; there's nothing out there" as we were launching. Then, before their taillights disappeared into the traffic, our rods would be bending into the first fish of the day.

Bomber Deep-A lures in the 4.5-inch size are the ticket for light-tackle trolling. We drift downcurrent with jigs and troll back upstream with these and catch many fish.

The best odds of finding and catching stripers will be from a small stable boat; canoes are too dangerous for icy winter waters. However, many local anglers who don't own a boat or don't run their boats during the wintertime can catch their share of stripers right off the town docks. The shore-based fishery centers around the town docks, but there are other locations around the harbor and downriver to the Dahl Oil Property, where people can reach the channel with a cast. It is necessary to be able to reach the deep channel in order to catch fish. This is

Trolling with wire and spreader rigs like this is the most productive way to catch bass.

not like summer, when the fish run up into skinny water to feed. The shore-based winter striper fishing in the Thames River is most productive after dark, especially during warm spells, thaws and warm winter rains.

On this particular Christmas-week trip, as soon as we hit the midchannel, a wall of stripers that was 20 feet thick, roughly 20 yards wide and over 100 yards long appeared on the fishfinder screen. We ran the boat upcurrent past the head of the school and drifted back with the dropping tide, over the top of the school, while we dragged an assortment of small jigs through the fish. All three of us started hooking up as soon as our jigs started falling, actually bumping down through the school of bass.

(My favorite winter striper jig is a half-ounce Road Runner jig with the hair trimmed off and tipped with a 4-inch Fin-S Fish or curly tail as a teaser. In stronger currents a heavier jig may be necessary to reach and skim bottom, but always use the minimum-size weight required.)

After the boat drifted past the end of that school, we were just reeling in our lines when a second school of nearly the same dimensions (except it was only 10 to 15 feet thick) materialized on the fishfinder. We dropped our jigs back down and continued to bail (and release) schoolie bass that were averaging 18 to 20 inches in length. To our surprise there was a third school, skinnier but even longer, a few yards downriver from the second, so we continued on, ultimately taking our drift from the center of the harbor downriver past the old Thermos Company before the fish finally petered out. In total, that's a column of stripers measuring over a thousand feet long, ranging from 5 to 20 feet thick and averaging 20 yards wide! There had to be tens of thousands of fish down there, and on this particular day it seemed like every one of them was eating. We didn't catch any drag screamers that day; the largest bass was about 25 or 26 inches. Often, on the days when high numbers of bass are landed and released, there will be a fish or two in the 30- to 40-inch range. Essentially this is a schoolie fishery.

Fishing was so easy: Open the bail; feel the jig being slapped by tails or bounced off the fishes' bodies as it sinks through the school; close the bail; lift the rod tip to pull the jig off the bottom and - bam - fish on! (That is, if one of us hadn't taken one on the drop.) It was the fastest, longest period of literally nonstop fishing (actually catching) that I have ever experienced as an angler, in fresh or salt water.

The fishing was so incredible (and me being a complete idiot at heart) that I pulled out a second rod, rigged both rods with a couple of fluke drift rigs with dropper flies that happened to be in the box of jigs - and I was hooking up four at a time, two fish on each rod. That got really confusing really quickly, so I only did it a couple of times, just for the heck of it, before going back to a single rod and bent barb hook.

Before the entire tide ran out, with all three of us hauling bass up to the boat and releasing them as fast as we could, the catch and release body count (without a single damaged fish, I might add) reached 176 stripers. When Al said, "Hey guys, it's been fun but I have to meet my wife for some Christmas shopping," there were no complaints. The sandpaper-like teeth of so many small stripers had nearly ground off our fingerprints so we reeled in the last triple of the day and headed back to the launch.

When there are so many fish, so densely packed, don't set the hook at every little tap or many bass will be foul-hooked. Intentionally snagging them is not only unethical, it's illegal, so wait for a definite strike and the weight of a fish at the other end of the line before setting the hook. Because just so many short fish may be caught during a good trip, crimp down all barbs - for their sake and yours.

That day was one of the best Christmas presents Mother Nature has ever given me. Not so much because we caught a ton of fish (actually, it was more like a quarter ton at an average weight of 1 1/2 to 3 pounds per fish), but because as a biologist I knew this was the turning point in the restoration of this wonderful gamefish. Not every day is that good; in fact, sometimes, despite "buildings" of fish below the boat, the fishing can be horrid. But even on the worst days, when the bass are turned off, it is usually possible to catch at least a few "de-skunkers" for the old ego. However, by paying attention to weather conditions and tides it is possible to improve the odds of having a productive outing rather than a tough one.

It's simple. The bass move upriver with the flood tide into the harbor, stack up and then drop back down with the ebb tide. Try to fish the ebb during low-light conditions whenever possible, and the stripers will pretty much do the rest. We normally drift and jig downcurrent through the schools, then run back up through them trolling 4 1/2-inch Bomber Deep-A's or other big-lipped deep divers. Captain Al Anderson, a friend who spends a good deal of time fishing the Thames and tagging the bass he catches for the Littoral Society, racks up higher catch totals using 20-pound-test wire-line rigs and trolling with small, multiple-hook spreader rigs. The spreader rigs also seem to hook a higher number of large (over 30 inches) stripers than our small jigs. Captain Al has placed tags in more than 20,000 stripers at this point, with more than 3,000 of the returned tags coming from the Thames River's wintering stripers.

Most of these fish are small because large rivers like the Thames are nursery areas that are heavily used by juvenile stripers. There are always a few larger fish mixed in; we've caught them up to about 30 pounds, though fish of this size are rare. Over the years we have averaged one 30-inch-plus striper for every 30 to 50 stripers landed. If you catch a 10- or 15-pound "dead of winter striper" from the Thames, then count your lucky stars.

Despite the incredible number of stripers that winter in the Thames, occasionally, when the barometric pressure rises steeply because of the approach of a windy arctic high pressure system, those thousands of stripers all seem to turn off like someone hit a kill switch. Under these conditions, which is a universal, year-round turn-off for fish, we have drifted over those same 20-foot-thick schools of stripers for a whole tide and only caught two or three fish. Once we even got skunked - and we were in the fish all day long!

On a good day, between December and mid-February, as long as the river is free of ice and the fish are biting, the Thames River's overwintering stripers can provide some of the fastest and most consistent fishing to be experienced anywhere in the North. Christmas is the time when the odds are best that Mother Nature will come through with a present for you.

Connecticut Coastal Fishing
Surfcasting From Public Access Land – A Look At Hammonasset And Harkness State Parks

By Bob Sampson Jr.

There are eight Connecticut State Parks and assorted other access points on Long Island Sound. While some have good fishing and others are marginal, two of the best state-owned surf-fishing destinations are Hammonasset State Park in Madison and Harkness Memorial State Park in Waterford. You won't find the crashing rollers of the South County Beaches in Rhode Island or the wild open spaces of the Cape Cod National Seashore. But both of these relatively large state parks have fishing areas that surf anglers in Southern New England should get to know.

Hammonasset State Park is an easy to reach destination that has its own exit (62) off I-95, which takes cars right to the main entrance. During the off-season, from October through May, the entire two-mile Hammonasset Beach and its bookend jetties are open to fishing. During the summer season when the beach is full of swimmers, anglers are limited to fishing the Meigs Point jetty at the eastern end and the West Beach jetty at the western end of this beach during the day between 8 a.m. and sunset. After sunset, the entire beach can be fished all night long.

The water off the beach is fairly uniform in depth and there isn't much in the way of bottom structure so the fish don't hold in one place for very long other than near the jetties at either end and Hammonasset Reef, which juts out into the Sound for a few hundred yards beyond the Meigs Point jetty. For this reason, schools of fish tend to move along the beach in the direction of the tide, searching for or pushing bait.

When there is bait in the area, blues and bass work around the jetties or along the beach during the off hours when anglers can cast there. There are probably fluke in close to the surf break during the summer, but the daily beach closure precludes much in the way of effective fishing for this species from the surf, except off the jetties.

West Beach jetty is the less fished of the two major landmarks on the beach. It borders the outlet of a creek where fish wait to ambush prey as it is flushed out. Some huge blue-fish have been taken here over the years, along with bass and the occasional weakfish and fluke.

Despite the presence of other species, I think of Hammonasset Beach primarily as a bluefishing destination. During the 1980s when I was working for the DEP on their Marine Recreational Fisheries Program, the largest bluefish of the thousands we measured and weighed during my years of creel census work was caught off the West Jetty, a 22-pound monster! Anyone who has ever caught a midteen or larger blue knows that big blues look much larger than they really are, this one was like a blimp with teeth. In fact, the excited angler thought he had a 30-pounder. The scale busted that bubble, unfortunately, but his huge grin probably lasted for hours after he went to sleep that night.

In fact, this is such a good bluefish spot that occasionally swimmers have been bitten by marauding choppers. During the worst attack, two women and a young boy were bitten severely, requiring 80 to over 150 stitches each. These are rare occasions of course and the people were bitten accidentally by bluefish that were crashing into menhaden schools in a feeding frenzy. The blues did not target the humans but were biting blindly into anything they encountered, including the odd hand, leg or foot.

But don't worry, you don't have to use your body parts for bait or chum to catch blue-fish at Hammonasset Park. Friends and I had one of our best ever bluefish trips while fishing from a boat along the marsh shore between Meigs Point and Clinton Point. It was the day after Hurricane Gloria hit the coast. Sun was shining and waters were calm. The blues had huge schools of menhaden pushed into this shallow indentation of the shore and were gobbling them up so fiercely that the air smelled of bunker oil and blood. The water was rust colored partly from the blood and partly from stirred up sediments. The fishing action was incredible, with blues that averaged between 8 and 12 pounds and the largest a bona fide 17-pounder!

The blues come in close to Hammonasset Beach during the late summer and fall, after the swimmers are gone for the season. Schools of choppers push the menhaden right up to the surf line. Anglers in the know will watch the birds and breaking fish and move along with the schools of fish, which will follow the prevailing tides, often hanging up briefly at the corners where the jetties stop their progress.

On one occasion, on a beautiful October morning, I was doing survey work and noticed two anglers spaced a few hundred yards apart in the middle section of the beach. I had a long walk to the first surfcaster, who had recently caught a 10- or 12-pound chopper, judging by the fact it was still breathing as I interviewed him.

I began heading east, the same direction as the outgoing tide, toward the other angler.

The rocky beach leading to Harkness Point is a great stretch of surf from which to catch bass, blues, porgy and blackfish. The sandy section to the east is a good area for fluke.

About 200 feet or so away from the guy, as I walked along, there was that distinctive odor of bunker blowing in with the onshore breeze. The glare was too much to see if a school was there, but the smell, which I've smelled many times in the past from schools of both bluefish and bunker, was unmistakable.

As I approached the angler, I asked if he'd caught anything. He was reeling up his line, mumbling something about being skunked, had no hits and was "getting the hell out of here." I could tell by his gear and actions that he was new at the surf-casting game.

"I wouldn't do that quite yet," I said

Almost defiantly he said, "Why?"

"Because I just smelled some fish a short way down the beach, they should be here any minute," I said.

He laughed and continued to pack his stuff away, probably thinking I was kidding him.

"I'm not kidding," I said. "You can really smell bunker and bluefish when they are thick in the water."

"Oh yeah!" he said, as he took one last, reluctant cast with a Hopkins Spoon. I could tell he was trying to prove me wrong but also hoped I was right. He became more focused when I told him that the fisherman to his right had just landed a fish. We could see his lure behind the second wave in the small surf when it disappeared in a big splash from a 12-pound blue.

After he landed the fish, that distinctive odor of fish once again permeated the air. I asked him if he could smell it and he replied, "Yeah, you weren't kidding." He didn't know it, but I never kid around when it comes to catching fish. He nodded with a big smile, took another cast out into the fishy breeze and immediately hooked into another jumbo chopper. After completing the interview, I told him to follow his nose and he could be catching fish until he runs out of beach at the Meigs Point jetty nearly a mile down the sand.

The Meigs Point jetty has all the elements to make for some very good fishing when conditions are right. The jetty itself is riprap that creates structure for blackfish to hide in. I've seen fish weighing up to five pounds caught literally from between the rocks. Offshore a few hundred yards from the Meigs Point jetty is a rocky reef that creates the kind of rip lines and riled waters that attract just about all the gamefish we see in Connecticut waters. Along with bass and blues you'll find scup (porgies) and blackfish here, and the water along the nearby beach is always a good fluke drift from a boat.

After dark, fishermen can walk the jetty slinging eels, chunk baits, live bunker, if they can catch them, or plugs to whatever happens to be around. Like most shore based fishing locations, Hammonasset runs hot and cold. Surf fishing is usually at its best during low-light overcast days or at high tide and into the ebb during the night.

Weakfish have been coming on pretty strong around the New Haven area lately, and at times they move east to Guilford and Madison, providing some lucky anglers incidental catches as they fish for other species at this state park.

A 45-minute drive to the east lies Harkness State Park, which is one of the most gorgeous pieces of real estate in eastern Connecticut. Willed to the state by the Harkness family of New York, the park's centerpieces are its gardens and mansion. This opulent home was constructed early in the twentieth century, when other tycoons were making their millions and building their "castles" in Newport, Rhode Island.

This park has barely a half mile of rocky beach that is closed to swimming, so there is no competition for anglers. The legend is that a member or friend of the Harkness family drowned while swimming there, so they requested that the public not be allowed to swim as part of the agreement when the land was turned over to the state.

The rocks that make swimming so dangerous also make it one of the better shore-fishing striped bass destinations in Connecticut. Where Hammonasset is a prime bluefish spot, Harkness is its equivalent in stripers.

In addition, this stretch of shoreline features some great fishing for blackfish, bluefish, summer flounder and porgy. Last summer, there were even a couple of false albacore reportedly caught from the surf at Harkness when they moved in close to the beach while feeding on abundant juvenile bunker.

At the western end of the property is a small tidal pond that empties into the Sound, scouring a hole in the process. It's an excellent little hole to fish for fluke by day and bass after the sun sets. To catch fluke here and along the beach, try using a small jig baited with a strip of squid and a live mummichog. Cast the jig out and slowly retrieve it at a slow crawl along the bottom.

For bass and blues, fish at dawn, dusk and after dark at this little outflow and along the rest of the waterfront. The entire shoreline here is a great place to cast soft plastic baits, shallow swimmers, spoons or poppers for striped bass and bluefish. Sand worms cast close to the rocks will often produce some porgy, while a green crab, which can often be caught from the rocks at the park, will probably nab a blackfish.

Hard-core surf anglers looking for big bass will walk and cast the surf at Harkness Park after dark, with either chunk baits or live eels. Hook the eel up through both lips and cast it like a living lure around the park's rocky shoreline – it's a deadly method that produces 30-pound-plus fish here every season. Last year there was a 45-pounder taken from a boat off these rocks during the early summer, the time that the big fish start showing up in good numbers along these Connecticut shores.

To reach Harkness Park, take Exit 72 off I-95 and follow Route 213; the park is on the seaward side of the road where it swings along the coast just to the west of the Eugene O'Neil Theater.Harkness is never closed to angling like Hammonassett Park. This means that when the skies are cloudy and the bass, blues and blackfish are around it's possible to catch them all day long from the rocks and beach. After dark the gates are closed, but anglers can park along the road and walk less than a half mile to the water, a worthwhile effort considering what can be waiting at the end of the road.

Late-Season Surf Casting
Along Rhode Island's South Shore

By Joe Lyons

A friend of mine used to say, "Watching the birds is for the birds." Of course, we all scan the sky for working birds, particularly in the fall. I think most everyone has done his share of bird chasing. I believe the point my friend was trying to make was that it's foolish to abandon our collective analysis of weather, bait and historical precedence – methods that serve us well all season – in favor of a bird's analysis. So, when fall arrives, I'm always surprised to see how many anglers switch their fishing strategies to a more observational method.

For Rhode Island surfcasters, the majority of our fall run still falls under the definition of night-fishing. It seems as soon as our Rhody beaches open to 4-wheelers, even popular rock-hopping nightspots see a significant reduction in pressure. If you, like everyone, it seems, have a 4-wheel drive buggy and just can't wait to get on the sand and chase the terns, you may want to reconsider. True, working birds are a good indicator of the presence of gamefish, but they don't fly on October evenings when trophies cruise the shallows of points and jetties and inlets to feast as they push south.

The same surfcasters who are overly eager in early April when there is little chance for good fish (and are exhausted by Thanksgiving when the odds are much better) tend also to give up on night fishing too early. It is understandable, after four months of night fishing; a chance to fish in the day can be seductive, but those in the know stay faithful to the night. My experience has been that Rhode Island night fishing for big, migratory stripers tends to holdup at least until Halloween, and often past Election Day. There are even those who know the Rhody surf well who night fish well into December.

It would be a foolish angler indeed who gave up on night-fishing too soon. If the weather cooperates, your best chance for the fish-of-the-season, or fish-of-a-lifetime, may come on the night tides around the new moon of October. There will be plenty of time for scanning the horizon with your binoculars later. I recommend switching your areas of preference southward, but not giving up the night –at least not just yet.

Early in October, stripers feed mainly at night. Their predictability is often dependent on, and tied to, the prevalent baitfish. When they are feeding on sand eels, silversides or peanut bunker, it is not uncommon to have repeat performances in one place for several nights in a row. When they are feeding on herring, macks or larger menhaden, they tend to have more one-night stands.

October's jumbo stripers are economical in their pursuit of migration calories, preferring large and wide-bodied baitfish and densely schooled smaller bait. For the Rhode Island shore angler, this means using large and wide-bodied lures and heavier tackle.

Classic autumn lures include Gibbs Dannys, Bombers, Needlefish, Atoms and Giant Pikies. Newer lures such as soft-plastic Sassy Shad, Slug-Gos or wooden offerings by Habs are all good choices. For night fishermen, eels and chunks are hard to beat.

This is the time of year when big stripers will test your tackle if you forget to. So, clean your drag and check your line for nicks and replace if necessary. October is definitely not the time for light tackle. A stout 9- to 10-foot rod of medium-heavy action, rated for lures of 1 to 3 ounces is best. Choosing line of less than 20-pound test is usually an invitation to disaster. Check your hooks for rust and your terminal tackle, including leaders.

Stripers tend to move down the Rhode Island coast in fits and starts, known among anglers as "pushes." You may not notice a distinction between the groups of fish mov-

ing through initially, as they often are nearly successive in nature or comprised of resident fish. Toward the end of the month, however, it becomes apparent that there are breaks in the action. A slowdown in the action is not an indication that the next group of fish will be small, however. The big fish could, and often do, come later in the month. Keep an ear out for information, and monitor fishing reports. Be attentive to reports from the north. If the fishing is good on the Cape and Islands it's just a matter of time before at least some of those fish arrive in Rhody waters.

When big stripers trap a school of large-bodied bait in a cove and you are there to capitalize, they will hit with abandon. A good friend of mine fishing a cove in Narragansett one night several seasons back got 47- and 48-pound fish on successive casts.

The regulars at the inlets and breachways will tell you that the dropping tides of October and early November are prime because juvenile baitfish begin to drop out of their salt pond nurseries.

It was right after dark, with a freshening southwest blowing, the fish were feeding on 1-pound menhaden, but he got both his fish on eels.

Typical striper feeding behavior during October is to corral bait along rocky bars, points, breachways and inside coves. At Block Island's Southwest Point there have been legendary blitzes when stripers corral sand eels along the rocky bar to the west of the point. I have seen stripers make slashing runs inside the bait and their actions appeared to be organized, with only a few fish at a time rushing the bait. I have had very good luck along breachway sides that abut the bathing beaches of Charlestown. Look to the first major structure along most any Rhode Island beach and you have found a fish trap. Gamefish will often chase the bait down the clean beach toward the structure and then attack. The east sides of Point Judith and Watch Hill, with their sweeping promontories allowing greater casting distance, are natural fish traps.

The regulars at the inlets and breachways will tell you that the dropping tides of October and early November are also prime because juvenile baitfish begin to drop out of their salt pond nurseries. Believe them; the lion's share of the trophies will come from either inlets or beachfronts that are heavily influenced by an inlet. Drifting swimming plugs or eels and slowly retrieving soft plastics are all deadly effective breachway methods.

Just where the best fishing will be in October is hard to predict. Unlike the spring, when herring and crustaceans are really the only significant food sources, autumn's fish have a smorgasbord to choose from and their movements are less predictable. There is no sure-fire method short of time on the water to figure out just where they will show. But for those willing to move around and try (not just look at) a variety of spots, the fish can usually be found.

If I had to pick one characteristic of the successful Rhode Island fall surfcaster, it would have to be mobility. By mobility I do not necessarily mean driving the beaches, though that can certainly work. A smart surfcaster with 20 miles of productive striper water to hunt through will not spend a lot of time in one spot if it does not produce. While all the better anglers have a few sure-fire fall places, they still spend a great deal of time tracking.

One of the best surfcasters I know meticulously plots out his trips to visit as many spots as possible in a single tide. He'll scour the south coast from Narragansett to Watch Hill, with two or three contingencies for each tide stage.

He hits each spot at precisely the right time but only briefly, often no more than 20 minutes. Beachfronts are tried at high tide, the sides of coves midtide, sandbars and inlet ends at low tide. He only stays at a location if he gets hits or fish. His philosophy is that he has so many places to fish that it does not make sense not to move. This Stick-And-Move methodology has served him well; he is one of Rhody's premier surfcasters. I'm not as aggressive, but I tend to have at least three spots planned for most October outings.

I'm not a believer in absolutely repeating what worked last year, but I am a proponent of repeating what worked in similar years. By this I mean either look through your logs or ask as to which previous year reminded anglers of this year. Though no two autumn runs are exactly the same, by finding the similar characteristics between years, we can come up with a much better starting point.

This October, because of the favorable tides, I would look to the breachways and inlets early in the month. All three breachways, Charlestown, Quonochontaug and Weeka-paug, hold fish and all are excellent places to start. October's new moon at Charlestown Breachway in particular has a long, storied history of producing autumn trophies. Look for the sharpies of Charlestown to be drifting eels in the outgoing tide and follow rotation etiquette on the breachway's productive end.

As we near the middle of October, the migration will begin in earnest. Fish can usually be found along most beachfronts each morning, particularly at false dawn. This season, high tide will occur around dawn at midmonth, perfect for beach fishing. Some notable beachfronts for autumn fishing include Green Hill, Charlestown, East Beach and Weekapaug Beach. Around midmonth I like to start my trips in the deep night and stay at least until the sun is full up. The fishing gets better closer to sunrise as the month progresses.

Tides should also be a consideration as to where you position yourself. I like the inlets and breachways around the time of the full and new moons because of the strong rips that develop. I like to fish the beaches during the quarter moons. Schedule your breachway trips so you are there for the last hours of the dropping tide, when the water exchange is greatest.

Structure and opportunities abound at the points and lighthouses.

One thing is certain: At some point during October, a push of large fish will come through. Most likely their presence will be detected by some anglers, but don't expect to hear about it until it is over. To pick up on just when this is happening you will have to be out there with your eyes and ears open. If you have done your fieldwork and put your time in, you may get one. Surf casting, when it's done right, is a thinking man's sport. Look for drag marks, blood and scales on the rocks, filleted-out frames.

October is fleeting, and soon November will be upon us and our night fishing strategies will become less and less applicable. The fish will be scattered along our southernmost beaches, and catching them becomes more a matter of luck than of skill. It's then that I become something of a birdwatcher myself. When I find myself on a beach chasing after a lone seagull, I know I'm almost done.

Stripers In The Snow

By David Pickering

It's the middle of winter and in the minds of most fishermen, stripers exist only as a memory of a fall fishing blitz or a hope for an early run in April. Most striper fishermen would not even consider wetting a line in the middle of January, let alone landing a bass. It doesn't have to be that way, though. Winter fishing for striped bass can be quite productive here in Rhode Island in an unlikely location: above the far northern reaches of Narragansett Bay in the Providence River. Stripers can be caught here, sometimes in big numbers, right through the months of January, February and March.

The reason that the fish are here in the dead of winter is warm water. Just north of the Providence Hurricane Barrier sits the Manchester Street Power Plant, and this plant has two warmwater discharges that pump a voluminous flow of 55-degree water into the river. This is a confined area and the warm water spreads out, making this entire area comfortable for striped bass all winter long and as long as the power plant is pumping water, the fish are active.

The boys and I fish this place regularly throughout the winter. This is our place to hang out and fish on a winter night rather than sitting at home and watching television. We have been doing this for the last six years and we have experienced some fantastic action at times. In fact, in each of those years we've caught at least 300 bass in those first three months of the year and I expect we will this year, too. This is not entirely a secret; I've met plenty of fishermen who claim to know about this fishery but few will venture out on a cold night in January to ice up a line. Which is just fine with us!

It has become a tradition for us to celebrate New Year's Day by catching a bass or, if we're lucky, many bass. This is not just a shot in the dark. Our logs of past years show that large numbers of fish arrive in this area during the last week in December as water temperatures in the bay plummet, forcing bass that are still around Narragansett Bay to enter the warm and comfortable waters of the river.

Last year things held true to form as we found big numbers of fish here during the last week of December. On New Year's Day we headed for one of our favorite spots, the sidewalk of the Point Street Bridge, and began casting. We were using Zoom Flukes mounted on jigheads and bounced them along the shadow line of the bridge and close to the edges of the rotted pier below. From sunset until several hours after dark we had plenty of action, more than enough to take our minds off the winter weather. The tally was 23 bass, mostly schoolies weighing a few pounds, but also a couple of fish that approached legal size. In the best possible way, a new year had begun!

One very important fact to keep in mind, and I'll be the first to admit it this area isn't for everyone. This is an urban fishing experience, with all that implies. Parking spots are often more difficult to find than fish. You won't be planting your feet along a sandy or rocky shore; rather, you cast from an assortment of man-made structures: bridges, abutments, sidewalks, piers, docks and walkways. Instead of lapping waves you'll hear the constant droning of traffic and the occasional siren as cars and trucks negotiate nearby Route 195. Weather can also turn this river of normally clean water into a smelly and unsightly mess. In times of extremely heavy rain, the city's sewage system cannot handle the excessive street runoff and the river turns a coffee-brown color.

But if you're willing to accept these negatives, the fact remains that fishing can be extraordinarily good. And sometimes the worst conditions can produce the best fishing. Two years ago on January 21, my son Ben and I went down to the river after an all-day rainstorm. The barometer was falling, the water was brown and a cold drizzle was falling, but final count was a total of 60 stripers. This remains the best January night we have had in this spot. When the waters cleared the next day, the fish were gone.

On another occasion several years ago, we were all home due to a snowstorm that dumped a foot of snow on the area and closed schools. We weren't going to let a little snow keep us inside, though, and as soon as the roads were passable, we headed down to the Hurricane Barrier walkway armed with fishing rods . . . and snow shovels! We shoveled an area to fish from and landed a bass on just about every cast. We've seen this happen a few times since then, and now when it snows and most folks are thinking about heading for the slopes, I think of grabbing my fishing rods.

Winter fishing techniques to use in the Providence River are simple, and you can fit all the lures you need in your coat pocket. This is a time for jigs fished on light tackle, and since most of the fish will be schoolies with an occasional small keeper, spinning setups of seven to eight feet are perfect. Line is your most important consideration. Monofilament tends to stiffen in cold weather, especially lines greater than 10-pound test. A good alternative to stiff mono is to go with braided lines; they are very limp, strong and sensitive. Many jig fishermen use braided line attached to a fluorocarbon leader and I think this is an ideal combination for winter jig fishing. Your leader should be a slightly lower pound-test than your braided line to allow break-offs should you get snagged. The best lures to use in the Providence River are light-colored plastic fish-like bodies on jigsheads of 1/2-ounce or less. I especially like 4-inch Zoom Flukes in albino color, although Storm lures, Cocohoes, Fin-S Fish and shad bodies also work well.

Another important aspect to this fishing is that nighttime is by far the right time to fish. The natural tendency of an inexperienced fisherman would be to try this place on a warm winter day. The thinking would be that the fish would be active during the warmest part of the day (afternoon) in winter, yet this is not the case. Remember, it is the warmwater outflow that controls the water temperature along here and not the sun. Just like in the summer, these stripers feed more actively during the night, and that's when you'll find the best action. Unfortunately, that usually means fishing during the coldest part of the day, but isn't bragging about fish caught under the worst conditions more fun?

The trick is to be prepared. Unless I'm absolutely certain it is going to be unseasonably warm I dress like I am going ice-fishing with layered clothing, ski pants and winter pack boots. Rarely is my body cold but keeping my hands and fingers warm and moving is a problem. Gloves that are warm may be too thick and will not allow the dexterity needed to cast. Gloves that are too thin are as bad as no gloves at all. I've used everything from neoprene gloves to hunting gloves, and I've found the best are ski gloves that are lined. Look for a pair that are warm, yet lightweight. Lined hunting gloves are a close second. I'm not high on unlined neoprene gloves. Also, try to get gloves that are waterproof, since rainy or snowy nights and wet hands can send you back to the car in a short amount of time no matter how good the fishing is.

Admittedly, there seems to be a cutoff point as far as the temperature is concerned when winter fishing. It's been my experience that temperatures below 25 degrees are very difficult because ice forms on the guides and the spool. Sometimes ice must be removed every seven or eight casts. Ice on the guides can be removed by swishing the rod in warm water or by blowing a warm breath on the icy guides but severe cold makes fishing impossible.

Finding the prime areas to fish near the power plant is easy because they are located right off Route 195. From Route 195 west, exit 2 will bring you to the Hurricane Barrier and almost right to the water. Imagine a big rectangle with the Point Street Bridge on one side, the Manchester Street Power Plant on another, the private docks and restaurant area on another and the Hurricane Barrier itself of the other side – this is the most productive area to wet a line. You can walk around about half of this area and fish from the many perches that rise above the water. Although the fish tend to stay together they have a tendency to move from spot to spot, so it's important to keep moving until you find them. Parking is available along the streets, most of it along South Water Street near bars and restaurants. Parking can be especially difficult on Friday and Saturday nights when you are competing with bar patrons for parking space. There is also a parking lot at the west end of the Point Street Bridge that has ample parking after business hours.

The Providence River offers a highly unusual, urban fishing experience for striped bass fishermen. It is a far cry from the pristine south shore that most Rhode Island anglers associate with striper fishing. But if you're one of those striper nuts who just can't stand the idea of waiting until spring, the striped bass are here. Where else can you catch a striper during a snowstorm in January?

Jon Pickering unhooks a schoolie on a snowy night at the Providence River. This is cold-weather fishing and you will need to dress as if you are ready for ice fishing. Warm, lined, waterproof gloves are a must.

April In Matunuck

By Joe Lyons

Now, just as they have each new season since the advent of the sport, anglers are making their way down familiar Matunuck Beach Road, past some of the last of South County's farms, beyond the last of the honky-tonk surf bars and 1960s-style beach trailers to a funky little place that the booming economy did not transform into a little slice of East Hampton.

After the fish make their debut at the West Wall, anytime from late March to the second week in April, their next stop is Matunuck. Matunuck's Deep Hole fishing area, Carpenter's Bar and the beach behind the Ocean Mist nightclub are all within walking distance of each other and each affords early season anglers with some great catch-and-release opportunities. Later, around mid-May, the area begins to yield bigger fish. In the fall, Matunuck sometimes produces whoppers. This is springtime, however, so I'll confine my discussion to early season fishing at the three areas mentioned. There is a lot of water in-between and outside of these three areas, so feel free to experiment.

Deep Hole

For many Rhody surfcasters the arrival of fish at Deep Hole signals the "real" beginning of the surf season. Even though the fish may arrive weeks earlier at the West Wall, many anglers refuse to fish there due to mortality concerns over the handling of the sometimes extremely small fish, and the fact that some of the people who frequent the West Wall early in the year are yahoos. It is not uncommon to see undersize fish taken and arguments over crossed lines develop among some of the neophytes. In short, the West Wall, though a very good spot, can be a zoo, particularly on weekends. To fish Deep Hole, however, one needs to own a raincoat and waders and be able to read a tide chart.

After parking in the DEM lot, make your way onto the beach and take a left. Deep Hole abuts the seawall and runs along a rocky sandbar, which quickly becomes exposed once the

tide begins to ebb. Deep Hole is literally just that: a big, steeply descending hole. On most days, when there is white water making up at the end of the sandbar, you can get an idea just how deep it is by observing the waves as they make up, then quickly expire. The bottom drops off so quickly it often appears as if someone pulled the rug out from under the waves.

The conventional wisdom dictates that Deep Hole is best fished on the lower end of the tide, roughly two hours after high until two hours before high. Though there is some disagreement, I like the rising water better than falling, but both produce. West, southwest and early stages of east winds are considered favorable, but the main thing to look for is white water.

Although you can catch fish all along the sandbar and even by the seawall, the best strategy at Deep Hole is to position yourself at a point on the sandbar where you can cast to the drop-off, right where the white water fades. There are usually several points along the sandbar where the combers break, with the farthest sets being the most productive. Wade out onto the sandbar parallel to the incoming waves, and then make your way toward the hole. Cast to the up-tide portion of the white water, take up slack, stay in contact and impart action as the sweep brings your plug, jig or fly by the hole's edge. In the turbulent water, with slack in the line, it is not uncommon to miss strikes. Keep an eye on your line and be prepared to quickly retrieve and set if a fish should hit early in the retrieve. It's not as simple as it sounds, however, and there are many nuances to fishing Deep Hole that only time on the water can convey. If you see someone else catching, take note of what he is doing and try it.

Most of the people who fish Deep Hole are experienced and friendly. They will readily share information about what color jig worked best or when they caught last. This is not the highly competitive, secretive crowd that will come later; the early season atmosphere is more like that of a reunion. When you are on the sandbar, give the people around you room so the "sweep" does not cross your line with theirs. This can be easily deduced by watching the anglers for a couple of minutes before you start casting. Everyone crosses somebody's line occasionally, but repeated indiscretions will label you as an ignoramus, so be polite. The surfers and birdwatchers who frequent the area should be afforded courtesy also, as they are often good sources of information about the presence of bait and gamefish.

For early season action, a medium-action rod with 15- to 20-pound-test line (to pull snags free) works well. If you've never done any wading in April, be advised that the water is very cold at this time of year. I recommend that you use insulated neoprene waders, a tight sealing coat, a wool hat and half-gloves.

A small white or chartreuse bucktail jig attached to a wooden-egg-style casting weight is the most common and most effective method. Tie the jig to the egg with 2 to 3 feet of mono and retrieve with a bouncing action.

When fly-fishing, I like a white and chartreuse Clouser Minnow on intermediate line, retrieved with a bouncing, jiglike strip-

At Deep Hole, the white water edges, where the waves collapse into the hole, is where you want to be!

ping action. I always use a stripping basket when fly-fishing Matunuck. Korkers or felt-soled waders provide good traction on the slippery rocks that cover the sandbars of Deep Hole and Carpenter's.

Every now and then at Deep Hole you will see someone way out on the sandbar, fishing in deep water. Don't assume that just because they can do this, you can also. There are a couple of very experienced anglers who use wetsuit-like outfits that enable them to fish the last, most productive sets. I don't recommend it, particularly for beginning anglers. The waves often come in from two directions and double up on you, and the drop-off, as I stated before, is quite steep. It's not worth risking life and limb over a few extra fish.

Carpenter's Bar

As you make your way to the right, toward the Ocean Mist, a popular beachfront bar and restaurant, you will come upon a point of land just before a concrete-block retaining wall. In front of this point a rocky sandbar is visible at low tide. It stretches seaward in a diagonal line for about 600 feet. White water can be seen making up at a narrow point at the bar's end. This is Carpenter's Bar. Carpenter's is similar to Deep Hole in that it is best fished on the lower stages of the tide, and the edges of white water are the most productive.

But unlike Deep Hole, where you have the exposed bar behind you, at Carpenter's you will be surrounded by water. Also, as you wade out, take note that the bar dips about halfway out and then rises again in front of the white water where you will be fishing. Keep that in mind so you do not flood your waders on the return trip to shore. Follow the bar to where the white water makes up, take up position as close to the white water as you feel comfortable, and try to cast behind the combers and retrieve through the whitewater edges. The number-one mistake people make at Carpenter's is not going out far enough; the best fishing will be out where the waves are making up.

Carpenter's is best fished with a partner, which makes fish handling in the deep water a lot easier. I like to use metal and surface stuff at Carpenter's, but most everything works. Carpenter's tends to lag behind Deep Hole slightly as to when the fish arrive, but only slightly. Wind conditions of light-moderate west-southwest are considered prime. When the fishing really gets going in May, Carpenter's gets the edge for early season keepers.

Carpenter's is not an easy area to fish, but for those with the skills it is a great spot. It is not uncommon to see some excellent fishermen out on the sandbar. A surfcaster should have scored a B or better in Surfcasting 101 before he attempts Carpenter's. The difficulty level, between getting to the best spot, navigating the deep water and knowing when to get off, tends to weed out the amateurs. Another important downside should

At Carpenter's, make your way over the partially exposed bar and fish the edges.

be noted also: For the most part, Carpenter's does not lend itself well to fly-fishing. Some may disagree, and there are exceptions, but I find the distance needed to hit the most productive water is almost always too great for the long wand.

Beach Behind The Ocean Mist

The beach behind the Ocean Mist is as easy to fish as Carpenter's is difficult. If you want to introduce a child or other beginner to surf fishing, this is one of the best places to do it. Again, west-southwest wind is preferable. Midhigh tide is best, white water is not necessary and the spot lends itself to fly-fishing quite well.

In addition to the standard bucktail jig, metal lures like Kastmasters and Hopkins work well behind the Ocean Mist. There is nothing to hang up on, so swimming plugs are very effective and a favorite choice. Good swimming plugs include the Yo-Zuri in fluorescent yellow and chartreuse. If you have any Swedish-style balsam wood plugs remaining in your plug bag, like Nils Masters, this is a good place to bust them out, as they work exceptionally well, also. For fly-fishing, Clouser Minnows, Deceivers and, later, poppers in bright colors will all work. Sinking line for all but the poppers is the order of the day.

If you are only going to fish behind the Ocean Mist, there is street parking available. Park in the designated areas. There is technically a two-hour limit, but this is mainly enforced during beach season; I have never seen anyone get tagged in the spring and fall. To get to the beach, cut through by the front door of the Ocean Mist.

There's a lot of surfcasting legend and lore revolving around Matunuck. The late Jerry Sylvester, who wrote one of the early sportfishing books, *Salt Water Fishing Is Easy*, reportedly suffered a fatal heart attack while fighting a fish on Carpenter's Bar. In *Reading The Water*, the popular book about fishing Martha's Vineyard by Robert Post, there is a section by the late Roberto Germani that details his experiences and the experiences of Andy Ray while fishing Deep Hole. In addition to interesting reading, there are some useful techniques woven into the story.

My favorite memory of Matunuck took place a couple of seasons ago while fishing alone on a misty Tuesday morning. There was no white water that day, but I decided not to heed my own advice and went anyway. I hooked an average school fish on a chartreuse Deceiver while fly-fishing at Deep Hole. It was the first fish of the year and the fish hit the fly close enough for me to witness the take. I played it, released it and then continued fishing. All and all, a non-event, it was just a typical school bass.

But that first fish of the year, that first take, then watching the fish swim from my hand back out, was such a wondrous experience. So much of our energy is focused on catching Mr. Big, we forget the joy of our first fish. Maybe it's a good thing there is an off-season. Because every year when I go to Matunuck and catch that first fish, I'm reminded of the reasons I fish, and I again feel a degree of the same joyous excitement I felt when I caught my very first fish.

Rhode Island's West Wall
-There's Rarely A Break In The Action

By Thom Pelletier

There are few places along Rhode Island's oceanfront that offer more opportunities to catch gamefish and food fish than at the West Wall at Pt. Judith's Harbor of Refuge. This long dogleg-shaped fish magnet extends some 3,600 feet into the Atlantic and can provide an excellent platform for the shore-bound angler or a go-to structure for boaters.

From mid-April, when the first school bass arrive along the outer wall, until mid-November, when the last schoolies are taken in the pocket at the base of the inner wall, there is not much slack time here. When the water temperature reaches their comfort zone, the first of the year's bass are drawn to this site. A few days of southwesterly breezes can have the wall teeming with fish. The presence of small bait, such as squid, will keep them in the area for weeks, from late April right into June. As the water starts to warm, there will be a good mix of fish, from tiny fish of 9 or 10 inches to the keeper mark and occasionally beyond. At this time a 1/4- to 1/2-ounce white or chartreuse bucktail or curly tail grub will often produce enough action to wear you out. Slug-Gos, Fin-S Fish and other soft-bodied artificials will often draw the interest of the larger fish.

The normal pattern of early season schoolies is to run along the wall while pushing the bait. You can track their movement as anglers to the left or right of your position hook up progressively in a domino effect. Even when the action really heats up, care should be taken in releasing these youngsters. They are just as vulnerable to internal injuries when bounced off the rocks as any other creature.

The next visitors will be the blues. When they are on the prowl and mingling with the bass, some of the jigs that you offer on light leaders are going to disappear. The first bluefish that arrive are usually small, "cocktail" blues. These 2- to 4-pound fish are often feisty leapers that are a riot on trout tackle. Frequently a charge of larger fish, long, lean and with a head that seems disproportionately large for the rest of their body, will buzz through. These 8- to 10-pounders will definitely kick the intensity of the battle up a notch.

An event happening with more and more regularity in recent years is the appearance of squeteague. They are drawn to the same feedbag that attracts the other species. Many of these squets will later take up residence within Narragansett Bay for the summer. While it is unlikely that these guys will ever inhabit our shores in numbers to rival the bass and blues, any return of this beautiful gamester is more than welcomed.

As the season progresses, other fish will provide sport and delicious table fare for anglers plying the wall. This man-made rock pile is one of the few places that offers a chance to catch fluke from shore. Those diligent enough to drag and bounce a baited bucktail on or very close to the bottom can often tempt a few keepers along the first leg of the wall's ocean side. The same method can also produce on the inner side of the wall, especially as the Salt Pond empties on a dropping tide.

Scup fishermen can count on the far section of the wall right to the very end to produce good numbers, again on the ocean side. Sea bass are often taken here, as well. Simple scup rigs with squid, worms or clams will take all the fish you want. Be sure to take enough bait and tackle, especially sinkers, as it's a long walk back, and this rocky turf can consume a considerable number of them. A helpful trick is to secure the sinker with a lighter line than your running line and hook leaders. This way when the sinker gets lodged in the rocks, and a few inevitably will, the lighter line will break first. Then you can at least retain the rest of your rig.

From a fisherman's perspective, the wall can be divided into two sections. The end closest to shore is lower than the far end after the bend. On this close end are many fishing stations, some of which are more favorable than others. The better ones allow an angler close proximity to the water without dealing with the perils of slippery, slime-coated rocks or having to take too many soaking wave splashes. When it gets crowded, however, you have to take what's available. I stick to this end when fishing for school bass because it allows me to reach and release them most efficiently.

The far end beyond the bend is somewhat higher off the water. It can also produce early school bass, but the distance down to the water makes it a struggle to unhook the fish on light tackle. Smaller fish, such as scup and sea bass, are much easier to deal with.

From late May to early July the inner base of the West Wall is a great place to soak a whole squid, sea clam or chunk of alewife for keeper bass. At the bend opposite the end of the short wall at George's Restaurant, the wall kicks out slightly to the west. These days there is an ever-increasing number of lobster pots near that spot. Dropping a bait in the eddies that form in this pocket as the tide starts to drop can be very productive, but landing a large fish can be a challenging endeavor. Casting swimming plugs and bucktails before the tide starts to rip is also effective, but when the salt pond starts to empty, you'll often have to deal with weeds fouling your hooks.

This spot also hosts numbers of hickory shad at daybreak just about all summer. These bantam tarpon look-a-likes respond to shad darts, tiny metals and small bucktails. When hooked, they'll put on quite an aerial show.

When the bonito and false albacore arrive in August, the wall is one of the premier spots to take them from shore. The entire length of the wall becomes the playing field as these fish harass schools of bait. The schoolie and bluefish action in this locale occurs mostly in the early morning or evening, but when the bonito and albies appear, the activity can take place at any time throughout the day.

Boat anglers are also drawn here during the early season. They, along with the jetty jockeys and surf crowd, also welcome the infusion of fish that hit the wall and the adjacent Jerusalem Beach. A show of courtesy here between the boaters and their less mobile counterparts can avert unnecessary confrontations.

While jetty-bound anglers often combine casting with waiting and watching, boaters have the luxury of trolling the area when visible action slows down. Small diving swimmers, such as Rebels, Bombers and Thunderstiks, will usually appeal to stripers and blues. Small umbrella rigs with 3-inch tube lures and smaller versions of 9'er rigs will often yield multiple hookups.

Boaters should also be aware that, in the fall, both albies and bonito can be found anywhere along the entire wall, inside and out. I've often run into schools as soon as I cleared the gut and entered the harbor. They regularly remain in the channel on a dropping tide and will chase bait right out into the West Gap.

To catch these mini-tuna while trolling the area in the vicinity of the wall, the swimmers mentioned previously will take a few. Metals such as Needl-Eels, Crippled Herring, Spro swimming jig and Deadly Dicks can also be cast or trolled effectively.

When the bonito, which are more discerning than the albies by nature, become even more finicky than usual because of fishing pressure and boat traffic, try this method. Start with a 3- or 4.5-inch Slug-Go if sand eels are present or a 4-inch Fin-S Fish if silversides (spearing) are the prevalent bait. Carefully thread the soft bait onto a 2/0 long-shank beak hook so that the eye of the hook can be hidden within the bait. You want a very slight bend in the bait, as this will cause the erratic behavior that often triggers reluctant fish. The trick is to not allow too much of a bend, as this will exaggerate the action too much and totally twist your line. For leader material I like 12- to 15-pound-test SeaGuar fluorocarbon. Three to four feet will normally do it. Quality swivels are a must.

When fish are in the area but not showing often, a 1/2- to 1-ounce bead trolling or keel sinker can be added. This will serve two purposes: It will get your offering down a bit and help alleviate the line twist.

Shore anglers coming from the north or south can find the West Wall by traveling Route 1 to the East Matunuck State Beach/Snug Harbor exit. This puts you on Succotash Road. When the road forks, bear to the right and continue toward the State Beach. At the entrance to the beach, the road angles sharply to the left. Proceed along the dunes and beach houses until you reach another left at a small traffic island. A little past the island there are several parking spaces opposite the dockside shops. When these fill up there is also parking farther down the road at the Jerusalem State Pier. Once parked, head back to the traffic island, where you will see the access road to the wall. There is no parking on this road and violators will get towed. It would be wise for first-timers to make a daytime outing to become familiar with the layout.

For boaters, there are several options in launching facilities. The state ramp in Galilee is the most popular. Follow the signs from Route 1 directing you to the Port of Galilee and the Block Island ferry. At the end of the Escape Road that leads to the village, take a right and the ramp entrance is just before the Great Island Bridge.

There are other public ramps but most are farther up the pond and a few lack adequate parking areas. Kenport Marina on Succotash Road offers, for a fee, a convenient private launching area and parking, plus fuel, bait and tackle.

Whether from shore or boat, this is one of the premier fishing areas along Rhode Island's South Shore. From spring to fall it seems there is always something happening at The Wall. But instead of taking my word for it, why not give it a try. ◄►◄

Breachway Bass

By David Pickering

B reachways are unique to Rhode Island. Everywhere else along the East Coast they are commonly called outflows or inlets, but along Rhode Island's oceanfront, these avenues of water that join coastal ponds to the ocean are known as the south shore breachways. They are highly productive places to fish, treasured locations where shore-fishermen sling eels, free-spool plugs and bounce jigs in search of big bass that feed in swift breachway currents. Prime time to catch large breachway bass and occasional big blues is on the nighttime dropping tides in October and November.

The Rhode Island south shore runs from Point Judith in Narragansett to Napatree Point in Westerly. It forms almost a straight run of roughly 20 miles of fragile barrier beach. As you stand on this shore, in front of you, to the south, is the pounding Atlantic; behind you, to the north, lies a series of large, protected tidal ponds. Only the breach-ways, by the names of Weekapaug, Quonny (short for Quonochontaug), Charlestown and the Galilee Channel, cut this south shore ribbon of sand to provide water links to these ponds. Each of these breachways has jetties bordering its outflow, and each offers the shore-fisherman public parking right along its flow, making for hassle-free access. One breachway, located at Charlestown, even has camping.

While the beach runs for 20 miles, most experienced fishermen know full well that the majority of fish will be found in front of, or near, these breachways on the outgoing tides. Large predatory fish, striped bass in particular, are drawn to the breachways like magnets. For much of the year, these predators use the breachway as a route to swim to the ponds under cover of darkness. There, they forage on the large amounts of bait, such as hickory shad, baby flounder, shrimp, silversides, worms, crabs and other delicacies that reside there. However, during the fall months when the predators are migrating, many prefer to lie in wait at that magical point where the breachway exits into the ocean. It is there that outgoing tides deliver many of those prey morsels, some of which are heading south for the winter. Whenever the flow moves out, it signals a dinner bell for large fish in the area to move into the flow for easy pickings.

Most experienced breachway fishermen know that the inside corner rock at the end of the jetty of any of the four breachways is the key spot to fish. For that reason, the end of the jetties can get mighty crowded on a nice fall night, especially during the early evening hours. Many of these bass fishermen will congregate on the ends of the jetty and fish in rotation when there is a crowd. They play almost a circular game of musical chairs, as fishermen take turns casting, free-spooling, holding their plugs in the currents and retrieving while constantly moving to the left of the line. Rainy and lousy nights will see few fishermen off the ends with no need to rotate. I never liked the rotation game, so if the ends of the breachways are crowded, I prefer to drop back within the narrow lane of water between jetties and fish in the breachway itself. Few want to fish this swift water, admittedly less productive, yet there is lots of room along here to move back and forth, and less competition for its fish.

Techniques for successfully fishing these places can vary from place to place, but there is a common thread to fishing the breachways of Weekapaug, Quonny and Charlestown, all of which are similar in makeup. One of the very best lures to use in these three places after dark is a large surface swimmer like those from Atom, Hab's or Gibbs in the 2- to 3-ounce range. These plugs are cast outward, off the end of the jetty, and free-spooled way out into the outflow. When the current begins to lessen, put the reel into gear and hold. You should feel the plug's side-to-side swimming movement on your rod tip as the current imparts the action. As the pull of the plug slows, reel it in slowly. Hits will determine the productive zone and how much line to free-spool outward. Live eels can be fished in these places using the same casting and free-spool technique. Another artificial with proven success in the breachways is the bucktail jig. Overall, that artificial catches more fish in these places than any other does, due to the fact it is the best daytime artificial and also works at night. The key to using the jig in the breachway is to get it working along the bottom. The weight of your jig will depend on the speed of the current. However, a jig of 1 to 2 ounces is a good size to use during an average flow of water. The best jigs will be all-white models. I like a big-eyed and bulky "popeye" jig, although I have also had success with hot lips, spearhead and flathead-type jigs. Make sure you add plastic curly tails or pork rinds to your jigs for additional action.

Fishing a jig in the breachway currents can be a tricky business because of the rocks that exist there, as well as out front. One needs to develop a feel for where that jig is at all times; those experienced at this can scratch it along the bottom with ease. Successful

The Charlestown Breachway. At times it can be quite crowded, looking like a porcupine. Get there early to claim a prime spot towards the end of the jetty. -photo by John Burke

jig-fishermen will cast crosscurrent or even upcurrent and let the jig drop before beginning the retrieve. With swift currents imparting the action, all that is needed on the part of the fisherman is a slow retrieve that will keep the jig off the bottom – expect to lose some jigs down there.

Another artificial that works well in the fast water inside the breachway is a swimmer, such as a 7-inch Mambo Minnow, straight-back Rebel or 6-inch Nils Master. My technique for using swimmers involves casting crosscurrent and holding in the swift currents. As the plug swings toward the shore, it digs deeper down. Most of your hits on the swimmer should come close to the jetty since that is where most fish will be foraging, close to the structure and safety of the jetty rocks. Using swimmers has worked well for me along Galilee's Short Wall and within the swift and narrow currents of Charlestown Breachway. I prefer light-colored swimmers in a pearl color or blue-backed models.

Probably my best "live" bait for a big bass in the breachway has been rigged eels. I pre-rig many of my dead eels with front wobble plates called "eel squids." These rigged eels also sport a hook in the rear. The front plate gives the rig weight to get it down, and its wiggle gives the eel a snakelike, back-and-forth swimming action. Cast these out crosscurrent, and let them sink. Just like fishing a swimmer, you want to hold them in the current and let them swing close to the jetty before retrieving. Using the rigged eel, I've taken many keeper bass in the Galilee Channel.

All four of the above-mentioned breachways are within a half an hour's drive of each other, and all of them are accessible from Route 1. The Galilee Channel is located off Route 108, or Point Judith Road, in the port of Galilee. There is public access and free parking on the Galilee side, along the Short Wall, which is opposite the famous George's Restaurant. Traveling south on Route 1, Charlestown Breachway comes next. It is located at the end of Charlestown Beach Road. Parking is available at the campground that borders the east-side jetty of Charlestown Breachway. Camping for self-contained vehicles is available here and is very popular with fishermen who have campers. Quonny Breachway comes next off Route 1 South and is located at the end of West Beach Road. There is a public parking area in the back of the breachway, and you must traverse private property to reach the breachway mouth. Usually there are few problems with this in late fall or at night. Weekapaug Breachway is the farthest south and is located off Route 1A along Atlantic Avenue. There is a public parking area by the Atlantic Avenue Bridge.

One final tidbit of information, which is important to bass fishermen who fish these breachways, concerns the lag or difference in current and tidal conditions between the breachway and the ocean. In Charlestown, Quonny and Weekapaug, the water will not begin to flow outward until two or three hours after the high is reached in the ocean. Galilee moves out exactly 45 minutes after the high is reached in the ocean. The currents continue to flow out of all, except Galilee, three to four hours after low tide. Galilee currents continue to flow outward from one to one and a half hours after the low is reached. Conditions, like the height of the tide, storminess and strong winds can all alter these lag times.

There is no better time to fish the south shore breachways for big bass and occasional big blues than the outgoing tides in October and November. While nighttime will produce the biggest fish consistently for those using large swimmers, eels and bucktail jigs, good-size fish can also be taken in these flows in the daytime using bucktail jigs. Rhode Island's south shore sports 20 miles of beachfront, yet you will find the majority of fall keeper bass in or around the breachways. They are where the bass are foraging and are prime locations for shore-fishermen to hook a trophy. ◆━◀

Exploring Cuttyhunk's North Side

By Captain Charley Soares

Fishermen are creatures of habit, but unfortunately not all of this conduct is of the beneficial sort. Anglers tend to imitate or chase success, even the most modest or dubious accomplishments, and consequently, many tend to become mired in mediocrity. They follow the crowd and exhibit a herd mentality, derived from the fear of striking out on their own and having to deal with what they consider failure. Remember, fishing is not a sport in the sense that basketball, tennis and golf are. There are no real winners or losers, just satisfied participants. I know quite a few fishermen who are comfortable explaining their lack of success by saying no one else caught anything either. Before we get any further, I should explain that I've had some very satisfying days on the water when we didn't harvest fish, but I'm a fisherman who sets out fishing to catch fish – everything else is a bonus.

Every weekend boats head out from marinas all along the mainland of southern Massachusetts, Martha's Vineyard and eastern Rhode Island and set course for the south side of the Elizabeth Islands. I've been fishing that area for quite some time and recall a period when we could leave Sow and Pigs an hour or so after first blush, where we jigged up bass and blues, then head east towards Quicks Hole. Once there, we'd make a few passes to top off or cover the bottom of the fish boxes before the return trip to Westport, Padanaram or New Bedford.

On most mornings we might encounter, at the most, a lobsterman working his gear or a sport or two casting lures into the stones a respectable distance from the shoreline. Thirty-five years ago most of Vineyard Sound and the rocky shoreline of the Elizabeths was relatively deserted. Most of the cruising and commercial traffic headed straight up the middle of the Sound. Life was good. These days, on any given weekend from mid-May through late October, the shoreline from Woods Hole to Sow and Pigs is crowded with boats anchored up tight to the beach, fishing cut bait while staking out some of the most productive bass haunts along the entire striper coast.

The west side of Quicks can be like a parking lot without an attendant, with boats of every shape, size and purpose anchored between the navigation buoys, fishing cut bait in the rip. If you go through there some day during a bite, you can watch the skippers engaged in a dangerous game of chess, as boats from the rear haul anchor to jump in front of boats in the lead, which have just boated a fish. Quicks was one of my favorite and most productive spots. Snapping a Sabatowski bucktail behind 150 feet of wire produced a lot of fish, but I'm sorry to say that, because of the crowds, I haven't been able to fish Quicks the way I like to in more than a dozen years.

For years, when the familiar glow of the red and white beacon on Gay Head cliffs began to fade in the nighttime sky, it was time to head for the protection of Cuttyhunk's outer harbor. The most direct route from the Pigs was due east, down the back side to the bell at Canapitsit, where we ran the gauntlet of off-station buoys, playing Russian roulette with the boulders in the very narrow channel. I've made that hair-raising trip enough times to appreciate the alternative of sliding through one of my slots between the bearded knobs and heading around the north side for the safety of Cuttyhunk Pond.

On some nights the fog was so thick I set the hook up tight to the beach and hoped none of the guides would travel in this close and end up wearing me for a bowsprit. On one particularly quiet night we heard the unmistakable sound of bass tails slapping the surface a short distance away. The live eels came off the bait-casting gear and were replaced with the big Atom B-40s. The chubby swimming plugs were launched out into the dense fog and hit the water with a splash. The lures didn't move very far before they were inhaled by members of a school of hungry bass, which were pushing bait up against the shore of the cove where we anchored. That night was the beginning of breaking a bad habit and the start of extensive explorations along the north side of the Elizabeths.

I spent the next 10 years exploring every north-side nook, cove and rock pile along the roughly 14-mile stretch from the West Island Pond on Cuttyhunk, all the way down to Woods Hole when the southwest wind made fishing the Sound side impossible. While not every promising location held fish, the first time I tried it I eventually caught bass, blues and an occasional weakfish in almost every section with noticeable structure. I learned that the north

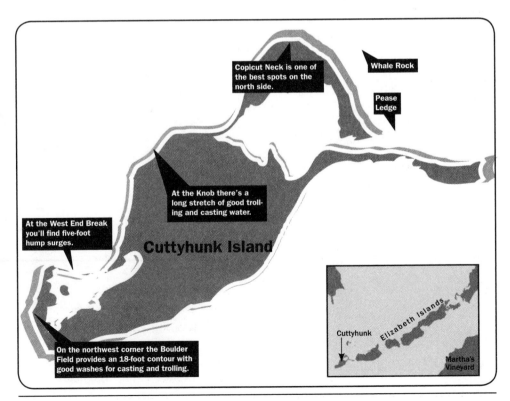

side was very similar to the weather side of the islands, right down to providing habitat and food for heavyweight linesiders with broad shoulders. It doesn't happen overnight, but over time you learn to read water and detect life when prospecting a familiar shoreline. I can work the north side, casting into certain holes while passing up others that don't appear fishy, with the confidence born of years of trial and error. Do I miss a few? Perhaps, but if I do, you can have them. In this game familiarity does not breed contempt; it enhances success.

Because of the nature of the dangerous structure along the north side of the Elizabeths, there will be no GPS or latitude-longitude coordinates provided because of the danger those coordinates might pose. The difference between 10 or 20 feet can mean the difference between a bent rod and grinding your hull up against a submerged boulder. If you are a stickler for explicit compass bearings, you will disagree with the first few locations we discuss, because, rather than being located on the north side, they are actually on the west or northwest corner of Cuttyhunk. For the purpose of this discussion, the back side will be considered anything north of Sow and Pigs Reef.

As you will notice when you peruse NOAA chart 13229 (Richardson's waterproof chart book for Buzzards Bay, South Cape and the Islands was my reference for this article) most of the productive coves, points and nooks along the north shore of Buzzards Bay were never named. They may have seemed insignificant to cartographers, but they are most important to striper hounds. If I'd been consulted, these locations would have such names as Bass Rock, Lunker Ledge, Cow Cove and similar descriptions that would start your bass fishing juices flowing. While I've given names to most of my favorite locations, those tags won't coincide with anything you will find on the charts. However, my descriptions of these places will put you right in the ballpark.

One of the many benefits of fishing the north side during a smoky southwester is that you'll be blown away from the rocky shores. Fish the south side in a stiff southerly breeze and you may find yourself on the boulders. The person who coined the phrase "between a rock and a hard spot" was obviously referring to time spent casting along the weather side of Cuttyhunk. Southwest Bluff at the tip of Cuttyhunk was one of my favorite casting locations, a piece of water from which we lifted a lot of big stripers over the rail, including numerous 50-pounders caught on bright summer afternoons as well as under the cover of darkness. There were a lot more trophy fish in the pond back then, but we experienced some close calls and hair-raising rides around that southern knob.

Since I began spending more time on the back side, I haven't noticed that much difference in size or production, and the fishing is much more comfortable

Skin plugs are deadly on both sides of the Elizabeths, particularly on the coves and rock piles of the north side. This 22-pound bass fell for a skin plug at early morning.

as well as a lot less crowded. Depending on where I travel from, I either begin at North Rock at the entrance to Quicks Hole on Nashawena or at the northwest corner of Cuttyhunk where the Gosnold Monument overlooks a boulder field, which I think the Good Lord created especially for striped bass.

If there is a problem with the north side, it's all the options you have to choose from. If I depart from Westport Harbor, I begin fishing the aforementioned boulder field approximately northwest of the Gosnold Monument. This is a very sticky place, where you must proceed with great caution, particularly with any wind from the northwest. On a typical afternoon with a sou'westerly breeze I troll up along the 15-foot contour and cast an eel or subsurface swimmer into the washes. If there is someone home, they will usually let you know with a tail slap or a big boil behind your offering. If they are not eating at that stage of the tide, I make a mental note to return here further along in the tide or around dusk.

What a difference low light or an increased rush of water makes in a fish's appetite and disposition. Trolling along this 15- to 17-foot contour line with a tube-and-worm offering will put some nice fish in your cooler. Just avoid cutting in too close to the shaded blue area on your chart where a rock could jump out and take a bite out of your skeg. Friends of mine fish parachute jigs on wire along the 20-foot edge and catch their share of fish, but I like working in closer, where the fish move into the stones to feed.

Anywhere there is an exchange of water, fresh or salt, is a preferred location that any bass in residence will visit at some stage of the tide. The opening to the West End (Gosnold) Pond is just such a location. Despite the shallow water (five feet at mean low water on the immediate south side of the break) it's a great spot to cast an eel or troll a tube. Although it may look pretty innocuous, there is a steep rise from 14 to 5 feet that creates a noticeable rip line where I find the bass lying on the island side of the shallow water. I never move over the five-foot mark (if you read under 10 feet on your fishfinder, you are in too close), because I want to avoid the ominous shadow my hull casts, which will spook a fish waiting in ambush. Once you invade the shallow water, before your lure or bait gets to the prime location, the predator(s) has vacated the area. Begin your pass in

Casting a live or rigged eel into the structure will produce bass from schoolies to heavyweights.

the deeper water, at 20 to 22 feet, and head directly to the 5-foot hump, turning northeast when you hit the 14-foot mark. Your boat and engine will not invade the shallows, and the turn will put your lures in the strike zone as you continue past the hump.

From the cut north, the shoreline is rather straight and ordinary until you reach the next pronounced knob, which protrudes and turns a corner. The depth at the beginning of this location is approximately 15 on in to 5 feet, with some impressive rocks thrusting out of the water at low tide. Casting and trolling along this entire edge to the break where the cobble beach marks the low-lying area just outside the anchorage in Cuttyhunk Pond is one of my favored and very protected locations. My friend Andy Fournier was aboard, casting a live eel on the point of the knob during a snotty southwester, and he put a 44-pound bass on the deck. Big stripers most certainly frequent the north side of the Elizabeths – just ask any Vineyard sharpie what he thinks about the productivity of the north side of his island.

The next prime area is both sides of Copicut Neck, which is a long stretch of boulder-strewn beach and washes that runs north-northeast around the knob and continues south-southeast towards the entrance to the north jetty and entrance to Cuttyhunk Pond. It's not uncommon to drift into one of the rocky coves and see the silver flash of stripers bolting from the edge where the bright sand meets the deep purple, as the shadow of your hull invades their lair. This is where trolling and casting will compensate you with bass, blues and an occasional weakfish, which take up residence here from August to early October.

Just east-northeast of Copicut Neck is Whale Rock, a huge boulder where an occasional bass or jumbo fluke hides in ambush in anticipation of an easy meal. What began as an embarrassing experience turned into a profitable lesson for a friend who got careless here. After you take a route for so long, you become neglectful in your rush to beat the fog to the jetty and you cut corners. Our friend strayed off course just a few yards and ran his rugged bass boat on top of Pease Ledge. His white oak keel and heavy bronze strut saved him from damage, other than the embarrassment he suffered when the word of his misadventure spread among the fleet. While stuck there in the fog, waiting for two hours of tide to lift him off his perch, he killed the time bottom fishing with sea worms from the flat he purchased in New Bedford earlier in the day. He appeared in Cuttyhunk Pond three hours later with a mixed bag of jumbo scup, sea bass, a doormat fluke and a case of wounded pride.

There is so much structure around Penikese Island that attempting to discuss it would not leave any room for the Nashawena shoreline. Over on the east side of Canapitsit Channel is a wreck symbol denoting an overturned vessel. In the course of 30 or so years I've seen at least five or six boats aground on that dangerous corner, and I pulled one man out of the water. The swimmer fell out of his boat as he was attempting to pet or grab the head of a whitetail deer swimming from Cuttyhunk to Nashawena. Fortunately it was almost slack water and he had shifted his boat into neutral. I believe he'll stick to bass fishing in the future.

Casting into that corner in early morning or late afternoon has almost always produced school bass holding just beyond the point, waiting to pounce on bait being swept along by the strong tides that run this dangerous gauntlet. I've never caught anything larger than school bass in these shallows, but a friend drifts for fluke on the east tide when wind and current combine for a good drift. I've seen some 25-inch doormats that have been pried off this interesting piece of bottom.

From this corner all the way to Knox Point, anyone with a nose for bass habitat can see where a well-placed plug or eel could get you a nice fish. Halfway to the point there is a great trolling spot that is highlighted on the charts. This is a hump that rises to 14 feet on the bottom of the tide where it's surrounded by 19- to 20-foot depths. Tubing this the first week of June resulted in nine bass in the 29- to 33-inch class, two of which were filled with choggies, scup, lobster and sand crabs.

Between Knox Point and North Point at Quicks is some of the best-looking water you could hope to find. In-between there is a large rocky cove you don't want to wander into, but it's a great place to idle up to and cast an eel into while the southwesterly wind pushes you out of harm's way.

There are fishermen who seek publicity for their accomplishments but will scream to high heaven if this attracts unfavorable attention. I avoid those guys like the plague. There are a few high-liners who operate in the shadows, preferring obscurity and the resultant tranquility. I know of such a man who made a living bass fishing at North Rock on the Buzzards Bay side of Quicks Hole. It seemed that every time I went through, there he was anchored up with three rods deployed. Over the years we became friendly and I asked if he ever went home. His answer was not during the bass season, but he did run back across the bay to sell his fish, catch his pogies and rush back to claim his spot.

From North Rock to the Lone Rock buoy is some of the best bass fishing in Buzzards Bay. The same shoreline from North Rock to Uncatena is also prime bass-fishing habitat that is worthwhile looking into.

Now for the kicker: Why would someone who has been labeled a hungry and a loner share this information with you? The reason is, I know that most of you will read this and rather than invest a little time conducting your own prospecting, you'll head for the same old spots and compete with the crowds on the south side, and that is just fine with me. Each time I set out from the mainland I leave behind some pretty fantastic fishing. I travel not just to catch bass but to seek the solitude the north side has to offer. Some fishermen are comfortable in crowds, but I thrive in quiet situations, even if it means making a modest sacrifice.

A friend of mine chides me about this idiosyncrasy by guessing that I feel violated when another boat enters my space. He's way off the mark; it takes at least two boats to move me off a piece of preferred bottom. With all the possibilities along the roughly 14 miles of the Elizabeths, there are plenty of nooks, coves, knobs, points and ledges at which to practice my religion along the north side of this temple of bass.

Fishing Under The Cliffs

By Fred Khedouri

The setting sun slips into a clear spot as the clouds start to break on the western horizon. I have been hiking for half an hour, picking my way along a narrow, rocky shoreline to the point where the northwestern corner of Martha's Vineyard rises up 130 feet from the sea. The leaden sky left by a storm has dulled the multicolored layers of clay, sand and stone that form the Gay Head cliffs, but now the land and water take on the intense golden reddish glow of the island's evening light, and the wind and seas are unusually calm. The water between the cliffs and the big green bell buoy offshore is just starting to churn and boil into the fierce rip it will become in another hour when the incoming tide gathers speed. I have a few minutes of light left to make the last hundred yards to a tiny cove formed by the 10-foot waves that winter storms have flung onto the cliffs for thousands of years. When the light is gone, I know the stripers will be here.

Sightseers have been admiring Gay Head since the first European explorers sailed past in the 16th century. But for those of us always on the lookout for a promising spot to fish, this area holds another attraction. Just as the pastures at the top of the Gay Head cliffs give no hint of the complex structure of the earth below, the ocean waters at their footings conceal a vast terrain of huge boulders, rock ledges and kelp beds. Look no farther out, for near-shore bottom structure makes an ideal habitat for striped bass.

Unfortunately, the same attributes that make this area a great fishing spot today gave it a fearsome reputation among mariners in years past when Vineyard Sound was one of the most heavily traveled waterways in the nation. The federal government first authorized construction of a lighthouse atop the Gay Head cliffs in 1799 – for good reason, given the hundreds of lives lost in shipwrecks in the area. The present brick structure replaced the first tower in 1856, and is still an active Coast Guard aid to navigation. Following a line due northwest toward Cuttyhunk Island across Vineyard Sound, the Devil's Bridge shoal extends nearly a mile from the base of the cliffs with numerous boulders only a couple of feet below the surface. Modern electronic navigation systems usually make for a safe passage, however.

To make matters even worse for passing vessels, the area is at the confluence of strong tidal currents moving up and down the Sound and in the channel between Martha's Vineyard and Nomans Land to the south. The currents further enhance the fish-attracting quality of the areas near the cliffs, of course, given the lazy feeding habits of stripers. Bait from near and far gets swept up and down the shore in water that is almost always moving and that stays nice and cool, even in midsummer. What better place to hole up in the lee of a nice big rock and wait for appetizing squid, bunker or sand eels to drift past?

Four miles down the shore, the southwestern corner of the island at Squibnocket Point offers a smaller, less colorful set of cliffs with similar undersea surroundings. This point also has a rock-strewn shoal extending out to sea. The currents are not quite as strong as they are off Gay Head, but the fish habitat must be just as attractive given the legendary productivity of the area.

The town in which the Gay Head and Squibnocket cliffs are located officially changed its name to Aquinnah in 1998. The signs have all been changed to read "Aquinnah," but naturally it is still common to hear it referred to as Gay Head, especially in reference to the cliffs. Aquinnah is by far the older name, being one of the traditional names used by the native Wampanoags, who still constitute a sizeable portion of the resident population of Aquinnah.

At the top of the cliffs the land is both publicly and privately owned. The area around the lighthouse is managed by the Vineyard Historical Society and is closed except for tours on Friday, Saturday and Sunday given in the summer beginning an hour before sunset. This is well worth doing, since climbing the tower steps gives a panoramic view of the western portion of Martha's Vineyard, Nomans Land and the Elizabeth Islands from nearly 170 feet above sea level, as well as a spectacular sunset over the water. Just west of the lighthouse, a small group of shops and the surrounding area are owned by the Wampanoag Tribe. Down the road a few hundred yards, the Martha's Vineyard Land Bank Commission manages a stretch of beach, beyond which the land is privately held, except for the Aquinnah resident-only beach. There is public parking for a fee near the Land Bank access operated by the Wampanoag Tribe and a trail down to the water. All of the land around Squibnocket Point is private, with the exception of a small parking area east of the cliffs just over the border in the Town of Chilmark that serves an adjacent resident permit-only beach.

For much of the season, the shore-fishing spots beneath the cliffs only produce consistently from dusk until an hour after dawn. The water on the Gay Head side drops off fairly rapidly on either side of the Devil's Bridge shoal, but the deeper water is beyond normal casting distance. A similar situation exists at Squibnocket. The fish move in very close to shore in low light and at night, however, following the baitfish into the 5- to 20-foot depths found within a few yards of the shore.

I prefer to use a 7 1/2-foot surf rod, relatively short by most surf-fishing standards, and a heavy spinning reel loaded with one of the new Spectra braid lines such as PowerPro in 30-pound test. The prevailing winds in the summer come from the southwest, so it is common to be casting into a moderate breeze. The ultrathin line helps quite a bit to maintain control and get some distance. I also find the braid is a bit more resistant to fraying from the inevitable brush with the rocks. Taking a hint from the offshore billfish crowd, I tie an 8-foot length of 60-pound-test mono to the braid as a leader. The main purpose of the mono is to have something to grab on to that won't give you the feeling you just picked up a razor blade edge-first. With an unhappy bass thrashing around at the end of your line, the ultrathin braid is capable of inflicting a serious cut to an ungloved hand.

The rocky bottom that makes the area a great fishing spot forces the use of surface plugs to get through the evening without losing too much tackle to snags. The shoreline is quite irregular under both the Gay Head and Squibnocket cliffs, forming a series of tiny coves marked by very large rock formations. You can fish these areas by walking out to one of the small promontories and then casting a search pattern in a fan shape to cover both the water at the far end of your casting range off the shore and the area right near the beach. I have used just about everything that floats at one time or another, but I generally stick with an Atom or an old-fashioned cedar plug in medium green or blue. Changing treble hooks for singles greatly reduces the odds of snagging weed without much impact on the hook-up rate.

Although lure makers, who introduce a new color pattern weekly it seems, may disagree, I have come to the conclusion that only three factors determine whether a surface plug will attract a strike. One is size, which you'll have to vary depending on what bait is in the area. The next factor is the action, which is primarily a function of the retrieve style. Since surface plugs are attractor-style lures, their job is to make noise and splash around to attract the attention of nearby fish, or in the case of Danny-style swimmers, to roll along slowly on the surface in the manner of a wounded baitfish. As always, it pays to experiment with different retrieve speeds and styles. The third factor is placement, which is especially critical when fishing under the cliffs. There are innumerable small holes, submerged boulders, ledges and other structure within yards of the shore. Sometimes casting a few feet in a different direction over a hole will make all the difference in the world, and experienced bass anglers know that large fish will often lie right next to boulders.

Despite the conflict with my self-image as an artificials snob who disdains the use of natural bait in any form, I have to admit to making an exception when fishing these rocky shores. Especially in the later part of the season, carrying in a bucket of eels is extremely worthwhile. I always use circle hooks because of their superior hook-up ratio and the fact that my fish are almost always lip-hooked. Snelled onto a three-foot fluorocarbon leader equipped with a ball-bearing swivel (both expensive items, but they help quite a bit in this setting), I cast the eel into a likely hole or near a boulder and leave it to fend for itself for a few moments. Then I retrieve it slowly a few feet at a time. The slow retrieve allows you to cover more water and it's slightly less likely that the eel will work its way too deeply into a crevice and snag, which they love to do if left on the bottom.

It is always a good idea to check the tide charts. Different areas below the cliffs fish well at different stages of the tide, and this is something you can only learn from experience, but in all cases moving water is better than slack. The steep and often narrow shore gives you an even more important reason to know whether the tide is rising or falling; you can easily work yourself into a position that might require a boat to escape at high tide. Although the tidal range is only about two feet or less, that is enough to force a swim if the tide comes in after you have traversed a ledge or spit of beach. Apart from the unpleasantness of being cold and wet, the mussel and barnacle encrusted rocks, slippery footing and strong currents can make escape by sea quite dangerous, especially after dark. Climbing the cliffs is not a practical, or even possible, escape in most spots, not to mention that it is illegal to climb the clay cliffs at Gay Head, which are protected as a national landmark and are under constant threat of erosion.

For the experienced or slightly foolhardy – choosing your weather very carefully – the

Squibnocket Point cliffs (not Gay Head, which is too dangerous due to the strong currents) can be fished from a kayak or inflatable on calm summer nights. I own what may be the world's oldest inflatable dinghy still in service, a 1977 eight-foot Achilles model that has the sea-keeping qualities of a Styrofoam beer cooler. On evenings with no wind, I have launched from the beach at Squibnocket and rowed along the shore out to the point. Casting into the rocks from this pneumatic perch or trolling under oar power can be rewarded with a low speed version of the Nantucket sleigh ride the early whalers experienced when they tied harpoon lines off to the bow of their small boats. A big striper can't drag you 20 miles, but you can lose some ground.

September brings the barely controlled craziness of the annual Martha's Vineyard Striped Bass and Bluefish Derby. Many shore-division competitors are regulars at the cliffs and competition for a good spot gets a bit more stiff, though still very manageable. But the best time to enjoy this beautiful setting to its fullest is after the derby ends in mid-October. The fish are still around, most of the people are gone and the birds are back. The cliffs at the western end of Martha's Vineyard are justly celebrated by another set of outdoor folks – birdwatchers. Even if your birding skills are limited or nonexistent (I can identify only birds found above schools of fish, such as terns), the spectacle of the fall migration is astonishing. Huge flocks of sea birds settle in the water, covering acres upon acres, and then take flight all at once, sometimes skimming the water so low that their feet throw off a fine spray. Dozens of hawks, owls and other predators ride the thermal currents above the cliffs. On those mornings, the fishing is always good, even when your entire catch consists of two mussels and a clump of seaweed snagged off a rock.

The Big Three
– Nantucket's Top Rips

By Captain Ben Tribken

Legend has it that you may enter as a young man, but you come out as an old man once you have fished the Old Man. I am talking about what may be the most famous of all shoal areas off of Nantucket, one that causes rips to form of monstrous and often intimidating proportions. Thus the caveat: You will age rapidly once you have spent some time fishing those rips. When the tide is running hard and the wind is opposite the tide, some parts of the Old Man will stand straight up as much as 10 to 12 feet. That's a lot of white water looking down at you, and keeping your stern to and out of that cauldron is a chore in itself, let alone dragging a hefty bass or feisty bluefish out of the rip at the same time. I am not discouraging anyone from fishing the Old Man; I am just saying that one must use care and good judgment and preferably go with someone who has been there and done that.

Another famous rip just northeast of Old Man Shoal is Standpipe Rip, so named because it runs southeast off the standpipe in Siasconset, a tiny village at the southeast corner of Nantucket. It is not a particularly long rip, but it has some unique characteristics that make it a bass, bluefish and, sometimes in the fall, false albacore magnet.

Last, but certainly not least, is Miacomet Rip on the south side of Nantucket, approximately halfway down the island. It is the only rip between Smith's Point entrance and Old Man Shoal and, as such, is a natural stopping off place for bass and bluefish in their feeding and migration patterns.

Let's start with Miacomet. How do you get there? From any harbor on the south side of the Cape as far east as Hyannis, the simplest way is to run through the shoals south of Muskegat Island and Tuckernuck. Care should be taken when doing so, and one must

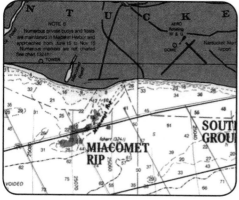

Try the shaded areas on the east-going tide.

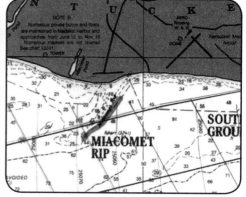

On a west-going tide this area of the rip is your best bet.

read the water and avoid the extreme shallows, which will be evidenced by breakers. After passing the Smith's Point entrance the rest of the run should be uneventful.

However, I can recall a time some years ago when the run down the back side of Nantucket was anything but uneventful. The back side is fully exposed to the open ocean and deep water, and nothing lies in the way to break up big rollers that can develop as a result of a strong, offshore wind or storm. At the time I was running my 31-foot Rampage, Amethyst II, and as I proceeded down the back side to Miacomet, the seas started to build and build from the south-southwest. Within a couple of miles the wave height

had reached 10 to 12 feet and the swells were coming every six to eight seconds, virtually eliminating turning around as an option. I knew immediately that Miacomet was going to be a nightmare – and it was. I had no choice but to go far out and around it to avoid 20- and 30-foot crests on the rip. The rest of the ride was no fun and it took over an hour to travel five miles to get out of the swells and into shoaling water near the Old Man. Always be aware that as a series of swells reaches Miacomet, the rip can build very rapidly and make it virtually unfishable. Typically, however, that is not the case, and one can usually be assured of some good fishing.

I prefer to fish this rip when the tide is running east and little pockets form and hold fish. Fish these pockets with 125 feet of 50-pound-test wire and a 10-foot, 80-pound-test mono leader. A 3- to 4-ounce bucktail or parachute jig with a pork rind is a proven lure; I like a white jig in the spring and dark green or black in the fall. A 4/0 Penn Senator on a soft tip jigging rod works well with this setup. If you fish the west tide, simply slide up and down the rip; it is relatively straight running and very visible. I find that when jigging the rip, the fishing improves as the tide moves harder.

On occasion both bass and bluefish can be seen cruising the rip and that is the time to break out the spinning or fly-fishing gear. Poppers on the spinning gear and Clousers sized 2/0 to 4/0 in chartreuse, all white or chartreuse/yellow with plenty of flash will take fish. Spinning

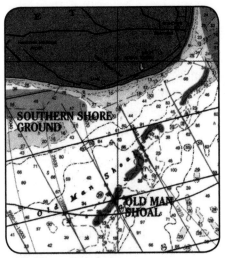

Try these shaded areas on an east-going tide...

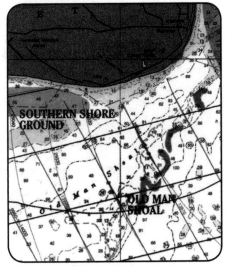

and these on a west when you're fishing the Old Man.

or conventional rods should be filled with 20-pound-test line, at least, to drag big fish out of the rip, and fly-fishermen will want to use 9- or 10-weight outfits with intermediate or fast-sinking lines. On my best day here I caught over 80 bass up to 43 pounds.

Next is Old Man Shoal, some seven or so miles to the east of Miacomet. But on the way, there is a hump running east and west that is commonly known as the Airport, so named because the Nantucket airport tower is visible. Throughout the summer, bluefish congregate over and around the hump. Slicks pop up and often bluefish can be seen tailing on the surface – and these are big bluefish, mostly 10 pounds or better. Poppers work well on spinning gear, but be sure to attach your lure to a wire leader or say bye-bye. The same holds true if you are fly-fishing; wire tippets are the rule. More often than not, when bluefish are in a feeding frenzy, they will go after anything that is moving and actually attack a lure that is already in another fish's mouth!

When you arrive at the Old Man you will surely notice that it is very distinctive. First of all, it is a long rip, often doubling and tripling throughout its length, and its length is some five or so miles. You just have to pick a spot that looks good where it's possible to control your boat (keeping it just out of the rip) and test your mettle. Both tides fish very well, but unlike at Miacomet, I like the west tide best. More pockets are formed and I find the pockets hold bigger fish. And I take my time and work each pocket thoroughly. Don't jump from pocket to pocket too fast; put your time in and it will pay off.

In the pockets, I use the same gear as at Miacomet, but if I fish the east tide, I increase the amount of wire to 150 to 200 feet with a 4- to 6-ounce jig. The east tide seems to fish deeper, thus the changeover. And if the fish are rolling in the rip or swimming in the curl, break out the lighter gear for surface or fly action.

I find the Old Man the most challenging of the rips because it offers so many minor, as well as major, variations. And as you fish it, you will discover something new every time. Wind direction, current and bottom contour all play a role as to how the rip will make up. As many times as I have fished it, I am still learning its little quirks. Just remember that it can be rugged out there at times, and your boating, as well as your fishing skills, are sure to be tested. On my best day I boated 70 bass, but no keepers.

The third of the big three Nantucket rips is Standpipe. This great rip fishes well on

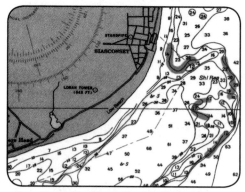

If you're at the Standpipe, try these areas on a west tide.

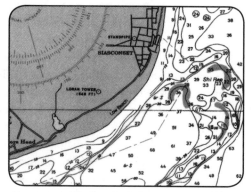

On an east tide the shaded areas are good bets.

either the east or west tide. You could spend the whole day right there with a fair amount of assurance that big fish will appear. Pockets form on both tides, and when it is running hard, the edges really make up and are easily seen.

I remember well a charter trip in the mid-1980s when running Amethyst I. On board were Don Pettit and friends and the late Frank Mather. It was blowing a good 25 knots out of the southwest with green water everywhere as we rounded Great Point to go down the east side of Nantucket. Finally we got to the rip and it was roaring with a west tide against the wind. Out went two wire lines to jig and one spinning rod (Frank never used wire line). Bingo! We had three on at once, and they were big bass, up to 30 pounds. And this went on for a couple of hours. Finally three fish were caught in the mid-40-pound class. This was a good day to be sure!

On this rip I use the same gear as at Miacomet; long wire is not needed, and often jigs on spinning gear are effective. The water on this rip seems to move very rapidly (perhaps because of its location at the southeast corner of Nantucket) and baitfish tumble in the white water. This is a "died and gone to heaven" place for marauding bass and bluefish, as well as for false albacore in the fall.

I like all these rips throughout the season. In late May and early June each year you'll find early season bass and bluefish with big heads and thin bodies. By July and August, you begin to see big blues, but not so many bass as the water temperature rises. But I find myself being lured to these rips the most in late September and throughout October; there is something about fall fishing off of Nantucket. Crisp bright days with graceful gannets diving into the rips mark the migration of big bass and bluefish. Dogfish also appear on the rips (not sought or welcomed by the fishermen) and on occasion big sharks can be seen feeding on them. You just want to be there – and that is what it is all about – catching the experience, as well as the fish.

Nantucket Around The Edges

By Dave Beaumont

Nantucket is only 13 miles long, but it is completely bordered by sandy beaches. Add all the nooks, crannies, coves, harbors and points to that and you get a lot of possible spots to try fishing from shore. There is also a variety of fish to pursue, from striped bass and bluefish to false albacore, bonito, Spanish mackerel, fluke, skates and sharks.

There are two sides of the island, the calm north shore on Nantucket Sound and the south shore with the surf of the Atlantic Ocean. I live on the west end of the island and fish out there a good amount of the time. In the early spring I like to check out the shoreline for potential fishing spots. After a few non-windy days I'll head to my favorite fishing grounds at low tide to survey the changes made by winter storms. I look for a steep wall of sand that you could ride down on your heels. There is usually a bowl-shaped area where this occurs, and this to me is a prime place to try a cast. By checking a long stretch of beach, I can locate a few such spots and thus have a chain of holes to fish.

On the south side are a few rips that form along the shoreline, and these are real fish attractors. One of them at the extreme west end of the island is Smiths Point. The water is always churning at the point. I often find fish on the drive out before I reach the point itself. I start fishing out there for my first bass of the year in mid-April and finish my year off there sometime into the second week of November. One year I caught fish every morning from Halloween to November 5. Four years ago on November 4th, I caught

On the south side of the island are a few rips that form along the shoreline, and these are real fish attractors.

fish from 7:30 a.m. until 12:30 p.m. Only one car drove by me the whole time. Usually I don't let people know when I'm into fish, but since it was only one guy and there were so many fish, I waved and tried to signal him. He must have thought I was being extra friendly or something, as he just waved and drove on by.

There are other rips that form up at Miacomet, Point of Breakers, Sconset and the granddaddy of them all, Great Point. It's a good name for that fishing spot, as it truly is a great place to fish. You can check out five miles of shoreline for signs of fish on the way out to an awesome rip that swirls at the tip of the point. Even if there are fish nowhere else along the way, there is always a stray fish or two in the rip. Since the point is at the tip of this spit of beach, there is also the Nantucket Sound side to explore. That's a lot of fishable beach here, and I've caught fish up and down both sides.

The north shore is the calm side of the island, and there are a variety of points and holes to try. Nantucket Harbor itself has the jetties, Brant Point, First Point, Second Point, the fingers, Polpis Harbor and Pocomo Point, which are all very fishy. Continuing along from the harbor west is Dionis, the Bathtub, the Knuckles, Billy's Bar and Eel Point, along with the inside of Smith's Point.

From late April until late spring, my shore fishing consists of tossing some sort of metal lure, such as a Hopkins, a Kastmaster or a leadhead jig. Then live eels come into play along with swimming lures, until the very end of the season when it's mostly metal again.

Though boats have a distinct advantage over shore-fishing, there are plenty of big fish taken from shore. My fishing log shows that a few years ago I landed 24 bass of 40 inches or better from shore, and so far this year I'm on pace to catch more than that. The biggest bass I've caught from shore weighed 49.5 pounds and I released one

The north shore is the calm side of the island, and there are a variety of points and holes to try.

that might have been bigger. These fish were taken by the grace of the fishing gods, by taking into account factors such as wind, tide, time of the day and the month, and by making the right choice of an offering.

I take most of my big bass after sunset to before sunrise. Even though I've caught many fish on windy nights, I still prefer the opposite conditions. Some of my best nights fishing the surf in the summer were when it was calm and the waves were small. In the spring and fall a south or southwest wind are good, as they warm up the shoreline waters, and in the summer I prefer a north or northwest wind to cool the water down. I like to fish the dropping tide down to low, and when I head out I will usually have a backup spot in mind to fish in case the wind is too bad or there is a lot of weed. Three years ago my backup spot netted me my biggest fish of the year, weighing a hefty 40 pounds.

To start the season I like to use metal lures because they're easier to cast when it's windy, and I get that extra distance that I can't get with a swimming plug. The single hooks also make for easy unhooking and releasing of the fish. But swimmers do work great, and adding a teaser can bring a few extra hookups or even double-headers. My best day this spring on metal lures was 20 fish, with 3 of them between 39 and 40.5 inches.

From late May through August I often bring live eels along. Some nights they just sit there and on others they are the key to catching a keeper. Sometimes I think they just bring you good luck. I was fishing the north shore with eels a few years back, and when I reached one of my favorite spots, there was a guy already fishing. I put on an eel and as I stepped into the water to cast, I saw a huge fluke come shooting into two feet of water. As kids we used to catch fluke with our feet and I knew what to do – step on its back and reach down and grab it by the gills. I did that and picked up the 3 1/2-pound fluke and showed it to the guy who was there. He couldn't believe it when I tossed it onto the shore, having caught dinner without taking a cast.

In the summer you can hook some good-sized sharks from shore using squid, mackerel chunks, bluefish or live eels. I catch them out of the surf quite often in August, usually after dark while tossing out eels for bass. On the north shore the sharks are there all summer, with Smith's Point, Eel Point and Coatue being very good places to try.

One thing that you'll have to deal with at times when shore-fishing on Nantucket

Nantucket is one of the premier surf-casting hot spots on the east coast. The island is surrounded by good-sized stripers throughout the season.

is sharing your fishing spot. Some fishing spots are pretty small, like Brant Point, and there's not a lot of room to cast or land fish. Sometimes there's a blitz of fish at Great Point and it can get crazy. I was fishing at Brant Point with a friend, back when the limit for striped bass was 36 inches, and a couple of other guys were there also. This kid walked up between us, casts out his eel and was instantly on. He was all excited and battled the striper for a few minutes, finally beaching his fish. One of the other fishermen measured it and it turned out to be only 34 inches, not a keeper. I told the kid not to worry about it, he'd catch a bigger one, but the words were barely out of my mouth when he grabbed his rod and fish and ran off down the beach. I certainly wasn't going to chase him, but I did get a good laugh out of it.

I believe that fishing is the one sport at which you keep getting better. You learn more each year, like how to recognize patterns and how to take advantage of them. Nantucket has so many spots to fish that each year I'm able to try a new spot to increase my repertoire. Having all those choices keeps it very interesting. So many spots, so little time.

Live-Lining Herring
A Nantucket Perspective

By Dave Beaumont

If striped bass could choose the bait you send down to tempt them, live herring would top that list every time. Herring are only available in the springtime, usually heading out around the third week or so of June. When the first legal-size fish arrive, they are hungry and are more than willing to fill up on herring drifting through their favorite hangouts.

Getting live herring on Nantucket can be very time-consuming; nobody sells them, so you have to get your own. The Second Bridge (Crab Bridge) in Madaket is probably the best spot, but herring can also be found at the right side of First Bridge, the entrance to Hither Creek and at Massasoit Bridge.

Throwing a cast net is the quickest way to get your bait, but it takes a lot of skill to cast a net efficiently. Most people (myself included) cast extremely small herring jigs or shad darts that weigh 1/32 of an ounce each. The trick to casting such a light jig is using two at once, tied about 10 inches apart, using an ultralight rig with a 4-pound-test line. Many experienced herring addicts remove half of the bucktail hair, or more, swearing it will increase their hits. The final item you must have is a live-bait well. Without one, herring won't last long enough to fish them live. I use a converted garbage can, and have a separate car battery that I keep in the back of my car only for use with the livewell. Even with a livewell, don't put too many fish in at once as they will start to die off quickly. The fewer you have in the livewell, the longer you can keep them alive.

When fishing from shore, I usually rig up a 4/0 hook (as sharp as possible) with 36 inches of 50-pound leader and swivel. Fishing from the boat, the rig is the same, except for when the tide is running hard and an egg sinker is needed to get your bait down. Herring are hooked in the tail or back unless there's weight on, in which case it's in the nose or mouth.

Any hole or drop-off can hold bass, and those are the places I typically look for. Over the years, the number of spots I've explored has expanded quite a bit. The bass are always somewhere. Some days they are easy to find, other days you have to test a few spots to find where they are hiding.

One hot June a few years back, I took a friend of mine, Stu, out in the late morning, and after the ritual of swearing he would not tell "my spot" to anyone, we headed to the honey hole. Stu had never caught a keeper and was more than just a little excited about the day's possibilities. We yelled over to the only other boat (a friend's) to see how his "luck" was. We were very disappointed to hear his "three hours and not a hit" reply.

We started our first drift and, boom! Stu was onto a good-size bass. He was fishing 14-pound line, and not only was the fish quickly emptying his spool, but there was also another boat coming fast and the driver couldn't see how much line he had out. I started up our boat. Stu jumped on the bow and started reeling like a madman as I quickly moved our boat before his line was run over. Fifteen minutes later we were bringing Stu's first keeper aboard: 46 inches long and 38 pounds.

Having sharp hooks is the key; you need to set the hook quickly and avoid hooking the fish too deeply. When I feel the telltale bumping of a strike, I put the reel into free-spool for three or four seconds, then I put the reel in gear and hit it hard. The hooks I use the most are Mustad freshwater hooks.

For me, herring fishing is a daytime activity. Since I work for myself, and springtime is very busy on "The Rock," this often requires deceptive measures. Usually I tell my co-workers I have to go do a bid or have to go to another job, when in reality I'm meeting another "boss" who is telling his workers the same thing.

One of my daughters was born in late May, which of course was very inconvenient for my fishing schedule, as my wife wanted me to spend all my free time at the hospital with her. When my buddy Paul called up and told me he'd get the bait and we could head out on his boat for just a couple of hours, I went for it. The trip was successful as I hooked up with my first keeper of the year. I release most of my fish, but I did want one for the table. However, my better judgment told me that my wife would not be happy with me for "playing" so I sent the fish back. At the hospital a couple of hours later, I was walking down the hallway toward my wife's room when a friend of mine stopped me in the hall for a minute to catch up on recent fishing. Of course I had to mention my first keeper, caught just hours before. Upon entering my wife's room a few minutes later, she said our voices had carried down the hallway and I was busted! I still haven't heard the end of it.

Bluefish might as well be barracuda when it comes to herring fishing, as they can quickly deplete your supply of bait. When we get a bait chewed up, we usually try a different drift unless the action has been really hot.

Last year I took a friend, Paul O'Rourke, out a few times, and our success had been good. It was later in June and the herring fishing that day was only medium. As Paul brought his bait back to the boat to start a new drift, a huge squid was visible, having latched onto his bait. I told him to pull very slowly and try to grab it. He did, and as he tried to grab the squid, it squirted him with ink and slipped away. When I stopped laughing we started our next drift.

Classic Striper Fishing Hot Spots On The Cape Cod Canal

By John D. Silva

The canal, the Big Ditch: Is there a better or more easily accessible saltwater shore-fishing area in New England? Not as far as I'm concerned. Although there are lots of opinions about what percentage of migrating stripers go around the Cape and how many take the shortcut north through the canal, there's no question that plenty of fish come through and plenty hang around all season long.

And there's every reason to believe that this year will be even better than the last. Gary Nelson of the Massachusetts Division of Marine Fisheries in Gloucester is the biologist in charge of the data analyses of striped bass for Massachusetts. When asked for a forecast for Canal area waters for the 2003 season, Dr. Nelson stated that while predictions and forecasts are always subject to change, Massachusetts' shorelines, and especially the Cape Cod area, should see increases in both the quantity and quality of striped bass landings, now and in the future. "The Chesapeake Bay 1996 year-class is still strong and they are growing in length, so anglers should expect to see many fish over thirty inches. Also, I expect to see lots of schoolies, because the Hudson River indices of young-of-the-year and age-one abundances have been the highest recorded. In the future, it is also expected that we should see large numbers of fish originating from Chesapeake Bay as the 2001 year-class (the second highest recorded since 1955) grows in length and they migrate north."

Many of those fish will be passing through the Cape Cod Canal. The angler's job is to locate the best places to intercept them.

Looking down from the Bourne or Sagamore Bridge, the canal looks like a large, featureless river, and it's fair to say that at one time or another there will be stripers just about anywhere in its 17.4-mile length, but some spots are consistently better than others. This is because the canal is lined with small rips, crosscurrents and back eddies that form around small points, underwater boulders and other structure. These places are holding areas for stripers and bait alike, and they are where you should concentrate your efforts.

The following locations are just a few spots on the Cape Cod Canal that provide easy access and are consistent producers of stripers. They may not come as much of a surprise to most experienced canal fishermen, but truth be told, these are areas that I find myself returning to year after year for the simple reason that they produce.

There are several good holes and rips you can fish in the area of the East End on the Cape Cod side of the canal. You can fish right off the pier next to the Lobster Mart, where the discharge from the shellfish company enters the water and attracts hordes of baitfish. Or working just a bit west, the east side of the entrance to Sandwich Harbor and Marina is one of my preferred locations. During the west-flowing tide, a nice rip forms just offshore where you can drift your bait or lure. Cast into the current and let your offering swing around into the slack water of the marina channel. And bring some light tackle along – depending on time of year, this can also be a good hole for mackerel, fluke, flounder and even an occasional cold-weather cod.

The jetty is another good bet; you might work the hole and rip at the base, or if you don't mind the walk, the end of this jetty can really get hot during an east-flowing tide at dawn. But bring your Korkers (studded sandals) because it can be very slippery, even treacherous, on those rocks at the end of the breakwater.

To get to this area from the mainland, cross the Sagamore Bridge and take exit 1. At the traffic light, turn right onto Route 6A toward Sandwich center. Look for Tupper Road, about 2 miles on the left, and follow the signs to the canal parking areas. There is a public parking area on each side of Sandwich Marina, as well as one at the eastern end of the road, which provides access to the stone jetty at the canal's east entrance.

To the west of the bulkheads and Sandwich Marina along the canal bike trail, you can fish the discharge canals at the Commonwealth Electric Power Plant. Stripers will stack up in the warmer currents where the plant discharges its spent cooling water. Some real nice swirls and rips form in those holes, especially during the east-flowing tides.

Heading west all the way to the other end, also on the Cape side, the mud flats and Railroad Bridge area at the end of Bell Road is one of the most popular destinations for die-hard canal rats. A consistent producer of large fish all season long, you'll find quality fishing along the entire area from the base of the Railroad Bridge to the end of the parking area (west) where the flats themselves are located. This is a fairly large cove off the canal itself, which holds plenty of bait all summer long. This area fishes best during the west-flowing, ebb tide. Once the tide drops down far enough, you may don your waders and venture out on the tidal flats to cast into the canal current. If you're looking to try some fly-fishing in the canal, this is one of the best places. In the last couple of years, fly-fishermen have even hooked up with false albacore here in the fall. Be very careful wading to the edge of the channel; the drop off is steep and dangerous. To get there, cross the Bourne Bridge and take the first right off the rotary onto Trowbridge Road. Follow this road for about 1 1/2 miles, then turn right onto Bell Road. Follow to the end and the large public parking area.

The West End of the canal offers many great striper spots.

Over on the mainland side, directly across from the mud flats, there is plenty of public access and great fishing at the Massachusetts Maritime Academy. You can cast all along the rocky shoreline of the parking area, or even bottomfish with bait if that is your preference. But the key spot here is the deep, swirling hole located at the far west end of the public parking area next to the pier where the tugboats tie up. You're not allowed to fish from the pier itself, but you can cast into the hole from the shore and drift bait or lures through the swirling back current. Fish here during an east-running tide. Finding this location is easy: From Main Street in Buzzards Bay, turn onto Academy Drive and follow to the parking area just inside the gate to the school.

The east entrance of the canal has stone breakwaters on each side. On the mainland side the long breakwater sits between Scusset State Beach on one side and the canal channel on the other, so your choices for fishing this area are many. You can fish from the surf on Scusset Beach itself, venture out onto the jetty, or explore other areas along the canal bike trail. From the jetty itself, you have the option of casting into the canal currents or the relatively calm waters of the bay (with two rods, one of which is rigged to bottom-fish, you can do both). If you can get a spot to fish on the very end, try casting a swimming plug or a piece of chunk bait out into the current during an east tide. Let your offering swing around the end of the jetty into the slack water. Generally, two hours on either side of high tide are best anywhere in the area of the beach or along the jetty.

To get to Scusset State Beach from the rotary on the mainland side of the Sagamore Bridge, follow Route 3A east onto Scusset Beach Road and proceed to the large parking area at the end.

There is also a 98-site camping area here that is very popular with trailer campers, open in the spring, summer and fall. Picnicking, bicycling, hiking, swimming and, of course, fishing are the main attractions. This is a great place to take the whole family for the day or longer.

To the right of the camping area at the far end of the Scusset Beach parking lot is a small dirt lot located at the beginning of the jetty. This is where you'll find a well-known canal fishing hole called Pip's Rip. Although this spot is certainly no secret and you'll have plenty of company, it is productive year in and year out. The shallow point at Pip's Rip becomes exposed during low tide and there is a fair amount of room for spin and conventional casters and fly-fishermen alike. Toward high tide during the west-flowing current, a rip is formed along the point while a deep, swirling pool develops just downcurrent. Cast a jig or soft bait into the rip, let it sink into the pool and hold on! Additionally, there are several decent holes within close proximity as you walk or bike west from here.

Probably the best known of all the fishing areas on the Cape Cod Canal is the Bournedale herring run. Located along Route 6 on the mainland side, there is ample parking, easy canal access and public restrooms. Motel lodging and seafood snack bars are directly across the street. Admittedly, the shoreline here can get very crowded with anglers during the herring spawning run as this is the only legal herring distribution station on the Canal for fishermen to obtain live bait. From late April to about the third week in May, a fish warden is on duty and is the only person legally permitted to capture herring in the run. Herring are distributed as individual allotments, depending on their availability and at the discretion of the warden. Anglers must obtain a permit at Bourne Town Hall, which must be displayed to get herring, and you can find the hours of operation at the run and days of the week that herring will be distributed. This may seem like a lot of hassle to go through, but hard-core canal veterans will tell you that swimming a live herring near the run in May is one of the best ways to take a trophy striper.

Once the migrating herring start to dwindle in number, the fishing crowds will begin to thin out at the herring run, only to be replaced in number by tourists, hikers, bikers and picnickers.

Personally, I'm not much for crowds, so I prefer to get my herring and lug them elsewhere. But for those without the means to keep bait alive over long distances, this spot is your best bet. Aside from the herring congregating here during their spawning season, this spot also tends to hold baitfish and juvenile drop-backs in the deep pool where the cool flowing river water discharges into the canal waters, so it is always worth a few casts even if the run is over.

Heading west on the canal service road (bike trail), The Cribbin, located between light poles 220 and 230, is identified by the stone retaining walls on the hillside border of the road. This extended area contains several nice points and rips that are often very productive, especially during the west tide. To the east of the herring run there is the mussel bed located below pole 170. During low tide the shelf is exposed, and like Pip's Rip and the Mud Flats, there is plenty of room for a fly-fisherman's backcast. Best fished during the east-flowing (flood) tide, a rip and a deep swirl form off the point and stripers hold there all season long, but this spot is especially productive in the spring.

All types of fish, bait or predator, congregate around structure, and in the Cape Cod Canal just about any man-made or natural structure of size should hold fish. The bridge abutments on the Sagamore Bridge, Bourne Bridge and Railroad Bridge are perfect examples. No real secrets here to unveil, just basic Fishing 101. Look for back eddies and breaks in the current, anywhere fish can find relief from the strong flow. Cast into the current close to the abutments and allow your jig or chunk bait to drift deep into potential holding areas. Be prepared to lose some gear, but the abutments are some of the most consistent fish producers in the canal.

These are just a few areas that commonly provide excellent fishing for anglers on the Cape Cod Canal. Most are well known, others less so. But by all means, don't limit yourself based solely on a few recommendations. There are scores of lesser-known holes, points and rips that are just a short walk or bike ride from these areas – explore and experiment. Low tide is a great time to go scouting. The points and shelves are exposed, and you can see how the hard structure of the shoreline affects the currents during different stages in the tide. You can mark these areas on your canal map (available at the Army Corps of Engineers headquarters in Buzzards Bay and at many local tackle shops) for future reference. Don't forget to note the pole numbers for accuracy.

Over time, you will learn when and where to be during certain tides and what methods and techniques are best. Observe the locals, don't crowd them and learn by example. As a rule, I fish during off-peak hours whenever possible, especially when fishing near areas with easy public access. Weekdays, and especially nights, are my preferred times to hit The Ditch to avoid crowds and hopefully secure my favorite sweet spot in a given hole. Fishing at night also results in better catch ratios once the weather warms and the fish become more nocturnal. Another rule is to always try and fish as close to the bottom as possible. Unless there are fish obviously breaking on the surface, chances are that they are down deep. So it's vital to use just enough weight in your lure or jig to get down to the bottom where the fish are but without hanging up in the rocks on every cast. Two to four ounces will usually do the trick.

Many of the locals look forward to breaking tides, those times when the current goes slack at dawn. There are a couple of days of leeway on either side of this event, which happens twice a month. This is the best time to fish big poppers on the surface. Consult the pamphlet of Canal currents, produced by the Army Corps, also available at their headquarters.

Once you think you've got it all figured out, it'll all change again. The fishing patterns in different areas of the canal will always shift and rearrange, so experience, flexibility and experimentation are always key. But year to year the areas outlined here are always a good place to start. Now go out and enjoy! ᕤᕥᐳ

South Cape & Popponesset Beaches
The First Stop

By Gene Bourque

An amazing phenomenon takes place every spring on Cape Cod along a short stretch of beach in the town of Mashpee. The striped bass return, followed a few weeks later by the first racer bluefish. This event is welcomed by fishermen and women, but it is not particularly remarkable taken by itself. What's remarkable is that every year, for as long as anyone can remember, this six-mile stretch of beach has been the place on Cape Cod to find the first arrivals, stripers from Chesapeake Bay, Delaware Bay and the Hudson River, and blues from points farther south. Hard-core, early season, striper nuts will keep an ear open for reports of the first fish caught on the Vineyard, usually taken near Wasque Point. Then it's off to South Cape and Poppy (as it's known to the locals) a day or two later to intercept the first schoolies of the year. Within a week the bass will spread north and east, into Cotuit Bay, East Bay in Centerville, and on up to Bass River. But those first fish have a special appeal, not unlike the first crocuses that poke through the thawed ground in March. They confirm the end of winter and the start of another Cape Cod fishing season.

Although no one knows for sure why the fish show here first, a look at a chart of Nantucket Sound gives some strong hints. Due north of Muskeget Channel, the open water between Martha's Vineyard and Nantucket, are a series of shoals and shallow water off Falmouth, Mashpee and Cotuit. The ever-stronger sunlight and longer spring days warm this water faster than much of the surrounding area, which in turn promotes the appearance of large and small baitfish. Many fishermen feel that the first migrating striped bass move outside of Long Island and south of Block Island and the Vineyard, then head up Muskeget Channel toward the Cape, where they find the warm water and a dependable food supply.

The beachfront of South Cape and Popponesset runs from the jetty that marks the entrance to Waquoit Bay on the west end, easterly for about six miles to the end of the spit of Popponesset. At the west end of the beach and along the South Cape Beach section, the bottom is small gravel and sand, and the prevailing southwest wind of the spring and summer creates moderate wave action and a steep drop-off of about three feet just below the low-water mark. Proceeding east, the bottom structure changes to a mix of rough gravel and cobblestone-size rocks. Along the section of beachfront adjacent to the cottage community of Popponesset are a series of small jetties, after which the beach runs for another mile to the end of the spit.

Jim Young, a native Cape Codder and manager of Eastman's Sport and Tackle in Falmouth, grew up fishing the Cape shores of Vineyard and Nantucket sounds and remembers when taking the first striper of the season ensured both bragging rights and local notoriety. Back in the days of a 16-inch legal limit for stripers, tackle shops around the Upper Cape offered prizes for the first fish weighed in, and the angler often had his photograph in the local papers. Certain fishermen seemed to win year after year and would accumulate some nice prizes by driving from shop to shop, showing off their catches.

April 15 was the day to break out the rod and head for the beach, said Jim. "Some years the stripers will appear a few days earlier, but they're never later," Jim said. "I don't think the weather has too much to do with it. It might be moon cycles, the tides, angle of the sun, who really knows? But the fish know."

Part of South Cape Beach is a state beach facility with a large parking area and easy access. From the rotary at the intersection of Routes 28 and 151, follow Great Neck Road south for about six miles to the parking lot. There is no charge to park here in the off-season. The Town of Mashpee has a large parking area directly adjacent to the beach here also, which is popular with anglers.

An energetic angler can make the long walk west, down the beach to the jetty at the entrance of Waquoit Bay. At one time a paved road ran down the middle of this barrier beach and the remains of this road give much firmer footing than the outside beach, but many fishermen like walking and casting on their way to the jetty. Fish can be caught anywhere along this beachfront, but some fishermen prefer fishing in front of the parking area, setting out a spiked rod with a chunk of herring on the end, sitting in their car and hoping for a legal-size fish.

This brings up an important point: Just about every early season fish caught along this beach will be well under the present legal size of 30 inches. Most will be in the 14- to 20-inch range and are much more fun on light tackle. We'll talk more about gear later.

The jetty at the Waquoit Bay entrance is a popular and productive spot, but the beach just

South Cape Beach in Mashpee, MA, offers plenty of parking and miles of fishable beaches.

inside the jetty has deep water along its edge and can hold just as many fish. It is a long walk from the parking area but worth the effort. As with all early season fishing, the best time to fish this area is usually in the late afternoon after the sun has had a chance to warm the water all day. I've had good fishing over the clear sand bottom of this part of the beach on a sunny April day, only to have the bite stop completely when the sun set.

To the east of the state beach parking lot, the beach begins to curve in a more northerly direction below the golf course at New Seabury. This part of the beach is called Succonnesset Point, and a very nice rip sets up on an incoming tide, quite close to the beach. A gravel bar extends off the beach here at about a 45-degree angle and is easily waded, if the tide is not high or running too hard. A small jig or fly cast out into the rip and allowed to tumble off into the deeper water will sometimes find stripers stacked up, waiting for an easy meal.

Walking and fishing along this beach in the early season is definitely a blind casting situation. Unlike during the late spring, there will be few signs that the fish are present. No birds will be working and there will be no telltale swirls in the wash giving away the presence of fish feeding on small bait. Because of this, it's important to keep moving. A cast or two will tell you if there's anybody home; these fish are hungry and aggressive. Active fishing will also help keep the blood flowing when the weather is blustery and fingers are frozen by the 40-degree water.

The beachfront along the communities of New Seabury and Popponesset features good structure in the form of a series of small jetties and riprap. The problem from here to the east end of the beach is one of access. In the early spring there should be fewer problems than in the summer, but be aware that this area is patrolled and there is very little parking. To find the small parking area, turn left off Great Neck Road into New Seabury and follow signs toward Popponesset. Follow Wading Place Road to the end where you'll find parking for three vehicles only.

From this point to the eastern end of the beach is the area known as the spit. Behind the spit is Popponesset Bay, a large, shallow expanse of water that is fed by the Mashpee River. This water warms very quickly in the spring and is a natural bait factory that attracts predatory fish all season long. It's entrance at the end of the spit is a fabulous fishing spot with a deep channel close to the beach where fish will hold, waiting for bait to be swept out of the bay. Stripers can be caught both along the outside beach and in the channel behind the spit, but be very careful wading here because the current is strong and the soft sand makes the footing treacherous. Still, this is one of the most popular and productive locations for early season fishing on the entire Upper Cape.

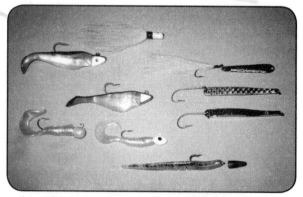

Jigs, soft baits and metal lures for early season stripers.

Although heavy surf gear and long casts will certainly allow you to cover more water, keep in mind that the first striped bass to arrive will be small, weighing just a few pounds. These fish are quickly overpowered by heavy gear and are much more fun on light- to medium-weight outfits. Also, most of the fish are caught very close to the shore, and long casts are unnecessary. The typical outfit used here is a 7- to 9-foot rod with a spinning or conventional reel spooled with 8- to 12-pound-test line. Small swimming plugs such as Rebels, Gag's Grabbers and Bombers will catch fish, but why bury a set of treble hooks in the mouth or gills of a fish you're going to have to release anyway? Many early season striper seekers use small grub-tailed jigs or rubber shads in 1/2- to 1-ounce sizes, Slug-Go-type rubber worms rigged with a worm weight and a 1/0 or 2/0 hook, or small metal lures like Hopkins, Kastmaster or Need-L-Eel set up with a single hook. These are all effective fish catchers and allow for quick and easy release of these sub-legal-size fish. Quite an assortment of these lures can be carried in a surfbag slung over a shoulder.

Fly-fishers will score well here, too, and the wide open beachfront leaves plenty of room for backcasts. Any flashy pattern will attract the stripers; Clouser Minnows, Deceivers, Brook's Blondes or Epoxy Minnows tied in chartreuse and white, olive and white, and all-white are local favorites. It's important to keep your flies small, no bigger than a size 1/0, to imitate the small silversides and sand eels that start to show up in April. An intermediate sinking line will serve well along the beach, but a higher density sinking line should be used in the channels at the entrances of Popponesset and Waquoit bays to get the fly close to the bottom.

The biggest challenge here may be the unpredictable spring weather on the Cape. Because the water is still in the mid-40-degree range, a day that may feature balmy spring temperatures well inland will be quite different along the shore. In the spring, the weather patterns begin to shift, and the predominantly southwest wind that brings warm, southern air in the summer blows over the cold water. This is an onshore breeze at South Cape and Poppy, and is anything but warm at this time of year! It's always best to check with NOAA marine weather forecasts and dress appropriately.

The tackle shops on the Upper Cape no longer offer prizes for that first striper of the year, of course, but many fishermen still make these beaches their first destination every spring. Some are there to push the limits of their fishing season, some are shaking the mental and physical cobwebs out of their fishing techniques, and some are there hoping for bragging rights, to be one of the first anglers on the Cape to catch a bass. In about three or four weeks, and with much less predictability, the first bluefish to visit the Cape will also be caught here. By that time the Sound will hold bigger bait, herring and squid, and fishermen will also have a shot at some much larger stripers. Blues will blitz these beaches, and it's not uncommon to see a line of surfcasters every evening casting big poppers to schools of hungry choppers. But the early season is a more solitary experience, almost like hunting. The reward will not be a trophy to take home but maybe a memory and the satisfaction of beginning another year.

Cape Cod Canal Early Season Bass

By Dave LaPorte

Unless you are fortunate enough to have the opportunity to pursue migrating striped bass from a boat along the Elizabeth Islands, the best chance for a shore-fisherman to take an early season keeper bass is near or around the Bournedale herring run on the Cape Cod Canal. This thin ribbon of seawater that pours into the canal is probably the most productive location for fishermen in Massachusetts to begin consistently catching striped bass. Why? Because hundreds upon thousands of these marvelous herring are entering this river, and the odor they emit, I'm told by the good old boys, will attract the bass from miles around.

The first surge of herring generally enters the river by the end of March. By the first week of May, the fish's diligent consistency dictates that the bass and bluefish should be putting on the feedbag, loading up with a high-protein diet of herring for their continual migration to the northern waters. Over the past several years the most productive part of the tide has been the last two to three hours of the east incoming high, and the first two to three hours of the dropping tide going out west. This window of time seems to produce the warmest water temperature, and at this time of the year the water temperature is critical; the water that's entering the canal at high tide is coming from Buzzards Bay, from the south. (Actually, in canal talk, the water is coming from the west.)

When I fish the early season with live herring, I keep a water thermometer attached to my herring basket. (The basket is a Rubbermaid 1 1/4-bushel laundry basket with a wooden cover secured to the top and a door and latch cut into the cover.) I check the water temperature once or twice an hour, noting that as the water temperature rises, the striped bass seem to begin to feed actively. I prefer it when the water is between 48 and 55 degrees. This seems to be the key ingredient at the herring run. (If you're taking a warm shower and someone turns on the water elsewhere in the house, there will be a rapid drop in temperature and your body notices the change immediately. Which one would you prefer, warm or cold? It's the same for striped bass.)

The first bass that are caught at the herring run are the schoolies. These are the long thin racers, known as "scouts." They are the lead fish from the massive schools of the first run of the northern migration. Within a week after these first fish are caught, the keepers begin to show periodically. After that there will be a surge of larger fish that filter through the canal in smaller, compact schools. Some of these fish travel directly through the canal without hesitating, while others take up residency and feed on the pre- and post-spawning herring that reside in the canal. If you decide to fish with herring from the Bournedale run, you will need a permit from the town of Bourne.

Now the fun starts. Hold the herring and hook the bait right through the eyes with a 6/0 or 7/0 bronzed, presharpened hook, number 94150 or 9174. Next, cast your bait as far as possible and slightly up-tide. When the herring lands, slowly release your line as much as possible, maybe 50 or 100 feet. If you have no strikes by the end of the presentation, either slowly reel in your bait, hoping for a strike on the retrieve, or rapidly reel in and repeat the procedure. (Note: Use a small rubbercore sinker, 1/4- to 3/4-ounce, to help sink the bait toward the bottom and into the strike zone, which is approximately two to four feet off the bottom. This method is usually done during the peak of a rapidly moving tide or current.)

It is key in bait-fishing to try to give the bait the most natural presentation possible. Often, before the strike, your bait will get nervous and skittish; this activity will generally translate to the tip of your rod. At times you will see your herring on the surface, skating and swimming for its life with the bass in close pursuit. When you feel the strike, dip the tip of your rod, let your line get tight, and then set up on the bass. Try not to set the hook so hard that you pull the bait away from the fish; let your line again get tight, and this time hook the fish hard. If you can master this technique, you will increase the number of live bait positive hookups. By doing this two-strike procedure, you will make the bass try to swallow the bait even more aggressively, which means more hookups and fewer misses. (Most of the bass are less than 15 pounds at this time of year.)

TECHNIQUES FOR FISHING WITH FRESH DEAD HERRING

Using iced-down fresh herring gives you the option of being able to move from one location to another instead of staying in one specific spot, as you generally must with live herring. Secure fresh live herring and immediately ice them down, still flopping and squirming, in a cooler full of crushed ice. Then, at your favorite fishing location, take a fresh dead herring and hook it under the chin and out through the top of the head. Add a rubbercore sinker onto your line, approximately one foot away. The sinker should be size 3/8 to 1 ounce, depending on the speed of the current and the water depth.

Throw your fresh dead bait out as far as possible up-tide, and let the bait sink toward the bottom or count to 5 or 10. As the bait sinks naturally toward the bottom, with the rod in your right hand and your left hand holding the line, pull the line approximately three feet to your left, away from the rod and reel. Lift the tip of the rod straight up, then release the line and let the dead bait again sink toward the bottom. Follow the bait with the rod, and dip the tip of the rod back down toward the water at a 90-degree angle. Repeat this process until the bait has reached the end of the sweep. Modification of this method and simple common sense will quickly educate you about this productive style of fishing. Another option is to release several feet of line by disengaging your spool and letting the bait and sinker free-float toward the bottom. These techniques work best on a rapidly moving current, which gives you the option of covering a vast amount of fishing area.

RODS AND REELS

An 8- to 10-foot spinning or conventional rod, capable of throwing 2 to 5 ounces of weight, is usually ideal for this type of fishing. (Conventional rods and reels are what most seasoned fishermen use.) The conventional reels of choice are the Abu Garcia 7000C3, Penn 310GTI, Shimano Calcutta or the Quantum Iron IR420CX. There are also a host of highly qualified bait-casting reels with level wind guides. Try to balance the reel to the rod. As for spinning reels, the Penn 7500SS, the Daiwa black-gold 7000 series and the Shimano bait runners seem to be the best. My advice is to fish with a rod and reel capable of handling 20- to 30-pound test, either conventional or spinning style. Whichever you feel comfortable with should be your choice of equipment. Remember also that the reels should be capable of spooling at least 150 to 250 yards of quality line.

EQUIPMENT

Your list of gear should include warm clothes, fingerless ragwool gloves for early season fishing, hip boots or waders, sunglasses, a hook hone, needle-nosed pliers, rain gear or windbreaker, and a small fanny pack to store assorted hooks, sinkers, measuring tape, etc. There is no need for toting around 500 pounds of fishing gear; basic equipment will do it.

PLUGS

Bring a few of the essentials, such as imitation or swimming lures. Rebels, Rapalas, Gibbs swimmers or stick baits in that style are all good. Favorite colors are blue and white or light brown with pearl white, plus black and silver. Although live and fresh bait will account for 95 percent of your fishing, plug-fishing should not be overlooked, especially when herring are not available.

THE HOT SPOT

The best fishing locations will be near or around the herring run. If, however, you think you will be fishing alone, better plan on finding another area. The run is the place to be. This is the Hollywood Hot Spot, and everybody knows it. Be prepared to be sociable and friendly because every fisherman in the world will be there. It's a performance close to a three-ring circus. Bring your camera; all the clowns will be there and you won't be disappointed.

Cabin fever is a dreaded winter disease, and the only known cure is a large dose of early season striper fishing at the Cape Cod Canal. Sharpen your hooks, dust off your gear and come on down – the fishing is fine.

Monomoy Island

By Steve Shiraka

The first time I ever set foot on Monomoy Island was some 20-odd years ago. It was a hot Friday afternoon in June and I had been persuaded by a friend to go to the Cape – I was living in Worcester at the time – and try a new location that his father and another guy had been fishing for a week and where they had been doing really well.

His tales of big bass naturally aroused my curiosity. There was one thing, though: He would not tell me where we were going until we got to Chatham later that afternoon. Maybe we were going fishing with Mr. Phelps – you know, "Your mission if you wish to accept it" kind of thing.

We were to meet my friend's dad at 5 p.m. at the dock at Horne's Marina and be ferried by boat to this secret spot. Because of the traffic jams and other circumstances beyond our control, we were late by an hour or so and my friend's dad, who was never big in the patience department, went on his way and we were left on the dock holding our rods, you might say. Also, it had become very apparent that a nasty thunderstorm was about to enter the equation.

Well, I figured that with the black sky and lightning and us missing the boat, it was all over for us on this trip. My friend was not to be outdone, and while I was taking refuge in my truck, he was negotiating some sort of deal with a local fisherman to get us out to the island. The guy seemed oblivious to the maelstrom from the heavens over the town of Chatham and agreed to take us out. "Now wait a minute here," I thought to myself, "No sane person would get in a small boat in a raging thunderstorm and get dropped off on some God-forsaken piece of real estate by someone he had just met, not knowing if we would make it in the first place!"

Well, that's just what we did!

The ride out was a nightmare, and after 20 minutes of racing through a fog and the coming darkness, never mind the thunderstorm, our man, the local, stopped the boat with no land in sight and told us, "This is where you get off." All I could see was white water washing over a sandbar, and fog. I looked at my friend and he looked back at me and the guy said to us, "You two go over the side, the water is about three feet deep here. Keep walking over that way" – he was pointing into the thickest fog I had ever seen – "about a hundred feet and you will be on dry land. If you go to one side or the other you probably won't be seen again." Great, just great.

It was now pretty well dark as both my friend and I, against better judgment, went over the side. As far as fishing for striped bass goes, it was the best move I have ever made. We walked along the top of the dunes in search of his dad and company. The storm had subsided, but the fog was awful.

After about 45 minutes we heard something ahead in the fog and dropped down to the surf line. The sound was more distinct now and we both knew immediately what it was. Someone's drag was groaning in the dark against a heavy fish that was bound for Nantucket! His father's friend suddenly appeared out of the fog and was in the process of trying to slow the fish down and was not being very successful.

Farther down the beach, my friend's dad was unhooking a fish that looked huge. The night had taken on a surreal quality. People were now just shadows in the legendary Chatham fog. I grabbed an eel, strung it on a 5/0 hook and let it fly into the night. On! My first Monomoy striper weighed in at a little more than 38 pounds. My friend's dad, it turned out, had a 54-pound bass. It was love at first sight.

Monomoy Island lies just south of Chatham at the elbow of the Cape. It is now a federal wildlife refuge. When I started fishing commercially for bass there in the mid-1970s, it was a wild and open place with hardly anyone landing on its shores and surf-fishing. A few townies showed up now and then, but most of the people fished it from boats in the rips offshore.

This island is now most famous for saltwater flats on the inside off South Chatham and Harwich. These flats were the result of the great storm of February 1978, which ripped the island in half. Although there were always tidal flats in back of the island before that storm, the area they cover now dwarfs what was available back then.

Today those flats are receiving recognition nationwide because of the fine saltwater fly-fishing they offer for striped bass and bluefish. Fly-rodding, although it is great sport and one that I have become addicted to, is not the only way to take advantage of what these flats have to offer. Nor do you need a fancy flats boat to fish this area successfully.

My fishing partner and I have been fishing the flats from his 19-foot center console for the last 11 years now with popping plugs, darters, etc., and have had great success.

If you would like to try fishing this area, I offer the following information and advice. The first problem is getting there. You can only get there by boat. If you are the proud owner of a watercraft, it should be a minimum of 19 feet in length because this will allow you to fish both the back (ocean) side and the flats.

Your closest access points are along the south side of the Cape at Saquatucket and Stage harbors. Stage Harbor is the closest in Chatham but has limited ramp facilities and parking. We use Saquatucket in Harwich; it has a great ramp, gas and plenty of parking for vehicles and trailers. It is about a four-mile jaunt to the midsection of the island from Saquatucket.

Monomoy is an area that should be experienced first with someone who has been there before. If you don't have that luxury, I would suggest you pick the best weather possible and get a recent chart of the place, study it, then go. This is no place for amateurs or beginners. Some of the nastiest water on the East Coast is here and the sea is not a forgiving environment to the unprepared.

The flats present great light-tackle fishing opportunities. It is perfectly suited to light spinning rods and fly tackle. One-handed spinning rods with 6- to 8-pound line make for an exciting way to spend a morning casting to bass in two to three feet of water. The lures you use are on the small side, but that does not mean the fish are of that stature. The flats ecosystem is geared toward bait that is suited to the conditions. In the shallow water, it is more likely that a sand eel or silverside will be found taking refuge than a three-pound menhaden, although they do just that at times.

Plugs can be the 1-ounce Gibbs Polaris, Rebels in the 4½- and 5½-inch sizes and needlefish. The water is usually crystal clear, and the fish become very wary as the season wears on.

As you drift across the flats at high water, you will learn to pick out the fish as they drift with the tide looking for an easy meal. They will appear as shadows with no sign of movement at times, and at other times they will be all around the boat, hunting in pods of 10 to 15 fish, clearly visible.

One of my favorite things to do is stand at the bow of the boat and scan ahead looking for fish as we cruise the shallows on a bright sunny day. My fishing partner, Eric, thinks I get more of a kick watching them than catching them. Not true.

The flats on the western shore of the island are bordered by the Chatham Roads, a natural channel that leads into the Stage Harbor area from Nantucket Sound. Several large fish traps are present from north to south in season, and you should be aware of the locations if traveling at night or in fog.

If you fly-fish, 8- and 9-weight rods are the order of the day. Brightly colored fly lines are discouraged. Monocore lines are suggested because the "slime line," as it is called, is nearly invisible in clear water. Longer and lighter leaders are valuable, as the fish are spooky most days. Small Deceivers and Clousers in light tan and white with chartreuse are more productive. Whispy flies with long thin hackles work well in the same colors. Crab flies work well here, also, coupled with a dead drift at a channel edge.

If wading is your preferred method, start by casting from at least 20 feet from the water's edge and work your way into deeper water. It is not unusual to see 30-inch-plus bass working the beach in four inches of water with their backs exposed. When wading, look for the darker colored water that spells out a channel or hole. Bass wait in these depressions for bait to pass by when the current is moving across the flat.

This is stealth fishing at its finest. It is really a combination of hunting and fishing. You hope to see them before they see you and get into position to present your fly so that it intercepts their path. You have to be quiet and place the fly with precision and not have it draw undue attention that will frighten the bass.

If and when you hook up, the fight is spectacular, as the bass in two feet of water has nowhere to go and panic sets in, with the fish showing a lot of white water and speed to rival any bluefish. I think they fight much better in this shallow-water environment than in any other. Be there at the break of dawn if you can, for this is the magic time when the fish are a little less cautious.

When the summer months warm the water to a comfortable temperature, a pair of surf shoes, a bathing suit and T-shirt are the perfect attire. Add your basket and a good pair of polarized sunglasses, and walk the flats and beaches unencumbered by heavy waders. Never forget a good hat, and make sure the underside of the bill is a dark color such as green or blue.

Next I will cover the back, or ocean, side of the island. Fishing there is totally different from fishing the flats and has its unique set of rules.

Back when I was fishing commercially on Monomoy Island, all the fishing we did was on the backside. We would land on shore and surf-cast along the beach, working from point to point with our backs to the dunes. At high water the waves would be lapping at our feet and, of course, we usually fished in total darkness. The draw of it was the chance of connecting with one of the numerous striped bass that made nightly forays into the surf along the beach. In the mid-1970s, it seemed there was an inexhaustible supply of stripers in the 30- to 40-pound class.

My tackle was rudimentary compared to what is available today: a 10-foot Lamiglas fiberglass rod with a Penn 704 loaded with 25-pound test and 7-inch super wind cheater Rebels right out of the package. Sharpen a hook? At first we had feather teasers, then Red Gills showed up. Ever hook into two 30-pound-plus fish at once? Fun, isn't it?

Being young and impressionable and able to equate poundage with dollar signs, it came to me that here was a veritable gold mine to be tapped. I had the best of both worlds: I was doing what I liked to do most and making money at it, as well!

The routine I followed then would probably kill me now. I would sneak in to launch my boat at Horne's Marina just after the owner had left for the day and put a chain across the launching ramp. This was a necessity because it was the closest ramp to Monomoy and it cut down the running time. Besides, it added to the excitement.

Our technique for finding fish was fairly simple. We would cruise along just outside the surf line and look for concentrations of sand eels. Once we found the bait, we would time the waves and bring the boat in with the motor unlocked and ride the top of a wave. Of course, it wasn't as easy when I was alone. Many nights would find me pulling up the boat, grabbing my rod and starting to cast right next to where I landed. On the best night I ever had there, I don't think I moved more than 100 feet from the boat. The average night was a five-to seven-fish pick. The average weight was 25 to 30 pounds. I would start with the white, 3½-ounce Gibbs bottle plug. If there was a full moon and the tide was running, I would walk from point to point and cast the plug up-tide at a 45-degree angle, just letting it come tight, and pump it as it swung through the arc. If fish were there, I would haul back and the rod would practically rip from my arms. These were the toughest fish of the season. On dark nights when there was a new moon, the fish would hang right in the back of the first wave.

Many times not only would I find sand eels but bass crashing among them, as well. These were the special nights. As I said before, it was grueling work, but at the time I never noticed. I watched the day end while casting to fish and greeted the next day doing the same. The moon rising out of the ocean was breathtaking, and on the new moon, the stars were visible from horizon to horizon.

Some nights I would practically drop from sheer exhaustion and would sleep where I lay down, only to wake up with the sun shining and my face half covered in sand. The dampness of the sand would make me stiff and I would run up and down the beach, back and forth, to get some body heat back. You would think any sane person would try this once and kiss off the whole proposition, but back again each night we went, knowing full well the discomfort that awaited us. I tell you, truly, you could bet on your mother's life that I didn't want to be anywhere else.

It was a free place 20 years ago, and I am glad I had the chance to experience it that way. Today the island is micromanaged by a number of state, federal and other wildlife agencies. Permits are required for parties over a certain number to land and fish or enjoy a walk on the beach. Don't even think about landing on shore when those cute little plovers are nesting, which also happens to be the best season for surf-casting along the shore. But be not discouraged, my friends. If you are persistent and don't mind bureaucratic b.s., you can enjoy this beautiful place.

Today the island is still a major destination for fisher folk seeking striped bass, although 99 percent of them fish from a boat. In a normal year, the fish will take up residence in the rips to the east of the island by mid-June. Starting from the rips at Bearse's Shoal adjacent to the red number 8 buoy and going south to east rips with names like Stone Horse and Handkerchief are storied bass grounds where many come with dreams of 50-pounders dancing in their heads. Some return the conqueror and some the conquered.

Drifting sand eels in these rips can be downright deadly. Employing a conventional rod and reel with 30-pound test, you can rig a 4-ounce egg sinker on your main or running line. This is tied off onto a good ball-bearing swivel in the 75-pound class. A 3-foot shock leader of 40-pound test is added on, to which a good-quality 4/0 hook is snelled. You can either hook your sand eels through the tip of the head and out the lower jaw or through an eye socket, and thread it onto the hook in much the same manner as a rubber worm used in freshwater bass fishing. Position your boat ahead or up-tide of the rip, and cast the rig out at a 45-degree angle toward it. Once the rig hits the water, let out about 10 feet of extra line, throw the reel in gear, and hang on. You will feel the sinker bounce across the tip of the bar and then, when it goes tight and stops bouncing, let it drift straight back until you either get a hit or it rises to the surface.

Drifting live eels is a steady producer of good fish. The best drifts are made close to the shore of the island, between the beach and the rips. Rubbercore sinkers placed above the eels keep the eel where it does the most good. The watchful angler will have one eye on the LCD fishfinder and the other on the boats around him. Look for mussel beds in 20 to 50 feet of water. Free-spooling as you go, keep in contact with the bottom, but avoid getting hung up. I must give credit where credit is due and thank Captain Ron Murphy, skipper of *Stray Cat*, for showing me the proper table etiquette when serving eels, and my fishing partner, Eric Lafleur, who is a master of this technique.

Several summers ago I was casting from a drifting boat stationed about 75 feet off the beach near Highbank, a famous bass spot on the island. The rip was not formed up as the tide had gone slack high. It was not a very productive time, so we decided to plug the surf from the outside. We chose this spot because of the steep drop-off close to the beach. There was no wind and it was flat calm except for a good swell breaking on the beach, rolling in from the southeast. I chose a P-40 Atom swimming plug and was casting it into the wash along the edge. On one particular cast, I overshot the edge and my plug ended up swimming back toward me in a flush of white foam about 10 feet from the edge. The wave receded, and there was my plug high and dry on the sand. Out of the corner of my eye I spotted a bronze-colored torpedo listing over on its side heading right for my plug. In the passing of no more than a second, she hit the plug and there I was, hooked to a 40-inch-plus bass that, because of the receding wave, was now high and dry. The fish was a good six feet from the water and I had to drag it back into the water and fight her to the boat. I was lucky Eric was there, nobody would have believed me otherwise.

I learned a lesson that day, and now we always plug the beach from the boat. Gibbs Polaris poppers and Danny plugs work very well with this method. Try blue and yellow for colors.

Fly-fishing is a popular technique for coaxing bass from the backside waters. From both the shore and boat, bass come readily to feather and flash combinations, such as Deceivers and Clousers. Slabside and Woolhead patterns will attract youngsters all the way up to the neighborhood bullies. Heavier rigs such as 10- and 11-weight rods are the norm. Manufactured shooting-head/running-line combinations in weights from 200 to 550 grains are required to reach fish holding in deep water along the beach or feeding in the rips offshore. Short and stout leaders 3 to 4 feet long will suffice. Often the leader need be nothing more than two sections, the butt end testing at 30 pounds and a tippet of 20-pound test, topped with a 40-pound-test shock leader that is less than 12 inches long to comply with IGFA-rated lines. The shorter leaders will help your offering sink with your shooting head. The fish, when in the feeding mood, are not that shy of the leader.

Fly size may range from 1 up to 6/0. Use the smaller sizes with flies tied to emulate the local sand eel population, and use the larger with imitations of blueback herring and menhaden, which are often found in these waters. In the late summer and fall months, bonito and false albacore are sometimes found alongside the bass and bluefish.

I cannot overemphasize that you should exercise caution when fishing this side of the island. Fog is almost a constant companion out there. Moon tides combined with a southeast or northeast wind should be avoided by all but the most experienced, and many experienced anglers don't go there in those conditions no matter how good the fishing is. Last year I saw a guide in his flats boat holding up-tide in a rip while his sport was casting from the poling platform with waders on! The angler obviously had a death wish and the boat's operator had "too little left on his spool." I urge you, though, to experience this wonderful place. Be smart and be safe and you won't regret having made the trip.

Good tides and great fishing to you all.

Barnstable Harbor

By Steve Shiraka

The first time I fished Barnstable Harbor was in June of 1971. The uncle of a kid who lived in my neighborhood in Worcester kept a boat at the marina there. The kid would take a picture out of his pocket that showed him holding a bass in the 20-pound range. He'd brag about how he caught it and I would drool with envy.

The kid's uncle was Lenny Hultgren and he ran the charter boat *Aquarius*. It was my sophomore year in high school and several of my friends and I decided to call Capt. Hultgren and set a date in early June. The day came and we were at the dock at the appointed hour expecting great things. We spent the day casting over what I now know were the flats on the east bar. It was a sunny, warm and beautiful day with no wind and no waves.

We drifted over the bars and caught a bunch of schoolies on 5-inch blue- and black-back Rebels. When the tide dropped enough that we had to get to deeper water, we went east and trolled for bigger fish, but it wasn't to be. I knew I had to get back to the harbor, though, and fish the place a lot more.

A few years later I met Captain Robert (Lucky) Singleton of the charter boat *Seawitch*. Over the next few years I mated for him when he needed an alternate, a week here, a weekend there. Lucky is as salty as they come. He knows his waters and he knows how to fish them. He was a great teacher when it came to bass techniques, be it nightime or daytime fishing, casting or trolling. You see, when you work on a charter boat, you have to learn to do things quickly or suffer the captain's wrath. Captain Singleton could dispense wrath with the best of them, and he hated to go fishless.

He was a master of navigation. He taught me to figure ranges and time over water by judging the tide against the course and speed. I thereby learned how to judge the distance between land and the boat. I remember coming into the channel at the entrance buoy at Barnstable one time and he asked me to tell him how much time it would take to get from buoy to buoy to the marina. I had answered several in a row correctly and was pleased as we passed each one when he told me I was correct. I screwed up, though, on the distance/time to the Beach Point buoy and was roundly cussed and then swatted with his sword-fisherman's cap.

Electronics back then were a flasher and VHF radio. Many times when we were caught in a fog so dense you couldn't see the bow from the cockpit, Lucky would look over the side, down into the water, and tell me exactly where we were. And he was right every time.

I learned a lot about the harbor then, and I still learn every year I fish there.

Barnstable Harbor has something for every type of striped bass fisherman. You can do just as well wading as from a boat. Conventional casting, fly rod, light tackle, trolling, jigging, live bait – all these methods work. Marsh and channels to the west and open water to the east attract bass. I'll start in the marshy banks and head east.

Scorton Creek connects to the Barnstable marshes. The creek gets larger as it meanders east and closer to the harbor proper. You can take bass far up into the marsh, but I start my fishing in the Calf's Pasture Point area where the bay proper begins. More reliable and not so tide-dependent, this area is fairly rocky and often the water is stained with suspended silt and aquatic vegetation. This is one of the first places to turn on in the early spring.

The more reliable fishing starts in mid-April, right around Patriot's Day. Fly-fishing works, but the most productive method is definitely a one-handed spinning rod with 10-pound-test line and a white grubtail jig. About three hours into the incoming tide is best. The first part of the outgoing is good, too, and fishing is consistent into early May. Wading is preferred as the fish cruise the shoreline, and it's not unusual to take 30 or more fish in a tide. It's "shake off the dust," fun fishing and worth the effort.

May sees the bass flooding in with each successive tide, in ever-increasing numbers as the days pass. Boat fishing shines in the area from Blish Point out to Beach Point. Schools of small- to medium-size fish range the harbor at dawn and dusk and if it's an overcast day, all day! This is where fly-fishermen have a distinct advantage. The bait of choice in the harbor is the common sand eel. Some years the channel will be stacked top to bottom with the things. On calm mornings, as the tide ebbs or floods and the surface of the water is like glass, the dimpling of the sand eels feeding looks like rain on the water. The swirls of the bass feeding on them look even better. An intermediate 8-weight mono-core line is perfect for gliding over the flats and fishing in two to six feet of water.

On most days you can sight-cast for them. Blind-casting is productive when the water

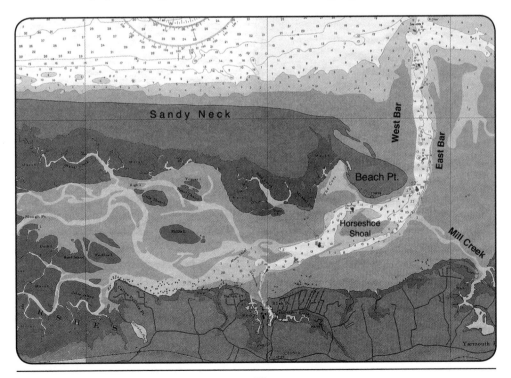

depth gets over eight feet and picking them off of the bottom becomes difficult. A Clouser in chartreuse and white (size 2) is great, as is a Hi-Tie in the same flavor and size. The east bar is the better area for this type of fishing as far as I'm concerned. The east bar is crossed by channels coming out of Mill Creek and Bass Hole. Mill Creek channel is a serious feeding ground for bass that stack up at the intersection with the main harbor channel. The depth goes from 3 feet over an edge to 40 feet deep. This edge is best fished with a 9-weight rod and a 300-grain, depth-charge-type sinking line. Cast upcurrent and let the line drift with the tide until it is at a 90-degree angle to the channel edge, then start your retrieve. Bigger flies are better suited to this and drifting them deep often results in a surprisingly large bass.

In the center of the harbor between Bone Hill and the lighthouse is a bar that, at low tide, lies fully exposed and at high tide is under four to six feet of water. This is called the Horseshoe Bar. At its western, or in-harbor, end it becomes exposed gradually and as the tide is dropping it forms a very noticeable rip, with a long, curving face. The main channel that leads into the harbor and up into the marina is on the west side, and a channel is also found on the east side. The east side channel of Horseshoe Bar does not go all the way around the bar and connect to the main channel. At dawn on a high tide this is a great place to drop flies on a weight-forward line. This is also a great place to cast swimming, surface swimming and popping plugs.

I have used plugs as small as a 1-ounce Gibbs Polaris and as large as their $3^{1/2}$-ounce Polaris and done really well. Danny plugs in yellow and white do well over the bar, too. Gibbs pogy-colored plugs do wonders and I can't tell you how many times I have caught fish on almost every cast on squid-colored poppers there. At low tide or, more precisely, about three hours into the drop, we like to head up-tide into the channel on the east side of Horseshoe Bar. We'll cast either flies or small Polaris poppers up along the exposed sides of the bar and, as we drift parallel to it, sweep the popper over the many small sandbars and holes on each side. With polarized glasses you can see the popper go across the surface of the darker water marking the hole, and as the plug is about to cross another bar, a bass will often swing up and smack that plug in an explosive strike. The fishing around the bar is reliable all season.

At Horseshoe Bar's tail end, leading out towards Beach Point, is a series of bars that do not become exposed at low tide. As the currents sweep around the Horseshoe Bar, they meet over these bars. Again, a fly rod with a 300-grain line is perfectly suited for use here. On a sunny day, using polarized glasses, you can see fish move to the side as your boat's shadow crosses over them. We call this stretch of water The Humps, and this is an extremely productive area when drifting eels in the dead of night. I have had good results here in the daylight casting Fastrac Rebels across the flow and reeling them quickly back to the boat, which drives them deep in the water, bumping the sand along the bottom. Jointed chartreuse with chrome sides is recommended.

Across from the Horseshoe Bar on Sandy Neck is a small cottage colony located along a wide, shallow cove. The area between the lighthouse and the start of the cottages is a channel. The channel follows the docks and bulkhead walls of the cottages, and when the tide is dropping, bait dumps out into the main channel. When the moon is at its fullest,

the cove will be almost dry at low tide. Be there when this lunar event happens at dusk or, even better, dawn. You can troll with light lines and small swimming plugs, like Yo-Zuris, Rebels or Bombers, skirt the moorings just outside the lighthouse and catch fish 'til your arms fall off in mid-May and again in the fall. Numerous small baitfish, such as juvenile pogies and silversides, seek refuge in the shallow cove waters and are forced into the channel as the tide goes out. You can pull your boat up and hop out and cast flies or plugs as the fish break at your feet.

Barnstable Harbor was custom-made for the wading fisherman, but there are risks in wading here. You must constantly be aware of tidal conditions. You are at the southern end of the Gulf of Maine in Cape Cod Bay and 9- and 10-plus-foot tides are the rule. The average tidal rise and fall for the Barnstable area is 6 inches every 15 minutes. If you have a full moon or new moon with plus or minus tides, the rise and fall rate is even more drastic. The area is made up of vast sand flats, cut by channels of all widths and depths. Most wading is done on the eastern shore, from Millway to Mill Creek and beyond. Three-quarters of a mile of bare sand shows at low tide, and to walk across to the channel edge to the better spots, you can cover a mile or more diagonally. Fighting a dropping or rising tide that goes up or down 6 inches every 15 minutes means you have to plan transit time and your fishing window of opportunity very carefully. When the fishing is good you can get into trouble quickly if you decide to try for "just one more fish" or if a sudden fog rolls in. Places like Bone Hill Road and Indian Trail off of Route 6A offer access, but you'd better plan when to come back before you go out there. For the first couple of times, go with an experienced hand to guide you.

Most wading fishermen these days are fly-fishermen. Neoprenes or breathable waders are suggested in spring, summer and fall. A stripping basket is another must. A small, pin-on compass is highly recommended, as is a flashlight worn around the neck. An intermediate line and a spare spool with a quick descent line should be in the wader pocket. If you are boating, you can pull up on the edge beyond Mill Creek where most waders who venture out from the shore fail to explore. The creek that empties out from Bass Hole is often very good. You can even follow the creek bed up onto the flats and take bass in shallow pools where they await the flooding tide. I especially like to fish the above area when the tide is flooding and fish can be seen cruising into the channels and shallows. A mono-core with a 10-pound-test fluorocarbon tippet and a size 1 chartreuse Hi-Tie gets 'em every time.

In the spring, drifting the channel with live herring from the Beach Point buoy to the bell buoy at the channel entrance can be deadly to the bass in residence. A small rubber-core sinker (about 1 ounce) a foot or two ahead of the herring is all that's necessary. The outgoing tide is more favorable than the opposite. Many fishermen prefer to jig the area with 150 feet of wire and a white 3-ounce parachute jig with a red pork rind trailer. We did that a few times last year and most days could not go farther than 100 feet after the wire was let out and we were on. The fish are generally of average size, but I have taken and seen some monsters come out of the channel that were fooled by a white parachute or a dark blue Jig-It eel. On many occasions, Lucky Singleton never left the channel while the other skippers were steaming east to Billingsgate; that was because he had marked fish while coming in from a trip. He would purposely delay leaving the dock until the others had gone around the bend so no one would see us jerking wire from the lighthouse to the bell buoy and back.

Over the past few years chunking has become very popular in the harbor and out in the channel. It's easy and can be deadly at times. Bass are suckers for chunk bait; they know a good thing when they see it. When chunking in the harbor became really popular five or six years ago, it killed the night-fishing with eels. The popularity of chunking has seemed to decline in the last two seasons, and this past season we had decent fishing while drifting eels in the dead of night.

Drifting eels at night, at least for me, is the best method to take big bass in the harbor. We start just after July 4. I look for a low tide that occurs at 10 p.m. and fish later each night until low tide occurs at just before dawn. The end of the lunar cycle through the new moon and the beginning of the next cycle to the quarter moon is best. We like to drift the water adjacent to and around the Horseshoe Bar. The best waters are the channels on either side, especially the east side. I look for water from 6 to 12 feet deep.

In the summer, the daytime traffic inside the harbor is heavy. But just before sundown the place goes dead. The fish respond by leaving the security of the deeper channels and come up onto the flooded flats to feed. The bass will hardly ever go far from the channel edge though. They skim the edges at the previously mentioned water depths and the eels are drifted away from the boat. The standard gear is a 9- or 10-foot conventional outfit with 30-pound-test line tied directly to a 5/0 live bait hook. The eel is hooked through the lower jaw and out an eye socket and fed back at least 150 feet from the boat.

We motor up-tide to the head of the bar, cut the motor and cast the eels back into the water. Feeding line back as the drift sets up, we stand in the back of the boat, keeping the reel in free-spool with a thumb on the spool and the line just ahead of the spool, pinched between two fingers of the other hand. If the eel gets hit, we just let the line go and keep slight thumb pressure on the spool. After a few long seconds we throw the reel into gear and wait for the tension before we set up on the fish. We use no lights on the boat except for a penlight around the neck and the dim light of the depth recorder, but we are on the lookout for other boats that might be out there. A careless light on the water can foul up the fishing for an hour or more until the fish get comfortable again. Only familiarity with the place in the daylight will prepare you for the experience of night-fishing the harbor. It's a totally different game after dark and a totally different place. Eel fishing peaks in September and you can have some big nights into October, but there are fewer with each passing day.

Many people like to rake their own sand eels and then either drift or anchor up and, with the aid of a small weight, send them down to the bottom to the hungry fish. You can purchase sand eels in most bait shops or buy a sand eel rake and rake your own at low tide in places like the Mill Creek channel. We once had a custom-made rake that was 10 feet long, and we would "power rake" along the sides of Horseshoe Bar. One of us would drive the boat slowly and the other would put the rake over the side and hold it tightly into the sand and drag it along for a good 50 feet or more. Most times it would come up absolutely crammed with the little critters. Usually only two or three passes were necessary to get all the bait we needed.

Most of the fish taken with sand eels will be small and it can get a bit monotonous at times, but it sure works. When hooking the sand eel, push a size 2 hook through the top of the head between the eyes and out the small, diamond shape that is golden amber in color. That spot is the hardest and most secure spot on the sand eel's body. If the bait is a little stiff, flex it a few times so it wiggles more naturally on the hook. This method is best in the channels around the Horseshoe Bar. Sand eels are not true eels, there are no minimum size requirements and you don't need a permit to rake them if they are for personal use.

If you trailer your boat you'll find an excellent ramp at Blish Point at the entrance to Millway Marina. Get there early, though, as the place fills up fast. In season (from June through September) there is a small fee to use it between the hours of 6 a.m. and 5 p.m. If you are wading, get a street atlas and look for any "town way to water" designations and check them out. Mid-May until the third week of June is prime, as is the month of September to the end of October. Fish can be had year-round if you work at it, but conditions can be miserable in the winter.

Two years ago on Columbus Day morning while fishing with George Ryan and another person, we were all buzzed by a 9-foot blue shark. It was nine in the morning and under a clear blue sky when George yelled the warning. I watched the shark come over the edge of the channel from green water into three feet of water over clear sand and head straight at me. As he was about three feet away he rolled over and eyed me with his black eye and brushed by. I could only watch in disbelief as it happened. It was a little disconcerting, to say the least, but that was the only time I've ever been shaken up while wading there.

That's Barnstable Harbor in a nutshell. There are many more areas in the harbor that deserve mentioning, but the places I have talked about are generally the most productive and easily fished.

Fall On Cape Cod Bay

There's A Buffet Going On, For The Fish And For You!

By Leo Bedard

When I think of fall on Cape Cod Bay, I think of stripers chowing down for their long trip south and the coming winter. They have to eat hearty. I think of eels, numbed by ice, dropped into schools of hungry stripers. The crowds have left, the commercial bass season is over and I know I'll find plenty of elbowroom at my favorite honey holes.

The water temperatures that seemed to take forever to get to 55 degrees back in May are still holding to the mid-60s, a perfect surface temperature for striped bass fishing. It's comfortable out there in a jacket, and the fishing is superb, whether you're fishing for stripers a mile or two from shore or flounder at the east end of the Cape Cod Canal.

With fall come fish blitzes on Scorton Ledge. The fact that the air is crisp and the sun is bright seems to have no effect on the feeding frenzy that is happening just below the surface. And it's amazing just how close to the surface they are. Last year a buddy and I were into 30-pounders, dragging red tubes on leadcore. We were three miles west of the target ship remains in Cape Cod Bay. No one else in the small group of boats was hooking up. What they didn't realize was that our leadcore was out only 1 1/2 colors, which is a mere 45 feet. The lines were less than 8 feet below the surface in 35 feet of water, and it was a bright sunny day. Just one of the experiences that make me love the fall on the bay.

This was not the first time we had been successful with such a short length of line. If you

The author lands another quality bass using a bunker spoon. This oversized net was made by the author to accommodate large fish.

know fish are in the area and you're not hooking up, don't change the color or the bend in your tube until you've first tried shortening the amount of line you have out. I know this goes against conventional wisdom, which says that more line out and a deeper presentation is the next thing to try, but things are different in the fall than they are in midseason. Stripers that have spent the warm summer months hugging the bottom and only feeding at night are on the move, and they're looking up, down and everywhere for their meals.

If you use plastic rather than latex tubes, a little trick for maintaining the right bend is to store the tubes with the trailer hook through the swivel at the head of the lure. Hanging them that way in your boat is a safe storage method that maintains a bend. Another trick is to store them in a bucket or pail. The length of the tube should determine the diameter of the container – the longer the tube, the larger the bucket. Experiment to see what radius works best for you. Be careful, though: too much bend and the hooks will have a propensity for finding the eye of the swivel while you're trolling. Many hours can be wasted dragging a tube that's in an almost perfect circle. The effect of the dangling worm (which is what this is all about) is lost, and the offering doesn't look appealing to any fish. The bend makes for more action in the water; the right motion can make the worm irresistible to the fish. Just be sure to use a high-quality snap swivel on the end of your leader. Without it, that spinning action caused by the bend can put some serious twist in your running line.

I frankly favor bunker spoon fishing, but two factors will get me to switch to tube-and-worm fishing very quickly. For one thing, in the areas that I fish in the bay, quite a few guys use big bunker spoons. I'm convinced that the fish get tired of them and thus become much more receptive to a trolled tube and worm. The other factor is the arrival of the bluefin tuna. Tuna like bunker spoons. One day, while trolling not too far off Rock Harbor, one of my two reels started screaming wildly. I usually troll with wire off one side of the boat and leadcore off the other; it was the rod with leadcore and a white bunker spoon that had been hit. I turned to shut off the motor (to prevent the wire from entangling the propeller) and by the time I turned back, the reel was spooled. I lost close to 50 dollars worth of line in about 3 1/2 seconds. My outfits were no match for that fish. The next day I switched to tube and worm and caught some nice bass, but that spot was crawling with tuna boats. It doesn't take long for word to get around.

The sun sets after 6:30 through September, so you can still get out in the daylight during the week (if you can come up with a decent excuse to leave work early). Just pick up a few eels, or grab some of those sea worms that you've kept hidden from your wife in the back of the fridge. Don't ever forget those things in there. Wives can be very unforgiving, even when they are avid fishermen themselves.

If the winds kick up, stay close to shore. For the last few seasons, the flounder at the East End of the canal have been abundant in September, and so fat that we've had to slice the fillets in half to use them in any kind of a roll-up recipe. And, if that weren't enough, legal-size cod can be found just a stone's throw from the south side of the Sandwich jetty.

September draws to a close all too quickly as far as I'm concerned, and October brings with it a new set of challenges. Less daylight makes it tougher to hit the water during the day after work, and the wind is often gusty and out of the northeast (the absolute worst direction in the upper area of the bay). But there is one big reason to look forward to October: the arrival of the biggest stripers of the year.

The big ladies have taken their time on their march south. They don't want to be involved with the schools of racers. "The bait that's left in the bay is like a buffet table to them," said Captain Bob Joyce. "I've always felt that the best weekend to pull in 40- and 50-pounders is Columbus Day weekend." Although Bob runs charters that weekend, he knows captains who like to keep that weekend just for themselves.

Eels are an excellent bait during this season, the best if you can't get large adult pogies. On one very calm day (unusual in October), using cold-stunned eels, I had the thrill of seeing my catch with two others at least as big following all the way to the point that I lifted the striper from the water. It looked like they were just hoping she would drop the bait. I was glad she didn't. Females grow significantly larger than males; most stripers over 30 pounds are female. When I was finally able to put that fish on the deck, my heart was pounding. I guessed I had caught at least a 35-pounder, but I was disappointed to find that the fish was a 1/2 pound below the 35-pound weight required for a state pin. And that's another thing we never outgrow. Those coveted pins are the pride of every fisherman. A few of those on your lucky cap, and you're dressed for any occasion that includes other fishermen. On Cape Cod Bay, the two most likely times when you'll earn one are early spring and – you guessed it – the fall.

Here's a tip for you boaters who, like me, like the versatility of a trailerable boat in the low 20-foot range but enjoy the use of a slip, especially when time is limited: A few marinas offer specials in the fall. Weekly slips are available for about the price you'd pay for two days in a transient slip during tourist season. At the Sandwich Marina, for example, Harbor Master Greg Fayne will give you a slip at three dollars per foot, for a week. That's an end-of-season rate that begins the third week of September. So for $69 you could have your 23-foot boat waiting for you at the dock for an entire week. This depends on availability, but there are usually many slips available, as most of the seasonal slip tenants have hauled out.

A lot of time is saved when all you have to do in the afternoon is walk down to your slip and start your engine. And you get to be pretty good at docking after dark. I never had any ambition to get good at driving onto a trailer after dark. Keep this in mind: In mid-October, the sun sets at about 6 p.m. You'd better start thinking of your work excuses now.

We shouldn't overlook the almighty bluefin tuna. It's not a fish that I choose to chase; the gear is too expensive for the amount of time that I could dedicate to the fishery. Gary Blake is a long-time tuna fisherman who started fishing the waters off Block Island and later moved to Sandwich. "Lately the tuna fishing has been spotty," Gary recently told me. "If you're in the right place, at the right time, you could be in for a couple good days of fishing in the bay. It's not like the old days."

There's a lot of encouragement in the fact that the footballs (immature bluefin) have been a regular visitor in late September and early October. These fish can swim at speeds up to 45 miles per hour. They come close enough to shore to pursue with a small boat at this time of year, and if you hook into one, you're in for the fight of your life. You'll see them at the surface, but they're comfortable at any depth. Assuming they aren't decimated by seiners or starved for lack of sea herring, they'll grow to become giants weighing up to 1,500 pounds. Some believe that the fact they're here now means the location is imbedded in their memory. Their presence is encouraging to me, and I hope that we'll once again see catches of 1,000-pound-plus fish within sight of the bayside beaches.

In the last few years the highliners from the Upper Cape have seen some good catches, but they have gone outside the bay to find them. Bait-fishing is the rule for giants; the experts use live butterfish, live whiting, chummed shad and live bluefish.

The tuna guys prefer smaller bluefish for live-lining, but there's just one problem – there are only big ones in the bay in the fall! And they're a blast to catch. I have a preference for stripers, but I'm not a bass snob. I carry casting rods in the boat and I'm always on the lookout for diving birds, which often give away the presence of big blues on the surface. While I spend most of the fishing season trolling, there's nothing like tempting huge blues with a surface plug. They don't bite; they slam the lure, and once hooked, they fight fiercely all the way to the boat. Pound for pound, they are the hardest-fighting gamefish commonly caught in Cape Cod Bay.

The skill lies in getting them to the boat. Getting them to hit in that frenzy takes no skill at all. They'd hit a pickle if you threw it out. (Yes, that actually happened – a friend of mine witnessed it.) Gulls won't even land on the water. Many of those who have are now standing on one leg because they don't have a choice. If you let a bluefish go near pot warp or your prop, you've lost that fish. They seem to somehow have developed the skill to wrap your line around anything in the water, and then to use that tension to break free. It's positively uncanny.

I realize I haven't done justice to bottom fishing. Now, I'm not one to give out numbers given to me in confidence by a fishing colleague. Friendships have been lost over such indiscretions, but last year I stumbled on this spot on my own. It's between Sandwich and Plymouth at N41deg. 59.724' and W070 deg. 29.754'. At these numbers, on two trips, in three hours each day, I caught 70 pounds of legal-size cod, sea bass, mackerel and pollock. On the second day tautog were in the mix.

I've always wanted to have a fishing hot spot named after me. So if you use this spot with success, please name it "Leo's Spot." If you're unsuccessful, still call it Leo's Spot; just put an expletive before "Leo."

This is a testament to the smorgasbord of fish available in the fall on the inside of this arm of land we call Cape Cod. The best advice I can give, as always, is to check with the bait shops in the area where you're interested in fishing. They're a vital part of the fishing network. Commercial hook-and-line fishermen head straight to the wholesaler with their catch. Recreational fishermen, on the other hand, head straight to the tackle shops. Having our fish weighed in and receiving the accolades is another thing we never outgrow. The information they gain from customers, and their knowledge of the sport, lets the tackle shop guys give you a well-educated guess of where the fish are, and what they're hitting. They'll also help you fill out the form necessary to receive that sought-after state pin that I mentioned earlier, if your catch is large enough to qualify. This is something you'll never get from a discount catalog or big box retailer.

Consistently successful fishing requires an intimate knowledge of your little section of the ocean. Fishfinders and chart plotters will only show ridges, bumps and holes. Knowledge of subtleties like mussel or scallop beds, weed patches, and mud or rock bottoms takes a network of friends and a whole lot of research.

I believe that my time has been more wisely invested than my money. I've spent thousands of hours on the water, yet every time I bring one of those trophies over the gunwales, I feel that thrill. How many thousands of pounds must you catch before that thrill goes away? When do you stop saying, "What a beautiful fish!" every time you gently lay one of them down on the deck? Never, I hope. ◄━◄

The tube-and-worm rig is a consistent performer on autumn stripers in Cape Cod Bay. Experiment with the running depth; sometimes you'll get more strikes in the middle of the water column than near the bottom.
-photo by Linda Bedard

Hot Spots In Hingham And Hull

By Ron Powers

The Cape Cod Canal has a well-deserved reputation as being one of the bona fide hot spots along the striper coast. Although the canal delivers the goods all season long, for many anglers, images of fishing the famous herring run take front-and-center stage in their thoughts. The possibility of hooking up with that first fresh-from-the-sea "keepah" of the year keeps anglers enchanted by the canal's potential.

Some of us who live in the Boston area and are a bit "geographically challenged" are not fortunate enough to visit that storied body of water as often as we'd like. However, the outlook is not as bleak as it may seem, quite the contrary, since a few minutes south of Boston, casters are blessed with an extraordinary bay area, fed by three different rivers in a five-mile stretch that all possess their own herring runs. A total ecosystem, the Hull Bay and its sister bay in Hingham host smelt, herring and alewife spawning runs that coincide with the arrival of the gamefish, and in fact may be the reason gamefish show up in the first place. Is there any mystery why this bay area would hold such promise for fishermen?

The herring runs are only a small part of the story. This bay is also bordered by open-ocean-facing beaches and contains numerous islands and parks. Besides bass and blues, shorebound or boat anglers can tangle with tautog, mackerel, smelt, flounder, cod and pollock, and often an angler can hook up with many of these resident fish all in one day. Once the herring runs have subsided, there are plenty of good reasons sportfish and the fishermen who stalk them stay around, not the least of which is the large population of forage species that make this area their home.

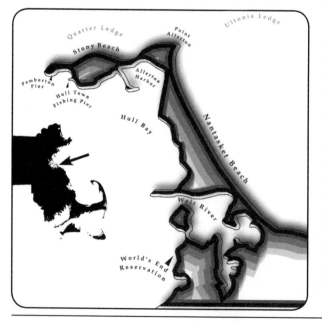

Located primarily in the towns of Hull and Hingham, Hull Bay is not only a herring and smelt nursery but also harbors juvenile winter flounder, sea worms and grass shrimp. In addition to these striper menu items, this area is exceptional in that it contains schools of adult herring that can be caught from shore or boat and live-lined, sometimes well into November. In the warmer months of summer, snapper blues frequent the rivers and are also effectively live-lined by regulars.

Hewitts Cove in Hingham is

one of the busiest lobster ports on the East Coast. When these lobstermen return from their outings, you don't need an instruction manual to figure out what they do with their scraps; they toss them into the sea. The continuous flow of chum calls fish in like a bird dog to a whistle. If by now you are getting the idea that this sounds like a smorgasbord to keep local gamefish populations fat, dumb and happy, you are about right.

Simply put, if there are bass out there, then there is a spot nearby where you will find them, regardless of the time of year. Let's get specific and point out some prime locations.

Starting in Hull, the westernmost point of this crook of land contains a number of great spots, one of which is Stony Beach. Stony Beach, as implied by its name, is a stone-covered beachfront that lies at the edge of Quarter Ledge. Typical of a ledge area, there is scattered rock structure that appeals both to crustaceans and the gamefish that feed on them. Not only is this a good place to cast to stripers, but it is also a spot where tautog often end up on the business end of a fisherman's line. Because deep water is nearby, courtesy of a channel close to the beach, this location has potential even during the dog days of summer. Travel along Nantasket Avenue through Fitzpatrick Way and follow this road to the very tip of Hull, just past clearly marked Pemberton Pier. Park next to the ballpark. If you are feeling energetic, walk the beach and cast, and be sure not to end the outing without working the waters off Pemberton Pier.

This area delivers the goods for both bait-soakers and casters alike. Chunking herring all through the season produces steady numbers of quality bass and blues. Tossing out metal, such as Kastmasters and Hopkins spoons, works well here. I always try to bring a few of each since they are effective at different water columns. I believe that the mirrorlike finish of the Kastmaster is what attracts gamefish in relatively shallow water, but the hammered finish of the Hopkins picks up and reflects sparse light, which is all that is available in deeper water, and it is there that I use that lure.

Since herring are a major food source to nearby stripers, don't forget to bring herring-imitating plastics. Swimmers and poppers work great when the fish are visible and near the surface. I always bring along a few soft plastic Power Pogies or Shad Assassins in both natural hues and high-visibility colorations, such as lime and chartreuse. When the gamefish are scattered they can home in on the luminous colors from a good distance away.

Due east of Pemberton Pier in Allerton Harbor is the Hull Town Fishing Pier. Easily

identified by the red, 40-foot-long buoy on the front lawn, the Hull Town Fishing Pier is the next logical place to try if your results at Pemberton and Stony are not what you were hoping for. The Town Fishing Pier is positioned right between the Hull Yacht Club and the Nantasket Saltwater Fishermen's Club. This harbor is a south-facing shallow basin (less than 10 feet deep) that attracts stripers because of an abundant bait supply, along with its sun-drenched waters, which

Pemberton Pier

heat up readily in springtime. Anglers casting sea worms off the pier have been hooking up with winter flounder with increasing regularity in recent years as this species begins to recover.

Just east of Allerton Harbor is Point Allerton. You can judge how productive Point Allerton is by the steady parade of fishing boats that at times can look like the "procession of the small ships" as they troll tube-and-worms nearby. Overlooking Quarter Ledge and Ultonia Ledge, Point Allerton benefits from being next to boulder-strewn structure and is in close proximity to deep water (40- to 50-foot depths).

To the shore-caster, the ominous no-parking signs that dot the streets make it plain that the welcome mat will not be rolled out by the residents of this well-to-do neighborhood. However, with a little derring-do you can fish this spot like you're on the VIP guest list. Park at the Daley Wanzer moving company parking lot at X and Y streets, just down the street from Point Allerton Avenue. Either walk the shoreline from Nantasket Beach or hike up the road to Point Allerton Avenue. On Point Allerton Avenue you can reach this spot via a public right of way to the water's edge. You can have access to prime

Point Allerton

casting waters, great views and not have to pay the high tax rate or be constantly cleaning the salt spray from your windows as the residents do.

Point Allerton is a jutting elbow of land that has two ledges, Quarter Ledge and Utonia Ledge. On the incoming tide the bass and blues move in from the deep confines of Utonia Ledge into the rubble-bottomed Quarter Ledge. Boat anglers must be ever vigilant of the large rock formations that lie just below the surface. The problem is that anglers must get as close to these rocks as possible to place the presentation where the linesiders lurk. Whenever I fish there, we assign one angler to lookout duty at the bow, even though we are quite familiar with the terrain.

With stripers in so close to the shoreline, Point Allerton takes on the role of a great equalizer, allowing shore-fishers to compete on equal footing with the boat guys. At dawn and dusk, a white-with-red-head pencil popper walked over the surface often calls them in. Just be sure to vary your retrieve. I always start with a slow walk-the-dog crawl and intermittently toss in a more aggressive retrieve with periodic snaps of the rod tip. Let the fish tell you how to put the pieces of the puzzle together. When the herring begin their spawning pilgrimages, they often cross in front of Point Allerton while en route. Experienced anglers know this and will soak herring chunks here in anticipation. Point Allerton also attracts schools of codfish from late summer to springtime.

Heading west along Nantasket Avenue you will come to A Street in Hull. Follow this street until you come to a pier. This is a good location to intercept stripers as they move along Hull Gut with the incoming tide. A Street is another area where herring are an ample bait source. A light spinning rod and a sabiki rig or similar combination of small shad darts will get you some of this striper candy to live-line. While fishing off the pier, keep an eye on the cove to your right where periodically bass will intercept schools of herring and drive them up against the shoreline. A swimming plug or popper chucked into the resultant blitz will get the stripers' attention.

Hull Fishing Pier

Nantasket Beach is a gorgeous, open-ocean-facing beach where shore-casters and boaters have the possibility of hooking into that moby striper all season long. A shallow beach, its sandy bottom is but a few

Nantasket Beach

strokes of a striper's tail away from the sanctuary of mid-40-foot depths. Parking is available along the entire beach. One of my favorite ways of fishing Nantasket is to wade into the surf and live-line herring, Cape Cod Canal style. I'll catch my bait at one of the nearby piers, such as A Street or Pemberton, toss them into an aerator in the back of my truck and head on down to Nantasket as fast as I can.

Spotting a fisher wading in the waters on the edge of the canal with a herring basket does not stop traffic. A surf-fisherman on Nantasket who strides to the water's edge with a modified clothes hamper in hand had better be ready to answer some quirky questions from beachgoers. One elderly gentleman approached me and wanted to know exactly what advantages there were to doing my laundry in the surf. I didn't know how to begin to answer him!

My experience has been that live-lining herring from this beachfront will give you the best shot around at consistently hooking up with seriously large bass. Oftentimes, when other anglers are messing around with schoolies at some of the nearby rivers, I am getting shell-shocked from the tail slap of 40-inch linesiders chasing herring yards from where I stand. This is a great beach to toss hardware, such as a SPRO bucktail dressed with a grub tail. My favorite is the 1-ounce green shad version topped off with a chartreuse 4-inch twister tail.

Nantasket is also a good beach to walk along and cast eels on a warm midsummer's night.

An effective eel container is one of those small, soft-sided coolers that come with a shoulder strap. Chill the eels into submission by putting a few cubes of ice on the bottom before you slide them in, sling the strap over your shoulder and you are now a highly mobile eel caster. Anywhere along Nantasket can bring fishy action, but my personal favorite is the southeast corner of the beach known as The Rocks. As the name implies, this spot contains a number of boulders that are havens for crustaceans and other forage that attract bass and blues. Not many anglers target tautog here, but the ones who do commonly tug in big ones. These buck-toothed bulldogs are often caught by accident while anglers fish for stripers or flounder with sea worms.

Heading farther inland to the town of Hingham, another fishing area worth mentioning is at the World's End Reservation. Just off Route 3A on Martin's Lane, World's End is a town-run reservation where a small fee is charged to park. You'll find that the minimal fee is well worth it. Situated at the mouth of the Weir River, World's End is like a funnel where herring, smelt and other baitfish must pass between two points of land that at the narrowest point are only a mere 25 feet or so apart.

As the incoming tide gains momentum, baitfish tumble along and are easy pickings for opportunistic stripers. Mariner's Cove on the south side of the reservation is a consistent producer, too. Shallow mud flats just outside of this cove hold plenty of sea worms – a great spot for doormat-sized flounder! Drifting a sea worm about five feet below a float can also result in some lively striper action. Boat fishers bag linesiders by trolling umbrella rigs or surgical tubes sweetened with a sea worm between World's End Reservation and nearby White Head Flats.

Hull offers plenty of choices but you "ain't seen nuttin'" until you've seen Hingham Bay. If you were to take the average angler on a whirlwind tour of the different locations available to a caster in Hingham Bay, it would not be unlike dropping Barney Fife into the busiest precinct in New York City. The term "overwhelmed" comes to mind.

Situated directly across from Hull Bay, and the beneficiary of the enriching flows of two channels, is Hingham Bay. Baitfish and gamefish migrate to this location through two channels: Hull Gut or West Gut. Flowing into the bay to further nourish this environment are the waters of the Weymouth Back River and Weymouth Fore River.

The Weymouth Back River is home to one of the largest herring runs on the East Coast. From the mouth of this river to its point of origin, Whitman's Pond, the Back River often resembles a herring traffic jam during May and June. Hot on their tails are the stripers. And you'll find plenty of parks and other access points along the river from which you can tempt these fish.

One such place is Bare Cove Park, a large recreation area located off Fort Hill Street. Even though you are within a few short miles of metropolitan Boston, there are no interstates or factories or other examples of urban sprawl nearby. This is not exactly the wilderness, but it is an amazing refuge so close to human habitation. A 10-minute walk will bring you deep into the heart of the Weymouth Back River area.

Eventually you'll come to the cove that gave this park its name. Lined with eelgrass, this is a premier spot from which to cast a few eels. Alewife-colored 9-inch Slug-Gos with

1/2-ounce jigheads undulated along the bottom imitate not only the eels that are present but also the herring that move along the riverbanks.

On the extreme right-hand side of the cove is a point where a caster can reach well into the middle of the river with his presentation. I've done very well here casting a 1-ounce white pencil popper or needlefish, racking up large numbers of bass when they are feeding on herring.

Another access area is just off Bridge Street. Traveling east on Bridge Street, turn right onto Beal Street; up the road a bit to the left is a ballpark. Park here and you're only about 1/4 mile from Bare Cove Park, which you can find by following the river.

Near the north end of Beal Street, across Bridge Street, is Stodder Park, a multi-acre park that is a point jutting into the Weymouth Back River. Numerous access points are available to the fisher. At low tide, vast expanses of mud flats are exposed on the western side of this park. As the tide rises there is a slough between the mud flats and the park where flounder move in to pounce on emerging sea worms. Striper addicts can find linesiders near the bridge and at the northern portion of the park, where it faces open water. Anglers soaking clams or sea worms may find their sand-spiked rods dancing to the rhythm of either a flounder or a bass at Stodder Park.

Just across the river from Stodder is Abigail Adams Park, where you'll find a boat ramp. This park is also a good starting point for the kayaking caster. Weymouth Back River is custom made for kayaking, and many of the coves and shallow-water areas off the river are best fished out of this type of watercraft.

Fly-fishers do very well here because of the huge population of silversides and mummichogs. Clouser Minnows catch plenty of fish, but any good thin-bodied baitfish streamer will produce.

Shorebound lure slingers toss out the usual suspects, including Yo-Zuri Crystal Minnows or Bomber jointed swimmers. On bright, sunny days stick to blue-back or green colors; at dawn or dusk tempt them with black plugs. Your best chances will be during the incoming tide, starting at the cove to your left and walking toward the bridge. The confluence at the bridge is a good place to drag a spoon through during the ebb tide. Smelters catch their favorite fish off the pier at the park in the spring and fall.

Reaching Abigail Adams Park is a cinch. Signs direct you to the park on the left-hand side of Bridge Street. If you're daydreaming visions of big stripers and cross the Back River bridge, turn back; you've traveled too far.

Directly across the street from Abigail Adams Park is Great Eskers Park. Great Eskers Park was once home to native peoples who for centuries took advantage of the bountiful sea life that thrives here. That same diversity of critters makes Eskers a highly regarded fishing hole. One of the premier locations on the Weymouth Back River to intercept the herring run, fishers

Great Eskers Park

can walk along a paved pathway that parallels the river and follow blitzing bass as they explode on herring. The herring move along so close to shore here that I'm often able to take all I need with a dip net. A Cape Cod Canal-style bicycle rig here would surely turn the local fishermen green with envy.

Farther north along Bridge Street, bisecting the Weymouth Fore/Back rivers, is Weymouth Neck. Accessible by Neck Street, Weymouth Neck has a boat launching area at the Wessagussett Beach parking lot. This boat ramp gives fishermen a direct, quick route to some of the better winter flounder waters in the state. Shoving off into the Back River, boaters are mere minutes away from Grape Island, Peddocks Island and Bumkin Island. Find a quiet, mud-bottomed cove and drop a flounder spreader spiced with sea worms. During cooler months codfish can also be caught in many of these spots and sometimes intermittently among the flatties.

Striper and bluefish hunters troll surgical tube-and-sea worm combos just inside of the ferry channel, all the way along Weymouth Neck up to Wessagussett Beach. One especially popular spot for trolling is Jackknife Ledge, which is adjacent to the easternmost portion of the beach.

Shorebound casters need not miss out on the fun since many of these spots are within reach of a surf rod. Wessagussett Beach is a productive beach from which to cast eels, particularly during low-light

Wessagussett Beach

conditions. Blitzing blues and bass, wreaking havoc among smelt and herring, often push the forage up against the sands of this beach. Nearby Jackknife Ledge, which is outlined by the seawall at the end of this beach, is a great place to hook into a keeper or two. Find the edge where the sandy bottom meets the ledge, toward the beginning of the seawall, and chunk some herring here.

Farther along Weymouth Neck, by way of River Street, you will find Webb State Park and its two coves, Upper Neck Cove and Lower Neck Cove. The first of these, Upper Neck, is a shallow basin with a gravel bottom interspersed with eelgrass patches. I'll often cast a Sassy Shad or some other soft plastic between the eelgrass patches in this area and hop it along the bottom. Stripers stalk the shallows for herring and eels and will seldom pass up a soft plastic swimming along in front of their nose. You won't lose much gear here because there are few if any obstacles to hangup your lure.

The Lower Neck Cove on Webb State Park is similar to the Upper Cove, except that the outermost point faces Grape Island. Watching the ferry boats skirt this outpost, it will be obvious that there is deep water a short distance away, and this channel, which permits the travel of ferries and lobster boats to Hewitts Cove in Hingham, doubles as a deep-water sanctuary for blues, bass and cod. Gobs of clam fished on the bottom will deliver cod and striper action depending on the season. During those exciting cusp periods,

when coldwater and warmwater conditions overlap, a strike can be an angler's
veritable roll of the dice to see whether
it's a codfish or a striper. Days when you
land a nice example of each species are
not unheard of. How many places can
make that claim?

Nut Island Fishing Pier

Avalon Beach in Quincy on the Fore
River is a local favorite that is definitely
worth checking out. The beach is between
Town River Yacht Club and Shipyard
Point. Marauding bass frequently pin
baitfish in the shallows where they literally have nowhere to go. This area holds populations of herring, smelt, sperling and mummichogs. With the variety of baitfish on hand, a
little "survival of the fittest" drama constantly unfolds here, with large baitfish feeding on
smaller baitfish. This may explain why dropper rigs tend to be so effective at Avalon.

For those who are unfamiliar with dropper rigs, they're little more than a teaser (streamer
fly or soft-plastic bait) tied off a few feet above a swimming plug. Perhaps the sight of
what appears to be a larger fish ready to make a meal out of a smaller one incites the
competitive instincts in a prowling striper or blue. I am always amazed at how often the
gamefish will grab the teaser and not the plug. But regardless of the reason, this technique
proves deadly on Avalon Beach and it is my favorite here. Incidentally, the Town River
Yacht Club is a great place to catch a couple quarts of smelt in the fall.

Nut Island on the easternmost point of Quincy features a large, comfortable fishing
pier that is in sight of Peddock's Island. Ferries and private boats are constantly shuffling
to and from Peddock's. The shore-caster working the same water all within sight of his
auto may think that he's got the best of both worlds. With cod, pollock, mackerel, bass,
blues, flounder and even tautog available, who could disagree?

Last year in June, my friend and light-line aficionado Denny Chan was drifting sea worms
off the pilings of this pier, hoping to connect with a couple of the pollock that congregate
here, when an 11-pound tautog clamped onto his hook. How he managed to land that
tog and keep it from slicing up his 8-pound-test mono on one of those barnacle-covered
pilings I'll never know, but he did land the fish, one of the largest I've ever heard of in
the Greater Boston area.

To find Nut Island, take Quincy Shore Drive to Sea Street past the police station, and
at the very end you will see the pier.

It seems that each and every time I go to the Hingham and Hull bays, I find another
great place to fish, and I never quite know what I'm going to catch. I haven't figured out
where the blue marlin are hiding out, but I'm working on it!

Chillin' With Boston Stripers
Midwinter Linesider Sport In The Bay State

By Ron Powers

If you're looking to grab a dozen pike shiners from any bait shop in the Greater Boston area this month, I suggest you get there early. There are certain patrons of the shops who go through these baitfish like chocolates on Valentine's Day. All the more peculiar is that this fisher is not a lover of hardwater and as a matter of fact couldn't care less about freshwater gamesters. So what midwinter pastime would cause such an insatiable appetite for big shiners? Well, if you are one of those still catching stripers, you know the answer!

Maybe you've seen one of these guys hunched over the railing along the Cambridge Parkway, peering into the black-water Charles River as if he's lost his keys. Then you notice the fishing rod and do a quick calendar check and wonder if he's lost a good deal more than that. But rest assured he is not crazy; this fisherman knows that when his bobber takes a nosedive, there is a good chance that a striped bass will be his reward. And these holdover bass are not all schoolies; fish that are well over legal size are landed here every winter.

Holdover stripers can be found in a handful of locations around Boston that combine certain crucial elements, and the Charles River above the locks is quite possibly the best. First and foremost, there must be some sort of artificial heating source to keep the water somewhat temperate, and if that is augmented by shallows that warm up on sunny days, so much the better. This is why this part of the river fishes well during the ebb – the outgoing flow brings warmer water, causing a spike in the striper activity level. There must also be a healthy ecosystem that provides forage, and this is the case after many

You may have to bundle up to hook up, but it is possible to land quality stripers in the off-season such as this one being released by Rick Holbrook.

years of restoration efforts along the Charles.

Of course, from a fisherman's standpoint none of this means much if there is no access. The Charles River in Cambridge aces all the requirements. Parking is a cinch and you'll usually have no problem finding a spot directly across the street from where you will fish. The hot-water discharge from the nearby power plant is easy to spot by the roiled water that flows out from beneath the retaining wall. This location is approximately 75 yards north of a pier that lies in the shadows of Longfellow Bridge. This water near the pier is often a good bet for a bass or two and is always worth a look. The most obvious place to wet a line is in the middle of the hot-water flow, but experienced casters will work their way along the sidewalk from the outflow toward the yacht club. A big lively shiner suspended four or five feet below a float is probably the best bet here. Some anglers go the artificial route and find success with soft plastics such as white/silver Zoom Flukes, four- to five-inch Storm Wildeye Shads and swimmers such as bronze-colored Yo-Zuri Mag Minnows because the forage here consists mostly of herring and smelt.

There is also a good possibility of an interesting bycatch from this location, ranging from white catfish to northern pike to largemouth bass. Being upstream of the Charles River locks, you will need a freshwater fishing license.

Landing a keeper here can be a little tricky. Some anglers do the "striper two-step" as they shuffle along the rail toward a pier about 100 yards away near the yacht club all the while trying to maintain pressure on the fish. If you have a buddy with you, bring along an umbrella-style landing net, which you can pick up at many nearby tackle shops. This type of net is modeled after an upside-down version of its namesake. A rope or cord is attached to the net and the exhausted striper is led onto the net and then lifted over the railing.

Next up on the list of wintertime linesider lairs is the Amelia Earhardt Dam in Everett. This location at the mouth of the Mystic River has been an off-season favorite for decades. The Mystic River itself is chock-full of bait in the form of alewives, sperling

Toss a bobber and shiner into the warm current of the Charles River off the Cambridge Parkway for holdover linesiders. Another option is to run-and-gun the bank with swimmers and soft plastics.

and smelt and the water is kept comfy by the downstream power plant. Although your chances of hooking a snowbird striper anywhere along the banks of the river are good, longtime sharpies know that the bulk of the fish are out in the channel. Fishermen who remember when there was a wooden railroad bridge that spanned the river can recall the amazing dead-of-winter fishing that used to take place off the bridge. The reason that the fishing was so good was that the bridge allowed you to present your offering directly into the channel. It was a sad day when they tore this bridge down, but the fish are still there – you just have to get to them. This can be accomplished by launching a kayak, pram or pontoon boat from the nearby park. The channel is located between the two pilings and a good plan is to tie up to a piling and work your bait in the outflow.

Stripers and sometimes bluefish winter over in the hot water discharge of the former Boston Edison Plant off Summer Street in South Boston. There is a convenient casting platform located on the plant side of the bridge.

The all-time best method of tempting bass here is to float a sea worm under a bobber in the current. Yeah. . . I understand that finding worms this time of the year is harder than finding a no-spin politician, but you'll find the effort worth it. If the fresh bait option is not feasible, try alewife-colored Slug-Gos. Although any striper this time of the year is a bonus, you may encounter some surprisingly large fish at the dam. I recall a particularly fruitful outing a few years ago with a buddy of mine, Jack Pagel. Although it was the middle of winter and we were fishing at night, the twin 15-pounders we caught made it feel as good as a midsummer day. During a thaw, bass will sometimes move through the locks and position themselves on the freshwater side of the dam. This section is worth a cast or two if the saltwater side doesn't deliver the goods; just make sure that you have your license with you.

While researching this article in December, I decided to check out an old favorite of mine: the area near the former Edison Plant off Summer Street in South Boston. A brand new bridge awaits the angler and makes an excellent casting platform. Before the roadwork prohibited access, we used to find willing wintertime bass hitting (of all things) surface swimmers and poppers. Part of the new construction includes a little nook on the eastern side of the bridge that looks juicy. I wondered with the new structure in place whether or not the fishing was still good. My answer came from an angler who had two surf rods leaning against the railing. I figured that unless this guy was a proponent of overkill, he most likely wasn't smelt fishing. When I asked him what was doing, he replied that a short while ago he almost had his rod pulled into the water but ultimately lost the fish. Sounds promising to me! Parking is available across the street at the FedEx building.

Directly in the middle of the hot-water flow was a legendary striper and even bluefish sanctuary in the middle of winter back in the days when you were allowed entry to this spot through the MBTA bus terminal on A Street. A fence has since been erected restricting access, but by the looks of the gaping holes in it a few stealthy anglers are still taking advantage of this fishery; if you can reach this section, the fishing is often spectacular.

Every year reports trickle in of linesiders caught along the Lynn Marsh during the winter months. But what many don't realize is that the fish aren't generally spread out here, they stack up by the hot-water outfall of the GE Plant in the tributary that is the Saugus River. Occasionally these fish wander and this is when the landings throughout the marsh occur. If you want to bump up your odds considerably, focus on the discharge itself.

Parking is available at the boat ramp across the street and next to the marina. If you've been here during the summer you probably had trouble finding a parking spot but the place is just about empty in the winter.

A walk along the banks of the north side of the river will lead you to the discharge. The good old sea worm under a bobber works well here and with a good population of eels in the river, casting live ones or imitations will yield results. Plan to fish here at dead-low tide, through the first few hours of the flood.

If the extent of your fishing exposure lately has been flicking between channels that feature guys kissing fish and others trying to out-yell each other, you could probably use a break. As befitting the season when all outdoor activities require some effort and planning, these fish don't come easy, but if you put in the time you will be rewarded.

Draggin' A Tube Through Boston's Channels -Fall's Last Striper Encounter

By Ron Powers

Like finned lemmings, they tumble forward from the rivers, estuaries and embayments of Boston Harbor, stripers of all sizes funneling along ancient travel routes with one thing on their mind – migration. Of course, this isn't completely true since they must satiate themselves in order to have enough fuel in the tank for the long, arduous journey. Out here along the channels and rips is where the prepared angler and the striper cross paths in what may be their final encounter for the season.

It is October and the carefree rhythm of summer is long gone and soon, so will the bass. The clock is ticking and if you would like to stack the odds in your favor, the game will take place along the rips that border the Boston Harbor channels and the method will be a tube and worm. Resident and transient linesiders use President Roads and Boston's North and South channels as underwater highways. Each of these thoroughfares pass a number of rips and each of them at one time or another will entertain a striper bite. But how does one pick which ones to target when in a three-mile radius there are probably 50 such rips? The answer is to fish the ones that have the most pronounced combination of current and structure. Year in and year out the rips of Deer Island, Nixes Mate and Bob's Bass Triangle are where experienced anglers catch those last cows of autumn.

Captain Lou Abate of Good Times Charters hauls in keeper stripers from these storied spots from April well into October. During the first few months of the season, Lou is partial to live-lining herring, but once that forage disappears the tube and worm comes into its own.

"When the herring are in thick and the water temperatures are still in the fifties it often takes a live one to get a strike," said Lou. "But once the fish become more active, the tube will out-fish live bait every time."

To work the tube properly you must have your lure in the strike zone, and this can often be a matter of inches. In Boston Harbor, using leadcore line of 45- to 60-pound test is the easiest way to ensure that the fish are eyeballing that tube, and having the right number of colors out is of paramount importance. Generally the stripers will be hunkering in 10 to 15 feet of water and will be situated a foot or two above the bottom. You want to present the tube a foot or two above the fish; at a trolling speed of 2 or 3 knots every color of line will take the tube down about three feet. This means that your best bet is to troll with 2 to 3 colors of leadcore out. Keep in mind that the channels of the harbor are often busy with boat traffic, so don't troll with an excessive amount of line out to avoid cutoffs from other vessels. If you find that the tube is ticking bottom, reel in half a color. A high-quality ball-bearing swivel is the essential connection between the leadcore and leader to prevent the old "twist and shout." A 10-foot length of 50-pound-test Seaguar fluorocarbon is my choice for a leader.

It is imperative that you maintain proper line control, which means that once you are plying the correct depth, keep your rod as rigidly in place as possible. Six inches higher or lower and you might as well be trolling in your kid's swimming pool. Try to hold the tip of the rod off to the side of the stern at approximately a 45-degree angle and keep the tip level with the top of the gunwale. This will allow you to control the rod and the fish when a strike occurs. And when that strike does happen, steel your nerves and refrain from setting the hook – oftentimes all that will do is pull the tube away from the fish. Stripers are notorious for short striking a tube and quickly hitting it again seconds later. The old adage of letting the fish hook itself certainly applies here. Probably the most important aspect of hiking the odds in your favor is to troll slowly; in fact, your engine can't motor too slowly for those lazy bass – at best you should be just making headway.

Don't be miserly with the sea worm portion of the tube-and-worm dance team. When the linesider closes the distance and decides whether or not to make that final assault, it is the worm that seals the deal. If you can get them, use a sea worm that looks like it's part boa; if not, thread two on the hook. You have already invested heavily in equipment and time, now is not the time to skimp. Pay attention to the weight of the rod in your hands. If you feel a gradual increase in weight, you may have mung hitchhiking a ride with your tube. Even a small amount of weed will ruin the action and the last time I checked striped bass had not turned into vegetarians. A sensitive rod helps out in the tactile department and a medium-action $6^{1/2}$- to 7-footer rated to handle 30- to 50-pound-test line is ideal. Of course, conventional reels, preferably with a level wind, are the only way to go here.

The ideal time to fish the rips is a couple of hours before and after high tide, when the current is roaring. Slack tide is the best time to break out that ham on rye you packed for

A tube and worm trolled slowly along the rips of Boston's channels is your best chance to hook up to the last big striper of the year.

lunch; you will find that the bass will not cooperate. When trolling through these rips most of your hits will occur as your boat moves in the direction of the current. Just like trout finning behind a boulder in the middle of a stream, the bass will position themselves just behind the structure and pounce on prey that is carried along by the flow. This is a good, natural presentation and when your tube passes over the bass, the fish will usually seize it.

Nixes Mate is located just east of Long Island and is marked by an octagonal pyramid of wood that is 20 feet high and painted black and white. The purpose of the pyramid is to warn vessels of one of the most dangerous shoals in the harbor. Long ago, pirates were hung from a predecessor of this landmark, but now you're more likely to see stripers hung from outstretched arms during photo ops. This one-acre shoal is extremely shallow during low tides and many a distracted boater has lost his lower unit there, but that same treacherous terrain forms a nice rip that is chock-full of striper-holding structure. It is best to approach Nixes Mate from President Roads channel at the tip of Long Island and work the northern perimeter of the shoal. Make looping passes until you connect with fish and pay attention to your route of travel and repeat it. At times the fish will set up right at the edge where single-digit depths quickly drop off to 20 feet. Other times, especially during low-light conditions, they will be shallower and in the thick of the rubble. If this is the case, try anchoring up and pitching pogie or mackerel chunks toward the pyramid.

Deer Island Light is located just south of the town of Winthrop and is about 500 yards from the Deer Island Reservation. Identified by the 33-foot brown fiberglass tower, a healthy rip sets up here where the 30-foot depths meet the boulder-strewn shallows around the lighthouse. This is the confluence of the President Roads channel and the harbor's North and South channels and you'll find a significant amount of moving water. Trollers do best by tubing as close to the lighthouse as possible. The location is pockmarked with deep holes and this is why some fishermen will troll an exaggerated "S" pattern, which allows the lure to drop down a few precious feet closer to where the stripers will be lying in wait. In addition to tubing, a tried-and-true technique that has resulted in many wall-hanger bass is to anchor just upstream of the rip and drift a surface swimmer into the moving water. This method is especially deadly at night and on the ebb; fishermen

The shoal of Nixes Mate is a productive spot to catch bass, look for the rip that forms just before and after high tide.

Being in close proximity to the harbor's major channels, Deer Island rip is a perfect ambush point for cow stripers, especially on the outgoing tide.

will let a Danny plug just sit in the current, weaving on the surface.

Bob's Bass Triangle is a 300-acre-plus menagerie of lumps, bumps and kelp that is perfectly situated between Boston's North and South channels. Roughly outlined by cans 5 to the north, 9 to the south and the split-colored red/green can that marks the confluence of the channels, the rips that form at the edges of the triangle make ideal ambush points for traveling bass. The only thing that makes working a tube and worm here dicey is the sprinkling of lobster buoys in the triangle. It can be enough to give you a coronary when you see the dorsal fin of a huge striper powering toward a lobster pot buoy. There are two things you can do to tilt the odds in your favor. First, never troll here with less than 50-pound line and do not under any circumstances pump your rod when under the pressure of a fish. If you finally hook that trophy and it seems to be drawn like a magnet to that lobster buoy, all you can do is clamp down on the drag and crank like heck. While pumping the rod looks good through the viewfinder of a camcorder, the slack that is created in between pumps will often give a cow just enough leeway to reach that buoy. As only a last-ditch effort, Captain Lou Abate will grab the line by hand and attempt to wrestle the fish "mano-a-pesce" until it's free of the impediment.

In case you haven't noticed, the clock is ticking louder than a bass drum. You can lament about how the season is over and dream about next year, but that would be a mistake. Drag a tube through the channels of Boston Harbor this month and your only worry will be whether you can get out there again tomorrow.

Great Fishing Along "The Other Cape" – The North Shore's Cape Ann

By Ron Powers

If you eavesdrop on a conversation involving long-time surfcaster Steve Papows, you're bound to hear "the Cape" mentioned frequently. But here's where things get a little tricky: you may start to think that he's talking in code as he mentions locations. After all, who has ever heard of Pebble Beach, the Gap and Halibut Point on Cape Cod? No one – because you're off course by about 100 miles. Steve and his fellow surf-fishing stalwarts wet their lines, not off Cape Cod, but rather "the other Cape" – Cape Ann, Massachusetts. Compared to Cape Cod, here the fishermen are few but, like Cape Cod, the gamefish are many!

What images come to mind when you think of Gloucester? Perhaps a gruff old commercial fisherman in a yellow slicker taking spray on the high seas or flannel-clad mates unloading boxes of freshly caught groundfish from a trawler. Probably not surf fishing! But there is a small cadre of local enthusiasts, such as Steve Papows, who see no need to fight the traffic to the National Seashore or wait for a ferry to the islands when they can fill their days and nights here, shore-casting for blues, stripers, flounder and even tautog.

We'll begin our tour with the marsh behind Nichols candy store, take it to the beach and end our affair in the rocks.

First up: the Annisquam salt marsh, which lies right behind the Nichols candy shop on Route 128. This is probably the earliest place where the stripers come a-knocking on Cape Ann. Expect to encounter bass here by the second week in April and no later than the third.

Are you shocked that stripers could be found this early in the season, this far north? Chances are, most of the fish are holdovers from nearby estuaries and rivers, but every day they are joined by migrants from the south. This estuary delivers mostly schoolies throughout the year, but an occasional keeper does muscle in. The marsh fishes best three hours on either side of high tide; once the rock pile in the

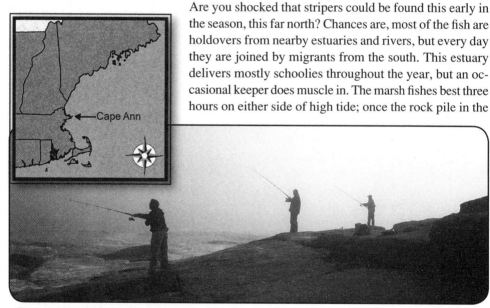

The rocky outcroppings and ledges of Cape Ann allow the shore angler to cast his stuff in the middle of the white water, where the cows forage.

channel begins to show, your time may be better spent hitting the candy store for a snack.

This is a nice place for light-line aficionados, as well as fly-fishermen. Since it is sheltered and the wind is seldom a factor, an angler can cast light wares without getting them blown back in his face. Fly folks do best with small Clousers in colors to imitate the abundant grass shrimp, and spin guys get them with small white swimmers. The only time that you don't want to go light is if you are soaking sea worms in the spring. The reason is that the Annisquam marsh is a major spawning ground for resident tautog. You may be surprised to learn that a "southern" species like tautog frequents Cape Ann; they do, and they are under-fished and big. Examples topping 12 pounds have been caught here, and usually by accident. I have hardly ever seen anyone actually targeting them, which is strange. You could be one of the first.

Next let's take exit 13 off Route 128, the Concord Street exit, and follow Concord Street to Atlantic Street. A right off Atlantic Street leads to Wingaersheek Beach. There is a parking lot right at the beach where you will have to pay to park from Memorial Day until Labor Day, but after 4 p.m. and in the off-season it's a freebie. And if you get there early (which if you're serious about catching fish, you should), there are free spots on the right side just before the gated entrance. What makes Wingaersheek special is the fact that it sits right at the mouth of the Annisquam River. The flow of the river has created a sandbar and a series of troughs and sluices, which attract bait, bass and blues.

If you're out for a day of family fun that includes fishing, but you also want to have other diversions close at hand, Stage Fort Park fits the bill very nicely. The park is located on the corner of Western Harbor, part of Gloucester Harbor, and is right off Route 127, quite close to the downtown area. In the summer a fee is charged until 4 p.m. to park in the large lot; after Labor Day the parking is free. You'll find some great fishing off the sea wall next to the Sammy Parisi baseball field. The water adjacent to the rocks from Stage Head down to the cove and out toward Field Rocks is also often productive. If family members grow tired of fishing, the park offers beaches and playgrounds; there are often evening concerts and food is available nearby.

Just north of the park on Route 127 is a bridge that crosses the Blyman Canal. This canal connects the Annisquam River and Cape Ann Marina with Western Harbor. You wouldn't want to fish this outflow at, say, noontime on July Fourth. But in the wee hours of the morning, you might want to float a sea worm under a bobber, drift an eel or let a big wooden plug weave in the current for some of the large bass that have been known to frequent this place. So respected is the reputation of this location as a big fish producer that you'll see anglers casting near the abutments, even as dozens of boats cruise back and forth through

If you like to wade, you'll find a 2$^{1/2}$ mile stretch from Niles Beach all the way out to Eastern Point.

the narrow entrance.

Continue north on Route 127, turn right on East Main Street and continue until it becomes Eastern Point Boulevard; before long you'll be driving along a crescent-shaped strand known as Niles Beach. This is a productive spot at first light, and is especially nice when there is a northeastern or eastern blow since you will be in the lee. Bass and bluefish often pin bait against this shore, especially in the fall when baby pogies take up temporary residence in the harbor. Chunking is a popular activity here, but if an angler equips himself with only a plug bag, he can work the 2 1/2-mile stretch all the way out to the Dog Bar Breakwater at Eastern Point.

If you prefer a more direct and convenient route to Eastern Point, you can continue on Eastern Point Boulevard until you get to the parking area at the foot of the breakwater. The segment of the boulevard leading out to the breakwater often has a guard on duty, since technically this is a private road, but there is a public right of way to allow access to the Audubon-owned parking area at Eastern Point. If you are questioned, simply say that you are going fishing and there will be no problem. In this era of tightened security, it's nice to know that, at least in this place, fishermen are still welcomed.

The 1/2-mile-long Dog Bar Breakwater is an easy walk, since it is relatively flat and has some convenient steps up to the top level. At high tide most of the nearby water is about 30 feet deep, but a short distance south of this structure water as deep as 80 feet holds cruising predators, even during the most oppressive days of summer. On overcast days, look for bass to head into Dog Bar Channel and seek out the crustaceans along the breakwater for a quick meal. In addition to stripers and blues, you'll find tautog here, as well as flounder. Flatfish numbers are spiking, and one of the reasons is due to the improvement in water quality in Gloucester Harbor. It wasn't that long ago that the harbor was a coffee-colored mess, but thanks to the two treatment plants in town, you can now see clear down to the bottom.

If the fish aren't cooperative at the breakwater, hoof it toward the Eastern Point Lighthouse at the Coast Guard Station. There is a good rock pile here (known by resident casters as The Spades) and it is always worth a cast or two.

Drive back down Eastern Point Boulevard, turn right onto Farrington Avenue and then left onto Atlantic Road, and you'll be on the mile-and-a-half stretch known as Bass Rocks (sounds promising. . . eh?). Don't let the trophy homes and nearby golf course fool you – this is not just a pretty view for the upper crust. There is fish-holding structure galore here: ledges, crags, coves and kelp beds are all part of the scene. If you cut your teeth at Newport or Narragansett Bay, you'll be right at home here. There are numerous parking areas on the side of Atlantic Road, where you are allowed to park anytime after September 15

Bait pours out from the salt ponds that form on Niles Beach all the way out to the east point, and bluefish are often waiting.

and during the weekdays all summer.

Don't forget your Korkers or similar anti-slip footwear. Target the pockets in the structure with plenty of white water; this is where you'll find bass on the hunt. Some of the rocky promontories make nice casting platforms; with polarized shades, you can peer right into the water and see foraging linesiders. Be sure to plot out a landing route. Don't wait until you are battling a 30-pounder to figure out how to reach the fish, and never, ever, attempt to land a fish when they are green. A big strong bass in close to the rocks means an inevitable cut-off. If you have the option, let the fish run and tire. If you can see your line, you'll know how close you are to the rocks and a potential break-off. This way you can make an informed decision on whether to ease up or continue the fight. Many experienced rock hoppers here opt for high visibility line such as Stren Hi-Vis Gold or Yo-Zuri Hi-Vis Yellow. For those who love braid, Stren Super Braid also comes in a sun-bright yellow.

At the southern end of Bass Rocks lies one of the more productive locales, known as Lynch Cove. You'll find parking along Grape Vine Road, which lies perpendicular to the shoreline.

Want to try one more great fishing spot in Gloucester? Try Good Harbor Beach, which can be reached by following Thatcher Street off Route 127A. With an estuary and salt marsh providing forage in the form of a fall run of smelt, along with sand eels, silversides and peanut bunker, this location is a favorite with local surfcasters. On rough days bass often forage upstream of the footbridge in depressions in the mud; the locals call these places "warm pots." During the ebb, drifting an eel or soaking a chunk on the ocean side of the footbridge is a good bet. Farther out, where the estuary meets the ocean, is a rock pile that's always worthy of a look-see. If you skirt the beach to the left you'll come to a rocky point known as Brier Neck, where you'll find a steep drop-off and churned-up water. Just before the neck you'll notice Salt Island. A bar connects the shore and the island for about three hours on either side of low tide. This island is a premier spot; in fact, one of the regulars caught a 53-pound cow here a few years ago on a live eel. Just be sure to keep one eye on the rising tide or you'll be fishing here for much longer than you intended.

If you are like me and prefer your bass battle-grounds to have plenty of varied terrain, Cape Ann just might be what you're looking for. Located a scant 38 miles north of Boston, you might be surprised at how few anglers share prime fishing spots. If you desire surf casting from a sandy beach, you'll find a slice of it here. If a marsh is your cup of tea – ditto. But what differentiates the Gloucester fishing experience from most others is its craggy shoreline. There is just something about the raw beauty of rollers crashing among ledges that make the "other Cape" someplace special. ◄═══

Some of the stripers among Bass Rocks are a handful (or maybe two handfuls!) as Matt Papows demonstrates.

A Tour Of Plum Island Sound

By Larry Backman

Plum Island lies at the northern edge of Massachusetts' coastline. It is a 7-mile-long barrier beach composed entirely of sand. Bordered on the north by the Merrimack River, on the south by Plum Island Sound and on its west by the narrow Plum Island River, the island is dominated by the open Atlantic Ocean to its east.

The island's character is formed by its long and mostly unblemished outer beach, most of which, at least the southern six miles, is an undeveloped wildlife preserve. While the northernmost mile has houses on the beach, they are set far enough back from the water that the surfcaster can feel alone, at one with the sea and the sand. The steepness of the beach, combined with the roar of the surf, helps to contribute to that feeling of isolation.

Plum Island is a surfcaster's mecca, one of the few remaining places where a fisherman can take a vehicle onto the beach (with proper permits) and prowl the margins of sand and sea, looking for signs of fish. Plum Island is a legendary place for big fish. With the Atlantic pounding its steep beaches, its proximity to the outflow of the Merrimack, and its position on the migration route of striped bass and bluefish, this island holds fish for six months of the year and, more important, attracts big fish during both the spring and fall migrations.

The island has varied topography, ranging from a steep beach at the northernmost end to a more shallow and gradual drop-off toward the southern end. At first glance, it is simply a long and straight sand beach with little structure breaking its length. However, if you walk the beach often enough, a great deal of subtle variation will start to stand out; you'll spot sandbars, steep drop-offs, crescent coves and sandy points. Walk the beach and fish those spots and you'll start to understand the underwater topography and how it relates to where the fish are.

I often think of Winslow Homer at Plum Island; the colors of the beach, the sea, and the sky, subtle shades of blue and gray, are colors that Homer used in his seascapes. There is a certain light to Plum Island – different from the ethereal brightness of Cape Cod, a harder and darker light reflecting Plum Island's connection to more northern waters.

When one talks of fishing this area, it's not enough to simply say, "I am fishing Plum Island." You must be far more specific. There are so many varied areas on this beachfront, its river mouths and its back bays, and each one is different. Let's take a look at the northern end first.

The Mouth of the Merrimack

Plum Island is a product of the Merrimack River, a mile-wide river that drains much of a two-state region. The barrier beach is constantly being replenished by silt brought down from the New Hampshire mountains. All of this flow rushes past the northern tip of the island, constantly carving and reshaping it from season to season, even from storm to storm.

There is a mile-long stretch at the tip of Plum Island that has it all: steep drop-offs, rocky edges, mussel flats, sandbars and even a long jetty at its end. This is the area for a novice to start an initial exploration of the island's fishing terrain; while it's not outer beach, it holds many fish in a reasonably small area that can be covered in two to three hours of fishing. Start your trip at the boat docks by the old Coast Guard station. The entire flow of the Merrimack rushes by this area on every outgoing tide and has carved a steep drop-off only a few feet from shore. There's no need to wade here, as striped bass can be found five feet off the shoreline. There's little surf or waves; however, you must be careful not to get too far into the water as the flow and the drop-off can sweep you away in no time. Always treat the Merrimack with extreme respect. It is a large and unpredictable river. I have seen trees, docks and even a deer sweep by my feet in its current.

Working toward the river mouth from the boat docks, you will soon come to a steep, sandy point with water screaming by a dozen feet below you. At two hours on either side of low tide, a long and narrow sandbar is exposed, extending toward the other side of the river, reaching perhaps a half-mile into the flow. The structure on this bar and just off of it is fantastic – gullies and potholes, two to three feet deep, broken up by parallel ridges of sand. When the water is boiling white in this area, you can be sure that stripers are hanging in those gullies and potholes, waiting to ambush hapless baitfish being swept over each sandy ridge.

This area offers prime fishing using a variety of techniques. Jigs, bait or even flies on a sinking line will connect with fish during low incoming or outgoing tidal flows. However, as with most superb fishing spots, there is a catch: This bar is extremely dangerous, in terms of both water flow and tidal rise. On an incoming tide, with a 10-foot variation, it can rise 6 inches in 15 minutes once it starts coming in. Wait too long and that casual splash through a puddle can turn into a desperate swim for your life against a strong current. Do not be either the first or the last onto the bar; follow the more experienced people here and leave when they leave.

Continuing on, let's retrace our steps back off the sandbar and move toward the mouth of the river. Walking along the riverfront we pass a series of sandy crescents, the first of which is a deep bowl backed by the sandbar. Each of these sand-arced bowls holds fish on the upper half of the tide. Eventually, we pass two small sandy points, both good spots to fish from, especially using the protrusion of the point to drag a fly or jig along the beach on either side of the points.

Closer to the river mouth, we pass or climb over a rock pile, an old jetty that alternately exposes and buries itself in the shifting sands. If the rocks are exposed – again a situation that can change from one storm to the next – this is a wonderful place to explore and prospect, especially on the higher side of the tide.

We have now hiked three quarters of a mile along the riverfront. At our feet is a steeply dropping sandbank, the beach falling away into the water at a steep angle with curls of current swirling a few dozen yards offshore. Almost directly in front of us lies the south jetty of the Merrimack River, extending in a great dogleg, perhaps half a mile out to sea. This area, the base of the jetty, is a prime spot for stripers in close and also for roving packs of bluefish 50 yards out in the channel. A short cast and deep retrieve will pick up stripers right at your feet; a cast the length of a football field, with a 10-foot surf rod, will put your lure in the reach of bluefish that enter the river on each tide from late June till early September.

This is the spot the experienced Plum Island surfcasters frequent at dawn, surf rods at the ready, waiting for steady signs of breaking fish. I learned to husband strength and energy by watching them half a dozen yards back – never a wasted cast, never an extra expenditure of energy. You'll see a lot of 50-year fishing veterans at this spot; these are the people to listen to and learn from.

The jetty is a place where, now that I'm in my 40s, I no longer venture to. Ten years back I used to scamper from rock to rock with never a fear and with little caution. It is a dangerous jetty. High above the water to compensate for the 10-foot tidal range, its crevices have 6- to 8-foot drops into black and slippery pits. At high tide, the base of the jetty where it connects to the beach is easily washed over by moderate seas from either the river on its north or the beach on its south. There is another low spot, about halfway out on the jetty, where the tide can cut you off in even more moderate sea conditions. With a 12-foot drop to the water at low tide, landing a fish here is extremely tough; this is not a jetty for inexperienced or careless fishermen. If you venture out, again, follow in the path of an experienced person, and be aware of the tide and sea conditions.

However, because of its length and because the entire Merrimack outflow runs down its side, this jetty can be an extremely productive spot. Try it at low tide on a calm day and you can actually reach its end and cast at the sandbar off that end, a place where tides and current bring bait, stripers and bluefish.

The Beachfront

Plum Island runs almost due north to south; the beachfront faces east and is exposed to the full force of the Atlantic. There are no towering sand hills here. Instead, the small dunes roll back from the beach in a series of gentle peaks and valleys, perhaps 20 feet high at most. Much of the beachfront is steep; the 10- to 12-foot tidal range of northern Massachusetts is reflected in the intertidal zone between low and high water lines, where the sand meets the water at a steep angle before dropping off quickly beneath the waves.

This is an outer beach in all of its majestic splendor, wind and wave dwarfing human presence. With its large tidal variation, and with the deeper water of the Gulf of Maine offshore and the frightening New England northeasters pounding directly on the beach, in the worst of conditions you can encounter 15-foot-high surf and waves. While this is not the norm, it is typical on a moderately windy day to encounter 5- to 6-foot waves crashing along the beachfront. Combine this surf with the steep beach drop-off and a heavy north to south current, dominated by the outflow of the Merrimack River, and Plum Island can be a dangerous place to fish. It's a place where a lone and careless wader can find him or herself in serious trouble in an instant. On the other hand, during the hazy, lazy days of midsummer, with a gentle west wind wafting over the dunes, the sea can be flat calm. A look eastward, over the glassy surface, can barely discern the boundary between sea and sky.

I think of the island's beach as being divided into three distinct zones. The first zone is the northern mile of beach, perhaps 100 yards wide from the water's edge to a series of cottages and houses lining the edge of the sand dunes. In summer this section is crowded with thousands of beachgoers. From this area you can look north past the great rock jetties at the mouth of the Merrimack and see the New Hampshire coast, backed by the looming mound of Mt. Agaementicus in Southern Maine.

The second zone is a five-mile stretch of nature preserve with few people and, with one exception, no sign of manmade structure. In this zone you can be alone with the sound of the sea and pretend you are alone on the planet. Here your view is eastward toward nothingness; the next stop is Portugal.

The third zone, the southern mile of the island, is where the beach extends south into Plum Island Sound, and is a flatter and gentler stretch of beach than the rest of the island. Your view here looks in at the towns of Ipswich and Rowley, at their brick houses and white steeples, and extends south to the point of Cape Ann, seven miles away. The very southern tip of Plum Island is called Sandy Point and is protected as part of the Massachusetts state park system.

Access to the beachfront is easy in the first zone. If you can find a parking space, you simply stroll down one of the many lanes and pick your way between cottages and on to the beach. The other two zones are inside the Parker River National Wildlife Refuge and require an entrance fee. This small fee gives you access to six miles of road, first tar and then dirt, that has seven small parking lots along its length. Each of these lots has a boardwalk leading over the dunes to the beachfront. Over-sand permits are available for part of the season and carry a steeper fee and set of requirements. Since Parker River is a wildlife refuge, beach access, both by foot and by vehicle, is restricted during the piping plover nesting season, roughly June through August.

If your destination is the southern tip at Sandy Point, you can tell the guard at the gate and not pay an entrance fee, as it is state administered. However, if you're headed to the point, you cannot park in any of the seven refuge lots along the way but must park in two designated areas at the very end of the island.

Make sure you bring insect repellent; the salt marshes behind the beach hold both mosquitoes and the even more ferocious greenheads. July and early August are the high season for the greenhead; long sleeves, pants and a hat are musts if you intend to venture onto the beach at this time.

With the scenery set, let's take a closer look at some parts of the island. First we'll turn north at the beachfront road and park in the church lot a mile from the northern tip of the island and walk over the dunes to the beach. Here the beach is so steep that from the dune grass at the edge you cannot see the water's edge below. As you walk down to the beach, you cross over two distinct terraces in the sand – one the high water mark from storm surge, the other the normal high tide line.

Standing below the high tide line, the beachfront appears as a series of scalloped crescent coves, each 20 or 30 yards wide. Each cove is in an arc of sand punctuated on either edge by a sandy point where the high tide line comes close to the water's edge in a sandy ridge. If you look at the water, you'll notice a deeper section in the center of the crescent, with shallower sections of water extending out from the sand ridges at the cove's edge. With the sandy terrain behind you as a guide, it is possible to mentally visualize the underwater topography and think in terms of structure that will hold gamefish. Each of the sand points extends under water as bars perpendicular to the shore. The tops and edges of these bars can be seen at low tide and in crashing surf; they are prime places to prospect for both striped bass and bluefish.

During the spring and fall migrations, schools of striped bass roam this area of the Plum Island beachfront. Sometimes, when the light is right, you can see them surfing the curl of breaking waves, hanging just under the crest and silhouetted in the clear water. If you cast out too far, you'll miss them. If you cast out past the first wave, parallel to the shore, and work a fly or lure along the back side of the curl, you can often catch fish until you are too tired to cast anymore.

The jetty by the Merrimack forms a steep corner that delineates the northern end of the beach. This corner can be an incredibly fishy place in crashing surf when the wind is out of the east. Baitfish are trapped by the junction of beach and jetty, and stripers will roam just outside the surf line, feasting on the helpless bait. Many of my most memorable high surf moments have been casting heavy metal lures as hard as I can into a blistering wind, waves breaking at my feet and spray flying over my head as I haul back hard against the power of a surfing striped bass in its element.

While the northern end of the island has easy beach access as well as excellent fishing, to really see and know Plum Island you must enter the refuge, drive its road, walk its trails and explore its beach. Turn south once you pass over the bridge onto the island, and within a few hundred yards you will come to the gate marking the entrance to the refuge. After you pass through it you'll continue perhaps half a mile before coming to the largest of the seven lots, parking lot #1. This lot has the only rest room in the refuge. If you walk over the boardwalk and onto the beach, you'll notice the same steep pitch that was at the northern end. However, should you explore this section of beach at low tide, you'll find a huge flat and exposed area that has pools of standing seawater running off through channels to the sea. Hit this spot on a falling tide with a calm ocean, and you can work those channels and find fish concentrated at the seaward end, preying on trapped bait.

Back on the road again and proceeding southward, you can look west over the vast and sweeping marshlands of Newburyport and see nothing but miles of grass, water and sky. The area behind Plum Island is as pristine and untouched a salt marsh as exists on the striper coast of New England. Parking lots 2, 3 and 4 are favorites of mine, more for isolation than for fishing. The crowds gather at either the first or last of the lots – the middle ones are often just you, the birds, the dunes and the sea.

I find these areas, centrally located in the middle of the long beachfront, to be hit or miss in terms of fishing. On one occasion I ambled over the dunes of lot 3 to find a bluefish blitz going on right in front of me, 8-pound bluefish slashing at anything thrown their way. But more often than not, I go fishless at these spots, rewarded instead by the solitude and quiet, as well as the mental well-being that accompanies a long and lovely beachfront walk.

On the other hand, lots 5 and 6, perhaps a mile apart toward the southern end of the island, are spots I associate with big-rod surf fishing. The beach is a bit less steep here, and at low tide the flats extend out well past easy casting distance. These are areas where a long cast is needed to prospect acres of featureless ocean. I have fond memories of the glory years of bluefishing in the early 90s, days when I would launch cast after cast with a big 3-ounce Polaris Popper, working 100 yards of water at a time, waiting for that electrically charged moment when a big bluefish would erupt out of the depths, crashing onto my lure in a spray of white foam.

Lot 7 is at the end of the beach, a few dozen yards before the island ends and the beach turns west to face Plum Island Sound. Right at the end of the beachfront a set of low rocks extends out, the only structure in seven miles of sandy beach. They are called Emerson Rocks, and they hold striped bass at all tides. Exposed during the lower end of the tide, covered during the high tide but swept with breaking water, these rocks can be worked with all sorts of techniques – fly, plug or bait. On calm days the rocks can be explored by fly-casting, standing off 50 feet and working a fly along their edges; on rough days a surface plug worked in and out of the breaking water will draw explosive strikes. At high tide, boats can get in close to the rocks and have good luck casting in against their structure. There is a deeper channel that heads in toward the rock, a natural feeding path for stripers on the rising tide.

Rounding the end of the beach, past the rocks, we come to the very end of Plum Island, Sandy Point. This is where the waters of three rivers – the Ipswich, Parker and Rowley – join to make Plum Island Sound and flow past the tip of the island. As with the Merrimack riverfront on the northern end of the island, Sandy Point is a spectacular mix of deep drop-offs and shallow sandbars. Combine this structure with the rushing tidal flow, and you have the perfect habitat for striped bass. Sandbars extend outward perhaps a half-mile into the center of Plum Island Sound and are accessible by foot during the lower portion of tide. Tidal flow has cut two- or three-foot-deep channels between some of the bars, easily crossed at low tide. As with the Merrimack sandbars, waders should be aware that the water can rise 6 inches in 15 minutes and should be careful not to get caught by the rising tide. Those channels, which are ankle-deep at low tide, will be waist-high with rushing water once the tide starts coming in.

How best to fish Plum Island's beachfront? Clearly, mobility is preferred, either by boat or cruising the beachfront or by over-sand vehicle along the beach. Then you can look for action, scan the water and sky for birds, and look for the splash of fish pushing bait up on the surface. Mobility allows you to range the beachfront – for somewhere on the 7-mile stretch fish will be feeding!

However, most visitors to Plum Island are restricted and must pick a single spot or, at most, two spots and work that section of beach. My recommendation is to divide Plum Island into the three zones previously mentioned. Select one of those sections for an expedition and work that area hard. The northern and southern ends can be covered on foot – a mile or so of walking the beach is good for you! The middle section can be covered by car, leap-frogging from one refuge parking lot to another, prospecting each area for signs of fish.

On another trip, plan to spend an evening on the beach and enter the refuge an hour or so before sunset. Assume a 30-minute drive to Sandy Point. You'll park and be on the beach just as the sun is setting over your shoulder. Now is the time to work the rocks and drop-offs along the point as the light fades and the stars come out. Big fish come in close to the rocks after dark. Plum Island is a true barrier island where schools of monster striped bass roam – at least one 50-pound fish a year is weighed in, taken off the beachfront!

Plan to explore Plum Island's outer beach in a series of trips. I have spent a number of seasons learning bits and pieces of the beach, as well as the techniques of how to fish it. Many members of the Plum Island Surfcasters have spent 50 years roaming its sand and divining its secrets. It's a wonderful place, an area where the more time you spend, the more you'll learn. ◀━━◀

The Mouth Of The Merrimack – Fall Fishing At Its Best

By Al DelDotto

Up and down the New England coast the striped bass fishing season has a particular rhythm and, while not always predictable, it is inevitable. The striped bass visit for a few short months and the farther they move up the coast, the shorter their stay. The bass spread out in the summer, but with the first few cool blasts from Canada, they gather like schoolchildren answering September's call to the classroom. In order to survive their southward migration, stripers need to feed, and they need the protection afforded by schooling up, which are two very good things for striper fishermen.

Fall fishing on the Merrimack River carries a certain sense of urgency. I never know when I have caught my last fish of the season. I always tell myself that I will get out there one more time, and I probably push the season more than most. Sometime late in autumn, when my skiff has ice in the bilge and the turkey dinner is a memory, I realize that the season is over and I have probably caught the year's last fish. But September and October usually offer some of the best action of the year.

The tides move salt water many miles upstream on the Merrimack, but from a practical fishing standpoint, I consider the mouth of the river to be from the Chain Bridge in Amesbury to where the Merrimack meets the sea at Plum Island, which is downriver approximately two miles.

The first bridge to cross the mighty Merrimack in Colonial America was located near Deer Island. Today Amesbury's Chain Bridge spans the river at the same site. In the middle of the bridge span, there is a small parking area, and from there anglers take a short walk through some woods and arrive at the end of Deer Island. Deep channels can be fished on the

The mouth of the Merrimack is usually a sure-bet for schoolie stripers.

north and south sides of Deer. The downriver side of the island is actually a cut between Deer Island and nearby Eagle Island. Both of the channels and the cut fish well in the fall from boat and shore. I grew up fishing with my father and younger brother, and in the mid-1980s, when striper fishing here was largely an exercise in futility, we would consistently catch bluefish from the shores of Deer Island.

Three additional islands lay immediately downstream from Deer. They are, in order, Eagle, Carr and Ram islands. All three will have fish nearby at the top of the tide. A variety of methods are used to fish this area. Some anglers anchor up and fish chunk bait off the bottom, while others troll light plugs or jigs. My favorite way to work these grassy outcroppings is to drift while casting either artificial lures, soft plastics like Slug-Gos, or flies.

The north bank of the Merrimack River, from the Chain Bridge through downtown Newburyport, consists mainly of salt marsh laced with creeks and feeder streams. Some of these creeks are extensive estuaries in their own right; others are little more than drainage ditches. In the fall, each outflow, large or small, deserves attention, especially during the dropping tide. Small fish, crabs and grass shrimp get flushed out of these creeks during the ebb. The largest of these feeder streams is Town Creek, which empties into the Merrimack near Ram Island. The "mini rip" that the outflow forms during the dropping tide has saved me from more than one shutout. This is another spot where I like to drift quietly by each creek mouth while casting.

A fair amount of duck hunting still goes on in these marshes during the winter. As a young man, my dad made many hunting trips to this area. In the days before Interstates 93 and 495, greater Newburyport was still quite rural, a world away from his home in Dorchester. Unfortunately, he gave up hunting before I was old enough to learn. The silver lining was that he fished more, and he taught me to fish; we still fish together often.

Downriver from the creeks and islands, the Merrimack runs under the Route 1 bridge and through downtown Newburyport. Many anglers anchor up and fish around the bridge, but I'm not fond of the downtown section because it's just too much of an urban environment, plus the water is tricky. The river narrows slightly and the current screams along; current combined with the increased boat traffic is not conducive to the light tackle and fly-casting that I prefer.

Past the downtown area, the river widens considerably. To the south, less than a mile from the Merrimack jetties, is Joppa Flats. Joppa is the premier location during the fall run. The extensive flat is composed of a dark sand and mud bottom, with several gravelly mussel bars and a few grass beds. At high tide, water depth ranges from about 4 to 10 feet, but at low tide a substantial portion of Joppa is high and dry. Woodbridge Island, a high grassy hummock, is located on the flats. Stripers can sometimes be found holding tight along the steeper banks of this isle. A rock pile off of Woodbridge's northwest corner also holds striped bass.

Joppa Flats also contains a boat mooring area. Fishing between the sailboats is consistently good throughout the season, and in the fall it is particularly productive. As with other sections of the Merrimack, Joppa can be fished in many ways. Bait fishermen often work the boundary between the flat and the deep-water channel. Light-tackle and fly devotees can motor up and explore Joppa's wide flats. Whether it be bait, lures or flies, drifting and casting is by far the most popular and productive method used on the flats.

There is also a place on Joppa for shorebound anglers. Wading fishermen walk to the flats from an old ramp on Water Street in Newburyport. There is a short window of opportunity, starting an hour before low tide and lasting about two hours into the incoming tide, when a boatless angler can walk out to fishable water. But beware: Once the tide starts its flood, the water rises rapidly and the wading angler must leave.

I found this out the hard way one August evening. The bite was great; the stripers would not stop eating my blue and white Deceiver. Finally, pitch darkness made me turn to leave. To my surprise, the water got deeper as I moved toward shore. I made it out O.K., but it was intimidating and physically exhausting having to walk half a mile over a soft bottom in water that was just below the top of my waders.

It was on Joppa that I first saw anglers targeting striped bass with fly rods. It was 1990. I had fly-fished in fresh water and I had fished for stripers, but I never thought to fly-fish for them. One night I parked on Water Street and watched and waited. When the fishermen hiked in, I picked their brains about the rods, reels, lines and flies they were using. Most of the guys were more than willing to share their knowledge; several of them even gave me some flies. I always repeat their generosity whenever someone asks me about the sport.

The Salisbury side, or Salisbury Drift as it is known to the locals, is on the north side of the Merrimack, opposite Joppa. In contrast to its more famous neighbor, the Salisbury side features a light-colored sand bottom interspersed with boulders. The water on the Salisbury side is much clearer and colder than Joppa, making it a must-try location during the fall migration. I used to be so focused on fishing Joppa that I completely ignored the Salisbury side. Then, one September evening after my brother and I had beaten Joppa to a froth without much success, we saw a handful of terns working the waterway off to our north. We motored over carefully and saw the unmistakable splash of fish feeding on the surface. We took more than a few of the small but very fat fall fish from the Salisbury Drift that night. These fish were obviously packing on the pounds in preparation for their long trip to their winter home.

The next spot downstream is the actual river mouth. The Merrimack River inlet is located between Plum Island Point on the south and Salisbury Beach to the north. Large jetties mark both sides of the inlet. On Plum Island, just inside the south jetty, there is a substantial sandbar; bait gets washed over the bar with both incoming and outgoing tides. Boating anglers prefer to anchor in this area and fish cut herring or mackerel. This is also a hugely popular shore-fishing location, and there is plenty of access on both sides of the river. Salisbury Beach State Reservation on the north side provides plenty of parking and a large tract of fishable beach and riverfront. Across the water there is ample parking at Plum Island Point.

The shore crowd employs many different techniques, including bucktail jigs, plugs and bait. A distinctly Plum Island method involves drifting a gob of sea worms along the bottom. In the fall, once fish are located, all of these styles will work. Any description of this area would not be complete without mentioning the fact that the Merrimack River mouth is one of the most dangerous inlets in New England. On a normal day, when river currents meet the incoming tide, some very large waves are created. On marginal days, walls of water are churned up just beyond the jetties. There are days, however, when the mouth looks like a millpond. Boaters who plan on running through the inlet must pick their days carefully and have a substantial boat.

Plum Island, which forms the south bank of the river mouth, is a seven-mile- long barrier beach. A great deal of Plum Island is encompassed by the Parker River National Wildlife Refuge, and the outer beach is a classic striper fishing hot spot. Like any outer beach, it should be scouted during low tide and the location of bowls, sandbars and depressions noted. When the water comes in, this beach structure is where the fish will be found. Because it is part of the National Wildlife Refuge, vast portions of this beach are closed during the piping plover season. The plover closings are usually just a memory by the time the fall striped bass migration gets underway, but anglers should check at the refuge headquarters for any information about late-season closures. For those who wish to run the beach, information regarding over-sand vehicle permits is also available at the headquarters. However, running over sand is not necessary; there are numerous parking areas on the refuge, and most fishing locations can be walked into without much trouble.

Schoolie stripers are just about a sure thing at the mouth of the Merrimack.

Finally, we come to the southernmost point on Plum Island. Sandy Point, as it is known, is state-owned land, and though it is accessible from the National Wildlife Refuge, it is not subject to the same closings and there is no fee. In addition to accessibility, Sandy Point offers perhaps the best fish-holding structure on Plum Island. Emerson Rocks is a good-size rock pile that extends into the surf at the southeast corner of the island. Every striper heading out of the river on its way south for the winter must pass by this rocky reef.

Last fall, two buddies from work went out to fish around Emerson's, a trip I had to pass on. Afterwards, they described a literal parade of striped bass passing beneath their boat. The fish were more occupied with swimming than eating, but still provided quite a spectacle.

The mouth of the Merrimack River, its estuaries and Plum Island are accessible from two excellent state-run boat ramps. These are located at Cashman Park off of Merrimack Street in Newburyport, and Salisbury Beach State Reservation in Salisbury. Both ramps are paved, double-wide and have floating docks. Both locations have parking for dozens of vehicles with trailers. These ample amenities are both a blessing and a curse for striper fishermen, for they lead to some heavy crowds on the weekends. After Labor Day the crowds are greatly diminished, but the fishing remains strong through September and into the first week of October. By Columbus Day, the season is just about over in these parts. So make no excuses – get out there now. Fall fishing, the finest kind, awaits. You never know when you will catch the season's last fish.

Maine's South Shore Stripers
– No Boats Needed!

By Al Raychard

Spring usually comes late to Northern New England, even along the Southern Maine coast. Sometimes it fails to come at all. Despite what the calendar says, winter jumps straight into summer some years, and virtually overnight the cold temperatures and snow that have plagued us for months disappear, miraculously replaced by warming sunshine, blooming flowers and the singing of newly arrived birds. Whenever and however the transition comes, spring has truly sprung when the first stripers arrive, and for a large contingent of fly-fishermen, it is time to wet a line.

Unlike waters south of Cape Cod and along the Rhode Island shore, where bass are often present in good numbers most years sometime by late April, certainly by early May, striped bass traditionally arrive late to Gulf of Maine waters. Although arrival dates vary, depending on spring conditions, water temperatures, food availability and other factors, it is an unusual year when fish are available to any large degree by the middle of May. Generally, things don't get really fired up along Maine inshore waters until around Memorial Day. Even then, the majority of fish are small schoolies. Normally it remains that way until early June, when water temperatures warm to the low 50s, then into the 60s, and the larger fish arrive and go on the feed. It may be even later than that before schools of large bass move inshore because those waters are slow to warm each year.

For die-hard fly-fishermen, however, it makes no difference. Once fish arrive and are being caught, regardless of size and number, word spreads like wildfire. Just as it does elsewhere along the New England coast, "spring" means stripers along Maine's southern shore, and within days, sometimes hours it seems, local enthusiasts will head for favorite hot spots from Kittery to Casco Bay with a passion. It will remain that way until well into September, when the migration south begins. During this period there is some excellent angling.

The interesting thing is, compared to Cape Cod and points south, fly-fishing for Maine stripers is a relatively new phenomenon. There's no doubt more and more folks are doing it these days, and more seem to join the fold each season. At times certain spots do seem crowded, but compared to the great masses typically found to the south, Maine's southern coast is unexplored territory. In his classic work *Inshore Fly Fishing*, Lou Tabory calls Maine a "sleeper" when it comes to working the brine with a fly rod. Lou may be right; there remains plenty of room to work a fly over good numbers of fish, but things are definitely waking up.

Maine's coastline is generally considered rockbound from stem to stern. Its ancient, exposed granite and crashing surf have been written about in poem and song and have long been favorite subjects among great artists. But the fact is, there are miles of beaches and dozens of estuaries and tidal rivers of various sizes and descriptions. These areas offer the same rips and holes, rolling surf and flat water conditions; the same submerged rock structure and currents, protected beaches inside bays and estuaries; and the same sandbars and shallow reefs as other coastlines to the south. Then there are the small tidal creeks and rivers with their grassy banks, deep pools, clam flats, undercut banks and outflows. There are the rocky points and jetties. All hold bass during the season. And the vast majority are accessible to the fishing public, although that access may be difficult to find at times. For the visiting angler, however, and the enthusiast just beginning to explore what Maine's southern coast has to offer, the question is, "Just where are these areas?"

Maine begins where New Hampshire ends, and that is at the Piscataqua River. Good striper water will be found the minute you cross over the big green bridge into Maine. Striped bass travel a considerable way upriver, but access is a problem. However, there is some limited access from the River Road off Route 103 in Eliot and in the vicinity of the boat launch in South Eliot. Those fishing from small boats can run upstream or down, but keep in mind this is a river with strong currents. There is excellent boat fishing in the area of Spruce Creek, and bass are taken at Seapoint Beach, Cresent Beach off Seapoint Road heading toward Gerrish Island and at Brave Boat Harbor; The end of Seapoint Road has lots of bass at times and is a great spot for small car-top boats.

Going up the coast, the Cape Neddick River is another good spot. There is a boat launch off Shore Road, on the left just before the bridge. From there it is possible to move upstream to take advantage of the extensive estuary area. There is good shore-fishing in

Maine's southern coast striper hot spots aren't as deserted as they once were, but they're still less crowded than points south.

the surf along Route 1A between York Harbor and York Beach. The stretch offers some rock structure, rips and productive holes, depending upon the tide. It should be noted that the Long Beach and Short Sands areas are popular with swimmers and other beach lovers, so the best times for throwing a fly are early and late in the day.

The Ogunquit River area comes next. This is a rather small, shallow area, but on incoming and high tides, bass move upstream a good distance on a brief feeding binge. It is well protected, so fly-casting is possible despite strong winds. I like it because it is rather intimate and easy to wade and work a fly, but it is also a challenge. The river itself can be one of those hit-or-miss situations; when the fish are in, it can be quite good. It is shallow and fish can be somewhat spooky, so some tact in the way you approach and cast is generally called for. This is one of those places where you hunt and stalk fish that can be observed feeding.

Schoolie bass are common in many of Southern Maine's small tidal rivers.

When no fish are evident, however, the river can be a waste of time. For that reason many enthusiasts seem to prefer fishing the beach area, particularly at the mouth of the river. This is a good spot on the incoming and outgoing tides, and with careful wading, it is possible to reach bass holding and feeding in the currents and rips offshore on the low tide. Fish will also be found in the surf along the entire 3 1/2-mile beach, which stretches all the way to Moody Beach. The whole beach is public and offers rolling or crashing surf, depending upon the tide, wind and season, as well as some exposed rock structure and other spots that hold fish. Access to the river mouth and lower beach is best off Beach Street from Route 1 in Ogunquit Village. Access is also possible farther north along Route 1, off Ocean Street.

Another great spot is the Wells Beach and Webhanet River marsh. The lower end of Wells Beach is reached via Mile Road from Route 1, just north of Wells. At the end turn left onto Atlantic Avenue, which leads to a large parking area. From there it is possible to access the beach, where you'll find good fishing in the surf and near rock jetties. Again, this is a popular swimming spot, so early and late in the day are best. Near the outlet of the river can be quite productive. The Webhanet River and its extensive marsh can be reached using Lower Landling Road, again from Route 1. It is a good-size tidal estuary but is protected, so small watercraft will help you do well here. Some wading is also possible.

One of my favorite spots is Parsons Beach, at the mouth of the Mousam River in Kennebunk. There is good fishing in the surf at the river's mouth and along the beach. The area offers good wading on the incoming or outgoing tides, and there is a mixture of rock structure, holes and pockets that seem to always hold fish. On the outgoing tide there are good rips at the mouth and fish are nearly always present.

Upstream the river drains a rather extensive tidal marsh, and fish travel well upstream of Route 9. The pools, undercut banks and shallow sandbars above the bridge can be fished on any tide from the banks and are all good places to explore. Limited parking is available near the bridge on Route 9. Below the bridge, the river meanders toward the beach, widens and eventually opens to a rather large pool when the tide is high, before it meets the sea. This pool holds stripers when full to the brim, but can be a challenge and difficult to work due to its size, depth, soft bottom in places and the fact that fish are often feeding offshore, beyond the reach of most casters. I have discovered it is best to fish the area on the rising tide, allowing the water to reach your knees and gradually working toward shore as the pool floods. To reach the beach area, turn off Route 9 onto the Parson Beach Road. After crossing the bridge, limited parking is available on the left at the end of the pavement.

Goose Rocks Beach is a good spot for fishing the surf. It faces the open sea, and wind can be a problem at times, but the beach tapers off gradually, allowing the angler to wade a far distance from shore, and at low tide some offshore structure offers good spots to find bass. The Little River dumps into the east end and can be easily reached by wading down the beach. Its name is appropriate. At low tide the river can easily be waded across, and even at high tide a competent caster can throw a fly from one bank to the other on the lower section. The bass also tend to run small here, but the action can be quite steady at times. Because of the easy nature of the place, this is a great spot to fish after dark, especially on an incoming tide. There is also some good fishing in the open salt along the rocky shore on the point on the east side, but caution should be taken. The rocks are slippery, and handling a big fish can be difficult. Access to this area is from Route 9, taking Goose Rock Road at Clock Farm Corner. At the end, turn right and the beach will be on the left. Public parking is available in this area but only during the early morning and evening hours.

Farther down the coast, heading toward the Saco River, Fortunes Rocks Beach offers casting opportunities from shore. The stretch of rocky beach offers a fair amount of structure within casting distance at low and mid tides and, though not well known, produces good fish among the rocks. The wading can be less than ideal, but some excellent fish are possible. Parking is available right along the beach. To reach the area, take Route 208 off Route 9, heading toward Biddeford Pool. After crossing a small bridge, turn right.

Another good spot in this area is The Pool at Biddeford Pool, which is on your left at the end of Route 208. Bass move into this area on the rising tide to feed on clams, crabs and the smorgasbord of other foods that are rich in the area. The best time to fish The Pool is on the high tide, and while shore-fishing is possible along Mile Stretch leading to Biddeford Pool, a canoe or small car-top boat is best. Getting afloat simply allows the angler to use the entire area. No formal launch site is available, but it is possible to get on the water near the small bridge on Route 208 or at Biddeford Pool. Just keep in mind, when The Pool empties, it leaves a bathtub ring of soft mud and exiting can be interesting.

Hills Beach, at the mouth of the Saco River on the west side, is a good spot to fly-cast for stripers. The spot offers a sand beach that tapers off gradually in most spots, and bass tend to congregate there before heading upstream. As the tide recedes it is possible to wade out a fair distance, taking advantage of available structure, holes and currents. Parking is limited but is available at the ends of several side streets off Hills Beach Road. The breakwaters on both sides of the river are worth exploring as well, especially on the east side, reached from Saco via Route 9 at Camp Ellis. This is one of the oldest and longest stone breakwaters on the East Coast. There is good fishing on the river side as well as the bay side, and in most cases bass are in rather close. This is a popular spot and may be crowded at times. Parking is available, although a fee is required during the summer season.

Saco Bay has always been a good spot for striped bass, and in recent years fly-fishermen have been discovering that fact. There is a good beach stretching from Camp Ellis all the way to Old Orchard, and during the late spring and summer months, once water temperatures warm in the bay, bass often move in close, offering possibilities in the surf at places like Ferry Beach and Kinney Shores. In places there are some exposed ledges and structure, and at Ocean Park the outlet of Branch Brook can be productive. The entire beach can be reached from Route 9.

On the east end the angler will find the Scarborough River and its extensive marsh and system of tidal creeks. This is a one of the top spots for bass in Southern Maine and offers both boat and shore opportunities. There is a boat launch off King Street for those who want to fish and explore the area by boat. For the land-based angler there is good fishing at the river's mouth at Pine Point from the beach or jetty. A lot of water flushes in and out of this large estuary and the fishing is often quite good. It is also possible to fish the Scarborough River by entering a dirt road leading to a steel bridge just before the Scarborough Nature Center on Route 9, heading toward Route 1. The river is smaller here, but it meanders and creates large pools, wide corners and undercut banks, all of which hold bass. If the angler doesn't mind some walking, there is a lot of water to fish here.

On the east side of the marsh the angler will find Route 207, which leads from Route 1 at Oak Hill to Prouts Neck. A few miles down, the road crosses over the Nonesuch River and just beyond the Clay Pitts Road, leads to a boat ramp. The area is highly tidal, consisting of quiet backwater, but it is excellent for stripers. If you continue on Route 207, it will lead to Ferry Beach and Western Beach, both of which offer good opportunities from shore. Higgins Beach at the mouth of the Spurwink is another good spot, but all three are popular with swimmers.

Needless to say, there are plenty of places to fish between Kittery and Portland. Many of those just mentioned are extensive and will take time to explore, learn and fully ap-

This striped bass taken on a fly from one of southern Maine's coastal rivers.

preciate, and typically each seems to lead to another, which is either part of the same system or are not far away. I have been fishing many of these areas for years on a regular basis, but I find I am still learning their idiosyncrasies and changing ways and at times wonder if I will ever learn all their secrets. I hope not. It is just one of the factors that keeps them interesting and draws me back season after season.

One of the more enjoyable attributes of many of the tidal bays and rivers just mentioned is they are rather small compared to counterparts to the south. They are almost always intimate. Small flies are the general rule, and unlike fishing the beaches and areas open to the sea where wind can be a problem, standard freshwater rigs, rods in the 8-weight class, equipped with matching lines and reels, are more than adequate. We don't even bother with specialized shooting heads, just standard weight-forward tapers, generally floaters throughout the season. Everything is simplified, lighter and easier, and a lot more enjoyable.

When working off the beaches, cliffs and jetties, a heavier 9- or 10-weight kit and longer rod of 9 1/2 feet will prove more advantageous. These rods allow for extra height on the backcast and increased reach. They are also better for beating against the wind and throwing heavier flies, which are often called for in these areas. If possible, because Maine's coast does vary and conditions change from tide to tide, having two outfits on hand is always a good idea. But even if you carry just one, it is possible to find a place to catch stripers along Maine's southern coast.

Chapter Two

Tackle
&
Techniques

In the last 50 years, there has been nothing short of a revolution in fishing tackle and the ways it can be used to catch striped bass. Whether you prefer the subtlety of casting a fly to stripers over a sandy flat, dragging a jig on wire line through a hard-running rip, or casting plugs or bait into the surf, understanding how to use your tools is mandatory for success.

"Big Ditch" Jigging

By Carl A. Johansen

After more than five decades of fishing the Cape Cod Canal, I have no doubt that jigs have accounted for more big striped bass than any other type of lure. But not all jigs are the same. Some work better than others in specific locations and knowing how to fish them over various types of bottom structure is essential. The right equipment is a factor, too.

You might look at the canal and see a body of running water that pretty much looks the same from one end to the other and conclude that the bottom is uniform in depth and composition. However, this is not the case; to be successful, the angler must learn to identify potentially productive areas to jig. We need to find structure like weeds and mussel beds, as well as obvious man-made structures such as bridge abutments and piers. The weed and mussel beds are irregular in size, shape and thickness. Generally, the thicker or denser parts of these beds are toward the center of the Big Bitch. Over time, the hard-running currents of the canal have dug out pockets or holes alongside these beds.

The same holds true around the bridge abutments and piers. One should try to locate backwashes and places around these man-made structures where the water appears to be moving slower than the overall flow; these indicate depressions, deeper places where trophy stripers like to lie in wait for their prey. It's no secret that big fish are lazy; they look for slow-moving water and won't move far from their holding area if they don't have to. Locating the depressions adjacent to the weed and mussel beds is more difficult because there are hardly ever visual clues. This is one of the reasons that you must fish your jig as close to the bottom as possible, and even the best canal fishermen lose many, many jigs every season to hang-ups. But if you can find these areas, your chances of catching a large fish are increased.

The Cape Cod Canal can be a very productive striper location, if you know how to work it. Those anglers that jig the "Big Ditch" properly can always find big fish.

There is a different set of conditions at each end of The Ditch. The bottom is mostly sandy in both places and bass use depressions in the sand, even quite shallow ones, to hide and take advantage of any bait that might get swept by. When jigging in these areas you must keep your jig bouncing along the bottom and adjust the controlled drift so the jig can fall into the depressions. This is where it is a huge advantage to use braid rather than monofilament, because every little bump and hesitation is instantly telegraphed through these nonstretch lines.

Having the right equipment and knowing how to use it is the first step. I use one of two rods, both of which are well suited to handling the style of jigging I employ, a Lamiglas SB121 3M and a Lamiglas GSB 120 1M. Both rods are 10 feet long and allow me to cast far enough into The Ditch to reach my chosen areas. Both rods also have plenty of backbone necessary to fight a good fish and move it off the bottom, and I can usually break free a jig that gets hung up. I use a Penn 980 reel on the 3M rod, loaded with 40-pound-test mono, and an Abu Garcia 7000CL loaded with 50-pound-test braid on the

Lead jigs have probably taken more stripers in the canal than any other lure.

GSB 120 rod. I keep my equipment highly maintained during the fishing season. I do not place any backing or spliced line on the reels; if I get into a trophy fish, I know that my line will do its job as long as I have the proper drag set on the reels.

Using your rod to put pressure on the fish as it runs is a judgment call, and once the battle is engaged, a combination of rod pressure and a well-set drag is the formula for subduing the fish. A heavy run is best countered with the rod at the 10 o'clock position to allow the line to peel off the reel and still maintain some control. If a fish is determined to take line, let it! That's what your drag is for – drop the tip just a bit while maintaining a tight line. Don't reel against the drag. Should the fish turn and go in the opposite direction, you will still be able to lift your rod and maintain pressure. Although stripers in the ditch will usually carry on the fight in the same direction as the current, they can and will swim against it, and you should always be prepared for this eventuality.

I usually use 4- to 6-ounce jigs, but the choice of style depends on water movement and where I am fishing. I carry Uppermans (flat head), No Alibis (open mouth, "Smiling Bill"), K jigs (the "Canal Special") and the Bug Eye (made by Charlie Cinto). The shape dictates the rate of drop and fluttering action, and each offers a different presentation. The flat and bullet styles will descend a little faster and, once on the bottom, will dance from side to side as they're jigged. The round style descends more slowly and then hops along the bottom as it is worked. You'll find these at the many tackle shops catering to canal fishermen.

It is worth mentioning that while most of the time you should keep your jig close to or on the bottom, there will be times when stripers will hit higher up in the water column. A change in style of jighead can put you in that strike zone.

You can enhance your offering by attaching a pork rind, strip of herring or mackerel to the hook. I use jigs with 7/0 or 8/0 hooks because large fish are less apt to straighten out a hook of this size. The standard colors of white, black and yellow will all take fish, but I have also taken fish using jigheads that were pink or green in an attempt to imitate bait present at that time. Bucktail jigging is most effective using the lighter colors during daylight hours and the darker colors at night.

Bucktail jigs aren't the only way to work the deep water in the canal. Spoon-type metal jigs such as Crippled Herring, Kastmasters, Hopkins, Deadly Dicks and diamond jigs are very productive. I recommend that you replace the treble hooks with extra-strong single hooks. Keep in mind that if the hooks are free-swinging on these metal jigs, then the hooks and singles are less likely to get hung up. And don't be afraid to make alterations such as painting metal jigs different colors; pink, red and green have all worked for me.

You will see many different approaches to jigging in the canal when it comes to presentation and how action is imparted to the lure. I would like to offer two ways that I have used with great success in my 55 years of fishing the Big Ditch.

The technique I use most often, and the one that may prove to be easiest to learn, starts with casting upcurrent into deep water and allowing the jig to hit the bottom. Keep the reel in free-spool or have the bail open, and control the line with your fingers (on a spinning reel) or your thumb (on a conventional) as you allow line to "bleed" out. This will ensure that your jig stays on the bottom for a longer period of time than if you engage your reel immediately after the lure hits the bottom. It is very important that you raise or lower the rod tip to help maintain contact with your jig as it works its way along.

The current flow will force the jig up off the bottom as it swims farther downcurrent. If you are using braid, it is easier to feel variation in the bottom and/or a fish picking up the jig. If you suddenly feel no weight at all, it could very well be that a large fish has picked up your jig and is moving against the current. If this happens you should immediately engage the reel and take up the slack before you strike. Remember, fish do not always take the jig or metal in the same direction as the water is flowing.

I try to work the jig as far as I can before engaging the reel because once this happens I know the jig will slide past the edges of the underground structures and out of the strike zone. How far you let it go can make the difference between catching a fish, coming away empty or even hanging up and losing your jig. This is where experience is the best teacher; you must put in the time to learn the subtle nuances of jigging. In any case, when you engage the reel and start the retrieve, do it slowly and smoothly to minimize hang-ups.

One more note on equipment. You'll be able to move the jig or give it more motion with a rod that has a stiff tip. Many of the stock casting rods that you'll see have soft tips, which are great for distance casting, but put a nice fish on the other end in deep water, along with a hard-moving current, and in most cases the fish will win the battle. Remember, this is not a beach where you will have the luxury of walking the shoreline as you battle the fish. You'll probably be planted on a slippery rock on the edge of the flow and you must do battle with your quarry without the luxury of being able to move. When you hook up with a large fish, the amount of backbone that your rod has will determine if you control its travel or it controls you. The more the rod moves under pressure from a large fish, the larger the hook's penetration hole becomes and the less chance you will

At times, metal jigs and lures will be your best bets.

have of bringing the fish to the water's edge. This is the critical point in the battle when the majority of quality fish are lost.

The second technique I use is what I call "walking the jig." This method is used in areas where the service road is relatively close to the water or when casting from piers where there are few obstructions. Simply put, what you're going to do is actually walk along and follow the jig as it bounces along. You can cover a lot of water this way, much more than if you stand in one place and cast. And for the angler who has some years piled up, rock hopping becomes a little harder to do, but this method can be employed safely. The first step is to be aware of people around you when loading your rod to make a cast; the canal is popular with walkers and bikers both day and night, and you'll need some room to utilize this technique to maximum effect.

Start by casting upcurrent and allowing the jig to hit bottom. Now it gets a little tricky because, depending on the velocity of the water, you can engage your reel or let it stay in free-spool as you walk along with the jig. If the water flow is slow, it's fairly easy to walk along at the same speed as the jig is moving, with the reel engaged, without getting hung up on the bottom. If the water is running full bore, allow the line to run off the spool with the least amount of thumb pressure (to prevent a backlash) as you walk. This will keep you in the strike zone a little longer.

A few more tips on using this technique. I find this method to be very effective during the top of the current changes as opposed to low-water current changes. Be sure to locate an area where you can land a fish without going down the rock embankment until you need to remove the hook. This is another time when having the right rod can greatly enhance your chances of lifting a fish under controlled conditions. And finally, as with stationary jigging, expect to lose some gear. Those of us who fish the ditch refer to this as "appeasing the canal gods."

The canal has many spots you can walk to and find fish, but being mobile will allow you to fish more spots and even find some solitude. The service roads that run along both sides of The Ditch are perfect for biking; rig one up with a basket and rod holders and you can hit many locations in one outing. A bike allows you to do some serious scouting, too. Learn where to fish a jig at low water and at high water. Look for outcroppings, sandbars, mussel beds and weed beds. Keep a log that notes locations you find to be productive and all the conditions when you caught fish. With a good pair of polarized glasses you can see some amazing detail quite a way out into the canal, especially during the "minus" tides, those low tides when there is a full or new moon. This will also increase your chances of discovering what type of bait the stripers are after. You can then select the appropriate jig and pork rind trailer colors to further your chances of success.

The Cape Cod Canal has no secret spots, but it does have plenty of secrets. No one angler can know the subtleties and variables of every location because each day is different, and the stripers' feeding habits can and often do change with the tide. Each fisherman who challenges its waters develops a style that works for him. Those who put in the time and learn from their experiences will ultimately be successful at catching quality striped bass. As in any fishing experience, it is important to keep a positive attitude. And when you've gained some knowledge and skill, don't be stingy about passing it on to the next generation of fishermen so they can begin learning the mysteries of fishing the "Big Ditch."

Cape Cod Canal Structure Strategies

By Carl A. Johansen

Everyone who has had the opportunity to fish the Cape Cod Canal has found it to be a very challenging place to catch large stripers. Volumes have been published regarding what works best, but in my opinion, formed over 50 years of being a canal rat, no one is an expert when it comes to understanding all the ways large bass can be caught from these waters.

Three bridges traverse the Cape Cod Canal. The railroad bridge has a center span of 544 feet and was completed in 1935, one year after I was born. The Bourne and Sagamore bridges have a center span of 616 feet and were completed in 1933. The railroad and Bourne bridges are located at the west end of The Ditch, and the Sagamore Bridge is located at the east end. These landmarks are important because large schools of bass migrate into the canal and feed around the masonry stone abutments that support the center spans. These abutments provide a safe haven and a place to rest for the large bass, which will hold on the lee side of the current and wait in the shadows for a food supply to come their way. These abutments also provide a habitat that is conducive to holding tautog and large fluke.

One note before we explore this fishery: The construction work currently being done on the railroad bridge has resulted in poor fishing because the vibration from the ongoing work is picked up by the fish and they keep their distance from the area around the abutments. However, after the workday is done, productive fishing resumes during the dark hours. When this work is completed, fishing in this area will return to normal.

All modes of fishing, if properly presented, can and do catch large fish during daylight and dark hours right around the time of current changes. Throughout the season, slack water at high or low tide is generally thought of as best, but at times (especially during the fall migration) the action may continue for the half-hour or so on either side of the turn and may actually get better. It is important not to quit fishing too early, and remember that every day is different.

The early migrating bass hit The Ditch in May and feed on herring. The bass enter from the west and will swim under the railroad and Bourne bridges along both sides of the canal. If you choose to live-line herring, simply cast the herring toward the downcurrent side of the outermost edge of the abutment and let the herring swim with the current. I try not to fish with live herring under the bridge itself because at times the herring will swim into an eddy, and if a large fish hits the herring, you will be cut off on the corners of the abutment. Live-lining herring can be effective during the west and east current swings, but I have found it to be more productive when the current is running east.

If you intend to fish the railroad bridge abutment on the mainland side, keep in mind that the west end of the abutment is not accessible; you can't get close enough to cast into productive water. Occasionally though, if the water is high, it will not be necessary to go beyond the edge of the abutment. Simply cast the herring into the calm water that forms inside the granite footing at that point. If a large fish latches on, make sure you stop it from turning the corner. Sometimes it helps to be some distance away from the abutment for a better angle when working the fish. This distance will vary depending how much water is flowing and the speed of the current.

After the initial arrival of herring, the Sagamore Bridge abutments provide better fishing during the period when the current slows, goes slack and then turns east. Again, position yourself and fish on the downcurrent side.

Once the herring have spawned and dropped back to the canal in June, the fishing around the abutments improves dramatically using cut bait, such as herring, mackerel, sand eels, squid, sea clams and pogies. One can drift bait or lay it on the bottom to catch a lunker. At this time I prefer to have my cut bait pulled under the bridge between the shore and the abutment. I find the east current to be the most productive.

Many who drift bait in The Ditch rely on one type of bait to catch bass and are disappointed when what they choose to use is not producing. My suggestion is to try other types of bait. As the fish spread out in The Ditch for the summer, they develop other tastes, which may or may not be related to the available forage. One thing is for sure, though, bass, especially big ones, love easy pickings, and all types of bait have taken their share of large fish. For those who prefer to drift fish, use large pieces, especially the head sections, for those big ones. Mackerel, butterfish, smelt, squid, pogies, silver hake (whiting), needlefish and flying halfbeak are a few species that will inhabit the canal during the warmer months.

It is also very beneficial to chum the water to bring the fish closer to you. The chum does not necessarily need to be the same as the bait you are using.

During the summer months the majority of these fish come in from the east end of the canal, and at this time of the year the Sagamore Bridge area is the most productive. For many years the only baits we used were mackerel, squid, sea clams and herring. Pogies became a hot item, but the decline in this resource has made it difficult to stock crunchies (nice firm, fresh menhaden) in the tackle stores. Mackerel is the better choice when fishing the Sagamore abutment, but the railroad and Bourne Bridge abutments will produce better on fresh crunchies if they can be found. The reason for this is that the majority of the mackerel come in from the Sagamore end of the waterway and the pogies come in from the railroad bridge and Bourne end. If you try to keep an open mind and do not get locked into using one type of bait all the time, I am sure you will be rewarded for your efforts.

Sometimes it helps to have a variety of bait on hand to make a different presentation when fishing. Try drifting the bait with a small leadcore weight. If this is not working, place a little more weight on the line or simply use a fish-finder rig with a heavy weight to keep it on the bottom for a longer period of time. This latter method works the best during the low and high slack current.

During the hard-running period of the tide, one will need to be farther away from the abutment to allow the bait to swing into the prime areas as the bait is pulled under the bridge. A distance of 30 to 40 feet should suffice, and as the current slows, move closer if possible, without interfering or intruding on someone else's space. This is one reason why a full spool of at least 30-pound-test line is needed on the reel in order to pull any large bass from the depths.

I have found that every abutment has a honey hole or sweet spot that will produce more fish than other spots once you satisfy the canal gods with a sacrifice. Expect to lose a few things until you learn where these honey holes are. I recommend using bait during the daylight hours around the abutments, but that's not to say that bait at night will not catch fish; I simply prefer other ways to catch stripers at night.

The use of jigs in the summer and fall around the abutments can be deadly during the early morning and evening hours. It is necessary to be farther away from the stone platforms when casting to allow for the sweep of the current. You want your jig to get as deep as possible.

Your jig will get quite a ride, depending what style and weight you choose. The Upperman, or flat jig, has more action on the way down through the water column and flutters when worked on the bottom. The No Alibi, or round jig, will descend to the bottom very rapidly and bounce up and down when worked. I strongly recommend that you fill your reel with one of the new braided super lines and that your rod be able to handle the jig weight you are casting. The braid allows you to be in touch with your jig and feel the slightest hit. I prefer heavy jigs from 3 to 6 ounces, and will use the heavier one when there is a full moon or when a storm from Buzzards Bay or Cape Cod Bay is pushing in more water, as the speed of the current increases during this time. The No Alibi and flat jig are the most common, but I use many other types of jigs, as well.

So here's the scenario: You're standing some distance upcurrent from the abutment on the shore. That distance is farther away from the abutment if the current is running hard, closer if it's slow or slack. You cast out (upcurrent, if there is any) and keep your reel in free-spool, allowing the jig to fall to the bottom. It is necessary to have a good idea where your jig is as you work it along the bottom and start your retrieve before it gets to the halfway point under the bridge. This will allow you to work the jig as you retrieve, and if a big one hits, you will have time to play the fish away from the shore. You can see that you are fishing in deeper waters than when live-lining and bait-fishing because you are casting farther into the canal. This is one reason not to get too close to the abutment, and how you position yourself in relation to the abutment is determined by the velocity of the current on that particular day. It is a safe bet that no two days will be exactly the same.

Color can affect your catch rate. You should keep several colors of each jig on hand. My preferences are all-white, pink, or black and green. Adding pork rind to the jig will increase its effectiveness. I use white, yellow, and red and white with the red side up for best results. The length of the rind can affect your distance, so if you are into fish at the far end of your cast, simply reduce the length of the pork rind a little to stay a little longer in the zone. Jigs work in the whole water column, but bouncing the bottom is best.

Although popping plugs will catch fish at night, I prefer to use swimming plugs around the abutments, especially at times of high water. This does not mean that the low water conditions will not produce fish, it's just that I've always done better at the peak of the tide. The majority of swimming plugs are light by design, so I try to use those close to the 2-ounce range and in some cases loaded with some steel or lead shot. It is important not to add too many pellets, as this will dramatically change the action. The wood swimmers, or needlefish, are a little heavier by design and at times better during a hard-running current. Try to work both sides of the abutments and be careful not to hit the stone abutments, which will do a job on the plastic swimmers. You will be fishing very close and in some cases parallel to the abutment itself.

Live eels or eelskins can be worked in the same manner, but I would stand a little farther away to work the front edge of the abutment. At times, casting a live eel at the abutment and allowing it to hit the stone and drop into the water can be productive.

You should always have a few larger surface poppers, especially during the early morning hours, because this is the time you will see large fish breaking on bait. When I started fishing The Ditch in 1946 it was not uncommon to see 40- and 50-pound fish caught with plugs as they chased bait. Those days are gone; in fact, for many years a big fish caught on a surface plug was almost unheard of. In the past few years we have started to see 30- to 40-pound fish on surface plugs. The turnaround of the fishery is not complete, but the increase in size has helped to increase the dreams of those fishing for the elusive trophy fish.

Safety cannot be overlooked when fishing around the abutments, so take your common sense with you, especially at night. Use appropriate footwear; those rocks can be treacherous, especially the weed-covered ones down near the water.

Not all abutments will be hot on a given night, so it is helpful to fish with a buddy, one on the mainland and the other on the Cape side of The Ditch. Communicating with your buddy was once done by flashlight and later by whistle. Unfortunately, it's harder to pick up where the whistle is coming from than it is to see a blinking light, which everyone else can also see. Today the cell phone is the chosen way, but I still like to use the whistle.

Experiment with different fishing methods and be both innovative and methodical in how you search the waters around the abutments under the bridges. Who knows, your number might be called and you will have an opportunity to catch a wall-hanger under the bridges that cross this man-made waterway.

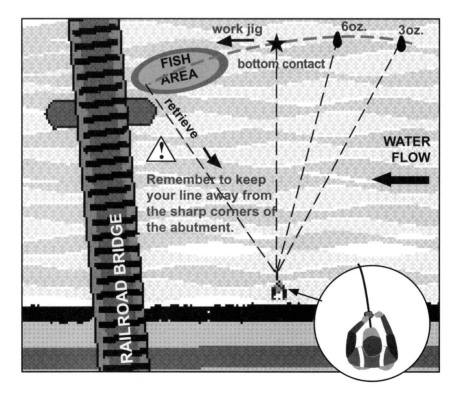

Jig 'Em Up!
Jigging Techniques For Bass & Blues

By Captain Mike Hogan

The actual act of jigging means different things to different people. In New England jigging can mean anything ranging from bouncing "metals" on the bottom to wire-line trolling. To most old-timers who have fished our waters for decades, a jig would be considered a metal lure cast from mold. However, if you walk into your local tackle shop and ask for something you can jig for bass or bluefish, you'll discover an extensive variety of options. You'll find that bucktails, soft plastics with lead heads, spoons and other hybrid variations all fall into this category, in addition to the more traditional diamond-style jigs. In any event, jigs are universally fished with sweeping motions of the rod, allowing the lure to dart, drop and flutter.

Very few techniques are as consistently effective as wire-line jigging for striped bass and bluefish, which makes it easy to understand why so many charter captains use jigging as their go-to technique. Though relatively easy to accomplish, there are a few tricks of the trade. To understand and be successful at this method, it is easiest to break it down into three components: your outfit, the jigging technique itself and the positioning of your lures over fish.

Due to the combination of its heavy weight and small diameter, wire line allows you to troll much more deeply in the water column without the use of heavy jigs. But since there is no stretch in wire line, all the stress associated with hooking and landing fish falls upon your gear. As a result, your outfit will need to be heftier than trolling setups used with monofilament or even leadcore line. For starters, you'll need a reel with a brawny drag system. I have always sworn by the Penn Senator 113HSP 4/0 reel, which is virtually indestructible if cared for properly. There are other conventional reels commonly used for jigging that are up to the task such as those offered by Daiwa, Shimano and Newell. Look for a reel that will hold at least 150 yards of 80-pound-test dacron backing and up to 100 yards of wire. Stay away from level wind reels, as they will make untangling backlashes difficult.

Your rod must have Carboloy or silicon carbide guides so that the wire doesn't cut grooves as it's let out and retrieved, which will happen in a surprisingly short amount of time with stainless steel or ceramic insert guides. Six- or six-and-a-half-foot rods are commonly used. Some jigging rods are very soft, meaning they are quite flexible, while others are fast, providing a stiffer action. I prefer the latter because I feel I have more control of the jig, requiring less rod work to keep the jigs moving. However, softer rods are more forgiving when fighting fish. There is less possibility of slack in the line if you drop the tip of your rod too quickly, and they are also easier on your arms if you're planning a long day of jigging.

The line setup on your reel consists of the backing, the wire line and mono leader.

Fifty-pound-test Monel or stainless single-strand wire is commonly used in New England. The backing is important as it helps cushion your rod and reel against the stress of the wire. People use either heavy mono or dacron for backing. I prefer dacron for my backing because I feel that mono allows too much stretch in the line, minimizing the effect of your jigging. You will need approximately 12 feet of mono connected to your wire to serve as your leader. Though traditional mono has worked for years, fluorocarbon material, which is far less visible under water, will help increase the number of strikes when bass are finicky. A minimum of 60-pound test is necessary for both a good knot connection and to prevent cut-offs by toothy bluefish. I use an Albright knot to connect the wire to the backing and the leader. If you are uncomfortable with tying this knot, tackle shops will tie it for you when you have your reels spooled up with wire.

There's more to jigging than just dragging a lure through the water. Learn the correct techniques and you'll be rewarded with big stripers.

Be careful when letting out wire as it has a tendency to backlash and kink if it's let out too quickly. Make sure you keep a thumb on your spool to prevent the spool from revolving faster than the line can go out, which is the number one cause of wire backlashing.

When deciding how much wire to spool onto your reels, think about where you will be doing the most fishing and how deep it will be. I prefer to use a premeasured amount of wire so the backing is all that is left on the rod when I'm fishing. This will minimize the wear and tear on both your rod and your line. It is a nice luxury to have multiple outfits spooled with ideal lengths of wire for different applications, but it's often more practical to have a couple shots of wire separated by dacron line in the middle. This will allow you to fish comfortably with only half your total capacity out. In terms of depth, the rule has always been 10 feet of wire to 1 foot of depth behind the boat, without a jig and assuming a boat speed of 2 or 3 knots. A few ounces of jig will add at least another five feet. To achieve greater depth without using more wire, try varying your trolling speed or even popping your boat in and out of gear. You want those jigs as close to the bottom as possible. Turns can also be made throughout your trolling pattern; your inside jig will fall while your outside jig will rise off the bottom.

Nine times out of ten, I will use a parachute-style jig, which is a variation of a bucktail jig. Basically, the only difference from a traditional bucktail is that the hair protrudes from both sides of the collar just below the head. This allows for more flutter as the jig swims up and down throughout the jigging cycle. I use the lightest jigs necessary to reach the bottom and seldom go over three ounces, but more may be necessary to compete with unusually strong tides or substantial depths. Generally speaking, you will be safe with 1.5- to 3-ounce jigs in your arsenal. Remember to tip your jig with pork rind. The large "sea strips" by Uncle Josh are a good choice and come in many colors, but the white/red version is the most popular. A jig with a little something extra will almost always out-fish one that is bare.

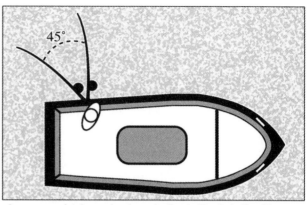

A common mistake made when wire-line trolling is to jig with motions that are too long. The tip of the rod only needs to move in a 3-foot span. Snap the rod forward about 45˚, and then let the jig slide back for about 3 seconds. Try to keep some tension on the line as it is dropping back since this is when most hits occur.

I can't even count the number of charters I have taken out where one or two anglers out-fished the rest of the party significantly with the exact same equipment. Though jigging is not difficult, it does require some finesse. Unlike most other lures, the jig's action and its ability to entice fish are dependent on the technique of the angler. To properly jig with wire line, the angler must be cognizant of both timing and motion. A jigging motion should be started with the tip of the rod at approximately a 45-degree angle outward and toward the stern of the boat. Some guys jig with the rod pointed down toward the water but this is fatiguing for the average angler and no more effective, in my opinion. Using a snapping motion, bring the rod back to a position almost perpendicular to your body, or just past it. Now, without generating slack in the line, let the tip of the rod swing aft, returning to where you began. With the same snapping motion, repeat the exercise with a relatively short interval between snaps.

A "three count" is a good place to start, but try different rhythms to find one that works best for the situation. This will depend on a multitude of factors such as boat speed and how much current you're pushing against, not to mention what the fish themselves prefer. Picture what your jig is doing under water. You want it to really "dance," darting up and down, mimicking a baitfish that is fleeing.

I think that the most common mistake is to jig with motions that are too long. I have seen anglers swing so far that the tip of the rod is almost pointing forward. While this is an extreme example, a long sweeping dynamic looks unnatural, and fussy fish will turn up their noses. The tip of your rod should not be moving more than a 3-foot span.

Wire-line jigging can be used in a handful of situations mainly associated with structure such as rips, rock piles, drop offs and wrecks. You will be trying to fish your jigs as close to the structure as possible. The golden rule of trolling states that you should always go against the tide. However, in an area such as Woods Hole with wildly strong currents, I'll break the rule and go with the tide. Otherwise, it will be difficult to stay close to the bottom.

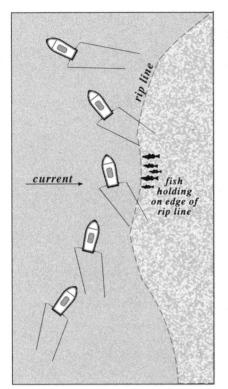

current

fish holding on edge of rip line

rip line

Bass love to hold in the turbulent water on the edge of a rip. When wire-line jigging, it's important to properly position your jig into the rip line. As you troll toward the rip, turn almost at the last instant, so that your lures will sweep over the rip as they swing around behind your boat. Ideally, they will settle in a location just behind the rip. This can be repeated by making a series of S-shaped turns.

Have you ever been jigging on the rips and noticed that some boats were hooking up consistently while others were not? More times than not, this is due to how well each boat's lures are positioned in the rip. The key here is to understand where the fish are holding and why. Picture a shoal and think about how the water moves over the raised bottom. As the tide begins to build in strength, the water will accelerate as it rises up and over the shoal, creating lots of commotion. A line of rough water can be seen as the rip "makes up," serving as a marker of the edge of the shoal. Both bass and bluefish will tend to hang out just behind the rip, waiting in ambush for the confused bait swept over the edge. Though bass and blues can be caught in the general area, the largest ones, particularly bass, will be holding just behind the edge of the shoal. So of course that's where you'll want your jigs.

To put them there, you'll need to position your boat up-tide from the rip so that your jigs will be behind you in the strike zone, just behind the rip. The tricky part will be to continuously position your lures so that they remain in the strike zone. This can be accomplished by making turns in front of the rip. As you troll toward the rip, turn, almost last minute, so that your lures will sweep over the rip as they swing around behind your boat again. Ideally, they will settle in a location just behind the rip. This can be repeated by making a series of S-shaped turns. Think about what is going on under the rip. Look for a spot where the bass will have the best location to ambush.

You must make just enough speed to gain headway against the tide. In such waters as Vineyard Sound in Massachusetts and The Race in Connecticut, you can be bucking up to five knots of current so the correct application of power can be a tricky thing. Also try different angles and approaches to the rip. Sometimes bass will expect bait approaching a certain way. Try periodically taking your boat in and out of gear to let your jigs drop all the way to the bottom, near or on top of the structure. Often you will get hits as your lures are falling. If you find you are not getting many strikes, try surging the boat. In an area that is very sandy, I will frequently let my baits skip on the bottom to create disturbances that draw fish.

When wire-line jigging over structure in smooth water, many of the same principles hold true. Although there isn't a defined rip to position your lures over, it's equally important to understand how bass and blues will be ambushing their prey. Use your fishfinder and look for structure such as drop-offs, rises and boulders. Stripers and blues will be holding close to the bottom, looking for baitfish trying to take advantage of the relief from the current offered by the structure. Careful timing in when to drop your lures is a skill that will yield more fish.

Sometimes jigging with wire just isn't practical, whether it's due to strong tidal conditions, fish holding too deep or lack of interest with wire, and vertical jigging can save the day. Though New England cod fishermen are quite familiar with vertical jigging, it's an underutilized technique for striped bass and bluefish. It's easy and can be done both at anchor and while drifting, and it doesn't require as specialized an outfit as is required for wire-line jigging. For the most part, any outfit that can handle the weight of the jig will suffice, even a heavy-action spinning rod and reel.

Vertical jigging requires somewhat different mechanics than trolling. Considering that the jig will be directly below you rather than behind the boat, the technique will consist of up

The next time you encounter small fish working under the birds, try tying on a jig and casting upcurrent of the breaking fish. Allow the jig to sink and work it along the bottom, where oftentimes there will be larger fish feeding on the scraps that the smaller fish create.

and down motions as opposed to the back to front motions of trolling. Again, the most common mistake made here is to sweep too far with the rod. A foot or two is all that is needed. Shorter snaps will make your jig look more like what you are imitating on the bottom. An effective modification of this technique is to let your jig go all the way down to the bottom, only to reel back up very quickly. This works particularly well on finicky bluefish. However, if you suspect bass are in the area, try the same technique, but reel more slowly.

If you are marking fish on your fishfinder, begin jigging just below their estimated depth. If there are no takers, reel in a few feet of line and repeat. Continue this exercise until you feel that you are no longer in the strike zone. Sometimes by adding a teaser you can greatly increase your score. It is very important to pay careful attention to each bump. Both bass and blues will hit a jig on the drop, but this is harder to detect than when you're trolling because your line will not become taut as quickly. Using a braided line will allow you to feel more bumps, especially when used in conjunction with a high modulus, fast-action graphite rod. If you're in an area with a lot of snags, reel in a crank or two as soon as you hit bottom to cut down on lost terminal tackle.

In an area where anchoring is impractical, repeated drifts may be necessary. Run up-tide far enough to allow sufficient time for your jig to drop into the strike zone as you pass over the fish. Drifting while vertical jigging is also an excellent way to cover a lot of ground. This is a useful technique if the fish are holding in a general area rather than over one particular spot.

If you come upon a school of breaking fish, vertical jigging can result in hooking the larger fish that are almost always positioned under the school. Pay attention to the direction that the school is moving and motor ahead of them. Though tempting sometimes, avoid chasing down the school, as this will only put down the fish and disperse the school. By sending your jigs down quickly, you improve your chances at bigger fish.

Casting a jig is an excellent light-tackle technique, especially when targeting fish holding near the bottom or on structure. Not only will the jig's weight help you achieve superior casting distance, but also you can fish at all levels of the water column by varying your reel speed. A fast-action rod that is stiff all the way to the tip works best. A softer rod will require more movement in your technique, as you will be compensating for the flex in the rod. A stiffer rod will also help you set the hook more effectively. Both conventional and spinning rods work well.

Casting jigs suit pretty much any fishing situation you can think of, ranging from the flats to working a rip. To fish a casting jig most effectively, let your jig sink to the bottom or desired depth. After taking all the slack out of your line, give your rod a snap. A motion of only a foot or so is necessary. As your jig begins to sink in-between strokes, crank in a few turns to give it some forward motion, repeating until it's time to make another cast. When casting on a rip, or any area with strong currents, cast upcurrent allowing your jig to sink as the current delivers it to your target. I've seen many large fish taken using this method, especially when bucktails are bounced over the edge of a rip.

Whether you are a light-tackle enthusiast or a fan of heavy conventional gear, jigging is a technique worth mastering. Don't forget to be creative. Jigging forces you to zero in on the fish, and when you master the different techniques, you will have the satisfaction of knowing you're fishing, rather than just dragging a lure through the water.

Bring The Excitement Back To Trolling
Give Light Tackle A Try

By Fred Khedouri

When I joined the ranks of boaters after fishing from shore for 30 years, I spent many hours exploring the range of techniques offered by my new means of access to the water. It soon became clear that for day-in-day-out results without the trouble or expense of bait, trolling was the way to go. That is how all of the successful inshore charter captains on my home waters off Martha's Vineyard fish most of the time when seeking striped bass and bluefish, and I soon followed their example.

Although my credit card was still smoldering from the steady stream of fuel and yard bills that are also a big part of boat ownership, my rod collection needed to expand. My first trolling setups were very typical of what you see all along the New England coast: sturdy 7-foot rods, moderately-sized Shimano TLD reels loaded with 30- or 40-pound-test monofilament line, or narrow Penn 49Ls filled with monel wire for deep-water trolling. I began to accumulate large and heavy lures, 4-ounce bucktails and spoons, 36-inch surgical tubes in various colors, umbrella rigs and large diving plugs.

This stuff worked well and easily handled the 6- to 10-pound bluefish and 30- to 40-inch stripers that we see most often at boatside. But I missed the excitement of the lighter tackle I used to cast from shore.

Taking a 10-pound bluefish on a surf-casting rod with a spinning reel and 12- or 15-pound-test line is great fun – and the fish wins a fair amount of the time. A 40-pound-class trolling outfit makes short work of a fish of that size. These nice-size fish are even more overmatched by stiff wire-line outfits. Of course, the traditional heavy trolling setup is quite sporting when a big one shows up – a 48-inch bass headed for the rocks takes a lot of persuading – but it seemed that some experimentation was in order or my light-tackle fishing would be limited to days when I found the fish feeding on top within casting range.

Over the past 10 years, I have tried a wide variety of equipment and techniques for using light tackle for inshore trolling. With the right combination of line, lure and trolling speed, some remarkably large bass and bluefish can be taken this way. Two years ago at the peak of our May run of migrating bass, I was bumping a 1-ounce white bucktail with a soft plastic sand-worm trailer off the bottom in 35 feet of water just west of Wasque Point. A fish picked it up and ran off at a moderate pace, barely noticing at first the resistance from my light rig with the drag set at 4 pounds. After 20 minutes of coaxing, I reclaimed 200 yards of line and a monster bass came into view (they do always look bigger through a few feet of water). The Boga Grip bottomed out past the 30-pound mark as I lifted the fish aboard. After quickly measuring the bass and removing the hook, I slid the fat 44-incher back in the water, moved it back and forth for a few minutes while it regained its strength, and watched it swim away.

There are still many times when standard trolling gear belongs in the rod holders. If the seas are rough and the wind is blowing, the added stress imparted by a bouncing boat makes heavier tackle mandatory. On the hottest days of summer, getting down very deep may be the way to find fish. Wire line and heavy lures are the only approach to reach the necessary depths of 40 feet or more. And then there are those mornings when I am fishing to earn my keep and use standard tackle to reduce the risk of losing the striped bass my wife expects to serve our dinner guests that evening. But on pleasant days in the late spring and early fall, after you've caught and kept what you need for the table, breaking out the light rigs can add a new measure of challenge and excitement. Here's how to get started.

A 6 1/2- or 7-foot casting or spinning rod with a long handle built on a glass or graphite blank rated for 15- to 25-pound-test line is the basis for the outfit. The most important quality to look for in a light trolling rod is that it have a "fast taper" so it doesn't get too loaded up and bend double just from dragging a lure through the water. Stay away from the heavy freshwater-style rods used for muskie and similar large species, however, as you will quickly find the guides and rod seats corrode. Most of the large rod manufacturers produce one or two models that will work well at the lightest end of their ranges of trolling-style rods. You are not too likely to find one at even a well-stocked tackle store in New England (these are normally considered "West Coast action" rods), but perusing manufacturers' catalogs will unearth what you need and most shops will gladly order one for you. Two good examples of this type of conventional rod are the St. Croix "Premier Saltwater" SWC70MF and the G. Loomis SWR84-16C. Spinning rods with similar line ratings are also a good choice. The choices are broader with spinning tackle because many of the shorter, lighter rods intended for surf or jetty casting will do just fine.

Scaling down your tackle will bring some excitement back to trolling for stripers.

My favorite conventional reels are non-level-wind casting models such as the Penn 975CS and the Shimano Calcutta 700S. Both are relatively compact and light, have fast retrieves, smooth drags, and will stand up to saltwater exposure. For those with an irresistible attraction to fine machinery and a sturdy credit card, the Accurate Boss B870 or B665H also make good choices. Almost any of the traditional trolling reels (assuming they balance well with your rod) can be put to use for light-tackle trolling since it is really the line that matters. The smaller reels will be a better match for the lighter rods, but larger conventional reels can be used in a pinch by spooling them first with heavy monofilament backing to take up space and avoid having to fill your reel with 2,000 yards of light line. With spinning reels, there are even more choices since just about any of the heavier reels with substantial line capacity will work. Good examples would be the Penn 704Z or 710Z reels, which are time-tested, simple, sturdy and not too heavy.

The choice of line is critical. Too much stretch and too large a diameter will compromise your ability to control the depth at which you are trolling. The new lower-stretch mono lines such as Yo-Zuri Hybrid in 15-pound test are a good choice. Technology has given a

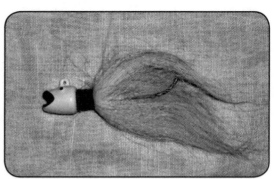

When the fish are holding a little deeper, my lure of choice is the bucktail, usually in the 1- or 2-ounce sizes.

big boost to light-tackle trolling with the widespread availability of ultrathin braided lines such as PowerPro. I have switched all my light outfits over to this type of line because it has virtually no stretch, even in very light weights, and because it is so thin that it creates almost no lift moving through the water. It also makes it possible to get a solid 300 yards of line on even the small bait casting and spinning reels, which is a good minimum. I use the 20- and 30-pound-test PowerPro, putting the lighter line on the spinning reels and the smallest bait-casting reels. These are roughly equivalent in diameter to 6- and 8-pound-test mono lines, respectively. Bear in mind that even though you might have a nominal 30-pound-test strength line, your drag should be set as though you had a conventional mono line of 12- or 15-pound test or you will risk damaging your rod and reel. The two biggest problems with this type of line are learning which knots work best (use the manufacturer's guidance) and the danger its thinness poses when mishandled – it can slice deeply into a finger in a split second when under tension. For this reason it's not a bad idea to bring along gloves like the hard-core offshore crowd.

The light-tackle alternative to wire is to put about 20 or 30 yards of 27-pound-test leadcore line onto a backing of PowerPro. Under the right conditions, this combination can get down to 35 or even 40 feet at slow trolling speeds.

A 6-foot fluorocarbon leader of 30- to 40-pound test with a good swivel (the tiny SPRO swivels are a good match) provides a bit of needed stretch and a stealthy approach. It also gives you something to grab when the fish is near the boat so you won't get cut by the ultra-thin braid. When bluefish are a likely target, get yourself some of the coated steel wire that fly-fishermen use for wire tippets. It is light and flexible and has sufficient resistance to teeth to prevent cut-offs. A 12-inch length tied to the fluorocarbon is usually enough.

In the early season when the fish can often be found within 15 feet of the surface or when trolling the edges of a school of breaking fish, I use the medium-size versions of Rapala diving plugs, Tony Aceta spoons, Deadly Dicks, and other lures that would often be used for casting with tackle of this weight. When greater depth is required, the lure of choice is the bucktail, usually in the 1- or 2-ounce sizes; 2 ounces is about the maximum the rods can handle. A 12- or 18-inch version of a surgical tube eel is good to have on hand, as well. If you're not inclined to go through the hassle and expense of procuring sea worms, a strip of red or green pork rind trailer on the lure will often make the difference. It's also a good idea to have on hand some of those somewhat malodorous soft plastic Berkley Sand Worms, preferably in the darker colors, for use as trailers.

To make light tackle work effectively while trolling, be sure to run slowly. You will find that these setups are much more sensitive to speed changes than the traditional heavier line and lures, so dropping your speed by half a knot often makes the difference between being in the feeding zone or being above it. When targeting bass, I usually let out about twice the water depth in line, with the boat just barely moving, until I feel the lure bouncing off the bottom. The no-stretch line makes it very easy to feel the bounce. Then accelerate to a speed of 2.5 or 3 knots, let out enough line to feel bottom again, and then reel in a few feet so you won't get hung up.

When using the PowerPro, it is very important not to get too aggressive in attempting to set the hook when you have a strike. Just pick up the rod and take up the slack quickly, applying steady pressure. Multiple hookups are usually a formula for chaos with light tackle because there is often much more line out while fighting the fish and thus more opportunity for tangled lines. Clear the deck of other lines in the water right away. It is usually necessary to put the boat in neutral and drift to avoid having the fish take an excessive amount of line given the light drag settings.

Some of my favorite targets are the large schools of bluefish that park themselves in the lee of Nomans Land from time to time. An 8- or 10-pounder is a real handful on one of these outfits. Their powerful last-ditch runs when they see the boat have had me doing laps around the console trying to keep the line clear. This is also the time when the track map on your GPS can really come into its own as a tool. Circling back and following the precisely same track at the same speed with the same amount of line out will almost always produce another fish.

Light-tackle trolling does have its limits. I carried the experiment a bit too far one day while pursuing yellowfin tuna out at "The Dump" southwest of Martha's Vineyard. Not much was happening, so I put a small cedar plug on my favorite 15-pound-class outfit and dropped it back in the spread among the lures rigged on 50-pound-class offshore trolling rods, thinking we might run across some dolphin (mahi-mahi) near the offshore lobster pot high flyers. Not long afterward, we saw a couple of petrels. Seconds later, we heard the pop of an outrigger clip and the sound of a screaming reel being emptied much faster than usual by what must have been a sizable tuna (my crew have probably turned it into a giant bluefin by now). With four other lines still in the water, we could not even think about backing down on the fish for several minutes. I exercised my captain's prerogative and picked up the rod. Sun glinted off the reel arbor's now very thin layer of line, and I took up the battle in earnest. I lost the fish a few seconds later when the last of the line disappeared and snapped. I've saved the light trolling outfits for stripers and blues ever since.

Win A Tournament
Use Bunker Spoons

By Leo Bedard

Captain Bob Joyce once told me, "When you're trolling bunker spoons, you're not fishing, you're hunting." That's exactly how I feel when trolling two lines, both rods pulsating, covering Cape Cod Bay at 4.3 miles per hour. It's more like hunting than fishing.

It was an unexpected early arrival for stripers in Cape Cod Bay this year. Generally the big ones don't show up until a week or so after the annual Cape Cod Canal Area Striper Tournament. This year, two weeks before the contest, the water temperature in Cape Cod Bay was approaching the striper comfort-zone levels.

I checked my 2001 journal entries and found that my striper season began on May 28 with a 40-pounder. This year my season started on May 4 with two at 12 pounds, one on May 11 weighing 15 pounds, three of keeper size from Barnstable Hharbor on the twelfth of May and a 38-pound fish off Barnstable on May 19.

I knew that this could be the year for the winner of the tournament to come from Cape Cod Bay, and I could hardly wait for it to begin.

My favorite spot this time of year is just a couple of miles outside Barnstable Harbor. What brings the stripers to this remote area with a relatively unstructured bottom are scallops. Scallop beds dot the area, as well as the eelgrass that attracts them, and baitfish. Although I've never recognized a scallop in a striper's stomach, I've found remnants of species of fish that are attracted to the scallops in those stomachs.

The author with a 40-pound striper taken on a bunker spoon.

My fishfinder marks neither scallops nor eelgrass in 6 feet of water, never mind 65 feet, where the beds are located. I just look for the draggers. Scalloping has been lucrative enough that some commercial fishermen stick with it through most of the summer season. In late summer some will re-rig their boats for other species, but you can pretty much count on finding at least one of them in this part of the bay on any given day.

As an added bonus, you may find one crew shucking their catch as they're dragging, which creates a chum slick that helps attract the stripers. Later in the summer, draggers are working deeper water looking for sea clams. This, too, has a tendency to attract the attention of big stripers.

Other species are attracted to these scallop beds. During the week of the tournament, I had a hit on one of the two bunker spoons we were trolling. As I was pulling that striper in, the other line sank to the bottom and was hit by a nice-size sea bass. That proves to me that bunker spoons continue to "hunt" even when the boat stops.

Bunker spoons are not usually used in Cape Cod Bay until after the mackerel leave. It seems suicidal, but mackerel will hit bunker spoons. Whenever you hear the complaint on your VHF radio, "What do these things think they're hitting?" you know that some fisherman has reeled in a lot of leadcore or wire, only to find a 10-inch mackerel on a 10-inch by 4-inch metal spoon.

What makes matters worse is that this always seems to happen when you're directly over that spot where you hooked up with a big striper yesterday or last week on this tide, and valuable time is wasted. Stopping the boat means no fishing is going on, so someone gets the task of pulling in a mackerel (that could be foul-hooked) while the boat is moving 4 to 4.5 miles per hour. Getting to the optimum depth in 65 feet of water requires 300 feet of wire, or leadcore let out to the backing. That's a lot of line to be pulled in under those circumstances. The manufacturer recommends that these lures be fished two-thirds of the distance to the bottom. And leadcore doesn't get you back down there as well as wire.

To avoid mackerel, a color change is sometimes helpful. Bunker spoons come in many colors. Silver, white and green are favored in Cape Cod Bay. Mackerel tend not to hit the green. I generally fish a different color from each side of the boat to increase my chances of a hookup. Once I've seen what works, I'll switch to that color on both sides to maximize my chances.

Rod holders that hold the rods perpendicular to the sides of the boat have proven to be invaluable pieces of equipment when fishing bunker spoons. I'm familiar with two companies: Reliable Rod Holders and Out-Rodders. They spread the lines another 10 or 12 feet because the rods are facing out and not toward the back of the boat. They also enable you to cover more territory. The spoons will draw fish from 10 to 20 feet away with their flash and erratic movement, and these rod holders spread that distance out so that you're hunting an area over 25 feet from either side of the boat.

These lures work well with wire line, but personally, I've had such good luck with leadcore that it hasn't been worth the hassle to switch to wire. I generally fish alone with two rods out, and when a fish hits on one rod, you can't let the other drop to the bottom if it's spooled with wire. The loss of a $30 lure that's caught on the bottom is small compared to the damage wire can cause to a lower unit should the boat spin in windy conditions. Another thing that is more likely to happen is that a fish being brought up will tangle in the stainless, causing a kink that turns your wire into a long thin piece of scrap metal. If I consistently fished with seasoned fishermen, I would probably switch to wire to take advantage of the 10-foot drop for every 100 feet of line that's out.

I rig my rods with 50-pound-test monofilament leaders and a 75-pound-test snap swivel.

The leader should be 10 to 12 feet long. The weight (keel) on a bunker spoon is adjustable and should be moved as far forward as possible for additional depth.

I know I have the right combination of balance and boat speed when my somewhat flexible boat rods are pulsating a distance of 3-inches at the tip with a constant 4-inch arch in the rod. Bass won't hit a spoon that's spinning. The rods should flex to a definite rhythm, a cadence that can actually be counted out. The "wounded fish" exerts a powerful pull and then an immediate release. When that beat is broken, say, with shorter, more rapid pulses, you've either picked up sea-weed or the speed of the boat has caused the lure to spin. Many times, though not always, seaweed will cause the bunker spoon to come to the surface. Monitoring the beat is critical, as is watching the water to be sure the lure hasn't surfaced.

Congratulations from officials with the Chamber of Commerce looking on.

We small-boat fishermen had two things working against us this year during the Canal Area Tournament: wind and work. The weekends, which were the only time many of us could fish, were windy or rainy. There were days when a 20-foot boat should have stayed on the trailer. The last day of the tournament was no excep-tion. Sunday had 25-knot winds out of the south, and my boat, *Fishfull Thinking*, was getting knocked around. Three miles off Sandy Neck beach in that wind, you're no longer in the lee of Cape Cod, you're in a fetch.

Persistence paid off. I knew I was into a big fish from the time it hit and made that reel scream. There was never a point that I wasn't confident I would boat that fish – it fought all the way and never tired. Finally, after a major struggle at the side of the boat, that striper was lifted over the gunwale.

Looking at it on the deck, it was even bigger than I had imagined. The excitement started all over again when I took out my scale and realized that I could possibly have a thousand-dollar fish in the boat. High-fives weren't enough. Watching my son and me carry on at that point was like watching a basketball team when a tie-breaking 3-pointer goes in at the buzzer. What an experience!

I've been striper fishing for 12 years. I've found that you never lose the exhilaration that you feel when you hook up and boat a large striper. This feeling was compounded by the fact that it all took place with my son looking on.

The weigh-in begins at 2 p.m. in the Canal Area Striper Tournament. The time that passed from when the fish was caught had to be the longest seven hours of my life. A look at the message board told me that the leader, Dean Lenling of Westport, at 43.25 pounds, was almost five pounds less than my fish weighed on the boat. On Thursday he had knocked out Jim Beneditto (42.75 pounds), another Sandwich resident who fishes Cape Cod Bay.

Numbers were given out to establish the sequence we would be called for weighing. I didn't have the heart to take my fish out of my Explorer. Contestants were proudly standing over, or holding, their stripers. Every fish there was a truly awesome catch.

I couldn't hold off any longer. My number was called and I carried the fish into the crowd. Every person there turned and gave their full attention to that striper. Forty-seven pounds, 50 inches long, and a girth of 28 inches were the measurements.

If you've never participated in this tournament, you're missing out on a real opportunity. Over 600 contestants compete for over $20,000 in prizes, and the daily prizes alone make it a worthwhile experience. There are divisions for men, women and youth in both shore and boat divisions. The cookout at the end of the tournament is a veritable "Who's Who," with some of the best shore and boat striper fishermen from on and off Cape Cod. It's a great opportunity to talk about the one that got away or, in this case, the one that didn't. ◄█

Fishing The Tube And Worm

By Captain Charley Soares

Every year it seems that someone introduces a new lure, or at least a variation of something that has been around for a while but either went out of production or fell from favor. Some of these contemporary lures are the result of the research of ingenious anglers experimenting and altering the action. Some are the work of a tackle company resurrecting an old favorite in a dozen new colors and sizes. Fishermen are lure collectors. It's a character flaw as obvious as our tendency to embellish the accounts and descriptions of our forays into the salt. This scribe is not being critical of these aberrations because I'm also swayed by these same tendencies, owning a collection of tackle and lures that would rival the inventory of many a small tackle shop. The aforementioned statement is not a boast but an admission of guilt.

Despite owning all this proven fish-catching tackle, if I had to catch a legal bass between the hours of sunrise and sunset, I'd choose a very simple rig, one that has experienced such an enormous growth in popularity and productivity over the past 25 years that it could be listed as a universal favorite. You could fuel the fishing fleet for the entire season with the energy generated by the debate on just what constitutes the best overall striped bass baits. For the purpose of this discussion I'd like to interject that it is not always the "best" baits that become the most productive, so I'm obliged to provide some insight into my reasoning.

Few knowledgeable anglers would argue against the popularity and fish-producing qualities of the menhaden or pogy, as we New Englanders refer to the oily forage fish that is currently in very short supply. Last season bunker was right at the top of the most-wanted list, followed closely by the live eel. The downside of these two baits is their variable availability and the difficulty for the average angler to capture and maintain them. A school of live pogies in some waterways generates almost as much interest as a school of bass or blues, and

Eddie Savje admires the only keeper of the day. It was caught on a straight tube and worm on a clear, calm, high-pressure August day when several other boaters from the same harbor fished pogies and didn't score a single fish. Never underestimate the power of a sea worm!

not everyone has a deep-water slip or dock where they can hide a supply of live eels during the heat of the summer. Although I seldom use pogies in any form, I'd never give up my live eels. Those serpents I potted over the years have paid for tackle, fuel and schoolbooks, and accounted for numerous bass up to 60 pounds. The live eel is still one of my favorite baits, but with that said, let me tell you about the most natural and readily available bait that accounts for well over 50 percent of all the bass, blues and weakfish we catch in a season, which stretches from April to late November.

The sea or sand worm might not be the most appealing of baits, but when I was a boy it was the staple of the winter flounder, scup, tautog, white perch and just about every other species that inhabits the salt water. For the privilege of rowing the old-timers along the rocky beaches of the rivers and bays, I learned an awful lot about the fish-producing appeal of the sand worm. Using Cape Cod or Niantic Bay spinners, we trolled quietly along the shoreline, hooking bass, scup and the occasional tautog on the tandem-worm rigs the old-timers attached to the tarred handlines, which were the workingman's choice of the day. We seldom accounted for any stripers larger than 10 or 12 pounds because their tackle and methods were no match for larger fish. Without the aid of a slip drag and the soft action of a forgiving rod, the big fish, and there were quite a few, tore off or broke the soft handlines. The trollers who used the old, stiff bamboo boat rods with the Ocean City or Penn reels did not fare much better.

The successful technique and results of these experiences were not lost on an inquisitive youngster who had plans of his own. Putting lively sea worms down where the stripers lived produced bass. Some of the haunts where the stripers were harvested were near my worm-harvesting grounds, so the broken worms the hardware dealer would not purchase from me were attached to a handline and cast out towards the channel. Other fishermen were using quahogs, steamer clams, squid and other strip baits, which were never quite as effective as the sea worms. These same stripers had been feeding on worms since their earliest migrations into these rivers, when they anticipated them engaged in feeding on the various worm spawns.

Some of the largest bass I've hooked and lost were tempted by the pervasive sea worm strung naturally on a single hook. At the time, we were fishing from an anchored boat, although I've achieved the same results fishing from the banks of a tidal river. Small 2/0 offset hooks were snelled directly to the 20-pound-test running line with little or no weight required until the current began to move, at which time we added pinch-on or rubbercore sinkers of the appropriate weight to keep the worms down in the striper's pantry.

The system was flawless whenever tide and fish combined, but for fish that held along rocky shorelines and other natural and man-made structure, trolling was the ticket. The Cape Cod spinners or blades and beads the old-timers fashioned worked in the rivers and bays, but the bigger fish I tended to hook along the oceanfront trashed the lures and broke us off more often than I care to relate. From my youthful experiences to this very day, I've learned that the sea worm was and still is one of the most natural and productive of all saltwater baits, and when presented properly, one that a trophy striper will seldom ignore. Here is just one last anecdote for anyone who might still harbor reservations about the importance of sea worms and natural presentations.

A few years ago I was hired to escort and assist a woman on a charter boat who was fishing in a contest. I didn't know the captain or the boat, but when I got a look at the condition and type of his tackle I was appalled, and walked back to my truck to fetch my rods and a container of sea worms. When we arrived at the rip, the skipper put out two beat-up 36-inch tubes with a very small piece of Berkley Power Worm attached to the hook. We trolled for an hour or so and caught a few small bluefish while boats around us jigging parachutes on wire were catching school bass in the 4- to 6-pound class.

I asked permission to try my rods and tubes with the sea worms and he said he didn't care what I did as he glanced at his watch, contemplating just how much longer before he could rid himself of these greenhorns. I put both wire-line outfits with small tubes and juicy sea worms astern and stuck them in the rod holders. We completed our first pass and when the boat turned, our tubes dropped deeper into the water column and both rods bent over. A few minutes later two stripers were being netted. We went on to catch 8 bass to 18 pounds and two small blues before the captain called it a trip. While we didn't win the contest, we ended up with more bass than did any of the other boaters who trolled large tubes with tiny pieces of plastic worms.

When a friend showed me some of the first tubes to show up in our area from Jersey, they were crude plastic rigs compared to today's models. But they presented the worms and held up to the abuse and punishment a big fish dished out when it tried to scrape the hook from its jaw. After some 30 years of numerous trials, experimenting and adjusting, I've come up with the tubes I employ today. You can purchase or make tubes of any shape, size or materials you desire, and if you have something that works for you, by all means continue to use it. The following is my description of a rig and methodology that has proven extremely successful for me, my friends and associates over the decades. At this juncture if you are not convinced of the prowess of the sea worm, I suggest you put the magazine down and begin building a holding car for pogies and eels.

Having witnessed just about everything from a stainless steel partial denture (courtesy of my dentist friend, Doc Riley) to numerous other wacky lures catch fish, nothing that has fooled a bass or bluefish would surprise me. With that said, it's obvious most of us are not interested in feats of extraordinary proportions; we just want to catch fish, big fish if they are in residence. But still some anglers feel it's necessary to apply or add something to the tube and worm to make it work. I don't believe that is necessary and hold to the KISS (keep it simple, stupid) rule, which I believe applies here. I know you've seen and probably fished tubes that gyrated and corkscrewed through the water and caught fish. If I've learned anything about fishing, it's

Hook the worms so that they flow from the hook naturally. Stick the barb an inch or so below the pinchers and thread the worm on so that the point of the barb comes out of the mouth. This will allow the worm to trail the tube naturally and not cause it to spin or twist.

to endeavor to keep my presentations, regardless of what type of lures or baits I'm using, as natural as possible. Unlike most wooden, metal or plastic lures that require some form of convincing "action" to imitate a wounded baitfish, the sea worm requires none.

My tubes are the conveyance that transport the most important part of this unique combo, the sea worm. I don't need or want to impart anything other than the natural movement of the sea worm as they swim through the water column. It's not necessary to twist, curl or distort the tube, because a worm does not roll or gyrate as it moves naturally through its element. Humor me and take a fresh sea worm and place it in the shallows or a white bucket of salt water. Observe the worm as its multi-segmented legs wriggle slowly and naturally in an almost straight line. My method presents the tempting worm in its most typical form. Certainly there are stripers and blues caught on all form and manner of tubes, but few if any of them account for wary 53-inch bass or fish in the 50-pound class in shallow water under bright daylight conditions. If you are catching 50-pound bass with a corkscrew or gyrating worm in the near-shore shallows, I'd love to present my tubes alongside you to that same class of fish.

This is not a condemnation of big, active tubes, quite the contrary. Over the years, in numerous experiments, I've fished large tubes in deep water and rips with great success. In those instances I required a larger, heavier lure to pull the stiff wire line from the reels. Do they work? They certainly do; just ask the charter specialists who account for large specimens of stripers with the heavier lures. I've made a long and detailed comparison of the thick and heavy, 24- to 36-inch tubes alongside my short, straight, soft tubes in the shallow near-shore coastal waters that I fish, and the smaller version outperformed the radiator hoses by a wide margin. These were not unsupported conclusions arrived at after a few random trials, but unbiased tests conducted over a period of several years. I can honestly report that I've never had a complaint from a deck mate who just landed a husky 30- or 40-pound bass about the lack of size and action of my little tubes.

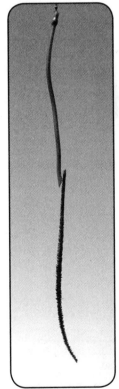

Most fishermen experiment to try something different out of boredom when the fish aren't in a feeding mode. The best time to conduct experiments is when the fish are eating; otherwise, you are just wasting your time. For experimentation purposes I've used a tube with two hooks. One hook is located at the customary location at the rear and the other affixed to the barrel swivel at the head to determine the primary purpose of the tube. We baited the rear hook and trolled through the structure where the fish were holding and caught three bass from 5 to 8 pounds on the rear, baited hook.

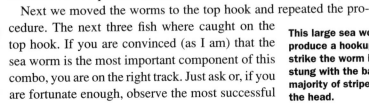

Next we moved the worms to the top hook and repeated the procedure. The next three fish where caught on the top hook. If you are convinced (as I am) that the sea worm is the most important component of this combo, you are on the right track. Just ask or, if you are fortunate enough, observe the most successful **This large sea worm is not too long to produce a hookup. Large stripers will strike the worm in the head, getting stung with the barb of the hook. The vast majority of stripers attack their prey at the head.**

live-eel and menhaden fishermen you can find, and if they are honest, they'll admit they are successful because they present their offerings in their most natural forms.

You don't have to own any expensive tackle to fish the tube and worm efficiently. Many conventional boat rods of 6 or 7 feet in length with a 4/0-size reel will get the job done. However, over the years my tackle has become quite specialized. I utilize a custom 6-foot conventional rod with a moderate to slow action that has Hi-Alloy guides and a size 16 tip-top. A Fuji reel seat and Hypalon grips with a gimbal butt complete this very efficient package. The rod is light for all-day use, forgiving when a big fish makes a strong surge, yet strong enough to beat any trophy striper and get it boatside without the angler having to walk to the opposite side of the boat. If ever a reel was designed or best suited for this duty, it's the Penn 330 GTI. It is strong, lightweight and has a great drag, and the level wind makes it perfect for expert and novice alike to retrieve line evenly in the excitement of battling a large striper. This is what I consider to be the best outfit for fishing the leadcore line I employ for fishing depths up to 30 feet in coastal shoreline situations.

If you are fishing rips, you will need a wire-line rod with carbaloy guides and a reel similar to the popular Penn 113H (4/0) reel filled with 40- or 50-pound-test stainless or monel wire. This will get the tubes down to the proper depths in the fast-moving water.

On my leadline rods we start out with 150 to 200 feet of quality 50-pound-test monofilament backing, which is connected to 5 colors (each color is 10 yards, or 30 feet) of 36-pound-test leadline via a bead-chain connector or small 50-pound-class barrel swivel. At the business end of the leadline I attach a 15-foot length of 50-pound-test leader material to which the tube is tied directly without any snaps or hardware. Don't confuse leader material with monofilament line because they are designed for different purposes. Mono line is manufactured with characteristics that make it suitable for numerous applications, including casting. The leader material is stiff and usually more abrasion resistant and permits the lure to fish more naturally. In many instances the leader material has made the difference between hooking and landing large aggressive stripers.

My tubes are constructed using a 16- to 18-inch length of soft latex or vinyl tubing, dyed a dark red or maroon. Using liquid laundry detergent as a lubricant, I insert an egg sinker from 1/2 to 1 ounce in weight in the forward end of the tube, pushing it about 1/2 inch past the opening. I then insert a length of twisted stainless trolling wire or 174-pound-test solid Sevenstrand wire through the opening and sinker to extend about 10 inches from the bottom of the tube, which is cut on a 45- to 60-degree angle. A quality 6/0 hook (Mustad hooks are fine, but I usually use a Tru-turn) is twisted onto the wire, then pulled back until the hook is snug up against the tubing. I cut the wire about 4 to 5 inches longer than the tube, then pull on the hook and bend on a 3/0 Rosco barrel swivel. The pulling action allows half of the barrel to fit inside the space between the egg sinker and the top of the tube. If that sounds like a lot of work, I can assure you it's not, and the effort will pay big dividends during the season.

Fishing a tube and worm is one of the easiest techniques you'll ever use. However, every boat and engine combination has different characteristics, so it is not possible for me to recommend a specific speed or r.p.m. for your boat that will put your lure at the optimum depth. Each skipper has to determine their own progress through the water using his or her GPS, loran or a reliable knot meter. Years ago the same fishermen who looked askance when

I suggested that trolling for bass at speeds over 3 knots would not tempt trophy fish have become believers. By keeping it slow and low down in the strike zone, you will be much more successful. Use the wind, tide, trim tabs, trolling valves or other devices to slow you down, including your second (trolling) engine, along with judicious use of the gear shift lever. Keep the rod in your hand to feel the nuances and strikes of bottom fish that might attack the worm. It's a misfortune if you've finally located the habitat of the largest striper in the area, then drag a barren tube or one covered with weed or grass by its nose, because it won't eat it.

You can't feel or see what's happening if the rod is stuck in the rod holder. With the rod in hand you must avoid the temptation to set the hook. If it's a legal bass, you won't have to set the hook; the fish will do it for you. Setting the hook prematurely usually results in the worm breaking away from the hook and the bass turning off because now it has the bait and you have a barren tube. Bottom fishermen initially have difficulty with this aspect of the game but eventually make the necessary adjustments. Only as a last resort, when I have a problem with someone who just can't resist setting the hook, I have them place the rod in the holder and instruct them to watch the tip. Large bass attack the worm right at the head and get stung by the hook, while smaller fish and blues begin biting from the tail end of the worm until they get to the barbed end.

Are you content to sit and wait for a bass or bluefish to find your chunk of bait, or are you the type of angler who enjoys hunting bass and making things happen? One of the most productive means of catching fish is to anchor over known habitat and chum and chunk. When fish are in residence they follow the chum to the baited hooks and swallow them. This method of fishing does not require a great deal of knowledge or experience, although the most experienced anglers obtain the best results. It's obvious that the fisherman who is accomplished in numerous disciplines is better suited to cope with the ever-changing situations we encounter in the salt water.

It is, however, easy to become complacent when we stop thinking and experimenting and fall into a rut. "Troll" might be a five-letter word that spells boring to the uninitiated, but if there is a more productive and interesting way to locate fish along a coastal shoreline, I'm not aware of it. While trolling, you learn to read the water, become intimately familiar with your surroundings and learn to recognize consistently productive striped bass habitat. An old-timer once told me that if you don't have faith in what you're doing, you won't do it well. I apply that theory to everything I attempt, particularly fishing, and it has paid tremendous dividends.

Thread a large, lively sea worm onto your tube and troll it low and slow into productive striped bass habitat. If you invest the time to master this technique, it won't be long before you are fishing these lures properly and catching more fish than you ever thought possible under a bright midday sun. Give the tube a fair trial and you'll become yet another disciple of the deadly combo.

The Versatile Cedar Plug

By Bill Brett

A cedar plug, sometimes called a cedar jig, is a simple lure that has been used for more than a century to fool offshore gamefish.

Cedar plugs are popular with tuna fishermen, who troll these wood-and-metal lures at speeds of 6 to 10 knots to attract school bluefin, yellowfin, albacore, skipjack and other tuna species. With a little modification, this age-old lure can also be used to fool inshore gamefish, such as striped bass and bluefish.

Cedar plugs are handmade using wooden cedar dowels and ordinary lead. No two plugs are exactly the same. Making a quality plug requires a considerable amount of labor and hand-finishing, but in spite of this, these lures sell for very modest prices. Unrigged cedar plugs retail for about $4, while the same plugs, painted and fitted with a large saltwater hook, sell for $6 to $10 dollars, depending on size and finish.

There are a few reasons why cedar plugs make good striped bass and bluefish lures. Cedar plugs are unbalanced, with all of the weight concentrated in the front tip of the lure. This causes the plug to descend when line tension is reduced and rise toward the surface when line tension is increased. A forward or backward sweep of a fishing rod is all it takes to make a trolled cedar plug swim like a wounded baitfish. In addition, these lures may appear symmetrical, but they are not machine-made with a high degree of precision. Rather, most cedar plugs are slightly off-center. This minor imperfection translates into a subtle wobble when these plugs are trolled or cast and retrieved. This side-to-side swimming motion becomes more pronounced as the speed of the lure is increased.

I discovered cedar plugs several years ago while browsing the aisles of a Green Harbor tackle shop that caters to the bluefin tuna fishery. Hanging on the wall of this shop were some unrigged cedar plugs that looked like miniature torpedoes. These 5-inch lure bodies weighed 2 1/2 ounces and were heavy enough for ocean surf casting and trolling. I purchased several of these plugs and planned to convert them into striped bass and bluefish lures. Three years later these cedar bodies were still sitting on a shelf in my basement, reminding me of my habit of impulse buying.

These plugs remained in their original packages until one snowy day last winter. I was drilling and wiring wooden casting weight/floats when it occurred to me that a cedar plug could be through-wired in the same manner. The lead tip of a cedar plug is pre-drilled lengthwise along its centerline to allow 130-pound-test monofilament line to pass through the metal portion of the lure. Plug makers also bore a larger hole lengthwise through the wooden portion of the lure in order to allow the shank of an 8/0 or 9/0 needle-eye hook to slide up inside the cedar body of the lure. If I increased the diameter of the hole through the lead tip, I would be able to pass a length of wire through the entire plug, form a wire loop on each end and attach a hook to the rear loop.

The lead portion of a cedar plug is just 1 inch long. This allowed me to use standard drill bits and a handheld electric drill to widen the pre-drilled hole in the tip of this lure. There is seldom a need to widen the hole running lengthwise through the cedar portion of the lure because this hole is usually large enough to accommodate wire of any diameter. I drilled out the lead tip starting with a 7/64-inch drill bit and progressed in 1/16-inch increments to a 13/64-inch bit. This made the diameter of the hole large enough to accept my wire twist. I used 16-gauge stainless steel wire for this project, but copper, brass or galvanized steel wire may also be used to through-wire cedar plugs.

I then inserted the free end of the wire through the lead tip and pulled the wire out the back end of the lure until my wire twist fit snugly inside the head of the plug. This gave me a wire loop on the front tip of the plug. I then twisted the free end of the wire to form a second loop at the rear of the plug. Before shaping this rear loop, I jammed toothpicks into the cedar body of the lure to keep the wire firmly centered in place. This trick ensured a tight-fitting rear loop. My cedar plug was now through-wired and ready for a rear hook. I'm not a proponent of split rings, but using them allowed me to change the hook without disturbing the integrity of my wired lure. When I was done, my cedar plug had a swinging hook instead of a fixed hook wedged into its soft wooden body.

I purchase unrigged cedar plugs by the dozen, and drill and wire them in lots of six at a time. Tackle shops that cater to New England's bluefin tuna fishery are the best places to buy these lures. Many dealers stock 6-inch and 8-inch cedar plugs weighing as much

as 3 ounces. When fishing for striped bass and bluefish, however, you will want to use a smaller plug. The Sea Striker Corporation of Morehead City, North Carolina, manufactures a 4-inch Junior Cedar Plug that weighs exactly 2 1/2 ounces, sans hook. This plug is a good size for trolling and surf casting. Most tackle shops can special-order Sea Striker cedar plugs for you. If your local tackle shop cannot supply you with this particular item, you may purchase these lures from Tackle Direct in Ocean City, New Jersey 08226.

When the baitfish are small I use a different cedar plug. The Strike Master division of Leadmasters, Inc., a family-owned business in Southern California, produces a slender 1 1/4-ounce cedar plug that is very effective when sand eels and silversides are present. These petite 4-inch cedar plugs are exceptionally well made and nicely finished and cost about $4 apiece. Strike

This small arsenal of cedar plugs features a variety of color schemes and feather types.

Master cedar plugs are available from CharkBait! of Huntington Beach, California.

Most tuna fishermen troll cedar plugs au natural, probably because color is unimportant when a lure is moving at a speed of 8 to 10 knots. When trolling at 2 or 3 knots, however, color sometimes makes the difference between fishing and catching fish. I like to paint my cedar plugs, particularly the lead portion of the lure, because I've never seen a baitfish swimming around with a metallic-looking head. Before painting my cedar plugs, I use a small file to smooth out any rough edges in the tip of the lure. I then sand the entire lure, end to end, with 220-grit sandpaper. Wear a disposable respirator when you do this because very fine particles of toxic lead are released into the air when filing and sanding lead. After sanding I apply two coats of Zinsser Bullseye 1 2 3 primer. This material adheres to metal as well as wood and gives the entire body of the plug a uniform surface. When the primer has dried, I sand again and paint my plugs with an oil-based enamel.

I painted all but two of my first batch of wired plugs using colors such as sunburst yellow, bright red, high-gloss black and super-gloss white. A few weeks later I remembered I had a small, unopened can of Rustoleum Hunter Green enamel paint in my basement. This paint had been purchased years earlier for a never-completed, home-repair project. To ease some of my guilt, I decided to use this green paint on the two remaining cedar plugs. This turned out to be a fortuitous decision. Hunter Green has out-fished every other color, including unpainted natural cedar. I don't know why this dark green color attracts stripers and blues, but it does.

I applied clear lacquer sealer to my second batch of wired plugs in order to enhance the look of natural cedar. Marine varnish and tung oil treatments also produce the same effect. These surface coatings really spruce up a dull, weathered-looking cedar plug, but they do little to extend the useful life of this lure. These plugs last forever without any protective treatment because cedar is naturally rot resistant, and lead is an inert metal that oxidizes and corrodes very slowly.

I initially used 6/0 hooks dressed with bucktail or tied with feathers for most of my cedar plugs. These natural fibers are effective when the baitfish is relatively large in size. Sometimes I even add a pork rind trailer to a cedar plug with a feathered hook. This combination looks a bit strange, but it really works. I used a plain bare hook on a few of the plugs because I wanted to experiment using soft plastic tails as trailers. It wasn't long before I was changing most of my bucktail and feathered hooks to bare hooks because soft plastic tails were so effective. When sand eels and other small baitfish are present, nothing beats a soft plastic tail on a cedar plug.

Last winter when I modified cedar plugs intended for tuna, I didn't know if these lures would fool bluefish and striped bass. I didn't have to wait very long for an answer. The first time I fished with a cedar plug I knew this lure was a winner. It was early June 2001 and I was in Cape Cod Bay near the mouth of the Pamet River trolling for striped bass using large plastic tails threaded on leadhead jigs. That year the bluefish arrived with the striped bass, and these toothy creatures were systematically destroying my favorite striper lures, one at a time. After four hours of trolling, all I had to show for my efforts was a pile of 9-inch Slug-Gos and 10-inch Fin-S Fishes that now averaged four inches in length. I hadn't lost any leadhead jigs, but neither had I hooked any fish.

I was fishing alone and decided to troll a different type of lure while I sorted out some gear before starting the 25-mile trip across Cape Cod Bay to my home port of Green Harbor in Marshfield, Massachusetts. I reached into my tackle box and grabbed one of my new green cedar plugs with a bare hook. I threaded a small Slug-Go onto the hook, tied my lure to a 3-foot piece of 40-pound-test monofilament leader, tossed the rig overboard and resumed trolling. I needed both of my hands free, so I placed my fishing rod in a holder. Within moments I had a strike. It was another bluefish, but this time something was different. Instead of swimming off with the latter half of my soft plastic tail, this fish was hooked. When I reeled in this fish I was surprised to find tooth marks as far forward as the lead portion of the lure.

I tagged and released this fish and continued trolling using the same lure and plastic tail. A few minutes later I had another bluefish tugging on my line. When I landed and released this fish I noticed tooth marks all over the cedar plug. The soft plastic tail, however, was still in good shape. Instead of chewing the soft plastic tail, these bluefish were attacking the cedar plug itself. During the next 45 minutes I caught eight more bluefish, and in the process I sacrificed just three small, inexpensive plastic tails.

The following week I had an opportunity to fish in Duxbury Bay. I was anxious to know if my cedar plug would also fool striped bass, so I began trolling a 2 1/2-ounce Strike Master Jr. cedar plug with a 4-inch Slug-Go threaded on its bare hook. During the next two hours I caught and released 10 striped bass ranging from 24 to 28 inches in length. These were not big fish, but they were typical of the school bass I catch in the shallow waters of Duxbury Bay.

During the next two months I experimented with cedar plugs on every fishing trip. This gave me an opportunity to try these plugs with feathered hooks, bucktail hooks, soft plastic tails of all sizes, shapes and colors, pork rind trailers and even live sea worms. Everything worked! Even cedar plugs with just a plain, bare hook fooled stripers and blues. I caught more than 100 striped bass and bluefish during my first season fishing with this modified tuna lure. The largest striper measured 31 inches in length and the biggest bluefish was 30 inches long. I'm sure larger specimens can be fooled with cedar plugs if these lures are fished at greater depths using heavier tackle and wire line.

After just one season, cedar plugs have earned a special place in my tackle box. These lures are great for casting and trolling because their streamlined profile and weighted tip enable them to fly through the air like a missile, as well as swim below the surface with minimum water resistance. Cedar plugs can be used with almost any trailer, including live bait. Best of all, cedar plugs can be used with inexpensive soft plastic baits to target striped bass in the presence of bluefish. I'm glad I discovered these versatile lead-and-cedar lures. ◄━━◄

Striper vs. Mackerel
– You Win!

By Leo Bedard

It just doesn't seem right to call it fishing when you're absolutely certain that you're going to be catching. That's how I feel when I live-line mackerel to catch stripers. I take fishing for both quite seriously, and when I combine the two, it's fishing nirvana.

I catch mackerel to help pay for my fishing gear every year, and I don't think that I have to tell you why I catch stripers. My commercial license allows me to sell the mackerel, or sometimes I exchange them for store credit at willing bait and tackle shops. They also make great bait for the 10 lobster traps that I keep in Cape Cod Bay.

Every year around the middle of May, mackerel come to my area of the bay. The Sandwich boat basin is an excellent launching area for that event, as is Plymouth or Blish Point in Barnstable. I will admit, I have an advantage over those of you who don't live near the water: Every morning on the way to work I drive past the Sandwich Marina on Cape Cod. On those early spring mornings when I see a half-full trailer parking lot (at 7 a.m.), I know that the New Bedford hook-and-line fishermen have received word from their dragger brethren that the schools of mackerel have arrived in the bay. It might not sound like much of an advantage, but it puts me on fish just a couple of days ahead of the fishing reports. It pays to be early in the mackerel run.

Those guys get an early start. One weekend morning I put in at 5 a.m. and Joe, the ramp attendant, told me that I was the twentieth boat in the water that morning. By 10 a.m. many of them are already coming off the water with totes full of mackerel. Actually, that was the last time I ever dropped the boat in at 5 a.m. for mackerel fishing. The fact is, it gives you no real advantage and I'd rather get an extra couple of hours of sleep.

The author displays a striper deceived by a live mackerel with a bait hook behind its dorsal fin. It was caught just off of the "CC" Buoy in Cape Cod Bay.
-photo by Linda Bedard

For your own planning purposes, you can pretty much figure on finding mackerel in the southwestern section of Cape Cod Bay on or just around May 15. Even as strange as last year was, with an exceptionally cold early spring with very cold water temperatures, they were right on time. Spring of 2003 was the coldest in 12 years and water temperatures in the 40s were common throughout the month.

Overall, the spring 2003 mackerel run was disappointing, but what's nice about using them as bait is that you don't need many to have a successful fishing excursion. Striped bass is the real target species.

If you're out there, you'll know my boat: I'm the one far away from the drifting pack of small boats. I'll also always have one extra line out seemingly doing nothing. That's for the big girls! "The Pack" will be drifting and then running, looking for the big school of mackerel. I'll start on a school and continue the drift. The fish will come around again, they always do. My reason for staying away is that I'll have one line run out quite a distance, with one of those live mackerel on a bait hook. The reason, of course, is that there are almost always some stripers under those mackerel.

The amount of patience that I have on any given day will determine how long I remain on one drift before I haul the lines in and run up to start another run. That and the activity either on the lines or on the fishfinder.

First, let's catch the mackerel. To some this may seem like pretty basic stuff, but I think I can offer some new tricks that will improve your catch, both of mackerel and of striper. First and foremost, I recommend mackerel rigs (also known as Christmas tree rigs) with small, thin, sharp hooks and a strong leader of 30-pound test or greater. You'll find out why later.

On the end of the mackerel rig I attach a diamond jig, the weight of which is determined by how quickly the boat is drifting; I want the line to be as close to vertical as possible. I keep three different sizes on board. In theory I could possibly catch a striper on that lure, but in all honesty I've never seen that happen.

I'll attach that entire rig to the leader at the end of the leadcore line left on the reels from the year before. I religiously change my leadcore twice a year. I have to because after the mackerel and before the tuna arrive, I use bunker spoons. The constant stretching from towing a heavy, action-packed lure like that weakens the leadcore. But for mackerel it's just fine, and I wait until after they have passed to change the line. Using leadcore is another way to keep my offerings vertical.

The key to catching a lot of mackerel is to have the line in the school as it passes. Leadcore changes color every 30 feet, so when my fishfinder shows they're at 34 feet, I'll let out one color. That plus my leader puts my offering just above the school, which is where I want to be. Mackerel don't tend to look down for their food. Keep this in mind and count your colors of leadcore to stay in the strike zone. And be sure to get down there quickly as these fish move fast.

Once the bite is on, don't pull in only one fish. With practice you'll know if you have one or many fish on. Leave the first one to hit in the water. He'll be thrashing around making others think he's having a feast. They'll join him and soon you'll be able to pull in two, three or four at a time. That way you'll have some for the tote and some for the baitwell.

Taking four fish off of a rig can be time consuming. In order to get them off the hook quickly (remember, you can't catch fish if your rig is not down with the school), grab your rod tip with your right hand and, over the tote, give it a snap; with any luck you'll have four in the tote. At any point you can carefully remove one or more for the baitwell.

Last May I was out on one of those rare, calm, early spring days and I was using this strategy. I had one mackerel on and I wanted to wait for others to join him for breakfast. The water was so calm that I could see all the way down to the one mackerel that was hooked on the rig at about 10 or 12 feet. They had been hitting close to the surface at that hour so I didn't have enough line out to even reach the colored leadcore. The mack was thrashing around, but it wasn't attracting any of its brethren.

All of a sudden, from the depths directly below beyond my view came a huge striper. (They all seem huge when you see them and know you don't stand a chance of catching them.) Straight up it came, its mouth open to limits I never thought they could reach! That small, sharp hook was no match for that fish. It picked that mackerel off as if it weren't hooked at all. In this instance, I didn't mind losing the fish; the surprise and the heart-pounding exhilaration made it all worth it. It did make me wonder, however: Why the heck did I have so much line out on the live-lined mackerel? The stripers were obviously willing to hit within 10 feet of the boat!

To understand the excitement of seeing a striper hit that close to the boat, you must have experienced having a lure or bait picked off that close to your gunwales. Even a 20-pounder becomes a formidable opponent. Unlike a strike far behind the boat, a fish close in is strong, rested and has seen the boat. And you have no advantage from the cushioning effect of having a lot of line out. Those were the visions that were going through my mind when I saw that fish grab the mackerel so close to the boat and I knew I had no chance.

So here's the methodology. Keep jigging, snapping the fish you catch into the tote and getting the rig back down there as quickly as you can until the school has passed. Then just let your rig down to the depth that has been productive and put the rod in a holder until you hear that alarm on your fishfinder go off again. You'll be busy in the meantime.

Pick a mackerel with no visible wounds, or perhaps you unhooked a couple rather than snapped them off the rig. The point is that mackerel are bleeders, and if you put a bleeder in your baitwell, the blood in the water will kill everything else in there very quickly. They would actually have a better chance of staying alive in the tote without water, but not for long.

If you don't have a livewell, float a round basket with a cover next to your boat. Use the same strategies for keeping them alive that Cape Cod Canal fishermen use with their mini herring cars to keep their herring alive. An advantage to this is that the constant flow of water prevents any blood from a wound you may have missed from killing the rest of the bait. The disadvantage is that, when you make your next run, what do you do with the fish? But, as I said, they'll survive longer out of water than they will in a container that is filled with bloody water. Simply pull the bait car from the water and either place it on the deck or put it in a larger vessel filled with fresh salt water. They won't be there long. Once you start your drift, put the bait car back in the water.

I do enjoy live-lining mackerel more than herring. Herring are very labor intensive. You must wait for a run to open, then take just what you're allowed and hope you can somehow keep them alive until you get to your boat. That, of course, means another baitwell in your car or truck. With mackerel, you just catch them, keep them alive for a short time, then put them on a hook.

Don't be afraid to select a fish that is fairly large for use as a live bait. I know that many fishermen like using tinker mackerel, but a striper's ability to take a large bait is really much greater than you may think. That mackerel that was taken from my rig that day was big! That incident changed the way I look at bait size. The size of that mouth opening and that cavernous cavity beyond, to me, was proof that the only restriction on size should be: Is the bait so large that it will spool the reel when it's in free-spool with the clicker on?

O.K., so now we've caught the bait. From this point, my strategies are different than the way I live-line herring. I never use weights to get the mackerel down. I simply insert a thin wire 4/0, 5/0 or 6/0 live-bait hook behind the dorsal fin. You must do this above the fish's lateral line or it won't live long. Then it's just a matter of lowering the mackerel

Chad Bedard has two mackerel on. He's waiting patiently for one or two more to hit before he reels them in.
-photo by Leo Bedard

into the water and letting it do all the work. Unlike herring, which often are reluctant to leave the surface, mackerel will almost always head for deeper water. I'll let out a little line, then put the reel in free-spool with the clicker on. The slight amount of drag that's created by having the clicker on keeps the tail elevated and that, combined with any forward motion from the drifting boat, sends the fish down. No weights are necessary.

You'll know when a striper is approaching. Normally, the baitfish will take the line out slowly. It might even find a depth that is comfortable and stop taking out line, although I can't be sure if comfort is the reason or exhaustion. When a predator approaches, that clicker will speed up its rhythm and you know things are about to happen.

You should check your line every now and again when you haven't heard the reel clicking for a while. The mackerel can become lethargic or die, and I've had occasions where the bait was picked up by dogfish and, rather than running, they just followed the boat. I had no way of knowing just how long that scavenger had been on the mackerel.

I've had good luck with dead herring when they were rigged right, but I've never had good luck with a dead mackerel. I believe the main reason is that I'm in much deeper water when I use mackerel, usually around 60 feet. Dogfish are common at those depths and they'll grab that listless bait very quickly. In the relatively shallow water where I use herring (20 to 30 feet), sand sharks are uncommon.

Suddenly, your clicker alerts you that your live bait has caught the attention of a hungry striper. The bait is getting nervous and may be trying to run. Then the reel goes off like a siren! When you're sure the fish has the bait, point the rod tip toward it and take the reel out of free-spool. When the line gets tight, pull.

This is not a method that the charter-boat captains would ever want to employ. They have to find a fish for each person on board, every four hours. In that amount of time, I'll boat two some days, and some days only one. But I will say this: They're always big.

So if you want mackerel for bait, the smoker, the table, the lobster traps or the money, and you feel the way any red-blooded fisherman feels about catching striper, try this method. It's a keeper! ◄

Saltwater Offerings
How To Identify "Prime" Bait And Keep It That Way

By Carl A. Johansen

When you buy or otherwise obtain your own bait, is it still usable when it comes time to fish? Does it stay that way for long? With the prices today, the prudent angler should take steps to keep his bait in prime condition. And it's just as important to be able to distinguish when bait is fresh and when it is not at the tackle shop. Every New England angler should be familiar with what constitutes good or not so good bait; it can spell the difference between putting a big fish in the boat or on the shore and going home empty-handed.

One of the more readily available and popular baits, and one of the most expensive, are sea worms. They are sold by the dozen or by the flat. A flat should contain 125 worms. Within the flat, worms are graded by size, from large to medium and small. Most worms come from Maine, and the mix of large to small worms within the flat depends on how far the tides go out when the diggers are working. If for example the tides are at a minus level, the worms in a flat should be larger overall than when the tide is normal. Worms that are dug fresh need to be "hardened up" prior to shipping for sale. This is done by keeping them on fresh, dry newspaper under damp, but not wet, seaweed in boxes at a cool temperature. Fresh worms at the bait store can be a week old before you buy them, but if the store changes the paper in the boxes daily and keeps them at the right temperature (about 45 degrees), they should remain in good condition.

One trick to tell if the worms have been maintained properly and will last a while is to place your hand inside the flat or box of worms and see if they try to bite you. Chances are that if they bite, they are not prime. Another way to tell how fresh the worms are is to lift the seaweed away from the paper. If the paper shows lots of a brownish or bloody liquid and the worms are biting, you will have a flat of worms that will not last the weekend and will not stay on the hook. They will also emit an odor into the water that many fishermen feel is unattractive to the fish.

If the bottom paper is only damp to the touch, simply replace it. If the seaweed is dry, take a small sprayer with clean salt water and lightly spray the worms. This will invigorate the worms and help to keep them alive longer in the box.

When fishing with worms for an extended period of time, place them in an insulated cooler. Place frozen ice containers on the bottom and separate the ice from the box by placing cardboard, newspaper or burlap bags between them. The idea here is not to freeze them, but keep them nice and cool. If the weed feels frosty, place more insulating material between the worms and the ice in the containers. You can always place a few small strips of wood in-between to get the right conditions The main thing is to remember that once the worms become wet, warm or frozen, they will have a short life span and not be very good for bait.

Herring, menhaden and mackerel are the next choices of many anglers, especially those targeting stripers and bluefish.

Most mackerel used for bait are caught by commercial draggers and in some cases are packaged at sea in flats and quickly frozen or vacuum packed. Once frozen, and if they do not undergo changes in temperature, they generally will be prime upon thawing. It is rare to find unfrozen mackerel, unless you go to a fish market and then the cost will be more. Thawed macks will be good hook baits for a few hours after they're thawed.

Menhaden and herring are more often sold in the unfrozen state, and one needs to determine the condition of the fish to judge its freshness. The condition of the bait is directly related to how it was handled when it was caught. Menhaden and herring are caught by commercial draggers or commercial bait fishermen in smaller boats using throw nets or hand nets. The fish should be chilled in a brine solution (salt water and ice mixture) because this hardens the flesh and helps to prevent decomposition.

Fresh unfrozen menhaden and herring should show clear eyes and little bruising, and should be firm to the touch. Upon cutting for bait, they should give off a crunching noise and not fall apart. The skin should stay on the flesh as each cut is made. Once menhaden and herring are chilled they can be placed in a cooler and layered with shaved ice. Keep the cooler drain open to allow for drainage. If you freeze them in this state they will still be prime upon thawing, as well. Freezing in a vacuum bag, along with freezing them evenly on both sides, will add a little more shelf life while in the freezer. I've gotten the best results thawing out frozen bait gradually in a refrigerator. This will allow the juices to remain in the fish and the more scent that remains, the better your bait will attract those large fish from a greater distance. The bait should have almost a sweet smell to it for best results.

Local fresh pogies are a sought-after commodity and a very hard bait to find. Only a few commercial bait providers actually use a throw net to catch them in Massachusetts. These throw-net-caught pogies are always in good condition when they come into the shop. Those that sell the "New Jersey Reds" try to get the "top of the boat," those baits that are on the top of the pile in the bait holds, but they are not given the same care as those caught locally with a throw net. These menhaden show more bruising and red eyes and tend to have flesh that is softer to the touch. In most cases they have already started to decompose by the time that they make it to the shops here in New England. It is still possible to get two pieces of bait from these, one from the head and tail. The cost for the local bait is greater because it cost more for the tackle store to buy them, as they are of a much better quality and in demand.

At different points in the season, typically from mid-season on, sand eels can be a very productive bait for an assortment of gamefish. Sand eels have about a three-day shelf life in an unfrozen state. Freshly raked sand eels are best and they too must receive care before they reach a tackle shop because they are fragile and decompose quickly. One way to reduce the loss is to clean them off in a cold saltwater bath. Inserting frozen ice packs into a container of clean salt water chills the water. Drain or spin-dry them and then use paper towels to finish the drying process. Place inside a sturdy Ziploc bag, one at a time, keeping them flat. Do not overload the bag. Put a layer of crushed or shaved ice on the bottom of your cooler, then the bags of bait, then another layer of shaved or crushed ice on top. Sand eels in this condition can also be frozen, but it must be done right away for them to be prime when thawed out. Fresh sand eels should be very firm to the touch and not have any foul smell in an unfrozen state. Again, defrost frozen bait in a refrigerator or a cooler, not in water, for best results.

Sea, razor and softshell clams are bait that many bass fishermen fail to utilize in their quest for big stripers. At certain times of the year these clams are very productive for many other species, as well. Normally they would be purchased in small cups or by the gallon, unless you raked your own or picked them up after a storm. The meat of the sea clam should be pink and have a nice sweet smell to it. A whitish appearance indicates old bait and one that was not processed correctly. It can still be used as bait, but it is not prime. Fresh sea clams should be mixed with kosher salt prior to use, to toughen the flesh. This will help the bait stay on the hook when cast. Mixing them with salt before freezing will also make them usable sooner, once out of the freezer.

Squid is one of the more inexpensive baits and is especially good if you are fishing with children because it stays on the hook better thaen most baits, and if you do not use it all up, it can be refrozen for another fishing trip. The squid most everyone buys is frozen and not caught locally, as well as being cleaned for eating purposes. The packaged frozen squid is white, unlike fresh squid that is almost black with pink tinges. The meat is white under the skin. It is almost impossible to find freshly caught squid, unless you catch your own under a light at night somewhere. It's been my experience that the longer squid is in an unfrozen state, the better it is for bait, but the longer squid is thawed, the harder it is to remove the smell from your hands. Slowly thaw frozen squid for best results prior to using.

Green crabs are mostly used by those fishing for tautog, but bass love them, as well. Good green crabs are another bait that should be handled with care by the bait dealer and the fisherman. These creatures have a smell all their own – you won't have any trouble knowing if there are dead ones in the batch. About the only thing you can do is keep them in a saltwater "live car" (a wire mesh trap that is tightly closed) to keep them alive or place them in a burlap bag that has been soaked in salt water. Dead crabs should be discarded on a daily basis, and in most cases, when you purchase them at a shop they will be in a damp burlap bag and refrigerated. This slows down their metabolism and reduces loss. Unless you have a bait refrigerator at home, it's best to purchase and use them as soon as possible. Never place them where food is kept.

You can keep them for a day or so in a cooler with shaved or crushed ice or in a bucket with ice around it if you're not planning to use them right away. Do not let the crabs come in contact with the ice. Crabs are cannibals so make sure you keep them asleep, but not frozen. As they are exposed to the outside temperatures they will become very lively and prime for cutting into bait. Fresh cut crabs will have more body fluids and more scent to lure those larger fish to the hook.

Eels can be used dead or alive and skinned for jigs. They are a good versatile bait for stripers as they can be cast, drifted in deep water or trolled. When purchasing eels you can assume that if the eel is swimming it is in prime condition. Your job is to keep them alive long enough to use, and this is a little trickier than it may sound. If you have kept herring alive in a livewell, the setup is very similar, except you must have a good cover on the container. One good bait holder for eels is a cooler that has a screen an inch or so from the bottom. It is important that the eels are not in any water, strange as that may sound – they live longer out of water than in a small amount of water in a confined space. Place ice packs on top of the screen or crushed ice under the screen. Try to get some seaweed for the upper part of the cooler; the more you put in, the better for the eels. What you are trying to do is put them in a "sleep" mode without killing them or freezing them before you get to use them. Make sure the container or cooler has some depth to it and a good cover. Live eels can jump out and I have seen them slither a few feet up to get out of an uncovered container. During the warmer months it will take more ice to quiet them down. You will need to experiment with how much ice they need for the type of container you plan to use. If you do the job correctly, it will be possible to hook the eel and not have a balled up "eel knot" before it hits the water.

Many fishermen throw their eels away once they have expired, but the prudent fisherman will save them to rig for another day of fishing or skin them for jigging. Small eels can be frozen and used on a tube and worm setup in place of sea worms or placed on a bucktail jig in place of pork rind. Save the larger ones for rigging, but rig them before they are frozen.

To skin a fresh dead (but not frozen) eel, cut the skin all the way around the body just behind the head. Nail the head to a board or perhaps a tree in the back yard, then pull the skin down and off with a pair of pliers. Keep the blue side out, clean off any extra meat from the skin and immerse it in brine. Skins should be stored in a plastic container that has a very tight-fitting cover and is long enough to lay the whole skin out flat. Place a layer of salt on the bottom and keep each eelskin separated from its neighbors. Once you have a single layer of eelskins, place another layer of salt and continue until you have filled the container. Finish the top off with another layer of kosher salt and spray a small amount of water on top and place in the refrigerator. Be sure to mark the cover indicating that the contents are eelskins! Every once in a while, especially if you have a frost-free refrigerator, make sure the skins are moist. If you keep them in this manner and use a tight cover, you should not have any complaints from the kitchen.

In general terms, when one purchases any type of frozen bait, whether it be sand eels, herring, menhaden or mackerel, it is important that the contents do not show any brownish liquid inside the packaging. This is an indication of bait that was already decomposing when it was packaged or was defrosted and refrozen. What you'll end up with is bait that for all practical purposes is better off used for chum as it will not stay on a hook and the crabs will make short work of it.

Many fishermen buy bait that is in prime condition, do not take care of it and then wonder why the bait did not last long enough to be used or didn't catch fish. They then dismiss this highly productive method. However, if one chooses to fish, it is important to keep an open mind and try to learn all the ways to catch that trophy fish we all seek. Using bait has its own rewards, just like working a plug across the water, but the first step is using the right bait that's in the best possible condition.

I have obtained my own bait by digging sea worms, raking sand eels and sea clams, trapping crabs and eels, and netting herring and menhaden. Those experiences, along with experiences shared by others, made it possible for me to write this article. I owe deep thanks to one person in particular who shared his experiences with me but did not want any credit. Perhaps you'll be lucky enough to find a fishing mentor who will teach you how to select, prepare and keep bait.

Sand Eel Fishing

By Steve Shiraka

When it comes to striped bass fishing, I've been exposed to many different disciplines over the years, from fly rods to live eels and anywhere in-between. I believe a truly adept striper fisherman should know all these techniques, and if need be should be able to switch to any one of them in order to ensure success while on the water. In my eyes, the measure of a good fisherman is not being the best fly-fisher or the best plug fisherman, but rather the one who has taken the time to learn all the various ways to tweak fish from the sea, and excels at each and every one of them.

There is one technique that offers a sure-fire attack on the local bass population, and that is bait-fishing with freshly raked sand eels. *Ammodytes americanus* is the Latin name for these long, slender fish that resemble eels in their movements; they differ from a true eel in that they possess segmented fins. They are the most prevalent forage fish in Cape Cod Bay, and likewise in many other locations around the Cape. Greenish-bronze on the back and lightening to silvery-white on the sides and belly, they can attain a length of six inches, and sometimes longer offshore. And they can burrow into the sand in seconds flat when alarmed, completely disappearing in front of your eyes.

Sand eels can be harvested with a special rake custom-made for that purpose, or they can be bought in most local tackle shops, both fresh and frozen; fresh bait is the best and frozen is a poor second. Raking sand eels for bait is an adventure in itself. First you have to purchase a good sand eel rake. There are two types available, and the difference lies in the handle. One type is made from a steel tube with a welded head. The other type has a wooden handle that is thicker than the steel tube type and has the added benefit of being able to float. Either type works well and will suffice.

The head of the rake is made up of about 30 steel prongs, which are sharpened to a needle point. The object is to locate the sand eels in shallow water, three or four feet deep. This may be along a beach, or where a salt creek enters a bay, or along an exposed sandbar. As you walk through the water, look at the bottom immediately in front of each foot as you take a step. If they are present, the sand eels will dart out in front and bury themselves again, making little puffs of sand as they do this.

Once you've found a good concentration of them, take your rake, and with one hand about a third of the way down the rake shaft, pull the rake toward you, keeping the tines sunk about two inches into the sand. Each swing of the rake should be about three feet. As you pull the rake from the bottom, the bait will be impaled on the tines. A fish tote (one that doesn't have any holes drilled into it and also floats) should be tied onto a short length of cord and secured to your wader belt. Bang the rake on the tote; that will loosen any sand eels off the rake, and they will drop in.

Another way to collect sand eels is power-raking them from a boat. If you are out on the water and notice a lot of sand eels as you are crossing a shallow bar, have someone drive the boat back and forth over the bar at about five knots and pull the rake along the bottom for 30 to 40 feet on each pass, if possible. This is a very effective way to harvest a large amount of bait in a short time without expending a tremendous amount of energy that should be saved for the actual fishing part of the operation.

Now that you have your bait, it will require a certain amount of care to keep it in a palatable state for the bass. Lee Boisvert of Riverview Bait and Tackle in Bass River goes to

extremes in the amount of care he takes with his bait before he offers it for sale to his customers. After receiving the sand eels, he carefully rinses them in salt water and then pats them dry with paper towels. Rinsing them removes the blood and prevents quick spoilage, and patting them dry with paper towels removes excess water and fluids, which otherwise could also accelerate decay. Next, Lee puts them in Ziploc bags and places them on ice in a cooler that has its drain plug open, which allows the melting ice to drain out. Although this may seem like a lot of work, the process produces a high-quality product that his customers can count on.

A sand eel rake

If you can't rake your own bait, there are some things you should look for when you purchase bait in a shop. Be fussy – if you're not, the fish will be. Freshly raked bait will have a firm feel to it. I always pick one out of the bag and squeeze it between two fingers; if it's old, it will be mushy and won't have a fresh smell to it. Sand eels are an oily bait and will smell like cut cucumbers when fresh. Now, on to the fishing.

One of my favorite places to fish fresh sand eels is Chapin's Beach in Dennis on the bay side. This beach, about a mile long, is bordered by Bass Hole in Yarmouth to the west and south, and Cape Cod Bay to the north and east. A system of sand flats stretches out for a half-mile or more from the actual beach, and the flats are exposed at low tide. The tide range is about eight feet, fluctuating with the phases of the moon. The front of the beach faces northwest and is best fished when the wind is in your face at that quarter. The snottier the better, and a good nor'west blow, with white water getting blown off the tops of the waves, can offer the best fishing to be had in the area.

Chapin's is accessible with a four-wheel-drive vehicle, but you must obtain a seasonal pass from the Town of Dennis, and that can be quite costly for nonresidents. With a large parking lot available and the short length of the beach, it is very accessible by foot. There is some equipment that will make your outing more enjoyable and more productive. A sand spike is mandatory for each rod fished. The tube type sold in most tackle shops should be avoided. A piece of 1½-inch PVC pipe, secured to a 4-foot piece of ¾-inch by ¾-inch angle iron and tapered to a point so it can be hammered deep into the sand, will ensure that a big fish doesn't take your rod down and out into the deep blue sea. Don't laugh – I've seen it happen too many times.

Whether you are fishing a conventional or a spinning rig, the rod should be 10 feet long with medium action, capable of hauling an 8-ounce chunk of lead with undue strain. At a minimum, 20-pound-test mono should be spooled on; if you're using a conventional rig, 25- or 30-pound is even better. Your reel should hold at least 200 yards of line, and the line should be an abrasion-resistant type. Terminate this with a 75-pound snap swivel.

Sand eel rigs can be purchased prefabbed, or you can make your own. Store-bought rigs are usually made of clear mono rated at 100-pound test and sport two 6/0 gold bait-holder-type hooks. These rigs will work well, but I prefer to make my own. I use 60-pound-test green mono, such as Berkley Big Game. I take a piece about 4 feet long and stretch it. About a third of the way from each end I tie in a dropper loop which extends six inches out from the main body of the line. To each of these loops I add a 6/0 Eagle Claw stainless steel hook. At the top I secure a 100-pound swivel, and at the bottom I tie on a 100-pound snap. I tie these both on with improved clinch knots.

I carry an assortment of sinkers from 4 to 8 ounces, both the pyramid and Carolina types. The heavier the surf, the greater the weight. Most of the fishing will be done at night, with high tides at dusk and dawn producing better than those in the wee hours. A new moon will produce better than a full moon tide and, coupled with a nor'west breeze, can only bring good things. A cyalume stick taped to the rod tip is a great indicator of a biting bass, and is a must as far as I am concerned.

Now that you're all rigged up, it's time to bait up and get the bait out to where it belongs. It is wise to first limber up the sand eel by bending the entire body; this will produce a more lifelike appearance in the water. If the sand eels you raked or purchased are of decent size, take the hook point and insert it through the eye, then thread the hook through the body cavity so the sand eel holds the slight bend of the hook shape as it hangs. Walk out from the beach as far as you can and cast. After your rig has settled on the bottom, take up all the slack you can, putting a slight bend in your rod. A current will be running along the beach as the tide rises or falls; the slight bend in the hooked sand eel will produce a movement from side to side as the current passes around it.

If the fish are there, they can show at any time of the tide. Watching your cyalume-stick indicator will be a dead giveaway as to their presence. Small fish will nibble at the bait, and this will be detected as you watch the cyalume stick dance in the darkness. Big fish nibble, too, but 99 percent of the time there will be no mistaking which is which as your rod goes over hard and the reel strains as the bass hooks itself and starts a frantic run to deeper water.

Some nights are better than others, and there are also other places to fish sand eels in the same manner, such as Race Point in Provincetown and Nauset and Scusset beaches. Wherever you do it, this is a highly productive method. I can recall one past summer taking 30 fish over 30 pounds in a 3-week period at Chapin's Beach, the heaviest weighing 49 pounds. And at times this method can be relaxing, as well. Give sand eel fishing a try; no doubt it will become part of your repertoire, too!

The Seductive Serpent

By Captain Charley Soares

My left index finger quivered from the vibrations being sent up my line by the gyrations of the lively 18-inch eel. After the initial surge of energy, the eel promptly headed for the bottom, seeking a rock or clump of weed to hide under. Large eels don't get to be that size by swimming on the surface or upper levels of the water column where they are exposed to predators. When a large bass eel (my preference is for eels in the 18- to 22-inch class) hits the water, they instinctively know they're vulnerable and head for what I refer to as the strike zone, that area two to four feet off the bottom. Most inexperienced anglers fish eels too shallow and retrieve them too quickly, resulting in their baits being well up out of the strike zone.

My eel had settled down and was being coaxed along "low and slow" when it began to pulse and shiver erratically. The tugs and quick short bursts of movement were an indication that my bait was being eye-balled by the stripers, which had signaled their presence by following and rolling behind our swimming plugs during the period just before sunset. Unlike the wooden imitations that require both experience and skill to produce realistic movement, my live eel's action was perfect right down to the stimulus of natural scent. Just then a sensation best described as a sharp rap curtailed the furious tugging, at which time I slipped the clutch on the old Penn Squidder into neutral as line began to peel off the spool. My offering was in tow. Some fishermen can't resist the tendency to strike as soon as they feel the hit, and while the predator might have the hook, just as often they don't. I prefer to allow the fish to begin moving off with the bait and let water pressure force the eel into the stripers large bony maw. Immediately dropping the rod toward the fish ("bow to the cow," as the surf crowd at Montauk says), I engaged the lever and lifted the rod tip. The sharp 7/0 offset hook bit and the bass took off on a long run toward the cover of the submerged boulders I enticed it from. By the arch in my rod and the way line was melting from the spool, I knew this was no ordinary striper.

Pinching the line between my thumb and the blank's cork tape ever so slightly, I was able to exert enough pressure to turn the fish and move her sideways to the structure. Shifting the boat into gear, I continued to apply pressure, knowing that if the striper reached her destination she would rub and chafe my line to shreds. Fishermen have a tendency to exaggerate, so when someone tells me that they fought a bass for 15 minutes, I chalk that up to a combination of excitement and enthusiasm. This bass surfaced just east of the clumps where the sight of her huge dorsal fin brought a lump to my throat. With four half-century fish to my credit at the time, I thought this striper might be my promotion from the Nifty Fifty to the Super Sixty fraternity of the prestigious R.J. Schaefer Salt

Water Fishing Contest.

Less than five minutes later my deck mate required assistance lifting the bass over the rail. Lying across the aft deck, the hefty striper was long but not as thick as I had hoped; however, both of us believed we'd broken the 60-pound barrier. Four hours later the weighmaster hefted the thick linesider onto the hook of the certified scales at the Linesiders Bass Club where it stretched the spring down to 58 pounds 8 ounces. Three more attempts at securing the hook in various locations along the big cow's gill plates did not amplify the original computation.

That incident took place in July of 1964, which I have often referred to as the year of the bass. Although marine scientists and fishery managers are anxious to declare the striped bass resource totally recovered, it is not and won't be until we have the combined ratio of divergent year-classes of bass that migrated to our shores during the 1960s. Are there any more 50s out there? You can bet on it. Just look at the results of last year's fishing contests and tourneys from Montauk to Maine and your question is answered. Over the past 26 years I have conducted a fairly accurate poll of charter skippers, tackle shops and high-line fishermen. My list for 2001 tallies over 15 fish in excess of 50 pounds up to 58 pounds, with perhaps a few more captured by sharpies who would rather give you the key to their safe deposit boxes than contribute information on trophy stripers. Even though there have been several stripers in the 50-pound class harvested this season, with the current status of our stocks supporting an unhealthy ratio of small and medium to larger fish, your quest for a 50-pounder should not be considered futile.

The dreaded eel-ball. Many anglers have been discouraged from using eels due to this acrobatic manuever.

Every cast I take, every pass I make, I believe that next fish might just be 50 pounds. Perhaps even a 60 that somehow eluded traps, weirs, nets, fykes and thousands of hooks and baits set in its path over 20 years of migrations. Some of my most memorable fishing experiences have been fooling trophy bass with artificials, but the reality of the situation is that if you are serious about hunting trophy bass, you can't beat live bait. Few knowledgeable anglers would argue that live menhaden, herring and mackerel are top-notch bass baits, but not everyone can catch or keep them, and that's just one of many reasons that moves the live eel to the top of my live-bait list.

Almost anyone can catch a striper when they are actively feeding, but it takes skill and experience to entice a resting or well-fed bass to take a bait. Low and slow is the technique to entice hits from resting bass. I can demonstrate this basic fundamental much better than I could ever explain it. Most inexperienced anglers retrieve their eels much too rapidly, which results in their baits being fished too high in the water column and well up and out of the strike zone. I've been targeting big bass for 40 years and I can count on one hand the number of jumbo linesiders that came up through the water column to attack my baits. In order to tempt bass into striking, you have to move your eel through their scullery naturally. To duplicate this method, take a live eel and place it in a large tub or bucket of salt water. Once the eel calms down, watch how it moves in the water, swimming slowly using its natural gyrating propulsion system. If you concentrate on your retrieve and recover your line slowly, you'll be able to walk your eels close to the bottom without the unnatural rolling or twisting that might discourage a savvy old cow from attacking.

When you've trapped live eels to supplement your income, as well as provide bass bait for yourself and fishing buddies, you come to appreciate the value of these unique marine serpents. From the time I caught my first striper on an eel to this very day, there is not much more additional information available on the biology of these unusual creatures. What many consider repulsive is one of the most productive striper, bluefish and weakfish baits in the world, and not just a few giant swordfish have fallen victim to the seductive serpent. Although eels are relatively plentiful in the early spring and midsummer, they become very scarce in the late summer and fall. When someone standing next to you at Race Point offers you $5 for a dead eel, you know you are fishing the right bait. As long as you have a bait and tackle shop that can provide a consistent source of live eels, you don't have to bother with catching your own, but I've always potted my own eels in an operation that offered much more pleasure and enlightenment than a commercial venture. All you need are a couple of round, galvanized wire eel traps purchased or home brewed (some people use minnow traps with extensions that catch a fair amount of eels), preferably baited with a piece of horseshoe crab to entice eels into your pot. When horseshoe crabs are not available, we use crushed mussels, clams or chunks of menhaden in an onion bag. This attracts chubs and silversides, which the eels enter the pot to feast on.

I set my traps at dusk and pull them before dawn to prevent them from walking off with someone who might stumble onto them in the daylight hours. You can set your traps alongside the edge of eelgrass in narrow river systems or alongside bridges and piers that allow the eels some form of protection. Although they are nocturnal and chase small bait at night, they are well aware they are also prey to larger fish that pursue them. I know a local police officer who was an avid bass fisherman who potted his own eels. Much to the chagrin of his fellow officers that shared the same patrol car, my friend would set three pots along the riprap of the bridges along Route 195 in southeastern Massachusetts on the Palmer, Coles and Lees rivers. Some mornings he called to show me as many as 50 eels, chubs, green crabs and small finfish he had captured in those traps.

When the wind blows and the weather turns sour, I do a bit of freshwater bass fishing for the challenge and an excuse to be on the water. The first plastic worm I ever saw was a purple jelly worm a friend from Jersey used to catch weakfish, so I tried the largest ones I could find on bucketmouths and they were deadly. At the time I had a storage container full of live whip (small) eels and I wondered, if the imitation plastic worms worked, what kind of response would lively eels elicit? It didn't take long to find out. I'd purposely been fishing small ponds where go-fast boats could not maneuver and had never broken the 5-pound barrier until I started flipping live eels into the structure. I won't belabor the point with the details, but the lunker-size largemouths I hooked with the skinny snakes hit with the strength and fury of ravenous stripers. I've learned a lot from talking to and observing successful sweetwater fishermen, but one of my Florida clients took a page from my eel book and played it out in his home state waters. Not long after his first trip with me for stripers using live eels, he began sending notes and photographs of lunker largemouths he caught in Florida waters on large eels. He boasted that he was catching bass twice the size of his normal catches on artificials in the very same waters he had been fishing for a decade. Eels are deadly baits in both fresh-and saltwater, and if you want to start a serious argument, just drag a lively eel within reach of a swordfish or skilly and you can add two more species that are just crazy for serpents.

It would take an entire article to do justice to the subject of hooks, so with that in mind the following are some of my personal observations on your main connection to your quarry. You can read about it in plenty of fishing articles, but I've found that only the most pragmatic anglers appreciate the importance of the hook. The standard offset J-hook (also known as an octopus hook) has always been my favorite for fishing eels, although I've been experimenting with circle hooks since the manufacturers began sending me samples before they first appeared on the retail market. Circle hooks can be an effective conservation tool, but when they first appeared, proponents were quick to point out their benefits while few anglers paid attention to the instructions about the learning curve necessary to

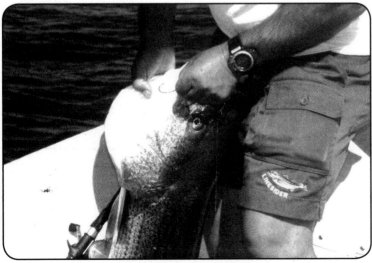

utilize them properly. The early hooks had points that curved around so much that the gap was closed so tightly you couldn't hook a proper-size eel and expect the hook to do its work. Revised models with less curvature and a slight offset allowed the use of larger eels

The right hook. Your only connection to a 38-pound bass has to stick and hold.

A nice magic-hour bass. Sunset and sunrise are ideal times for slinging eels.

and worked fairly well as long as the angler did not attempt to set the hook. Most of us have been conditioned to rear back and set up at the first hint of a strike, and all this accomplishes with a circle hook is pulling the hook and bait out of the fish's mouth. Even if you let the fish run with an eel for a while, you must tighten up on the fish gradually rather than hit back hard. I take people fishing for a living, and I've found it's much easier to teach someone how to fish with circle hooks without any preconceived notions about how to use them. While I've had numerous hookups in the corner of the fish's jaw with the original circles, I've also had some gut-hooked bass while waiting for the fish to take up the slack. I've also cut leaders for my clients who allowed a fish to run too far with a circle hook that ended up stuck in the fish's stomach.

In this fisherman's not-so-humble opinion, the Octopus Wide Daiichi Bleeding Bait hook in 6/0 (#D16Z); the Owner Super Needle Point Offset style SSW, size 6/0 (model 5315-161); and the Mustad black offset (92553BL), all in offset-eye configuration, are the very best live eel hooks you can use. If you are using another type and brand with success, by all means continue; these are my personal favorites and hooks that have accounted for numerous bass in the 40-pound class.

Fish send us subtle messages and we have to acquire the experience to interpret them. It can be very frustrating when eels are cast into a boulder pile or reef and the bass just grasp them. These fish don't run or eat the baits, but if you inspect the eel closely, you can tell where their miniscule teeth have scratched the eel's glossy skin. If the scratches are along the body, well beyond the head, those fish are not eating. Maybe they pick it up because they just can't help themselves. Don't keep showing them the eel because soon they will ignore it completely. Move to another location where there might be more fish in residence, and this is where the competition for a bait, no matter how well fed the fish may be, will get you a strike as they compete for your offering. I'll return to those locations, where fish demonstrated they were in residence but not ready to eat, on the next tide or wind shift and have those same fish attack the eel with a vengeance.

This scenario repeated itself for two weekends recently, and my deck mates could not believe I was pulling out of a boulder field with bass that were reluctant to eat. Just before the top of the tide, the wind shifted from north to a brisk southeast, and before long the tide changed as evidenced by the angle of lobster buoys. We returned to the same location, but this time the first casts resulted in solid hits and runs. The fish attacked so quickly, my guest with the spinning reel could not get the bail open in time on three successive casts.

Although I thoroughly enjoy sharing fishing experiences with friends and clients, I enjoy fishing alone where stealth can put me in positions where I can actually observe large fish holding in the shade of a boulder or ledge. Because I must land large bass without assistance, I use custom 7-foot fast-action conventional rods with Penn International 965 or 975 spooled with Maxima gold or Berkley 20-pound-test Big Game with an 18-inch shot of 50-pound-test leader material between my hook and a barrel swivel.

Although I'm a big fan of the large Frabil landing nets, slipping a 45-inch fish into a net alone is a daunting and often impossible task, so I employ a razor-sharp 5-foot Pompanette gaff. I do most of my fishing in Massachusetts and Rhode Island where gaffing is legal. Remember a gaff is a tool, not a political statement, and anyone who sinks a gaff into an undersized fish deserves to have one planted in his backside. I've seen too many trophy bass lost at the boat because the netter bumped the bass or snagged the hook, or the angler attempted to lift a large fish into a hoop better suited for crabbing than landing trophy bass.

The tube and worm is my bread-and-butter method, but when there is grass or weed that prevents trolling, when the fish are extremely wary, or there is so much fire in the water you can't move a lure a foot without leaving a cometlike trail, then try dead-drifting or casting and free-falling an eel and you will catch fish, big fish, when others can't even come close. Ask the surf sharpies who fish The Race and oceanside beaches, which get choked with mung after storms, what their favorite bait is. If they are honest and you can get them to respond at all, they will tell you a live eel is their hands-down favorite. There will be a few 50s and some 40s making their way south this fall, and a live eel is your best shot at hooking up with what just might be the fish of a lifetime.

Eeling For Surf Trophies

By John Skinner

The life-altering experience occurred in the wee hours of a crisp October morning. As a surfcaster barely out of my teens, I naively thought I was well positioned for a trophy bass. The 22-pounder dangling from a rope attached to my surf belt only helped to reinforce my ignorance. I worked the water in front of me with the 7-inch swimming plug that had fooled that fish, as well as several others in its size range. Only two other anglers were nearby, both throwing live eels, and neither had caught as many fish as I had.

As the hits became less frequent, fatigue began to set in, and I decided that it was time to go. I vacated my casting perch, politely said good night to the other guys and headed for my truck. The angler nearest to me seemed somewhat pleased that I was leaving, and his next cast would be delivered from the very rock that I had stood on for the last three hours.

My back was turned to him, and I was only about 50 feet away when I heard him grunt, "I'm on," in a strained voice. That irked me a bit, since I hadn't had a hit there in quite some time, but there was plenty more frustration to come my way. The angler worked the fish on a stout conventional outfit that hastened the battle.

The scraped up eel hanging from this 43-pounder's mouth had already caught four other bass when this trophy came along in the fall of 2001.

"Good fish" was all I heard, as his buddy helped with the landing. Almost not wanting to know, I asked, "How big?"

"Over forty," he responded. It was pushing a beach scale to 43 pounds as I walked over. The guy seemed to sense what I was feeling, and offered some advice. "Fish like these don't care much for wood or plastic."

On the drive home I couldn't help but wonder how many times I dragged one of my plugs right over that fish's head. At the time, that was the largest bass I had ever witnessed caught from the surf, and I wanted one like it. With the angler's advice echoing through my sleep-deprived thoughts all the way home, I told myself that I would not only learn how to fish live eels properly, but I would also strive to master the technique.

It would be less than a year before I slipped my hand under the gills of my first 40, while my eel hung from its mouth. And many others would follow.

Live eel casting is a nice compromise between plugging and conventional bait soaking. They're best fished like a slowly retrieved plug, allowing the angler to cover a lot of water with an offering that bass find hard to pass up. This combination of mobility and effectiveness makes a live eel an excellent bass-hunting tool.

If you can put the eel within striking distance of a decent bass, Mother Nature will often take care of the rest. It's been theorized that bass attack eels not only for food, but out of a response born from some sort of competition between the two species on the striper spawning grounds. While we can only guess at a striper's motivation for striking at something, I've landed bass that had little chance of being able to eat the eels that they hit.

One night while reaching into the mouth of a striper that weighed almost 30 pounds to remove my eel, my hand hit something that didn't belong there. When I flipped my light on, I was amazed to see the tail of a nearly 2-pound bluefish sticking out of the gullet of the bass. I carefully eased the bluefish out to find the front three-quarters partially digested, while the tail section was in good condition because it was too large to fit in the bass's stomach. This bass could not possibly have been hungry, yet it still hammered my 20-inch eel.

Suffice to say that bass often find eels irresistible. The challenge is to get the eel in front of a big bass, and then convert the strike into a landed fish. The ability of the angler to do this is influenced heavily by equipment and eel selection.

I have two outfits that I like for fishing live eels. For relatively shallow water with slow to moderate current, I use a 9-foot graphite rod that was built from a 10-foot Lamiglas GSB1201L blank with one foot cut from the butt. The rod is balanced nicely with a Van Staal 200 spooled with 30-pound-test Spiderwire Stealth. The outfit is ideal for casting eels up to about 18 inches, and with a properly set drag, does a fine job handling large fish.

For deeper water applications, or where there is substantial current, I opt for an 11-foot graphite built on a Lamiglas GSB1321M. This rod is well matched by a Van Staal 300 or Penn 706 spooled with 50-pound-test Spiderwire Stealth.

I always fish the eel without weight, and the terminal rig couldn't be much simpler. I prefer a 40-inch length of 50-pound-test fluorocarbon

Eeling is a technique that focuses on quality over quantity. An otherwise slow night changed quickly into a memorable one when the author beached this 45-pound bass on a live eel.

with a size 1 barrel swivel on one end and a 7/0 octopus-style hook on the other. I grasp the eel firmly by the head with my burlap rag and whack the tail end hard against a rock several times. This does not seem to be at all detrimental to the effectiveness of the eel, and it allows me to work it more slowly along the bottom without getting hung up. In shallow areas, I usually start a slow retrieve as soon as the eel hits the water.

Hits on an eel typically feel like a couple of sharp raps. When I feel this, I drop my rod tip, wait for the line to tighten, then set the hook hard multiple times. The elapsed time between the hit and the hookset is only about three seconds. By hitting the fish quickly, I'm more likely to get a firm hookup in the mouth instead of catching the hook on softer tissue that might tear during the fight. This is also better for fish that will be released. Another reason I strike early is to pull the eel away from smaller fish that I don't want to waste my time or eels on. Since some of my largest stripers have fallen to eels that were dead or nearly so from having been hit by several fish, I use my snakes until they stop producing.

If you miss a fish cleanly on a hookset, you've got a good chance of having another crack at the same fish with a well-placed cast to where you had the hit. I'd always felt this was the case, because on numerous occasions, I'd have hits on consecutive casts after having gone a long time without any. Of course, I could never prove that the hits came from the same fish until something rather bizarre happened.

I had gone about 90 minutes without a hit, when I dropped a fish (and lost my eel) after a very brief hookup. I gunned the next cast to the same spot and within seconds I was on again. As I got the 20-pound fish close, I was glad to see that my eel had slid up the line. I was very confused when I reached down to grab the fish and another eel hung from its mouth. Apparently this was the fish I lost on the previous cast, and the tail end of the eel was still in the fish's mouth. When I set the hook the second time, I drove the hook through the tail of the first eel and into the fish. So I caught the fish, got both my eels back, and gained some reassurance that I had been right all along about missed fish coming back on subsequent casts.

By hooking the eel through the lower jaw and out just behind an eye socket, you'll rarely lose an eel.

Unfortunately, bluefish will also exhibit the same behavior. I once had a night of very good bass fishing interrupted by frequent bluefish strikes that were decimating my eel supply. The interference came to an abrupt end when I landed a bluefish that had one of my hooks in it that had been cut off an hour earlier. After removing that one fish, I was bluefish-free the rest of the night. Since then, I have switched to plugs on a few occasions to get unwanted bluefish out of the way. Of course, this strategy only works if there are a few blues around, but that is often the case where big bass in good numbers are feeding. I have also dealt successfully with bluefish by taking a short break. Once the scent and sound of food slapping the water were removed, the bluefish moved on. If there are a lot of bluefish in an area, you may have no choice but to fish elsewhere.

It would be pretty unreasonable to walk into bait and tackle stores and ask for some eels of a certain size, like the 19- to 22-inch ones that I prefer for inlets. This is where having a well-stocked home livewell becomes very important. Since eels will live in fresh water, maintaining a home supply is rather easy.

My home livewell consists of a 30-gallon container that's aerated by a pair of fish-tank pumps that would be suitable for a 30-gallon aquarium. The pumps are connected to plastic tubing with 6-inch air stones on the ends. Instead of letting the eels swim freely in the tank, I pack them into a covered 5-gallon black bucket with holes drilled into it. This bucket is submerged in the main tank. By constraining their movement, the eels stay thicker because they expend less energy. These eels cast better than skinny ones because they're a bit more aerodynamic. I use a black bucket because I prefer darker eels, and to some extent, eels will take on the color of their surroundings. This setup will easily support up to 75 eels, provided you change the water every couple of days or so.

Eels will live for quite some time out of the water as long as you keep them damp and somewhat cool. I transport my eels from home to my fishing destinations in a bucket with holes drilled in the bottom. These drain holes are important so that the eels don't suffocate in their own slime. This bucket is placed in a second bucket to catch the drainage. Eels will live for a day or two in this setup if sprinkled with crushed ice.

When fishing, I usually keep my eels in a small mesh diving bag tucked under my surf belt. The bag needs to be dunked once in awhile to keep the eels from drying out, especially on windy nights.

The most important thing to take with you when you go eel casting is a big-fish mind-set. You must make a commitment to stick with the technique and accept the fact that you might have to endure hours of hitless fishing to have a shot at a quality fish. This requires ignoring the smaller fish that are often readily available with other methods. This can be difficult in the beginning, but patience and determination will eventually lead to success. With that success, you'll acquire your most important weapon – confidence. Once you have confidence, and you're convinced that it's only a matter of time before you tie into another big fish, you'll be in an excellent position to consistently convert live eels to trophy stripers.

Win With Skins!
Making And Using Eelskin Lures

By Joe Lyons

Every striperman worth his salt knows of the deadly effectiveness of the eel, and most are devotees. Eels are highly versatile; you can fish them on the bottom, three-way them, troll them, sling them live and rig them. These prehistoric creatures are extremely hard to kill and work well even after they have passed into the eel afterlife. In the practical sense, they are the only live baits a surfcaster can use with regularity because most coastal bait shops stock them from May through the fall run. But next to an eelskin jig, probably their least-used incarnation is as a peeled accompaniment to a lure: the skin plug.

Like the long walk to a good fishing spot, or the night without sleep as you wait for the wind and tide to turn in a more favorable direction, making skin plugs takes effort. As in life, the willingness to work is one of striper fishing's great divides, separating those who merely want success from those who are willing to do what it takes to achieve it. That, and the fact that most people are not too keen about the word "skinning"! Fortunately, for those averse to skinning there are a couple of places that sell eelskins.

What are eelskin plugs you ask? Simply put, an eelskin plug combines the castability and permanence of a lure with the lifelike representation of an eel. This is achieved by skinning the eel and then sheathing and lashing the skin to the host lure. After this process is completed, you have a new type of lure unlike any other, one that incorporates qualities of the eel and the lure. Wooden, metal-lipped surface swimmers, in sizes of 4 to 6 inches, are the ones most commonly utilized, but needlefish, darters and subsurface swimmers are also used. Locally, the Gibbs Danny is the preferred lure, but Habs and Lex swimmers are excellent picks, as well.

It takes some work and time to fashion and keep skin plugs, but it is not nearly as time-consuming as building your own lures. It is a nice, simple craft for those who are challenged in the handyman department, like me. Once you know how to do it, you can produce one in about five minutes. The type of angler who takes the time to learn how to make and use a skin plug is in elite company; some of the best striper fishermen I know are die-hard skin plug enthusiasts. Like all things striper-related, if it takes time, effort and practice, you can believe it works. First we'll look at making and testing the lures and then how to use them.

First, you'll need to decide which lures you want to use as skin plugs. One word of caution before you enlist your favorite lures for eelskin duty: If you use and reuse wooden lures with eelskins, by the end of the season they will be waterlogged and infused with salt to the point where they will be ready for the trash. For this reason, I prefer to use lures that have been around the block instead of new ones.

Then, you'll need to get some skins. If you don't want to trap and skin them yourself,

eelskin plug materials:

- a suitable lure
- 50-lb-test dacron
- durable plastic bags
- pliers and hook cutters
- eel-skin (sized to match the plug)
- smaller replacement treble hooks
- razor blade or Exacto knife
- wax dental floss
- duo-lock snaps
- kosher salt

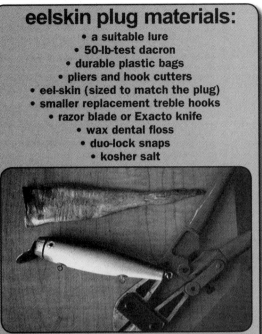

Figure 1: Cut the hooks off and carve a groove behind the swim plate.

Figure 2: Sheath the skin up the lure, and tie to the groove. Tie first with dental floss, then dacron.

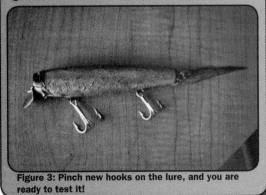

Figure 3: Pinch new hooks on the lure, and you are ready to test it!

you'll have to purchase them. The eels that you typically get for striper fishing are far too small – you will need skins from fairly large specimens. Two tackle shops in southeast Massachusetts that sell eelskins are Red Top Sporting Goods and Maco's, both in Buzzards Bay. To my knowledge, there are no shops selling skins in Rhode Island.

The tackle shops are good about letting you pick which skins are most suitable to your needs. The size of the lure you are going to dress will dictate the size of the eelskin you'll need. Keep in mind that you will only be using the tail end of the skin; for a six-inch lure this means about the last nine inches. Inspect the skin for tears and decomposition. The eelskin should be able to slide up around the fattest part of the lure while leaving about three inches to wobble off the tail end of the lure. This is important, because not enough skin off the tail end defeats the purpose of using a skin plug, while too much degrades the lure's castability and presentation.

Now comes the assembly:

1) Cut the hooks off your lure and file a notch around the entire body of the lure (this assumes you are using a wooden lure) at the place where you will tie the skin on. The notch should be straight and at least 1/16-inch deep. See picture for an approximation. More striper fishermen prefer to use skin inside out (the blue side) rather than right side out, feeling that the inside color is more attractive to the stripers – decide for yourself after you have been using them for a while. (*Figure 1*)

2) Work the skin up around the plug to the notched area leaving about three inches to dangle off the rear.

Using a length of old-fashioned waxed dental floss, make several wraps around the top part of the lure. Tie the floss snugly into place, making sure the wraps fall into notch. Trim off the excess, and repeat the process with the dacron. Overhand knots are fine for the floss, but use a surgeon's knot to fasten dacron. A drop of superglue at the knot is a good idea. *(Figure 2)*

3) Using a razor or an Exacto Knife, cut small slits by the hook hangers and pull them free. Attach new trebles to the body only, forgoing the use of a tail hook. Because of the added weight of the skin, most anglers will elect to go down one size on the treble hook.

At this time you can attach your treble hooks *(Figure 3)* if you are going fishing immediately, but if you are preparing them for later use, it's better to do so at that time because the kosher salt used to preserve the skin will rust the hooks. Place the finished lure in a heavy-duty plastic bag, sprinkle with about a tablespoon of kosher salt (per lure) and place in the coldest part of your refrigerator. Never freeze eelskins, as they will become brittle. The salt will keep the skin from becoming rancid. After using your lures, rinse them with cold water, pat them dry and reapply some kosher salt. The skins should last for many uses or until a bluefish tears into them.

Now that you have made your skin lures you will need to fine-tune them – as any process of lure modification tends to impact the lure's action. Most sharpies will seldom fish a metal-lipped swimming lure straight out of the box – and this is especially true with skin plugs. Other factors like where you plan on using the lure will also play a role.

Rhode Island surfmaster Steve McKenna has been using these lures for close to 30 years and he always tests them. "If I'm going to use the lure in a current, I'll bend the eye up so the plug digs into the rip and does not broach on the retrieve. If I'm going to be fishing a shallow, bony area, I'll bend it down so it rides higher in the water," said Steve.

There are a lot of ways to tune a plug, maybe enough for an entire article, but bending the eye up to make it run deeper or down to run higher in the water are the most common. If you are unfamiliar with plug tuning, keep it simple or enlist the help of someone with a little more know-how. Avoid bending the lip on metal-lipped swimmers.

It should be noted that there are several highly competent anglers that prefer lures other than lipped surface swimmers for their eelskins. There are some Cape Cod surfcasters who swear by needlefish skin lures. The Super Strike needlefish is a favorite because the head of the plug is grooved below the eye, which greatly facilitates attaching the skin. Wooden diving swimmers outfitted with eelskins have more than a few Rhody fans.

The eelskin jig is a favorite at the Cape Cod Canal and with boat, breachway and beach fishermen. The eelskin jig, an even more specialized tool of a smaller contingent of anglers, is highly productive. If you like to fish deep rips or you are looking for an eelskin presentation to troll in deep water you would do well to acquaint yourself with this time-tested lure. There are several competent local lure builders who pour and craft their own skin jigs. They are available through many local tackle shops, particularly those near the Cape Cod Canal.

Eelskin lures are best used as a daytime offering. This may come as a surprise, as eels are most often thought of as a traditional nighttime bait, but nonetheless they are predominantly a daytime lure. Skin plugs are typically used in situations where your first thought would be to use a popper, situations when you have calm water and want to cause a commotion to raise fish or when you have slower wave sets with discernible foam lines. Surfcasters do well with skin plugs, particularly at first light and during daytime hours at major points like Point Judith, in May, when herring are dropping out of the Narragansett Bay. Steve McKenna related a story about taking a 38-pound striper at Point Judith in May on a skin plug.

"The fish hit just as I was picking up the lure to get ready for the next cast. It almost pulled the rod out my hands. It scared the heck out of me."

Some friends of mine who fish the Elizabeth Islands with Capt. John Christian tell of stripers coming up from depths of 40 feet to take skin plugs.

Eelskin lures seem to work better when used with a duo-lock snap, as opposed cross-lock or tying direct. Use a typical lure leader: a quality swivel, three feet of 50-pound monofilament leader material and the duo-lock. Try a variety of retrieves, but whatever you do, fish each cast out. A lot of fish will follow this lure in, and then hit it as it wobbles in the wash of the first wave, just before you go to pick it up. If you ever find yourself in a situation where you are sight-casting to finicky stripers – pull out the skin plugs. Skin plugs seem to work best when nothing else will.

At times they will even out fish live eels. I'm not going to speculate on why fish do what they do, but for some reason they display very aggressive feeding behavior toward skin plugs. Either they hate them or they love them. I don't know. I only know that when they hit, make sure you are holding onto the reel stem with a white-knuckle grip. Fishing topwater lures for big stripers at first light is about as exciting it gets and a big reason why so many smart anglers use skin plugs. It just does not get any better.

Six Rules for Eelskin & Skin Lure Storage

1.) Don't freeze them, ever!

2.) Do rinse and dry skin lures after use.

3.) Don't leave skin lures in a rod rack.

4.) Always store skins and skin lures with kosher salt in the coldest part of the refrigerator.

5.) Skin plugs can be put away with skin on.

6.) Be sure to warn family members about those strange-looking things in the bag in the back of the refrigerator!

So as we approach the new season and you find yourself champing at the bit to have at the hordes of school fish that will soon invade local waters, just hold on a moment. If you really want to catch a large fish, like you profess, you may be better off forgoing an early season trip or two in favor of fine-tuning your tackle and making a half-dozen skin plugs. I found out the hard, tired way that it is often better to stay home and prepare than it is to pound away when there are only small fish about or when conditions are poor. Be ready when the big baitfish arrive and you find yourself on a sandbar casting skin plugs to trophies some June or November morning.

New Wrinkles On Fishing Plastic Baits
Expert Tips On Rigging, Technique & Tackle

By Robert Sirois

It was 1989 and most of my freshwater bass tournaments were behind me and I had enjoyed incredible success with a newly introduced plastic jerkbait called a Slug-Go. I was amazed at how it worked on freshwater bass and was itching to try it in the salt for stripers. It probably comes as no surprise to the anglers of today who use that bait that it proved to be deadly on stripers. There was just one problem. Fishing from a boat designed for bass lakes, a Bass Tracker Tournament V17, out of Scituate Harbor, presented its own unique problems and challenges, but I was especially frustrated during windy conditions or when offshore storms were tracking by. The heavier surf on the ledges I liked to fish between there and Hull sometimes prevented me from getting in close, which, combined with the wind, made it impossible to cast a plastic bait where I wanted it. My love of tackling stripers on freshwater bass or light saltwater gear compounded this problem, making casting distance something I was constantly looking to improve.

Then one day I was in a tackle shop I frequent specifically for their custom hand-poured plastic baits and I happened to explain my problem to the owner. He stepped from behind the counter to show me a new plastic jerkbait he was making, but what caught my eye was the odd way it was rigged, on a hook I'd never seen. The bait was very simple, nothing more than a wedge of plastic about 6 inches long and the hook I later learned was a 5/0 Owner saltwater series 90-degree jig hook, with a cutting edge point. It was incredibly sharp, unlike the hooks I'd been using, which usually had to be sharpened before use. I also liked the wide gap, as this I hoped would solve another problem, a high percentage of missed fish on hookset with narrow gap hooks. Wrapped along the shank of the hook was some lead solder, which he explained was for weight and enabled him to fish the bait more deeply, but I saw it as something that would increase my casting distance. I later learned that this weighting method offers many other advantages beyond additional casting distance.

So I stood there turning this bait over and over in my hand when I realized there was something else quite different about it. With only the hook point embedded in the bait, what was holding it on the hook? It certainly wasn't rigged anything like the Slug-Gos I'd been fishing. Upon closer examination I found that it was held in place by a little corkscrew-type device made of coiled wire that was clipped onto the hook eye. The "corkscrew" was turned into the head of the bait. The design was very simple (the current patent holder markets them under the name HitchHiker) yet it turned out to be a remarkable little device for holding plastic baits on a hook. Later I would discover that the life of my plastic baits almost doubled as this device prevented baits from being ripped apart so quickly, unless of course a mouthful of razor-sharp teeth might be involved. It also eliminated the need for superglue; the baits remained in place until they were no longer usable.

Of course, nothing worth perfecting comes quite that easily and it took me well over a decade to fine-tune the method, but I still marvel at what I had in my hand that day and cringe at the thought of being without it today. That one change in rigging alone was responsible for a tremendous increase in my striper catch. The other innovation that allowed a quantum leap forward in my ability to fish plastic effectively for stripers was the introduction of modern braided lines. In my opinion, anyone serious about fishing plastic for stripers must use a good quality braid and there are many available today. I firmly believe that braid almost doubled my hookup rate. This is due to the main characteristic of any braid, no stretch. I could feel the subtle taps I'd been missing due to the inherent stretch of monofilament and hooksets became a snap.

As with any system there are many parts making up the whole, all contributing to the overall effectiveness of that system. A good quality graphite rod is critical to telegraph to the angler what is happening at the business end. If you're going to fish from a boat, I recommend a 7-footer, with a fast tip and good backbone, but one rated specifically for the weight (plastic, hook, solder) you intend to fish most of the time. Now, if you're fishing a full range of plastic like I do, from little 4-inch Split Tails to 13-inch Mega Jerks, this will mean a couple of different sticks. I'm very partial to the Lamiglass GW series as they have a thicker wall than a lot of the higher-end graphite blanks and will take a beating better. My primary boat plastic rod (GW84ML, for lure weights 3/8 to 3/4 ounce) is actually rated below the weights I typically fish, but I've found that I can really load up this rod and get the most distance out of the 4- to 6-inch baits I usually fish.

If you're planning to wade, a good quality 8-footer would probably be the best bet, with an 8- to 9-footer fitting the bill for the jetty jockeys. Remember you will get the maximum distance from a rod rated at or maybe just shy of the weights you will be throwing; too heavy a rod and you will not be able to load it properly to achieve distance. All the anglers I see struggling with distance have one of two problems: The rod is a poor selection for the baits being thrown or they are hesitant to really load up the rod before letting a cast fly.

A reel is a tool to hold line and to fight the fish, and generally you get what you pay for. However, certain reels are, in my experience, just better at handling braid. My favorites are the Shimano Stradics; they handle the braid well and have excellent drags. If you wade and tend to dunk your reels on occasion, this might change your choice of reels, with a sealed design then becoming a priority.

With braid there is a learning curve, but I can give you a couple of tips to avoid some headaches. Have your reel spooled up at a reputable shop, unless you have experience with braid. If you opt to do it yourself, make sure to either put on a small amount of mono backing or several wraps of electrical tape before starting. If you don't, the braid may spin on the spool and this can be very frustrating if there happens to be a fish on the other end. To avoid the dreaded loop knots that can occur with this type of line, close the bail manually after each cast. I always do this and then either visually or with my fingers check to make sure the line isn't across the top of the spool. Some will go one step further, pulling out a short length of line against the drag, which also ensures any loop is eliminated. Distance and comfort are a trade-off in reel sizes; larger spools will gain you some distance but at the cost of added weight and balance. I use the Stradic 400 series reels on the boat, and the same or the 500 series when wading.

After I paid my dues initially, I stuck with the line I started with many years ago. Today

I'm still using 30-pound-test original Spiderwire, which, according to the manufacturer, has a diameter equivalent to 6-pound-test mono. The fine diameter and soft, limp nature of the line are major factors in gaining distance with the smaller plastic baits. Many friends of mine are high on other lines, Fireline and Power Pro, to name a couple. The key is to keep the diameter down; you want to gain the advantage of no stretch and sensitivity without sacrificing distance by going too high in rated strength. It's important to comparison shop, and there is a wealth of information out there in cyberspace that can save you many headaches in this department.

I carry a permanent green marker for coloring the line as it fades, marking some sections, leaving short lengths between untouched, sort of a camo effect. If the line looks a bit fuzzy at the end of a season, I will reverse it on the same reel or another of similar size.

The connection between braid and the leader is another personal choice. Many fishermen I know tie braid directly to mono, but I prefer a Spro 80-pound-test swivel. If you tie the braid directly to the leader, some of the popular ways to connect the lines include the surgeon's knot, Albright knot and a double uni. The consensus is that adding some turns in any knot is advisable with braid.

I prefer a swivel because many times I will be working only the first 1/3 of a cast and will reel in quite fast after the bait is out of the strike zone, which may twist the line with certain bait designs. The uni knot is the best way I've found to tie on my swivel and I continue to use it today, while others I know swear by the Palomar knot. Between the swivel and hook I use an 18- to 30-inch piece of Seaguar 30-pound-test fluorocarbon leader, although early in the season I might go with 20-pound test. If there are blues around I'll go with a heavier pound-test. In addition to the virtual invisibility a fluorocarbon leader gives you, it's important to have something other than braid to grab on to while landing a fish, as braid will cut you to the bone. The hook is tied on with an improved clinch knot. The head of the bait is then screwed on to the HitchHiker until it is close to flush with the hook eye. I then hold the hook shank with the bait hanging alongside, so I can see where the hook needs to penetrate the bait so it hangs straight. A slight bend is put in the bait so I can push the hook through the right spot and I'm good to go.

The Owner 5319 Saltwater 90-degree jig hook is my favorite in 3/0, 5/0 and 7/0 sizes for fishing plastics of 4, 6 and 9 inches, respectively. Daiichi offers a similar 60-degree jig hook with the HitchHiker pre-rigged and others offer similar designs. It's important to find one designed for salt water because freshwater types will not last as long and are also of very fine wire that can easily straighten under the weight of a large striper.

Weighting the hook is a crucial step when rigging the corkscrew type of plastic baits. I use lead-free rosin core solder of approximately 1/16 diameter, which you can find at any hardware or plumbing supply store. Wrapping the solder is an easy task, but it's important to wrap toward the bend of the hook. Wrap to the hook eye and then wrap back over the first layer, working back toward the hook bend again. That step locks the solder in place, preventing fish from pulling it down the hook or loosening it. Preseason, I might get fancy and paint the solder black to match the hook finish or red to hopefully trigger some strikes, but midseason any replacements are plain solder. You can vary the weight of the hooks two ways, either by varying the diameter of the solder or how far back down the hook you wrap the second layer. You have to be careful not to go too heavy on the solder, as it will close the gap of the hook and start to make hooksets more difficult.

I discovered a few other advantages the solder offers over putting plastic on a jighead as most anglers do today. First let me say, I have pounds and pounds of jigheads on my boat and in my shore bag, as there are times the vertical presentation a jighead offers is more effective. I discovered early on that spreading the weight out over the length of the hook allowed me to work my baits in more of a horizontal presentation, even while fishing depths to 20 feet, which I do at times. This is key to the success of this weighting method: Weight can be added for distance or depth considerations, without radically altering the inherent action of an unweighted plastic jerkbait. With a jighead that lends itself to more of a vertical presentation, there is very little erratic side-to-side movement, which bass find hard to resist. An unweighted plastic bait has this motion, and my rigging method only affects that action slightly when worked properly.

Consider what happens when you stop your retrieve when working a piece of plastic on a jighead. It goes basically straight to the bottom as all the weight is up front. When rigged with the weight spread out, baits fall at a more gradual angle and on more of a horizontal plane. In the case of my Ledgerunner split tails or similar wider-bodied baits, they will actually spiral in a 5-foot circle when given slack line. I am constantly on the lookout for my bait coming back to the boat (good polarized glasses a must), because I'm looking beyond it for following fish. If a fish follows but doesn't seem inclined to strike, stopping the retrieve and feeding some slack can be very productive. There is something so natural about bait spiraling down in front of a striper and few of them will pass up what appears to be an easy meal. I get such a thrill out of watching a large fish rush forward suddenly and suck in my bait.

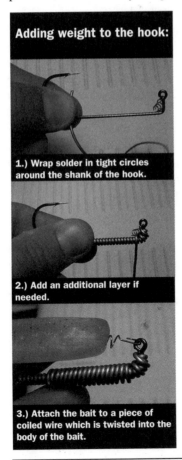

Adding weight to the hook:

1.) Wrap solder in tight circles around the shank of the hook.

2.) Add an additional layer if needed.

3.) Attach the bait to a piece of coiled wire which is twisted into the body of the bait.

The traditional jighead is also very likely to snag when fishing rocky bottoms. I lose so few baits on the bottom that I almost consider this rigging snagless. It's not, of course, but in comparison to a jighead, it's as close as you can get. That is a big advantage when fishing shallow rocky waters when you still want the additional weight for casting distance but don't want to be constantly losing terminal tackle. Look at the picture of the rigged bait. This rigging exposes so little of the hook that it is very effective in weedy water, as well. I don't hesitate to throw one before going to look for cleaner water. So with some creative weighting and presentations, you can work your offerings from the surface to a depth equal to your patience without sacrificing too much inherent action.

I try to experiment hour to hour, as bass will reposition themselves with changes in current, sun and cloud cover, wind, bait movements and even boat traffic. I vary depth with weight, line diameter, bait size and shape, counting down after a cast before I begin the retrieve. If I don't have success, I make changes in this order of importance: presentation, bait size, bait shape, weight, color and then location. When I start to get hookups or strikes, I make mental notes. Was that fish holding tight to the structure or well off it, was it on the up or downcurrent side, what was the approximate depth and how was I working the bait? I try to duplicate what works at other locations offering a similar set of conditions, too. Patterns change quickly, so try not to get stuck in that proverbial rut, repeating all day what worked at first light.

Here are some of what I've found to be the most effective presentations for plastic.

Twitch-twitch-pause is at the head of the list for all jerkbaits. I try to vary the way I twitch the bait, from subtle movements of just the rod tip using my wrist to the other extreme using the large muscles of the forearm, combined with some upper body movement. I vary the length of the pause, sometimes waiting longer to either gain depth or maintain a depth I'm working.

The dead-stick approach, allowing the bait to sink slowly and drift on its own without imparting any action, can be very effective at times. Casting upcurrent on the edge of a rip or seam is a prime example of a good time to try the dead-stick approach. By doing this you are allowing the current to impart action and to present the bait.

A weightless surface retrieve can be deadly when bass are feeding shallow or up on the flats. A variation is to purposely rig the bait with a bow in the belly, as opposed to hanging straight, which allows you to skip it across the surface or on harder pulls, jump it clear of the water. This works best with wider-bodied baits. I might vary from a slow steady retrieve to adding some pauses or jerks along the way, with a rapid high-speed retrieve sometimes drawing explosive strikes.

Drifting and allowing wind and current to move your boat over structure can be a great way to fish humps and ledges with sufficient water over them to allow for a safe drift. I love to cast and work a jerkbait because the hits are somehow that much more intense, but windy conditions sometimes beg for drifting or another presentation called strolling (see below). Whether you use a weighted hook or jighead depends on the depth of the structure and the speed of the drift. Some experimentation might be needed to get your bait into the strike zone, but once dialed in, this method can produce on each drift over the target.

Swim baits like soft plastic shads and curly-tail grubs are best fished on jigheads because a constant swimming retrieve is needed to trigger the action built into the tails of these very effective baits. These past few years I've become a big fan of large grubs and I've had tremendous success swimming a basic smoke/glitter 8-inch grub on a 1-ounce Owner jighead. There is something about a large grub swimming slowly through Mr. and Mrs. Roccus's home that they simply can't resist. It's also a great way to cover water, and by counting down before beginning your retrieve and varying the speed of the retrieve, you can easily work it to depths of 30 feet without too much effort.

Strolling is a term I believe was coined in the freshwater bass tournament scene and describes the use of the trolling motor for trolling. (In most bass tournaments trolling with the "big" motor is against the rules, but using the trolling motor to move the bait through the water is kind of a gray area.) Anyone with a rig equipped with a trolling motor like mine should definitely give this presentation a try because a lot of water can be covered but at a very slow speed, which is almost mandatory to catch big bass. Jighead weight, body size and shape, line diameter, amount of line out behind the boat, current and the speed setting on the trolling motor are what control the depth at which the bait will run. People fishing the Thames River all winter will see me "strolling" frequently, while dragging a 4 1/2-inch split tail on a 3/8- or 1/2-ounce Kalin jighead. I set my trolling motor on 50-percent power and run it intermittently to give the bait some vertical movement. I keep my finger on the line, giving the rod tip a sharp snap every so often to impart erratic movements. In that situation I prefer 6-pound-test Stren fluorocarbon; this light line lets me gain additional depth without too much stretch. In season and closer to my home waters, in the morning when the surface feed slows or stops and I am still marking fish below, strolling an 8-inch grub will usually trigger several more good hits.

If you are just getting into throwing plastic, here are some of my favorite baits. A well-stocked box should contain a selection of 4-, 6- and possibly 9-inch stick-type jerkbaits, 4- to 7-inch forked-tail wider-bodied jerkbaits and some 5- and 8-inch grubs and swim baits. Colors that will cover you for most situations are smoke, pearl or white, yellow, olive, black, purple and bubblegum or red. These can be solid colors or combinations of two in laminated baits. I'm a strong believer in the "K.I.S.S. principle" (Keep It Simple, Stupid), especially when it comes to colors, and I'd be 100 percent confident with a box full of smoke/glitter baits. My favorite color has a smoke top with black glitter over a clear plastic belly with a good amount of holographic glitter, which will throw many hues of colors. The dark over light is a pattern we all see in most baitfish and it remains a high-confidence selection of mine.

On the hardware side of things, a selection of 60- or 90-degree saltwater hooks with strong shanks, sharp points and wide gaps are the way to go. Medium and large size HitchHikers will fit the 3/0 and 5/0 sizes. I look for jigs with the same high-quality hooks ranging from 3/8 to 1-1/2 ounces.

If you've never had much luck with soft plastic baits, I hope you will dust off that box or start putting together a new one and hit the suds with a fresh perspective. Don't forget to set the hook, and tight lines. ◄■◄

-Bob Sirois is owner and manufacturer of Ledge Runner soft plastic baits.
www.ledgerunnerbaits.com

The Art Of Plugging

By Dave Manzi

I have been fishing on Cape Cod for many years and have gone through many phases. From tossing bucktails in the Cape Cod Canal and diamond-jigging for mackerel and pollock as a kid, to jigging up squid and dunking worms for winter flounder and cod when I was a little older, along with the occasional trip to the sands of the Big Beach with my father and later with my friends, the Cape has been my classroom. Along the way there were other adventures – running Plum Island in an old Scout and fishing the Elizabeth Islands when I had my boat were times I'll never forget.

But my true passion is plugging along the Outer Cape beaches. This is an angling art form that takes years to understand and master to the point that you can expect to hook up consistently. It's all about putting in the time, because that is the only way to learn to read structure and make a good guess as to where the stripers will be, figure out what they're eating, and therefore what to throw at them.

I don't claim to know everything – nobody does – but what I'm offering is what I've learned over all those nights on the sand. I'm not promising you'll catch fish right away, only that you'll have the right starting points and maybe I can shorten your learning curve.

The first thing to understand is what type of bait is available to the stripers that visit the Cape, and when it shows up. We usually start fishing seriously in late April when small bait starts to get active in the estuaries. We look for grass shrimp, spearing and worms; when they are around, you can be pretty sure that there are at least schoolie-size stripers in those places, too. But come May, it gets serious. The big bass show, and they are on herring. Along the Outer Cape and in some of the harbors, sand eels start to show. In the waters of the Upper Cape, squid are in deeper water and on the rips; mackerel should show by the third week of May, heading down Vineyard and Nantucket sounds. They aren't a big part of the bait mix on the Lower Cape, but the stripers are used to looking for them so they figure into our plans as far as which plugs are used.

Later in the month, hickory shad appear and stay into June in some of the bays. At times marauding bass and blues will push Atlantic sea herring on shore. Bunker will show later, and in late summer the small herring dump out of the lakes and ponds.

All of these baitfish are different sizes, shapes and colors, and they move in different ways. Knowing what each one looks like and its habits is the first and most important part of your lure-selection process.

Let's start by looking at colors. Although they don't exactly match any bait, solid colors are a good bet. The three basics are white, yellow and black. You can build from there, and yes, color and combinations of colors do matter. Some of my favorites are yellow and white, black and gold, black and purple, white and pink, and pink and silver blue. If you review the bait types listed above, take a look at them in a book or, better yet, in the flesh; you'll see why I like those color combinations. And don't be afraid to paint your plugs to your liking. An intangible but vitally important component to fishing with plugs is that you must have confidence in what you are throwing, and if you believe the color you're using is a close match to the bait that's around, you'll fish it longer and better. I will go into depth on color as I talk about each type of lure.

Plastic lures such as Bombers, Yo-Zuris, Mambo Minnows and Megabaits are readily available at most tackle shops (compared to some of the wooden plugs I'll be mentioning). You'll see dozens, maybe hundreds, of colors and sizes of these lures on the wall of your local tackle shop. Some of them, even by the same manufacturer, have very subtle, almost imperceptible variations in their color scheme and construction. Take the Bomber, for instance, in variations of yellow. The yellow and white that is being sold now and the older yellow and white (when Bombers came in a box) are not quite the same. The older Bombers had a seam along the top and bottom; I can tell you from experience that they swam differently. You'll also see one with a black back and a yellow belly, and there is another with a black back that has a lime-yellow belly. Nearby will probably be one called School Bus that is mustard yellow with broken lines on the side. And you'll see similar color schemes on lures by those other manufacturers. As you can see, there are a lot of choices and nuances involved just in one color; you'll find the same thing with the other basic colors.

The author works his plug magic along the Big Beach.

Why so many colors? Is it just a scheme by the lure manufacturers to empty your pockets? I don't know, maybe that's part of it, but consider this: They wouldn't keep making all those variations, year after year, if they didn't catch fish. That's the bottom line: Sometimes the fish will show an unmistakable preference for one color, and an identical lure with a tiny bit different color scheme won't get a look. The truth is, you'll have to carry a few variations. Then your job is to determine which one the fish want.

Here's how to approach that task. Let's say you are going to stick with Bombers only; it's a bright day and the sun is going to drop in a few hours. You're going to cycle through your plugs, being sure to try specific presentations with each one. We'll imagine you're fishing over and around a sandbar. (I will get into how to work structure later.) Starting with the yellow and white Bomber, which is a good choice on a bright day, reel the lure in without imparting action to the rod. Make four or five casts; if you don't get results, try working the plug with short pumps of the rod, with an occasional pause for another few casts. Next, drop your rod tip to the sand directly in front of you, sweep the rod back toward the side, move the tip back in front of you, reel in the slack, pause and repeat this process a few times. Then it might be time to try a dead drift – just cast the Bomber out, reel in just enough to keep a tight line between you and the lure, and let the wave action push it along, giving it an occasional short rip or twitch. Some nights the bass will eat the plug only when it's stopped; at other times they may want the Bomber's lip digging in the sand with short rips imparted for action. Remember, sand eels are the staple food on the Cape for bass, and sand eels spend most of the time hiding in the sand.

If I were fishing after dark, I would add a slow crawl with an occasional twitch to these alternative retrieves. One of them will work if there are fish around. The point is to work each differently colored plug in this manner until you find the color and the action that triggers a hit.

As the seasons pass, you'll accumulate more colors by different manufacturers; always remember to fish methodically and vary your colors with a logical sequence rather than just grabbing anything in the bag and always fishing it the same way.

Besides color and the movement you impart with the rod and reel, you have to consider the action that is built into the lure. Is it what you want, and if not, how can you change it? In other words, does it move like the bait you're trying to imitate? Is the side-to-side motion tight or loose? Does the plug roll, which is an unnatural movement?

A wooden Danny plug is a good example of a lure that can be "tuned" to have a specific action. Let's say you want your Danny to stay right on top because that's where you've seen the bass feeding. You would bend the eye down, but you have to be careful bending the lip down because too much bending may cause the plug to roll rather than undulate from side to side, which is the best action for a surface-running Danny. You can bend the lip just a tiny bit; there is a sweet spot on every plug, a point where a combination of a slight bend of the eye and the metal lip results in a perfect swimming action. You may want that plug to dive; if so, the trick is to bend the eye up. That will make the plug dig, and if you bend the lip up a little, that too will help it dive; you will notice hardly any roll. Take into account that you may be tuning the same plug a number of times to make it do what you want because the amount of current varies at different stages of the tide.

You're kind of stuck with how plastic swimming plugs like Bombers run, but you can change them a little by heating up the lip and bending it down. This will make it run right on top. You should replace the hooks and split rings (I like a 2/0 VMC treble in front and a 1/0 VMC as the back hook) because the ones that are used by the manufacturer tend to rust. But don't use anything big; doing so will kill the tight wiggle that you want with this type of lure. This is why I use the smaller hook in the back. Adding weight in the tail will slow the action down, which can be a good thing if you're throwing Pikies and want a lazy tail wag but is not desirable with plastic swimmers.

If you plug the surf on the Outer Cape, you have to be throwing wood; one of my favorites is the Pikie-style swimmer. Unfortunately, you won't find these in many tackle shops because they are made by custom plug builders who sell only small lots in a few shops. Quite a few surfcasters turn their own, and you may be able to score some if you attend the annual Rhode Island Saltwater Anglers Association or Massachusetts Striped Bass Association shows. Or you could join one of those groups, meet some of the members who make plugs, and learn how to make them yourself.

The best time for Pikies is in the spring and into June, when herring and shad are around. You can also sometimes do well with them at sunup during the summer along the outer beaches. In late May they work well around rocks and in fast water. Big fish love them; any Pikie in blue and silver is hard to beat. I have been tossing a Pikie made by Mike Fixter that is dark green on top and light blue on the sides, fading into a creamy pearl belly. This plug has been producing for me since May. I paint mine olive with a gold belly, with a purple hue on the sides and black fogged in around the eyes. I came up with this color combo; it works at night and during the day under cloud cover. If you want the most important basic colors, go with all-yellow, blue and silver, and olive and white.

These plugs are designed to work on or close to the surface. The action is like an injured herring; I vary my retrieve and pop the tail up out of the water just after a very short pause. You can also work these plugs with short pops, varying the amount of time between them so that the retrieve is erratic. This should be done with a stout rod and braided line so that you have complete control over the action, have no slack in the line and can set the hook hard when a fish hits. Using a conventional setup rather than a spinning rod helps in this regard, too. I also use a very large snap (not a snap swivel) because it allows the plug to move in a natural manner from side to side. Be sure to check your leader often. These lures tend to tumble when they're cast; you will foul-hook one from time to time and the hooks may fray the leader.

My other preferred surface swimmer is the Danny-style wooden plug. I tune them to stay up in fast water, so that just swinging the lure in fast water with short pumps will impart a bit of action. There are a few ways to work a Danny. If the bass are boiling on the plug but not taking it, a short pop may get them to hit. I drop my rod and snap it, as I want the Danny to roll slightly and pop. We call this "ripping the lure." If the bass want the lure just below the surface, tune it to dive as I described above and use the same rod action.

Sometimes, when the bass are just nipping the tail, you can drop your rod and pause to get a hookup. I usually work a Danny with short pumps but a slow retrieve to impart some action on the lure. Sometimes I will drop the rod about six inches and pop the lure, then continue a slow retrieve, then repeat in a swim/pop sequence. Don't forget what I said at the beginning: Try different retrieves and swap out lures after a set of retrieves, but do it methodically!

The best colors, the ones that will cover most situations and imitate most of the baits, are solid yellow, solid white, white with a pink stripe, blue and silver. Go with black, gold and silver for cloudy days.

In the general category of wooden swimming plugs, we shouldn't forget the new Mr. Wiggly. The originals were made by Tony Stetzko Sr., and I still have a few in my shop and my surfbag. His son, Tony Stetzko Jr., is selling a modern version, still made out of wood, that is a proven fish catcher. They are jointed, designed to swim under the surface, and they remind me of a large, jointed Rapala but are shaped better. I fish them in places where a sandbar runs parallel to the beach. I toss it out into the shallow water over the bar, then drag it into the deeper water off the edge. If a striper is holding in the deeper water, the lure gets slammed.

So far we've looked at Bombers, Dannys and Pikies, including how I fish them, along with which colors have worked for me over the years. I have a few other favorites, though; some are relatively new and some have been around for decades. They are proven winners and I wouldn't hit the beach without them.

The predominant bait on the Lower Cape is sand eels, so naturally I started using soft plastic lures as soon as they began to show up in the local tackle shops. Many different companies offer soft baits that are dead ringers for sand eels and I've tried them all, but as far as I'm concerned, the three key players are Ledgerunner, Slug-Go and Storm. There are many color combinations to choose from, and more all the time, so your best bet is to start with basic, solid colors and build from there. These would be pearl, white, pink and yellow.

Ledgerunner baits are a little fatter than Slug-Gos, and while the Slug-Gos are probably a more exact imitation of sand eels in terms of profile, the Ledgerunners are tougher and last longer. They are great lures to use on leadheads and are available in 6-, 9- and 13-inch versions. The larger sizes can be rigged without weight and cast quite well. I use a large hook, about a 7/0 or 8/0; the ones sold for use with the 9-inch Slug-Gos work fine. Be sure any hook you use is very sharp. When I'm rigging these baits I wrap fly-tying thread around the hook and then glue the soft bait on the hook; they can slip down the hook without glue. I like slow-set superglue, as it does not "burn" the plastic, which can be a problem with the instant-set variety.

For 6-inch soft baits I use 1/2-and 1-ounce leadheads for fishing the surf. When I fish the Cape Cod Canal, with its strong currents, I step up to 9- and 13-inch models on 2- and 3-ounce leadheads.

Although they don't last as long, the advantage of Slug-Gos is that they are a softer plastic and because of that they have a tad bit more action. They are great in places with very little wave action and current, and I'll often fish them without weight. I do still use them in the surf at times, though, especially if a particular color is hot. If I do, I rig them like the Ledgerunners with leadheads or rigged on a small bucktail jig.

If I'm not trying to imitate sand eels but still want to use a soft bait, I turn to the Storm lures. They are great in early spring when herring and shad are around; they have worked for me in April and May when no other artificial lure will get a look from the bass. Ledgerunner also makes some shad bodies and split-tail-type soft plastic that is deadly around rocks.

The basic colors I mentioned will get you by most of the time, but before long you'll want to add some of the combination colors made by the manufactures mentioned above. When juvenile herring and menhaden are around, you should try a blue shad color or something in blue and silver. Olive and white can be a winner, too, especially if you fish around rocks or anywhere that it's likely eels will be found. If you get totally into soft baits, don't be surprised if before long you're either pouring your own custom colors or having them made for you – that's what I do.

Although there are exceptions, I go with yellow during the day and under a full moon, and pink seems to work well under cloud cover with the slim-bodied baits. Pearl white is a great all-around color. I usually work all three colors when I am targeting bass with soft plastic. When I'm fishing shad-bodied soft lures in the spring, I like pearl white and anything I can find that is close to bunker color; these are killer on the bass. I also like chartreuse in the smaller sizes, though it does not match anything in nature. Who knows why the bass fall for chartreuse, but they do.

I've picked out my colors, I've rigged up a few soft baits, now how do I fish them? Let's say I'm fishing the sand. Imagine a hole or bowl with a bar on one side that curves out and runs almost parallel to the beach. On the other side of the bowl is a sandbar running almost straight out. It's the early morning, just after the sky has started to brighten. I'll use a 1-ounce leadhead with a pearl-white 6-inch Slug-Go, or a similar size and color Ledgerunner, and fan cast to every area along the edge of the curving bar. Fan casting is nothing more than covering all points within my casting range. I'll hit both the smooth and the white water. Starting in close to shore, I'll cover every bit of water I can, then take a few steps down the beach and repeat the process. I'll be casting to some water I've already covered, but the lure will swim away from the edge of the bar at a different angle, which may be what the fish are looking for. It's important to take up slack quickly; that way I won't miss any hits. What I do is let the lure sink for at least 10 seconds, then pump the rod, and reel in just enough to take out the slack. I really don't want it to rise much in the water column, just have a straight line to the lure and impart a jigging action. On the drop or just as I start to raise the rod is when the hit will come most of the time. If that does not work, I will cast back out and reel straight in and impart some action with the rod, three- or four-inch twitches every few turns of the reel. I may do this for five casts and then toss the lure into the deep water in the bowl and work it back in with erratic action.

If nothing is happening in the bowl or along or over the curved bar, I'll try the other side, where there is the bar that runs straight out, being sure to cast over both sides of that bar. While I'm working both bars and the bowl, I'll be swapping out colors, too, but always in a pattern. This is just another example of what I have already talked about: cycling through my casting routine in a methodical manner. Before long you will develop your own routine as you spend time on the beach, and figure out which colors and retrieves work in different conditions.

Here's an assortment of topwater plugs that should be in every surfcaster's bag. From the top: Yo-Zuri Hydro Pencil (similar to the Zara Spook), Creek Chub Popper, Gibbs Polaris Popper, Gibbs Pencil Popper, and, last but not least, the deadly Hab's needlefish. (Note: Not all needlefish are designed to float. Many models are intended to be fished below the surface.)

The point is to make every day or night on the beach a learning experience.

Although working a swimming lure is a big part of the art of surf casting, there is nothing like topwater action. Most of us live for the strike on top. Chances are you'll take more fish with subsurface lures, but the sight of a huge striper crashing a popper is what you'll see when you close your eyes and relive your fishing experiences as the snow piles up this winter. You should always have a few poppers in your bag, and there are plenty of good choices. Some of my favorites are the Gibbs Polaris and the "canal special," which is a pencil popper with the bottom flattened out. Although not really a popper, Mike "Tattoo" Dauphin of Rhode Island makes and sells a Zara Spook-type topwater lure that is fished with a back and forth "walk the dog" technique that the stripers just hammer. And good old chuggers like the Creek Chub and the Atom take their share of fish every year.

When I fish a Polaris popper, as soon as it hits the water I quickly reel in any slack and go tight to the lure. This is because there are times when a bass will whack it almost the instant it hits, and I don't want to miss the strike. I then start a series of short pops that stay consistent during the retrieve. When the plug nears the surf that's breaking on the shore, I continue working it – and I've had plenty of strikes almost at my feet!

If this doesn't get results, then it's time for a change of retrieve styles. I may try a chugging, steady retrieve for a few feet, then a hard rip of the lure across the surface, followed by a short pause, then a repeat of that sequence. With this type of retrieve, I usually get the hit just as I give the lure that hard rip by way of a sharp upward or sideways pull of the rod.

I like to work these lures out a good distance. If I were using a popper in the area described above, I would start by working the far end of the bowl and then work the bars to the left and right. If I am fishing rocks, I cast well beyond them and work the plug along the ebb or down-tide side of the rocks. I work rips in the same manner.

Pencil poppers are a little different. First of all, they're not designed to give the big splash of a popper with a wide, flat or concave mouth such as a Polaris, Creek Chub or an Atom. The most common retrieve should be one that "walks" the lure along the surface, which is accomplished by using a fairly high, side-to-side motion with the rod tip. A steady rhythm should be kept.

If there are no strikes, I will rip the pencil popper and go right back to the steady retrieve. I will say, though, that the slow side-to-side retrieve will result in some missed strikes. But here's the good news: For some reason, fish will often come back and hit a pencil popper again, which is something that doesn't happen too often with other types of poppers. With pencil poppers, it is much easier to impart variations in action by using your rod rather than by increasing or decreasing your retrieve rate. But that's the fun of it – I think that pencils require the most finesse of any poppers, and you have the most control, which is why I like them.

I keep my color selection very simple with poppers; my favorites are solid white and solid yellow. Yellow with a red head is a great combo; blue and white, and blue mackerel and green mackerel round out my everyday collection. Stick with the medium sizes for both the pencil and the Polaris. This will get you going and catching fish, and you can build your collection from there.

I've saved the best for last. I love to catch stripers of all sizes – who doesn't – but don't we all want that trophy fish? When I've got poundage on my mind, then I know I have to fish at night, and there is just one lure that out-produces all the others put together when the sun goes down – the needlefish! I will readily admit that I have hundreds of these lures and build more of them all the time, in a huge variety of colors and in many sizes and weights.

The thing is, for most people the needlefish does not inspire a lot of confidence. It has no "built in" action and it looks more like a stick than a lure. But that is the secret of why it works so well – the person holding the rod is totally in charge of how it performs. Once you learn to make it do just what you want, there is no better lure out there for taking big stripers. My best last fall was 45 pounds!

If you don't make them yourself or have a generous buddy who does, you'll find that there are only a few needles out there. The ones that are available are very good fish-producers, though, and they are each quite different and have specific uses. Here are some needles you should have.

The Big Four, as far as I'm concerned, are Gibbs (large size); Hab's (both large and small); Beach Master; and Super Strike (both sizes). Start with all-black and olive/white colors on all of these; then, as your budget allows, get some in pink, purple, and especially the Super Strike in lime green and dark green.

One of the main reasons that you'll want to have as many of these as you can is that they sink at different rates, and this can be crucial to how you will fish them in a variety of surf conditions. The needles I make have three sink rates: floaters, slow sinkers and fast-sinking models. All of the commercially made needles will sink. But if you need one of them to stay close to the surface, the trick is to begin your retrieve by reeling very fast so that the lure rises to the surface, then go into a painfully slow retrieve. This is far and away the most common way to work the needlefish, and often the most effective.

If I'm working a floating needle in calm water with very little tidal movement, I start with a steady, very slow retrieve. This is more difficult than it sounds! Put another way, you can't go too slowly with a needlefish. After about 10 or so casts I may start to impart a little action to the lure. I usually drop my rod two or three inches and lightly twitch the rod tip. The main thing is to resist the temptation to reel quickly.

It's not uncommon to get a strike and not hook up; this is where the fun begins and your discipline will be tested. Wait to set the hook until you can actually feel some weight. If the bass does not take the lure and you get some more bumps, rip the lure in a one-foot burst and then go back to that slow retrieve. Don't be surprised if the bass waits until you're about to pull the lure out of the water to hit. See what I mean about the discipline?

In faster water or when there is a little surf I go to a medium or fast sinker. Hab's or Super Strike needles work very well in these conditions. I will use the above techniques, but I'll also let the lure swing across rips and bars with no added action. A Super Strike is deadly in white water if you use some short pumping (ripping) of the rod. Don't forget to fan cast and work both sides of any bar, and concentrate on troughs or eddies around rocks. Always be on the lookout for rips and white water.

A trick you can use, and this works very well, is to add a black or red pork rind to the tail hook of a Hab's needle. Another is to cast out a fast sinker like a Super Strike, let it sink to the bottom, then work it with a very slow retrieve with some short rips of the rod to mimic sand eels jetting out of the sand.

When the surf is up, fast-sinking needlefish are the way to go. You can cast out and let the lure swing and bounce along, making sure you have a tight line to the lure; reel it in as it gets parallel to the shoreline. This will look like an easy meal for bass running in the current – be sure to reel the needle as slowly as you can.

Although that maddeningly slow retrieve is almost always the key to catching with the needle, and you should never abandon it too soon, there are times when it may help to mix things up a little. It won't happen often, but there will be nights when the bass won't even look at a slow-moving needle.

Swap out colors after going through a set of retrieve styles, giving each retrieve at least 10 tries. Even during the darkest nights, color can play a role in whether you catch or go home skunked. I put away my swimming plugs or poppers and tie on my needles at sundown or just after. I start with light colors, then go darker, and if there is some moonlight I will try yellows, greens and multi-colored lures. If there is a quarter moon and it's heading toward the new moon, then I use dark colors. Fishing during the full moon is not my favorite, but if you must, try solid yellow or yellow and white.

You'll find that many of the needlefish on the market have a tendency to float or run just under the surface. This is especially true of the smaller versions, so be sure to have some large ones that sink quickly. Don't use a light floater in a heavy swell; it will be on the beach before you can even work the water. The opposite is true in calm water: A heavy sinking needle just can't be worked slowly enough to be effective without sinking to the bottom. This is when you should use your floaters.

Fishing the big beach can be discouraging – there's so much water to cover and it's easy to fall into the habit of changing lures too quickly and using a totally random presentation. But, if you stick to a plan, fish the structure, do most of your fishing in low-light conditions and use the lures I've listed, then before long you'll find success more often. And even if you come home empty-handed, I guarantee that you will learn something every time.

Treat 'Em Like Trout
Nighttime Fly-Fishing For Stripers

By Gene Bourque

There's a sound that stripers make when they feed after dark and I think it has to be one of the sweetest sounds there is, kind of a slurp-pop-splash. The first time I heard it, I flashed right back to fishing on the Madison outside Ennis, Montana; it was the same sound, and the rises looked the same in the moonlight, only much bigger, of course. Since then there have been many, many nights in estuaries and the narrow entrances of salt ponds near my home on Cape Cod when I've listened to that wonderful sound and caught plenty of fish. The key to catching them is almost always the same – just think of stripers as overgrown trout! A measure of faith is required in this fishing, especially in midseason. For shorebound fishermen along the New England coast, after about the first week of July, the chances of taking many striped bass (especially big ones) during the daylight hours is slim, at best. So we become night owls, and here's where the faith comes in. You arrive at your favorite estuary in the early evening and it appears to be devoid of life beyond some dimpling baitfish. But you have to believe in your heart of hearts that things are going to change when darkness falls. And assuming you're there at the right stage of the tide and there isn't a lot of boat traffic, it will. Where do they come from? Downstream or in from the bay, who knows? Maybe both. It doesn't really matter because the fish will be there if conditions are right. It might be just a few but it might be a whole school, and the best part is, you'll probably have them all to yourself. Night-fishing is not practiced by raw beginners or casual fishermen.

Although I occasionally catch a few fish during the incoming tide, I always have the feeling that those fish just happen to grab my flies on their way somewhere else. Dropping tides are by far a better choice, and if high tide occurs just after dark, so much the better. Late night turns of the tide fish well, too, although most of us have to function the next day and a tide that begins dropping at midnight means some lost sleep.

The first three hours of the drop are best, but I've caught fish almost until the bottom of the tide on dark, overcast nights when the fish weren't jittery in very skinny water. If there is any light, though, even starlight on clear evenings, the fish will move out as the water level drops. It's during those first three hours that most of the bait will dump out, too, another reason I like that time period.

The first similarity to trout fishing that you'll notice is that after dark, many stripers take up feeding stations just like trout in a river. If there is a steady flow of baitfish, you can sometimes even time their rises, just like a trout sipping mayflies. Take a little time to observe the rise pattern and rhythm, then cast well upcurrent from the fish. Try to estimate when your fly is over the fish, and be ready! The hardest part of this is the observational phase; it takes a strong-willed fisherman to not start casting right away when good fish are feeding just a cast away. But those extra minutes may mean the difference between taking many fish or just a few. Plus there is the added rush of having a fish hit when you know you put your offering in precisely the right place at precisely the right time.

I learned this one night when I arrived at my favorite marsh just after dark and found the conditions about perfect. It was an hour after high tide, there was smooth water with no weed, a good tidal flow a couple of nights before the new moon, and plenty of bait in the water. The strange thing was, I could only spot what appeared to be two fish working. I walked way around them in the marsh grass and approached the water about 30 feet upcurrent from where they were feeding. The bait appeared to be tiny silversides and the fish were rising at regular intervals, almost in tandem. I tied on the smallest, sparse white Deceiver in my box and cast toward the far bank and let the fly drift to the fish. Again they rose together, but the one closer to me took the fly so softly that I hardly felt any weight at all on the end of the line – it just kind of stopped in mid-drift. Resisting my usual bad habit of hitting back hard when I feel a fish, I tightened up on the fish and off it went. Ten minutes later and well downstream, I had a nice plump 32-inch striper on the grass bank, the first of 11 between 32 and 36 inches that I caught in the next two hours. It was the best single night of fly-fishing from shore that I've ever had.

The reason everything worked out was because I kept returning to the same upstream spot after landing each fish and I made sure that the fly was over the fish when I expected the rise to come. If I'd cast right at the fish or let the fly plop down over them between rises, I think it's likely that at the very least I would have caught fewer fish and at worst I would have spooked them out of their feeding station. As each fish was hooked, it would take off downstream and another would take its place until they moved out with the dropping tide. Although I've never been able to duplicate that night in terms of numbers of large fish, I've taken plenty of

The right fly plus the right presentation will produce some fine fish after dark.

others of various sizes by employing this drift-to-the-rise method.

We're all guilty of slipping into using the same retrieve over and over. Part of what makes fly-fishing so attractive is the rhythm of the casting, which is easily followed by a rhythmic strip, stop, strip, stop. I readily admit that this is what I do most of the time, but I do occasionally vary the length of the strips and the stops without much thought. After dark, this may work, but there is a better way for most fishing situations when there is a moderate current running. Trout fishermen know this one, too – it's called the dead drift. In striper fishing, though, this type of a non-retrieve is more accurately described as a con-trolled drift, very similar to crosscurrent nymphing in a trout stream. Older fishing books describe this as the "wet fly swing" and it really works for striped bass. Cast directly across the current or slightly upcurrent, strip a couple of times just so you are sure that you have a tight line to the fly, then let it swing across the flow. The hit will come at a point about half way between directly across and directly downstream as the fly starts to accelerate and climb toward the surface. You'll be tempted to give the fly a little strip or move the rod tip a bit as you start to feel it accelerate, but resist this temptation or do it only as a last resort. For some reason, fish find that steady across and up movement irresistible after dark and I've found this to be especially so toward the latter part of the fishing season when you're dealing with savvy fish that may have been in the estuary for months. The take will often be solid but try to wait a heartbeat or so before you set the hook. One of my fishing partners describes what the fish do as "kissing the fly," and a quick hookset will often pull the fly right out of the striper's mouth.

One variation of this retrieve that has served me well when there is little current (those few days between the new and full moon when there is little tidal exchange, or at the top of the tide just after it turns) is a very slow but steady hand-over-hand. I can't stress enough how important it is to keep it slow, though; exaggerated movement will be ignored more than it will produce.

When the fly reaches the end of the swing directly downcurrent, allow it to sit there for a few seconds before you retrieve and start the sequence again. Sometimes a fish will follow the fly for the entire drift, trying to decide whether it looks good enough to eat, and that fly hanging in the current is just too easy a target. I've always found it interesting and perplexing that I have hardly ever caught a fish as I'm stripping the fly back to me, even when I know I passed over an actively feeding striper. I have no explanation for this, but that's what makes fishing great, isn't it?

How many patterns do you carry in your fly boxes? A dozen? Two dozen? Maybe more? I used to, too. Now I just carry about a half dozen, each in a couple of colors and sizes. The most obvious differences in most folk's flies are the colors, because, after all, most saltwater flies (with the exception of crab and squid patterns) are variations of the basic streamer used by trout fishermen for hundreds of years. These consist of a tail, upper and lower "wing," some sort of body wrap and a head built out of thread with eyes applied before the final finish. But I've come to the conclusion that after dark, color is just about irrelevant. Shading, however, can be crucial. After many years of using dark plugs for stripers off the beach after dark, I figured that black flies would be best. Sometimes this is true, especially on dark, moonless nights, but just as often I've used all-white or chartreuse and white flies with success in the late night hours. My admittedly unscientific method is as simple as it can be: If I'm in a spot with actively feeding fish, I'll give a dark-colored fly a few dozen casts and if after trying a number of different retrieves nothing happens, I'll go to a lightly colored pattern. Then if nothing has happened I'll go to Plan Two, which is to adjust the size of the offering.

The patterns I use are pretty dull and ordinary, but I make no apologies – they catch fish. Clousers, Deceivers, Brook's Blondes and Tabory Snakes are pretty much it. You can go crazy changing flies when you have too many choices and this is why I keep it simple. The absolute most important aspect here is not pattern, but size and movement. The trout guys, and I believe it was Ernest Schweibert who penned the term, understand the importance of matching the hatch.

An example: In the summer around the end of July, baby silversides leave their birthplaces in the salt marsh with an extreme tide, floating out with the dropping tide in waves. Some fishermen call these 1- to 2-inch babies "rainbait" because that is what these schools of fish look like as they swing toward the ocean – sheets of rain dimpling the surface. If you're lucky enough to be there when this happens, the fishing can be phenomenal. I've seen hundreds of stripers feeding at once on these tiny fish. But forget about your big bulky flies. Very sparsely tied white Deceivers, Brook's Blondes or Clousers will do the trick in size 2 or 4. Anything bigger and you might as well be throwing a 4-ounce popper! And here again, the controlled drift is the key. Size, profile and movement are the order of the day.

What about those times when everything looks right but there are no fish obviously feeding? This is a good time to try Sliders, Gurglers or even small poppers. If there are any hungry stripers in the area, at the very least you're likely to get a swirl at one of these surface patterns and possibly a very good fish. I consider these patterns to be a last resort as they are harder to cast and control, at least for me. I have friends who swear by surface flies after dark, however, and even though they don't catch as many fish as I do on a night-to-night basis, the ones they do catch are large by anyone's standards. So there may be something to it.

Most hard-core after-dark fly-fishers would agree that if you are only going to have one fly line, make it an intermediate (slow sink) and my preference is the clear, monofilament core variety. In most cases you'll be fishing relatively shallow water but you also want the fly to sink a bit, so high-density sinking lines and floating lines should be second and third choices. I fish a 9-weight rod because even after dark there are nights that the wind just won't lie down and this rod works well in my battle with the breeze. I know some excellent fly-fishers who do just fine with 7- and 8-weight outfits, so this may be a function of my casting deficiencies rather than a need for a "big gun."

Always remember to wade carefully and walk softly along the banks as you approach feeding fish. Trout fishermen working spring creeks often approach and cast to feeding trout from their knees. This probably is a bit extreme for stripers, but the theory is valid. Another conundrum that I've given much thought to is, if this stealthy method is necessary to approach stripers feeding close to grass banks and in shallow water (and it is), why is it that a hooked fish that charges around and splashes on the surface often has no noticeable effect on the other feeding fish?

Don't forget a small flashlight for changing flies or getting the hooks out of all the fish you're going to catch, but for goodness sake, turn away from the water when you're doing these things! One beam of light flashing across a narrow outflow can put the fish down for an hour, possibly for the rest of the tide. And forget about those headlamps that you'll see in some of the magazines. No matter how diligent you are about turning away from the water, all it takes is one splashy rise behind you as you're changing flies. Any red-blooded fisherman just has to sneak a peek over his shoulder and the result is like a spotlight from the guard tower at the state penitentiary.

Night-fishing for stripers is one of my main fishing passions. It's about peaceful surroundings and solitude. It's about anticipation mixed with frustration. And it's about that wonderful sound, which is only equaled by the music of the drag as a big striper heads for the open ocean and the fly line disappears into the dark.

Spin-Fishing The Worm Spawn

By Bob Sampson Jr.

O f all the angling waypoints along the marine fishing season, the one I enjoy most takes place during a couple of weeks in May when the worms come out of the mud for an orgy that Caligula would envy. Anglers often refer to this event as the worm hatch, but nothing is hatching at all; it is the annual spawning ritual of a small cousin to the sand worms (actually clam worms) used for bait – I think? (The buggers are difficult to identify.)

Confused? You should be. Even marine biologists have a tough time identifying the myriad worms that inhabit our local marine environment. There are literally thousands of species worldwide, with dozens if not hundreds of them found in New England's coastal estuaries.

Many species of polychaete worms go through swarming behavior when they spawn. Evidently, coming out of the mud and up into the water column is evolutionarily worthwhile, despite the worms' vulnerability to predation when they do, or they wouldn't be doing it. Swarming behavior helps them find mates. It also may increase the odds of fertilization as they use a broadcast method when they reach the surface, seeming to burst as they release their genetic material at the climax of this ritual.

There are various spawning swarms throughout theNortheast, so the one you've seen may not be the same species being discussed here. Regardless of the species, it appears that all of the major tidal estuaries from western Connecticut through Rhode Island experience some sort of swarming spawning behavior from a small species of polychaete worm late in the spring or early summer. Worms swarm in some places on a monthly basis during the summer; others only host this event once (when it is noticeable to anglers) each year. It is likely that in most locations there are swarms from the larger sand worm species that are dug commercially for bait. Years ago, I witnessed and fished a worm spawn with these large, bait-size worms on the Housatonic River with John Posh, owner of Stratford Bait and Tackle. There are probably minor worm spawns that go unnoticed due to locale, species or a habitat that does not hold the incredible number of worms it takes to create a spawning event such as the ones that take place in Ninigret Salt Pond or in the Mystic River.

For the sake of accuracy and out of personal curiosity, I have tried to positively identify the worm species that I have seen swarm by the thousands in Mystic River and Ninigret Pond (Charlestown Salt Pond, Rhode Island). None of the scientists I talked to could tell me exactly what they were, preferring to rely on what could be called common knowledge. In other words, in the way that I could tell someone who saw a huge mass of foot-long fish moving up a small tributary stream that they were seeing an alewife run, simply by timing and description, no one could tell me what species of worm I'd find at Barn Island or in the Mystic River.

Using Howard Weiss's book *Marine Animals Of Southern New England And New York* as a reference, by matching key features such as jaw structure and shape of the parapodia (little swimming legs) to the diagrams in this informative publication, the species this article deals with appears to be *Neres succinea*, the yellow clam worm. Some anglers refer to this as a cinder worm, but there was no reference to this local name in this fairly comprehensive book.

Right or wrong, regardless of species, all a fisherman needs to know are a few facts about worm spawns in general to help determine when a fishable hatch may occur in a given area. Bear in mind that most worm spawns are short-lived and easy to miss, even when you're watching for them. A couple of windy or bad weather days at the wrong time and, from an angler's point of view, it would be like the spawn never happened.

These swarms occur in shallow, tidally affected estuaries and river mouths. The larger the shallow-water area, the better the odds of the place being able to produce a fishable worm spawn of some sort. The fact is, beginning some time in May and lasting from a couple of days in some areas to a few weeks in larger habitats, these worms begin to spawn. I have read articles on fishing worm hatches that say the worm spawns coincide with full moons or new moons, but I have never found this to be true.

According to my records over the past decade, the short-lived but intense worm spawn in the Mystic River and nearby Palmers Cove lasts less than a week, usually only two to four days, tops. This short window of time generally occurs within three to five days on either side of May 22. This event has never even come close to falling on a full moon the times I have

witnessed it. Last year it was right on schedule, May 22 to 23. The fact that it occurs around the same date every year indicates that it is probably influenced more by daylight, which equates to temperature more than moon phase. The full moon shifts around the calendar while this event always seems to fall near the same date.

Worm spawn activity may start late in the afternoon, with a few scattered worms shooting around like little missiles. I've seen the first ones out and about as early as 5 p.m. when the sun was still bright in the sky. However, as daylight fades they begin swarming in huge numbers, peaking at or just after dark.

My personal observations, which are limited to a few days fishing each year for the past 8 to 10 years, indicate that the worms begin showing in the water column when water temperatures reach 60

This striper was feeding on worms. An example of one is pictured here below two 3 1/2-inch Slug-Gos. Note that it is breaking apart; the worms are delicate and difficult to handle.

to 65 degrees. They increase in number for a few days in a given area, finally peaking on an evening when there is an incoming tide that starts around dusk. Cold nights or chilling rains will shut the hatch off temporarily or end it if it's toward the end of the cycle.

The first worm spawn I witnessed in the lower Mystic River about 10 years ago was an eye opener. I had heard about these events but never experienced one firsthand because I had no clue how to anticipate it. It was an accidental discovery, like penicillin.

While talking to Al Fee, of Shaffer's Marina, he complained that he and a friend had been terribly frustrated by the stripers on the previous evening. Al said they saw hundreds of rises but couldn't get anything to take his Atom Popper, just a few short hits and swirls.

Curious about what was going on, my wife Karen and I showed up at Mystic the next night armed with light, freshwater-weight spinning gear and a load of soft plastics in various sizes and colors. During the late afternoon, schoolie stripers were present but sparse. Karen caught one doing one of her warm-up rituals where she tosses the lure about three feet from the boat and plays with it to check out the action. That was in the first five minutes, but things slowed down from that point. We caught only a half-dozen small schoolies in a couple of hours. Karen, who had worked the third shift the night before, asked me to drop her back at the car so she could nap. Being a seasoned striper fisherman, she urged me to keep fishing. We had driven for over an hour and she said there was no reason why I should miss the "witching hour," as she calls the blitz that often occurs around dusk.

As I headed back toward the main river, following the shallow channel north of Mason's Island, I saw what I thought was a small fish scoot by the boat in the flat, calm water of early evening. I went a few feet more and there was another, then two, then many. As I approached a rocky point near the main channel, there was a definite boil. It wasn't the blast of a predator hitting a school of fast-moving baitfish; it was more like a toilet flush. In the shade of the tree line, light-colored worms were scooting around all over the place, but there was plenty of space between them. The bass were keying in on their presence. As darkness fell, it looked like every worm that swam by was eaten by a striper. I had to look for the worms, which were plentiful but spread out.

All I had to do was lob a 4 1/2-inch Slug-Go to visible swirls and there was an almost instant hookup. Within two hours I caught about 21 more stripers between 16 and 30 inches. The fish were all extremely fat and in great physical condition.

That was it, my first worm hatch experience, and I loved it! It was a new type of sight-fishing, which for me has always provided an added degree of excitement to any angling situation.

The next evening found me back at the Mystic River once again, this time with my constant fishing buddy, Eric Covino. Intrigued by the experience the previous evening, it took about two seconds to convince him we should make a trip. We were armed with every conceivable lure that might possibly match that hatch.

Despite our preparation we were not ready for what happened. Just like the night before, as soon as the shadows lengthened on the water, worms began showing, but in larger numbers. Early on, while the sun was up, we caught some school bass. However, an hour before it got dark, worms were like snowflakes in the water column. As darkness fell, the bass showed up in force and began swirling, popping and feeding in earnest. This time, rather than dozens of worms scooting past the boat, there were literally thousands of them, dimpling along the surface, making a visible wake, often leaving clouds of light-colored genetic material in their tiny wakes.

It was incredible! Stripers were feeding everywhere. It was impossible to scan the water without seeing multiple breaks from bass, ranging from typical schoolies to fish of scary proportions. If we peered into the gloomy, black water it was possible to see the flashes and shadows as fish swam by the boat like striped vacuum cleaners, sucking up their quarry. But we couldn't catch them!

It was tremendously exciting, but tremendously frustrating at the same time. It was like hitting a May fly hatch on a trout stream, an equally frustrating event where there is so much food available that the odds of a fish selecting your artificial lure from among the glut of real ones within their field of view can be a long shot. Where I had easily caught 21 fish the previous evening by simply casting toward the comparatively few visible fish, this evening, despite many more visibly feeding stripers, it took dozens of pinpoint casts before one was hooked. We caught something like five or six fish as the action heated up and only two or three combined after that. A slow but thrilling evening of fishing.

At about 10:30 p.m., as the tide was nearing high slack, the swirls subsided noticeably. We hadn't hooked a fish in over an hour, but noticed that the worms were still like snowflakes in the water column. Curiosity took over and out came the million-candle-powered beam light to see what was happening. We began a slow chug back up the channel toward the launch in awe, as we ran through what had to be hundreds of thousands of teeming worms. Every hundred feet or so a striper could be seen, swollen as if it had swallowed a cantaloupe. Most were typical schoolies, but one fish of at least 35 to 40 pounds was observed barely moving in three feet of water amid a cloud of mating worms. We concluded that the action had stopped because there was a limited number of stripers and unlimited worms. The bass were satiated and had simply shut off.

We were back two nights later, but the worms weren't. We did not see a single worm scooting beneath the surface. However, the bass were present in good numbers at all the usual spots along the lower river channel. We caught 10 to 15 each, but it was nowhere near as much fun as the previous night when it was possible to see the fish swimming by the boat, slurping worms as they passed.

That was the beginning of what has turned into a passion for fishing the worm spawn. Now it is the event I most anticipate each year as spring progresses toward summer. It is hot summer temperatures that finally turn the worms off. Stripers may persist in these food-rich bays and estuaries throughout most of the summer, but in numbers far below the huge crowds of bass that are attracted to these places by the super-abundant spawning worms, which are an effortless source of food.

A couple of years after that first experience in Mystic, a few friends began chasing the worms over at Ninigret Salt Pond, with great success and for a much longer window of time. While Mystic's worm spawn builds, peaks and disappears in less than a week, the fishing in Charlestown lasts as long as three to five weeks. I believe that this is because the worms come out at 65 degrees or so, and because this area is a huge sprawling system of shallow channels and coves, different parts of this salt pond reach this magical temperature at different times, hence the protracted spawning period. If it was triggered by the full moon, it would all occur at once, but it does not. One week the fish may be active in one pocket, across the bay from there the next, but nearly everywhere in the pond during the climax of activity just before it all ends.

Initially, the articles I read about worm-hatch fishing were written by and for those guys fishing fly rods. It is easy to tie a marabou, velvet or pipe-cleaner fly that is a dead ringer for these little worms, mimics their unique, floating, scooting action, and is readily castable with the fly equipment.

Early on in my experimentation with worm spawn fishing, I figured out that soft plastics are the spin fisherman's key to tempting worm-feeding bass. When rigged properly, spin fishing can be as or more productive when fishing the worm spawn, which used to be the sole domain of the fly-rodders.

The size of the lure and presentation are of prime importance when fishing the worm spawn. The objective is to match the hatch. The best clone for swarming worms is a 3 1/2-inch, Lunker City Slug-Go, with 4 1/2-inch Slug-Gos and Bass Assassins a close second. The absolute best color matches are Texas chili, red gold and fire perch. When the worms are extremely plentiful, or when the light is fading, bubblegum, Merthiolate or white color schemes may draw attention due to their high visibility.

Other productive soft plastic options include short pieces of Berkley Power Sandworms, Lunker City's 3-inch Helgies or any 3-inch piece of narrow, soft plastic material in the tacklebox. Herb Reed, inventor of the Slug-Go, says some saltwater anglers fish a tandem rig with a 4 1/2-inch Slug-Go for added casting distance, with a 3 1/2-incher to catch the fish.

The trick is in the delivery system. Here is where typical saltwater tackle and bait-casting rigs, no matter how light, become ineffective. I have a specialized spinning rod combo that can cast these light offerings without any added weight. I use a 7-foot, freshwater-weight, medium-action spinning rod, balanced with a quality reel, but the key is the line. In the days before Fireline, it was necessary to spool up with 2-, 4- or 6-pound-test monofilament to throw these light offerings. Unfortunately, this meant losing many larger fish to break-offs if they tangled in eelgrass beds where worm spawns often occur.

A few years ago I discovered 6-pound-test Fireline, which is gossamer-thin with the great casting qualities of 2-pound-test mono, but actually performs much better. Its incredible tensile strength and low stretch make it ideal for light and ultralight applications in the ocean. Any decent rod as described above and a reel spooled to capacity with this stuff can cast a 3 1/2-inch Slug-Go, with either a 1/0 or 2/0 light wire Mustad Aberdeen hook or a 1/0 Texposer hook, 20 yards or even more with a tailwind.

With this spinning tackle there is a definite advantage compared to beating the water to a frazzle with a fly rod and its requisite fish-spooking false casts as a fish moves past. If a bass swirls, the cast is off in an instant. Pinpoint casting is often necessary for consistent success.

Sometimes, spray casting an area works well when the fish are sparse and not showing their positions every few seconds. However, when the swirls are constant, it's much more effective to hold off casting until a fish swirls within range, then nail it with a quick, accurate cast. Often bass will feed in a linear fashion, making a swirl, then another four or five feet ahead of the first. This is the ideal set up; simply plop the Slug-Go right where the next swirl should be.

Retrieve with a slow erratic action that causes the Slug-Go to break the surface, just like the worms. To help make these lures plane up toward the top on the retrieve, string the hook about 1/4 inch from the nose, and be sure the SlugGo is absolutely straight on the hook with no curls, twists or bends. It must glide straight and swim like the real worms, or strikes will be reduced significantly. I have had good success by holding the rod tip high and swimming the lure along the surface, making those small vee wakes like a surfacing worm. To maximize hookup odds, cast to a visible swirl, retrieve the lure slowly about half of the distance to the boat, then reel in quickly and wait for the next swirl. Under these conditions stripers don't usually follow lures very far. Strikes are often within seconds of the lure landing. If there is a bulge behind the bait or a short strike, continue the retrieve all the way to the boat.

When the worm spawn is on, I bring three or four light rods that are all capable of casting the 3 1/2-inch Slug-Gos. One or two will be rigged with alternative baits, new stuff for side-by-side taste tests. One of the remaining rods will have the classic Texas chili Slug-Go, the other is usually rigged with a bubblegum-colored one or some other high-contrast color for increased visibility at dusk or when the worms are super dense.

Prowl calm waters looking for worms or telltale swirls. Birds often give the hot spots away (but not always) so keep searching for activity of any sort. If one place is not turned on, keep moving and stay alert. We have hit the mother lode of worms on the way back to the dock because someone saw a single dimple or boil and decided to try for the classic "one more fish," or in one case a de-skunking fish.

When the worms are out, the bass will be everywhere, often in only a foot or two of water. This means this is a small-boat fishery, and small aluminums have a marked advantage over the big glass boats that dominate the waters outside, off the beaches and reefs.

Access to Ninigret Salt Pond is limited. There is one pretty miserable, shallow, high-tide launch in Charlestown. The best bet is to pay the launch fee at the Ocean House Marina and search from there. Many anglers are using kayaks to fly- or spin-fish the shallows. Others use canoes to get to the action, sometimes beaching their crafts and working a hot shoreline in waders.

In the Mystic River, access is even more limited. Shore-fishing options are few and not close to the best worm activity. Launch for a fee at Shaffer's Marina, Mason's Island Road, Mystic, or at Wild Bill's, Noank, and run up inside the river from there.

Narragansett Bay, Rhode Island, and the lower Thames River, Niantic River, Poquonnock River near Bluff Point Groton, and Little Narragansett Bay, where the Pawcatuck River meets the Sound, are a few places in southeastern Connecticut to check that are known to have worm spawn activity in May. Start looking about midmonth and especially around May 20.

Every major coastal estuary has some sort of worm hatch, so there is almost certainly one near you somewhere, sometime. The trick is monitoring the temperature and watching water until it happens, then mobilizing that instant. There is no waiting for the weekend if the spawn is peaking in a given area on Tuesday. The worm spawn is by far the most fun I have fishing striped bass every spring. I don't even bother with the big water and reefs (which are also coming to life at this time) until it is over.

Walking & Wading The Estuaries

By Jeffrey Joiner

If there is a fly-fisher's heaven, it must look a lot like Cape Cod, with its countless bays, harbors, rivers, ponds and estuaries. I'm not sure if my own perception of eternity would afford enough time to truly know each and every one of these places. And most are only minutes away, no matter where you live on the Cape. In the 15 years that I have lived here, I have probably fished most of these spots, although I can truthfully say I know only a few of them well. That is the thing about fly-fishing: It eventually demands study, but the rewards are great.

To me, estuaries are like a university of fly-fishing. In these invariably gorgeous settings, life begins, thrives and ends. It is easily observed. We must determine what the food is, where it is, when the fish are feeding and how best to approach and make the cast. There is the wind to consider, and the flow of the water. The process of working out all of these elements can be fulfilling, and most of the information will be useful, no matter where we fish.

The gamefish we seek to catch, and usually release, have only two reasons to be anywhere: They are moving to or from somewhere to feed, or they are migrating to or from somewhere to spawn. As salmon fishers well know, spawning fish are a challenge to hook. They are not feeding regularly, if at all, and they choose where they lie for comfort. They are, however, territorial in the sense that they will try to protect their spots, and they can sometimes be tempted to strike at a well-ingrained image.

Feeding fish are opportunists. Most schooling fish work together to make feeding easier, giving us general patterns of behavior to work with. But it is often odd behavior on the part of the bait that triggers the strike. Fly-fishers who have experienced the so-called worm hatches can tell you how frustrating it is when there is too much bait and your fly looks like just one of millions.

It can be fun and fulfilling to take fish on an exact imitation, but often something altogether different is more productive. Fish come to our estuaries because of the varied menu. In almost all of Cape Cod's estuaries, they can seasonally find, among other things, several species of shrimp, sand eels, herring, alewives, silversides, mummichogs, needlefish, menhaden, American eels, many worm species, and hermit, sand and blue crabs. Each bait has its own behavioral patterns and can be tide and location specific. It's important to remember that these baitfish have the same jobs as gamefish, feeding and spawning. There are many good books on this subject, and scientific information can be an important part of figuring it all out. But walking, wading, watching and fishing are still your best teachers.

Learning to "read" the water, tides and shoreline will make the biggest difference in degrees of success. This is simply the process of learning to recognize where the fish might be at any given moment and where we might get at them most easily. Shallow, grassy coves near a dredged channel provide a roadside café for foraging fish and are easy to wade. There are rarely casting obstructions. Here, cover the water carefully after watching for signs of life. Always make a few casts before stepping into the water, particularly at dawn and dusk. At midday, under a bright sun, we can usually pass over these places.

Fishing salt-marsh creeks on an outgoing or low incoming tide is much like any river fishing. Look for undercut banks, often found at a bend in the channel. Here, a fast-sinking head is most helpful. Cast down and across the flow, keeping the line as belly-free as possible, and dead-drift the fly past promising lies. (More about the dead-drift later.) The strike will often come at the end of the swing. Don't waste time false-casting as it will only serve to dry the line and the fly, and tire you out.

Expansive, open bays, seemingly devoid of structure, can be deceiving. If there are no birds working, look for bars and channels. Also scan the water for slicks, which can be caused by large concentrations of baitfish. They will appear as a calm spot on the surface or perhaps just a dark patch of water. Judge the direction of flow, and cast so that your fly drifts into and alongside the slick, letting the fly sink and drift slowly at first. Again, always try to keep your line taut, with no belly, so that you will feel a strike. An intermediate-density line is the most useful searching line here.

Learn to use the wind to your advantage. The wind can help you achieve the distance and presentation you need if you don't try to fight it. Because most estuary fishing is wide open, longer casts of, say, 60 to 80 feet are helpful. However, if you can only cast 40 to 50 feet effectively (by which I mean consistently able to straighten out the line and leader), all is not lost; you need only choose your casting position more carefully. The ability to cast farther can be learned; it is not a strength issue, but rather one of technique. The more relaxed you are and the better you use the wind, the farther you will cast.

Probably the most useful fishing method in estuaries is the dead-drift method. Rather than being a type of retrieve, it is more a presentation of your fly, one that leaves you with the most options. The fish get more time to notice the fly, which will be acting much more like the bait it is suggesting, subject to the flow of water. Choose your casting position, as described earlier, out from and slightly down the flow, or direction, of water movement. Keep in mind that the water will often appear to be moving in another direction due to the effects of wind or cloud reflection.

Let your fly settle, keeping the rod tip low and pointed at the fly as it drifts with the current. Learn to mend the belly of your line back up above your fly. This is achieved simply by raising the rod tip slightly and throwing the line, but not the leader, back up-flow (upstream or up-tide). Practice mending until you can do it without moving the fly.

Let the fly swing freely with the flow, simply keeping the line straight. As the fly swings at the end of your cast, pay attention! It may hesitate or appear to stop. If it does, strike! If you see a swirl behind it or feel a bump, strip the line with a short jerk or raise the rod tip slightly. You may be rewarded with a strike. If nothing happens, let the line straighten downcurrent, raise the rod to get most of the line out of the water, and pick up the cast, placing it back up and across the flow. No false-casting should be necessary. After two or three casts, take a few steps downcurrent and begin again.

If you work through an area you are sure should hold fish but have no takes, change to a different pattern, size or color. Walk through again. There is no better way to cover as much water. Spend a whole morning or afternoon walking around areas you intend to fish. Stop and watch the water movement for a few minutes. If you see bait casually dimpling the surface, it does not mean you have also found the gamefish you are looking for. Relaxed bait movement implies a lack of danger, and you must look farther.

Look for areas of backwash or rip lines. These form over shoals or bars and are perfect spots to find gamefish lying in wait for bait to be brought to them. Here again the dead-drift technique serves well to search out fish. Cast above the rip line and let the fly drift through, as would a stray baitfish struggling against the current. I often fish two flies through rips, with a shrimplike fly on a dropper above either a sand eel or silverside pattern on the point of the leader.

A dropper is nothing more than a few extra inches of mono at the joint of the leader midsection and tippet. Leave the heavier midsection mono longer, trimming only the tippet back at the knot. The stiffer midsection will help keep the dropper fly from tangling with the tippet. Adjust your casting slightly to accommodate this rig. Make your loops more open, back-casting by moving your whole arm up and back, then dropping your elbow, moving into the cast smoothly and avoiding the snap as the backcast turns around. Keep the rod tip high, around 10 o'clock, as the forward cast straightens out, then drop the cast and the rod tip down to the water. Control the line flow with your line hand. If you can't double-haul, simply hold on tight with your line hand, following the movement of the rod. And, by the way, this is all good advice for wet-fly trout fishing, as well. Fishing a cast or two or more wet flies is a centuries-old technique.

If you know you are over bluefish, you must make the fly move faster. Dead-drifting is less effective on blues, except when both the fly and the blues are hugging the bottom.

Fly-fishers are a curious lot, myself among them. Because ours is a pastime subject to great amounts of controversy and emotion, all but the most generalized of opinions will evoke both adamant support and vehement disapproval. That being said, I should add that I base my theories only on the thousands of hours I have spent on the water. I happily recognize differing opinions based on experience! My grandfather's favorite saying was "The best fisherman is the one having the most fun." I embrace this notion above all.

There have been countless books written on fly dressing, and more specifically on imitating estuarine species. The quest for exact imitation, whether or not you believe it to be more effective, can actually be its own separate pursuit. For that reason, as a fly-fishing guide and fly-tying instructor, I choose to promote generalized imitation, and even suggestion, as the quickest way to achieve some success.

Novices, far outnumbering the experts both in fly-tying classes and as sports who hire guides, want to catch fish NOW. If they endeavor to first learn the techniques involved in adequately fishing the fly, they will be farther along than if they fish an exact imitation poorly. There is plenty of time later to further challenge themselves. In other words, how we choose to fish the fly can be as, or more, important than what fly we choose to fish with.

If we broke down into general types the flies needed to successfully imitate the prevalent baits found in the Cape's estuaries, we would actually need to carry only a half-dozen or so flies. And if we fished these patterns expertly, we could expect as much success as anyone, anywhere, anytime. But, of course, we don't have to economize that much!

Basically, we need flies that cast well, swim well, drift well and hold up well. We need them in a few sizes, shapes and colors. We need the ability to fish them deep (and get them there quickly), and we need to effectively cover all the water in-between. Let's look at the basic types one at a time.

Swimming flies represent swimming baits such as sand eels, silversides, herring, etc. There is an obvious difference between trying to represent a sand eel and representing a herring, right? Well, actually, maybe only in its size, the silhouette we create by its bulk and the way we fish it. A Lefty's Deceiver tied slimly on a size 2 or 4 hook is a pretty fair sand eel imitation, and if tied full and bulkier on a 2/0 hook it will certainly serve to imitate or suggest a herring, alewife or menhaden. However, these bigger flies are not much fun to cast on the lighter rods that are preferred when walking an estuary for hours. Lefty Kreh can cast a whole fly line without a rod, using just his hands, and he can probably do it with his car keys tied to one end, but if our goal is comfort, efficiency and fun, big flies and light rods are not a good combination.

The Deceiver-type flies are an excellent choice because they rarely foul, they swim and drift well, and they can be fished to represent a variety of baits. In my experience what they do not do so well is fish the bottom, or sink quickly through a heavy flow of water. This is where the next type – the Clouser Deep Minnow – shines.

The Clouser, with its weighted eyes and upturned hook point, avoids snags on the bottom very well. And, commercially tied, it sinks like a stone. In larger sizes, Clousers are not much fun to cast, but when used appropriately they are extremely effective. However, they are next to useless for dead-drifting in all but the strongest currents. They are essentially a bucktail jig.

Clipped deer-hair flies, such as the Muddler Minnow, can be wonderfully effective imitations of all kinds of estuarine fare. They are light to cast, can be fished from top to bottom, and can be reshaped easily while fishing in order to more closely match the size and shape relevant at the moment. Because they also "push" more water than other types do and can therefore be detected in slow-moving water from farther off by many predatory fish, they can be powerful attractors. They can be tied to represent great bulk and to give the impression of greater size without adding unnecessary weight. Depending on your choice of pattern and materials, they generally swim and drift well, and tend not to snag. To fish them deep requires a fast-sinking shooting head or fly line.

Perhaps the most effective type of fly with which to fish our estuaries is also the least specifically representative. These are the rabbit fur, or Zonker Strip, flies. They are a delight to cast, can be instantly altered for size while fishing, and can be fished to represent almost anything. If you like to walk the shore searching for fish, these flies should be in your arsenal. Tied on smaller hooks, say, size 6 through 2, they can be comfortably thrown 60 to 80 feet on a 7- or 8-weight line.

The last type I will mention is the simple bucktail, or Brooks Blonde, series of flies. I personally group the Blonde types with all the bucktail, epoxy-and-hair and bendback flies. They are durable and easy to cast, and they swim and drift well. They tend to foul and snag unless they are tied specifically not to do so, and they have the least amount of inherent action. But they react well when manipulated by the fisher. Of all the types, they can suggest the slimmest of baits most accurately. Most of the so-called "exact imitations" are of this type.

Novices are often confused after talking to more experienced fly-fishers about fly choice. Understandably, most experienced fly-fishers adamantly believe in their own methods and choices. After all, the more faith you have in a particular pattern, the more you will use it and the better you will fish it. But remember, no two people fish exactly the same way, or at the same place at the same time, or with the same tackle. Therefore fly-fishers' opinions, which develop from their own personal successes, can be wildly contradictory. I am, after all, merely expressing my own!

Most anglers who have fished the waters of the Cape from shore have seen the most common bait we need to suggest here. Sand eels – long, thin and silvery – are probably the most obvious bait fly-fishers hope to represent. Over the years, the options for sand eel patterns have grown to an amazing number. Twenty years ago an effective pattern was nothing more than some white or green yarn wrapped around a long-shank hook (often a flounder hook) with an inch or two of yarn left as a tail. This was actually a pretty reliable pattern.

Another older pattern, Don Brown's Silversides, is a bucktail with its wing tied down. This is still an excellent pattern. Now, with epoxy-bodied and silicone flies, it is easy to make a sand eel pattern that looks just like the real thing. My own favorite sand eel, when I choose to be so specific, is a simple pattern. Any long-shank hook is acceptable; on it tie a tail of white Fly Fur (a synthetic bucktail-type hair) about two inches long. Flank this with a strand or two of pearl Flashabou. Wrap the shank with more pearl Flashabou up to the head. Add eyes if you like. Some sort of protective covering helps its durability; five-minute epoxy, clear silicone or superglue work reasonably well, but I usually over-wrap the body with clear mono, which makes the fly almost indestructible. Size 2 or 4 hooks make this pattern a joy to fish on a 7-weight line. To date, my biggest striper was taken on this very pattern, and on a 7-weight line. Fifty-four pounds!

As unscientific as it may sound, I usually fish the same fly pattern to represent sand eels, silversides, spearing, etc. When doing so, I find the Zonker Strip flies hard to beat. These flies have so much inherent action and are so unspecific that I find it very rewarding to try to figure out more ways of fishing them. They are simple to tie. Standard or long-shank hooks work fine; use your favorite. Simply tie in a four-inch piece of fur, usually one-eighth of an inch wide. Tie it to the tail of the hook at the point where the shank starts to bend down to the barb. Leave an inch or two as a tail, you can trim it later if need be when on the water. Wrap the rest around the hook shank, leaving no space between the wraps until you get to the eye. Make a head, tie off, and either seal the thread with cement or apply eyes and epoxy. Now take it fishing!

There are obviously many variations of this pattern. You can alter it almost any way you want. You can add flash, brass eyes for weight or whatever. I have tried adding nearly everything and the flies all work, but not noticeably better than the simplest version. That's the one which I generally stick with now. In my experience this is the best dead-drift fly in existence. I have used it tied in a variety of sizes, from 1-inch versions on size 6 hooks to represent shrimp (tan or olive works great), all the way up to 6-inch-long versions on 1/0 hooks, which in gray, black or brown suggest an American eel as well as any fly I have ever tried.

To specifically represent silversides, baby herring, alewives, etc., modifications of the standard bucktail patterns are the most common choices. Freshwater fishers familiar with the Mickey Finn or Black Nose Dace will find these same flies, tied in seemingly more appropriate colors such as white, blue and green on sturdier stainless hooks, to be quite effective. However, in my own experience color has little to do with success. It is the transparency of the color, the contrast between colors, and the resulting silhouette that matter more. Again, particularly in large sizes, a Lefty's Deceiver fished appropriately works well.

The most difficult baits to represent with consistent success are shrimp, crabs and worms. I'll stick my neck out again and say that, in my experience, how our suggestions of these baits are fished is more important than the patterns themselves. I'm sorry to say that most of the fly-fishers I have taken fishing, or even observed fishing, have trouble when it comes to being patient. Laying out a cast efficiently and mending the line to control the drift and depth is apparently not nearly as much fun as frantically stripping the fly back. But let's get back to the subject at hand. The shrimps are probably the easiest of the group to master. Almost any simple bucktail can work. A good example is a Honey Blonde. Tied well, with the wing cocked upright, it can be easily fished to suggest shrimp. Al Brewster ties a very realistic grass shrimp pattern that has burned mono eyes and a plastic shell back. I have good luck with his pattern; I use two at a time, with the smaller size on the dropper.

To this day one of my favorite shrimp (and general purpose) patterns is one my grandfather showed me in the late 50s. It is nothing more than clipped deer-hair, leaving a short tail. Tied on hooks from size 8 to size 2, it is a natural for shallow water and drifting.

There are some terrific-looking crab patterns out there today, and you can find them easily in any saltwater recipe book or catalog. Here again, a deer hair fly, perhaps clipped to the general shape of a small crab, could be useful. I personally have had little luck with the beautiful epoxy and silicone imitations on the market now, but I know some people have done great things with them on the flats down south. Shrimp and crab patterns are probably the most difficult types to fish well. Trial and error will be your best teacher. Watch the naturals!

Worms are both dreaded and anticipated by Cape Cod fly-fishers. Perhaps the greatest amount of debate revolves around whether to use worm patterns when fishing during the so-called worm hatches. Here again, how you fish will be more important than using exact patterns. Through the years, my own success during worm swarms has been inexplicably inconsistent. I have tried all kinds of flies and techniques, kept records faithfully, and spent many hours just observing. I can only offer you my current thinking. I have had the most consistent success with flies having a lot of inherent action. The Blossom series of flies, simple but effective marabou streamers, have worked well for me. But I will give you a secret: During worm swarms, I most often fish a worm pattern on the dropper with something that appears to be predatory on the tippet. For this application, a simple small fly tied from a short section of red, pink or orange yarn, similar to the San Juan Worm, on a size 4 or 6 hook works fine. The tippet fly, which appears to be after the worm fly, is usually something like a Deceiver type. I have often taken a fish on the dropper, although not exclusively. I guess it makes me more confident to think that with this rig I have twice the chances of hooking up! Good luck with the worms – they can drive you crazy.

The last type I will address here is the big stuff. Casting herring, menhaden, squid and other baits that grow big (over six inches) can be a problem for the angler walking an estuary because of our tackle. Spending several hours casting a 10- or 11-weight rod while waist-deep in water, in the dark, is not my idea of a good time. Out in a boat it's a different story; big flies are much less of a problem. You search for fish and you cast. However, I have managed to come up with a few good patterns, or pattern alterations, that make it possible to represent large baits well and use them with an 8- or 9-weight rod. While it is possible to cast a big bunker fly a reasonable distance with these line weights, my theory has always been to make the experience of wading and casting as much fun as the fish catching. Therefore, I tried making the deceiver-type flies lighter by using less but bulkier saddle hackle. These are known as schlappen. They are the webby, opaque feathers that freshwater streamer fly-tyers usually use to strip barbules for beards or to wing soft palmered throats. I personally began fooling around with this stuff twenty-odd years ago, and there were already plenty of other tyers doing the same thing.

Four of these feathers, two to a side, will make a deceiver-type fly six inches long on a 1/0 hook, and weighing about a third less than a standard deceiver of the same length on a 3/0 hook. I further reduce the weight by surrounding the fly with Fly Fur rather than real bucktail. It takes a little experimentation to get the balance right, but the result can be a fly that suggests a much bigger image than it actually is. And, best of all, you can wade and cast the things at night without feeling like an F-16 is buzzing by your ear with every cast.

There are many successful patterns and types that suggest the larger baits, such as Bill Catherwood's, Lou Tabory's and a host of others. I suggest you try them all on your own tackle and see which types work best for you. Be patient. If you are new to fly-casting, take your time and cast smoothly with a fairly open loop at first. Spend more time hunting the water than casting. That is generally good advice whenever you are looking for big fish.

I have rarely found the need for these big flies in the estuaries I fish most. But I do find them valuable very late at night in the spring and also in the fall, when I always have a couple with me just in case. As I have said, I am discussing walking and wading estuaries, not fishing from a boat. I know many anglers embrace the "big fish equals big fly" theory, and I know a few who are exceedingly successful! My own experience, having caught many fish over 30 pounds on flies under 4 inches long, leads me to my own conclusions. And that, of course, is the whole point: Fish and study enough to be confident in your own methods. That is the surest way to consistent success and fulfillment as a fly-fisher.

There is far more than is written here involved in fishing the estuaries – more techniques, more study of baits, tides and seasons. It can be a lifelong study. But careful and thoughtful observation will bring results quickly. Just bear in mind that there is always more to know. All the rules have exceptions, and just when you think you have it all figured out, the tide changes and everything changes with it. I guess that's why we call it fishing instead of catching.

Chapter Three
Striper Tales

⟫•◈•⟪

The documented history of recreational striped bass fishing in New England goes back more than 140 years. In that time, much has changed, but some things have remained the same: the thrill of catching the fish of a lifetime, the love of the boats that take us to the fish, the wonderful obsession that every hard-core striper fisherman feels.

The Night Of The Big One

By Charles E. Cinto

It's 2004. Who would have thought I would be writing a story about the night 37 years ago that I caught my 73-pounder? A lot of water has passed under the hull since then, and many more bass have been caught, quite a few being 50-pounders. With the help of my wife Annette, who is also my typist and editor (!), I'll tell you what happened that night. Over the years I've heard plenty of misinformation about the event and I thought it was time to set the record straight.

My story begins 75 years ago. I was the first-born (oldest of 17 children) and I would have to say that I have been fishing for 76 years, since my mother told me I was fishing before I was born! My grandfather, Eric Anderson (on the Swedish side), was the best fisherman of us all. I was brought up on the Anderson Farm in South Foxboro and was very fortunate to have him and two uncles who took me hunting and fishing, and taught me many things about outdoor sports. They are long gone now but are dearly remembered.

On June 15, 1967, at about 5 p.m., I jumped in my beach buggy, picked up my friend Russ Keane and headed for Fairhaven to pick up Captain Frank Sabatowski. After a cup of coffee, we headed for the dock and prepared to get on board the *June Bug*, his custom Brownell bass boat. Got all our gear on board and headed out of the harbor, setting our course for Quicks Hole. By habit, I always sat on the deck in the stern, all the gear with me, making sure the hooks were sharp, rods and reels in good shape. Frank and Russ shot the breeze. We always tried to get to the islands before dark to look over the situation, and having fished with Frank and Captain Charlie Haig for quite a few years, I had some idea what to expect.

As we pulled into Quicks Hole, the tide did not look too good. So we headed for Gay Head.

It started to get dark as we approached the rip. Russ on one side, me on the other, we let the plugs (big 3-ounce Goo-Goo Eyes swimmers) slide back into the rip on the wire line. Frank continued to work the boat back and forth. WHAM! Russ was on! Before he even had his fish on board, I was on, too. This went on for a couple of hours until the tide let go. At least a half dozen weighed 30 pounds. Time to make a move.

At approximately 11 p.m. Frank suggested we go into Cuttyhunk Harbor and get a couple of hours sleep before heading to Sow and Pigs Reef for the 2 a.m. tide.

Rough ride back to Quicks Hole – the boat went up, I went down, and now another kind of "wham" – my nose against the boat. Blood running down my face, we finally pulled into Quicks, went around Nashawena and into Cuttyhunk Harbor. Anchored up and crawled into the cabin for a snooze.

Two a.m., Friday, June 16. Time to rise and shine. It did not take long to get to Sow and Pigs reef. The tide and wind were perfect.

Getting right down to business, we let those big Goo-Goo Eyes slide back into the rip. It wasn't long before we were into fish, which continued for 1 1/2 hours, resulting in several 30- to 40-pounders.

Then it happened – the hardest hit yet and I was on! This fish took off down through the boulders like a freight train. Finally slowed a bit, but I could feel the head shaking, trying to scrub the plug out. The fight went on for quite a while, but I finally got it to the boat where Russ was waiting with the gaff. The next thing I heard was, "Look at the head on this fish! Give me a hand!"

Putting my rod down, I helped Russ pull the fish aboard. Let me tell you, we all looked at that fish for a few minutes and agreed that it had to be in the sixties. I was one happy camper – feeling that I finally got my "sixty." Put it in the box, and again, back to business. We caught several more fish before the tide let go.

Gear put away, deck washed, we headed back to the mainland. As we passed Cuttyhunk, Frank suggested we head in and weigh that big fish. Pulling up to the dock, who was standing there but Captain Bob Smith, a Cuttyhunk skipper and official I.G.F.A. weighmaster. Bob right there, we hung the fish on the scale, which he set at 75 pounds! (WHAT?!) He set the scale two more times and finally said, "I can only give you seventy-three pounds." Holding the official I.G.F.A. form that he had given me to fill out, of course I said, "Sign right here!" Believe me, we were all numb for a few minutes. We put the fish back in the box and headed for the mainland, all three of us grinning from ear to ear. I don't think it had really sunk in yet.

Unbeknownst to us, Bob had called ahead and the word spread fast. As we pulled into the harbor and up to the dock, we were surprised to see quite a few spectators, plus photographers waiting for us. For the next few hours that poor fish was in and out of the box more times than I could count.

Stopped at Frank's house, celebrated with a cup of coffee, then made sure the fish was packed in ice. Russ and I then went to taxidermist Wally Brown's house in Falmouth. I asked Wally to determine what the fish had been feeding on. Most of the stomach contents were dissolved, but, to my surprise – there was a big sea robin! If you don't believe they will tackle anything, then it's time to give up.

Yes, it was another great night of fishing the islands – quite a few fish from 20- to 40-pounders, and, of course – THE BIG ONE.

There have been many exciting moments in my 55-plus years of striper fishing, but there is no fish more important than family and friends who have touched my life along the way, supporting and sharing my love of this sport.

Wishing you all fair winds and good tides, Charles E. Cinto.

Charlie Cinto on the ride back in with his 73-pound striper.

The Monomoy Blitz

By Dave LaPorte

Every fisherman can remember one occasion, whether from the boat, the beach or your favorite fishing hole, when the conditions were perfect, your stars lined up and everything came together. Some call it a "blitz." Whatever you call it, it's when practice and patience pay off and the fish gods smile down on your salt-soaked face. I've had these nights on Monomoy Island, providing fish tales and memories.

I was first introduced to beach-fishing on Monomoy Island in the late 1970s; the introduction was through a close friend of mine and was strictly by accident. I had asked him if he would like to go shad fishing.

"Why do you want to catch five-pound shad when you can catch twenty-, thirty- or even forty-pound bass from the beach at night and be able to sell them, to boot?" he asked.

Hearing this, I proceeded to grill him, begging for any information he could offer. He told me that he and a friend had been going out to Monomoy Island in a small tin boat, and every night that they fished they would catch at least a half-dozen bass weighing from 10 to 40 pounds.

I found myself out on the beach the very next night. That first night that I beach-fished Monomoy Island, I caught seven fish; the biggest was about 35 pounds and the smallest was about 20 pounds. I thanked him for revealing his secret and I never looked back. I became a "Monomoy Sandman" – a night-eyed sand dog, waving his tail at every breaking wave as he ran up and down the beach.

Monomoy Island is a thin, fragile sand spit on the southern side of Cape Cod. It is approximately seven or eight miles long, running from Chatham southwest toward Nantucket. The width of the island varies from as little as a couple hundred yards up to a mile. In the late 1970s, a winter storm split the island in two, making South Monomoy the larger of the pair and separating them with a cut-through of approximately a quarter to a half mile wide.

Because of the ever-moving sand, the island itself was always changing. Where there were deep holes one week, there would probably be sandbars the following month. Pleasant Bay would fill and empty past North Monomoy on a timely schedule, the tide bringing with it the feeding fish that followed the schools of sand eels, herring and pogies. As the bait passed by on every tide, we sand dogs would be waiting with rods in hand.

On most nights the fishing was good; it depended on how long you could last since eventually the bait or the bass would have to come by you. We fished as a group. When the fishing was slow, some of us would take a break, but at least one man would keep fishing while the others would rest. After all, it takes a lot out of a man to stay up and fish all night! On most nights, keeping going was a matter of insanity or endurance, or both.

The fishing would start around the middle of May. Usually by Memorial Day the schools of migrating spring fish would be gorging on sand eels and herring as their main food sources. Some nights the sand eels were so thick that on every cast of my Rebel plug I would hook two or three of them. On those nights I knew that eventually the bass were going to find the baitfish. Every night was a new learning experience; we were like infants learning to walk.

I can remember one night in particular. There was a large group of fishermen working the shoreline with various types of plugs. One fellow, who was fishing toward the north end of the island at a location known as Mud Banks, was using a Rebel plug with all the paint scraped off, which he'd achieved by scratching it up with his knife and rubbing it in the sand. The plug itself looked as though it were all white. That night he out-fished the rest of us by a margin of three to one. Of course, the following day we all searched around for solid-white Rebel plugs but could not locate any. The solution was to take a plug and dip it in white ceiling paint, hooks and all. That night those whitened plugs out-fished every other lure we fished with.

One night my friend Dan Morin was fishing the beach and hooked a racer bass, and he played the fish for at least half an hour before landing it. When the fish finally washed up on the beach, Danny shined the light at the plug and realized why it had taken so long: He had hooked a 40-pound bass in the dorsal fin.

The fog on some nights would be so thick that it reduced our visibility to just a few yards. On those nights we would not venture too far out into the water for fear of losing our bearings in relation to dry land. This potentially dangerous situation had already caught two of my fishing friends. On that night, I was on shore when I heard my friends hollering for my help. I hollered back, "What's up?" Their response was, "Keep talking and shine the light in the direction of our voices!" Out of the fog I saw my fellow fishermen emerge, holding onto each other and telling me how glad they were to see me. Apparently, they had been out on the shallows fishing about waist-deep into the current and had gotten turned around by the thick fog; every direction they tried to walk in, the water would get deeper. That's scary.

When fishing with plugs, we would throw the plug out as far as we could and slowly turn the reel but let the plug swing with the tide. Sometimes, just prior to lifting the plug out of the water, a fish would hit and scream out our line; if the drag was set too tightly, the fish would certainly break off or be lost. On the first run, most of these spring fish would take at least 50 to 100 feet. The fish were fast, lean and hungry. We called them freight trains because at times there was no stopping them.

My fishing equipment was at first caveman-crude, at least compared to the rods, reels and assorted accessories of today's typical beach-fisherman. My spinning reel was a Daiwa 7000 silver series with a skirted spool, which helped keep the sand and salt from the waves (which were breaking in my face) out of the reel. My rod was a $40 Spag's special, the most sophisticated rod of its time. Mounted on the reel was 20-pound-test line. The types of plugs we used in the springtime were the floating 7-inch Rebels in the blue-back, black-back, and blue and green mackerel patterns, as well as all-white and occasionally a pink-colored Bomber. These plugs were all used right from the box – we never sharpened the hooks. I wish I knew then what I know now about presharpening all my hooks!

I believe that the reason why these plugs worked best in the springtime was because there were massive schools of sand eels lying offshore in the shallows and on sandbars a mile or two off the north end of Monomoy Island. And when the sand eels were there, so were the bass. Another effective lure was a fly teaser, or dropper fly, appearing in many different colors to represent the sand eels. We also used the Blue Fox and Red Gill teasers; their shapes and swimming motion looked exactly like a real sand eel. It wasn't unusual to hook and land two bass at a time with this plug-and-dropper type of rig, although sometimes we'd land only one and either the plug or the teaser would be gone.

I wore a pair of quality chest waders with a good raincoat and a military-type utility belt to go around my waist in case I caught a wave in the face, which happened quite often. Hanging off my utility belt would be a small canvas container capable of holding a half-dozen plugs, as well as hooks, leaders, needle-nosed pliers and all the other accessories needed for a night on the beach. Also hanging off the belt might be a one-gallon plastic container, with holes in the bottom for drainage and a cover, used to store a dozen eels. I would also have a small hand gaff to help drag the fish up past the high water mark on the beach, and a rope to drag my fish along the edge of the surf after a night's fishing. Bear in mind that dragging three to six fish on the beach is similar to taking a rope, tying it around your fishing partner and dragging him on the soft sand!

The most important piece of equipment I carried was a good, small handheld flashlight. I would use a Duracell double-A style with a shoestring taped around the housing, and I would put it around my neck for easy access. A good rule of thumb was to use the flashlight as little as possible, making sure to never shine the light in the water off the beach. And the more times you turned on your light, the better the chance that if you were catching a fish you would soon have unwanted company, since we often signaled each other when we were catching fish.

The boat I used was an aluminum, deep-V, 14-foot Sea Nymph with a 20-horsepower motor, and it was ideally suited for two or three men with equipment. We launched the boat from Claflins Landing or Stage Harbor. If we could, we tried to launch from Horne's Marina, as that was closest to Monomoy. Hopefully the winds would be calm, but even then it would take us half an hour to reach the north end of Monomoy. After landing the boat, we would pull it up past the high tide mark, then suit up in our boots and all our gear and either start moving south down the island or toward the mud banks to the north. We fished and walked until we found bait, other fishermen or fish.

Some nights on the beach, when there were a lot of fishermen, we would stack our fish in a pile like cordwood as we fished our way up and down the beach. Each fisherman would make a circle around his fish, with his own particular markings to distinguish his fish from other fishermen's catches. Driftwood sticks or sand hills worked for me. Most times the other fishermen would never think to touch another man's fish; it was a rule of etiquette, as well as of honor and common sense, that nobody touched another man's catch.

The fishing would slowly drop off by mid-July, but if we stayed with it, we could always pick up two or three fish a night off the beach. By August it would get really quiet, and at that point most fishing was done out of the boat. By the end of September the water had started to cool, and the fishing would pick up again. The shorter days and longer, cooler nights triggered fish into a feeding frenzy; this would be their last chance to gorge themselves on available food sources. By October, the bait, as well as the bass, were moving south. The fall migration had begun, and Monomoy Island was directly in its path.

Every time I set foot on "Fantasy Island," a new adventure began. One that sticks out in my mind was a weekend in mid-October. Bob Forget, Dan Morin and I packed up my truck, and with the boat on the roof, and rods, reels and associated gear in the back, we headed out for a Monomoy weekend. The previous week we had done pretty well, so we were expecting to hit fish this weekend, too.

After launching the boat at Horne's Marina, we eventually landed at the north end of Monomoy Island and pulled the boat up past the high tide line. We geared up and began moving south along the beach. I walked the shoreline for at least half an hour before making my first cast. After fishing for a few minutes with no hits, I continued to move south down the beach, eventually finding three other fishermen. Not wanting to crowd them, I stopped about 100 yards from them and proceeded to fish, and there were fish present. However, after about an hour, the three other fishermen disappeared and so did the fish. I started my journey back north to the boat, bringing along my catch of three large bass on my drag rope. I ran into Bob and Dan and we exchanged notes; they had seen, heard and caught nothing up north, so we decided to fish down south at the break the next night. That day we rested as best we could, considering that we were three guys living in a truck for the weekend.

We returned to Monomoy later on Saturday, landing at the north end of the island at about four o'clock. We pulled the boat up past the high water mark and still had plenty of daylight left. Strangely, we were the only people on the island. We put our boots on and got our gear and paraphernalia together, then counted our eels and headed south down the beach for the night to fish at the break. The sun was heading over the horizon and we were almost to our destination when I noticed there were big fish breaking in the surf just in front of us, less than 50 feet from the beach. I grabbed an eel, threw it out and hooked up on a bluefish. I called to the guys, "Hold up and save your bait – they're only blues."

When I looked to my left, my friend Dan was on. His rod was bent like a "U," and his reel was screaming out line. His response was, "Dave, this is no bluefish!" and off he went, moving down the beach with the fish and the incoming tide. I put another eel on and ran down to the water, noticing that fish were busting no more than 30 feet from shore. I could see sand eels jumping out of the water with the bass feeding on them just under the surface; this is known locally as the dance of death.

Casting my eel no more than 40 feet, I was on with the first crank of my reel. They were all large fish, and they were breaking all around me; I just wanted to land the fish and get right back out before they disappeared. I pushed my rod, reel and line to their limits and beached the fish as fast as I could. It was still daylight, perhaps 20 minutes before dark – time seems to stop when you are into this kind of fishing. I pulled the fish up high on the beach and, unhooking the bass, saw that my eel was still good, so I ran back down the beach and threw another cast out. I was on again. I had thrown three casts and hooked three fish. Realizing that my time with this school could be limited, I pushed my gear to the max and landed the fish.

The fishing was unbelievable. I had 4 bass between 30 and 40 pounds landed in less than 20 minutes. I was in a sweat and froth. I would try to get the fish at the top of the first breaking wave and, with a little timing and a little luck, pull it right out of the surf. As I was dragging a fish up to the pile I had started, my friend Bobby said to me, "Dave, can I please stand in your spot?" I looked at Bob and said, "Help yourself Bobby, I'm kind of busy." As I dragged my fish up the beach, I looked back and saw that Bob was on with his first cast in this holy spot.

As I reached my pile of fish, night had taken over, and off in the distance you could see the lights from the Harwich beaches. Finally Danny came back with a fish that had to weigh 45 pounds. As I was unhooking my last fish and talking to Dan, I could hear Bobby yelling, "Dave, Dave, help me, help me – I need a hand!" I put my rod in my sand spike and ran back down to Bobby. He had a fish on and his line was tangled. Pulling out my flashlight, I followed his line up to the second largest guide, where I saw a tangle the size of a softball. I said to Bob, "You're in trouble pal – give me your arm." I took the line that was connected to the fish and wrapped it around his arm about 10 times, then cut the line with my teeth and started to do my repair work.

During this whole time, Bobby kept hollering at me, "Davey, Dave, hurry up, quick, quick, hurry up, please!" The reason behind his sense of urgency was that the fish was pulling on the line, and his arm was hitting the first guide on his rod. He would pull back like he was in a tug of war, trying to hold the fish. It was quite a show, watching the fish pull and yank on Bobby's arm. I managed to tie a crude blood knot in his line with as much speed and precision as I could muster and told Bobby he was back in business.

I raced back to my rod to get back into the blitz. We had been fishing for only 20 to 30 minutes, and I had landed five fish, all monsters, Bobby was on and Danny had a 45-pounder at his feet – if that's not a blitz, I don't know what one is. The fishing continued at this pace for the next couple of hours. We could see the bass breaking the surf and hear the distinctive sound of busting fish chasing bait.

The fish were in the first wave in front of the beach. At one point Bobby hollered over to me that he had a fish on and was holding another one on the sand with his foot. The beached fish had washed up in the first wave and was behind him, but he couldn't hold onto it, and on the next big wave the fish was washed back into the sea. There were so many fish around that we would throw out the eels, either half or whole, dead or alive, and when we hooked a fish, we would put our rods over our shoulders and, when the fish was in the top part of the wave, run up high on the beach. It wasn't pretty but it worked.

We only had 13 eels that night, and they were as precious a commodity as golden eggs. Danny would reach down the fish's throat into the stomach to find his hook, as well as his eel. When the fishing slowed down, we would move a couple hundred yards down the beach and it would start again. We moved with the incoming tide and continued to catch fish.

We fished until about 11 o'clock, and as the fishing began to slow down, we decided that because we did not know how far up the tide would go, we would bury the fish for the night, go back to the boat, get some rest and come back for the fish in the morning. We were fishing at the "cut through" at high tide, and the water was in front of us, as well as flooding in behind. Fearing for our safety, we decided it was better to stop before it was too late.

At sunrise I launched the boat, and as we approached our fishing location at the southern end of the island, we could see four or five obvious-looking sand piles high up on the beach. The seagulls were beginning to eyeball the bass for breakfast, but fortunately we got there in time. Uncovering a sand pile, I loaded the boat with a dozen fish, plus Danny and all the equipment, and headed back to the mainland to unload the truck, then headed back out to the island with the boat, motor and a 6-gallon gas can. I remember moving through the water like a speedboat. Finally reaching Bob, we loaded the rest of the bass into the boat, gave one last look at the islands and headed back to Horne's Marina.

When the boat was fully loaded with bass, Bob and I had only six inches of freeboard, and the boat sat very deep as we moved slowly through the water. Pulling up to Horne's Marina, another fisherman came over and looked into my little tin boat. He made a comment to his buddy that I'll never forget: "Hey Louie, you want to get sick? Take a look at this."

We loaded the rest of the fish into the pickup truck, secured the boat to the roof and headed back to the fish market to unload our catch. I will never forget looking at the piles of fish on the floor of that fish market. We took a total of 37 bass that night – 15 for Dan, 7 for Bobby and 15 for me. The largest fish was a 49½-pounder, which, by the way, was the one Bobby caught while he had the tangle in his line. The total combined weight of our catch was 1,110 pounds.

This was a fishing adventure that is branded into my mind; the pleasure and camaraderie of being with close friends, fishing side by side and helping one another, form a relationship that is blood deep. This was a magical night when three sand dogs received their wish of fish tales and memories, the night of the blitz on Monomoy Island.

Epilogue...
In January 1987, a severe winter storm caused a breach at the skinniest part of Nauset Beach, directly across from Chatham Lighthouse. The resulting changes in tidal flow caused shifting sand and shoaling in Pleasant Bay, all the way to Chatham Light. In essence, this changed the contour of the bottom, as well as redirected the flow of water from Pleasant Bay into two separate estuaries. The effects at North Monomoy Island were devastating. As a result, no longer do we have the same flow and heights of the tide that occurred prior to that winter's breach. No more are there massive schools of bait and predator bass that would use those precious waters for their feeding grounds and escape routes.

Monomoy Island is now a wildlife sanctuary with closed areas and rules and regulations that are strictly enforced. I would recommend that you check with the local authorities before venturing to the island. The fishing on Monomoy as I remember it is gone, but I feel privileged to have had the opportunity to beach-fish this island with my friends, and to have walked the solitude of that sacred sand.

Fifty Years At The Race

By Dave Peros

There are certain beaches on the Cape and Islands that have taken on almost mythical status in the minds of surfcasters. There are anglers who fish Great Point on Nantucket, Wasque Point on the Vineyard, Nauset Beach, Nauset Inlet and Chatham Light exclusively and worship the sand, rocks and waters that make them so productive.

But one area is revered not only for the quality of its fishing, but also for the sense of family and camaraderie that has developed over the years. Right on the very tip of Cape Cod is Race Point, and it stands foremost in the list of great Cape fishing spots.

Despite some writers' assertions that The Race was discovered as a hot spot in the 1970s, the truth is quite different, according to veteran Race and backside angler, George Carlezon of Milton. Still a spry and enthusiastic surf fanatic at 80, George has been fishing the beaches from Provincetown to Truro for 50 years, and no one has more praise for the productivity and beauty of this region. Although he has never been able to convince Mildred, his wife of 57 years, to join him on the Cape, George spends an average of two months a year between May and October in Provincetown.

"She won't come across the border, but I come down for about twelve days and then go home for a week or so to cut the lawn and take care of things at the home. I call every other day to make sure everything is okay and she's always been very supportive of my fishing."

When George got out of the service in January 1946 (he served in the Navy as a SEABEE), the first thing he did was go to Filene's Basement to get a new overcoat. Then he went to Raymond's and bought a fishing reel.

"The salesman thought I was crazy for buying a reel in January, but I had the bug," he said. "I didn't have any decent tackle at the time. I did some fishing in the canal and my son and I went to Nauset, as well. That April I bought a Model A from a neighbor who wasn't using it. Back then we didn't have four-by-fours, and the Model A was the way to go."

Despite using what he called "some of the raunchiest equipment imaginable," George was into surf fishing big time, eventually making his way up to the backside and landing in Provincetown.

"I had a tent at Peaked Hill where I kept all my tackle and left it there when I went home. No one bothered with it; in fact, during a storm, one of the regulars would drop the center pole on the tent and shovel sand on it to keep it from blowing away."

As time progressed, four-wheel-drive vehicles began to supplant the bread trucks and other live-in vehicles the surf-fishing fraternity used to extend their stays on the beach. George, part of the trend, bought a camper.

What George liked about the Provincetown scene was the freedom it offered.

"Back many years ago, a small group of dedicated fishermen, including myself, fished the beaches around here. On weekends, the townies would join us. We got along good, except they spoke some Portuguese and I couldn't understand what they were saying. They could be discussing where they were hammering fish and I was left out. I didn't like that."

Because it is so wide open, The Race falls victim to constantly shifting sand. One of George's friends had a cottage at The Race and lost 65 feet of beach in one season. This constantly moving sand meant that moving to find fish was critical, which at that time wasn't a problem.

"There would be maybe a dozen of us and we would start down around High Head and keep leap-frogging each other until fish were located. Then everyone would get together to fish the schools that were found."

Eventually, George and his cronies lost their freedom of fishing the beach to what George called "originally a Godsend" – the Cape Cod National Seashore. The brainchild of Senator Leverett Saltonstall and created with the signature of President Kennedy in 1961, the Seashore was opposed by many Cape Codders because it took properties, infringed on their businesses and limited their freedom. But George saw it as a way of curtailing the threat of development, which he recognized back in the late 1950s and early 60s.

What he and others didn't envision was the closing of huge sections of the Back Beach, including sections of The Race, to protect the dunes and piping plovers and roseate terns.

"They've gone too far," George says today. "Right now, almost five miles of beach south of the Coast Guard Station to High Head are closed, and the waters there are loaded with fish but we can't get there. We don't want to hurt the birds; in fact, we used to put sticks around their nests to mark them."

Further restrictions came with the dune buggies, which are often confused with beach buggies. The former has one purpose: going fast and flying over dunes. If you asked George, you'd know that he and the rest of the mobile crew that drove the beaches in search of fish wished that they had chosen a different name for their chariots. The Seashore administration, to keep dune buggies from ripping the dunes apart, restricted use of all motorized vehicles in the park.

Now the only territory that is open to vehicles is an eight-mile stretch from High Head to Race Point. But the Seashore administration may close down any of that to protect nesting birds. In addition, the Seashore established "self-contained vehicle" areas to the south and north of the Coast Guard Station, where there's a limit of 100 mobile homes allowed at any time. A vehicle must undergo an inspection at the ranger station at Race Point for proper tires, jack, board to support the jack, tow rope or chain, shovel and tire gauge.

While the latter may seem like an odd item to the uninitiated, tire pressure is critical at Race Point. The sand there is a fine granular form often called sugar. Vehicles that run the beaches can weigh up to three tons or more, and if the air is not let out of the tires to give them more surface area, the vehicle will sink into the sand no matter how much power is applied.

The speed limit at The Race is 15 m.p.h. except in the self-contained vehicle areas where it is 5 m.p.h. to protect the families enjoying themselves there. You want to float over the sand, not plow through it. And as George said, "If everyone ran at fifteen pounds average, we wouldn't have the ruts and holes that spinning wheels cause."

George is quick to point out that he resents the huge 35-foot-plus campers that take up space and whose owners have no interest in fishing there. "They don't belong here. They're just a sign of excess that we're guilty of today. Heck, one of the wheels and tires you need to run sand in one of those things cost $500 to $600, and you have to buy them from special shops like in California."

But George is happy to talk about the fishing opportunities and techniques The Race is known for.

"Back when we started, we used plugs pretty much. I didn't have a lot of money, so I used to turn my plugs on a lathe at work."

The Atom 40, the Creek Chub Jointed Pike Minnow, often called the Jointed Eel, and other large swimming and popping plugs held sway at The Race, but before long George and his friends began to throw rigged eels and eventually turned to bait. Nowadays, the two baits most popular are sand eels and live eels.

"We bottom-fish sand eels with a rig that has a long leader about thirty inches leading from the eye of a swivel and a shorter leader from the other eye to a bank sinker which is drawn across the bottom. A favorite hook is a 6/0 offset Mustad hook with bait holder slices on the shank. The sand eel is placed right up on the hook and is held in place by the barbs on the shank."

There are also special sand eel hooks, and some favor hi-lo rigs, but fresh sand eels, the most common and prolific bait in Provincetown and the rest of the backside, are a must regardless of the rig.

"Sand eels are pretty delicate and don't last that long. You can salt them to make them last longer, but I prefer to wipe them with a paper towel to dry them and then place them in a bag on ice. Getting rid of the excess water makes them last longer," said George.

Sand eels used for bait vary in length from four inches early in the season to 8 to 10 inches as summer drifts into fall. Some of the regulars rake them, but bait and tackle shops carry these thin pieces of gold.

George really enjoys fishing eels at night. "We hook them live through the bottom of the jaw and out one eye. They're unweighted, but they still drag the bottom because that's where they're going to head. Fish them slow and wait for the bump indicating a pickup. Drop the rod tip to the fish and let the line tighten. Then set, and you'll usually have a hookup in the corner of the bass's mouth. It's not like the rigged-eel fishing where the fish slams the eels."

And as George said, if you're fishing eels at night, which is the best time, you hope the bluefish aren't around. "I don't mind catching bluefish during the day. They fight great and seeing big bluefish ripping up the surface is incredible. Right now, we're catching them by blind-casting, but I sure don't want them around at night chopping up my eels!"

For lures, besides his own plugs, George speaks highly of Bombers. Color doesn't matter to him that much, although he prefers a dark plug on a dark night and a light plug on a light night.

"I do think yellow, whether popping or swimming plugs, is a good color. Not being a fish, I can't tell, but some scientists say yellow changes in the water and attracts fish." He also likes black or green needlefish lures that he makes himself, which he fishes slow and straight, with an occasional small twitch.

George never sold plugs on a large scale because it "was too much of a headache. I worked in the machine shop business for over fifty years and was able to make the lips myself, as well as treating the rolling wire used to rig them to make it flexible. Making plugs was more a hobby for me." He has more than 4,000 plugs of every size in his basement.

While he once preferred long, 11-foot rods when fiberglass was the material of choice, nowadays he uses 9- to 10-foot graphite rods, which he finds stronger and lighter and which require much less effort to cast.

George uses both spinning and conventional gear, with 17- to 20-pound-test mono on the former and 50-pound on his conventional gear, which he uses to throw eels. He recently spooled a conventional with 45 Assinippi line he found in a drawer. "I used to test line for the guy who made it. It was a seven-strand mono weave that was coated with beeswax. Even after all those years, and it wasn't made after the sixties, it still works great," George said.

There is a constant flow of water to the east around Race Point, which often forms a rip as it butts heads with a current working west from the backside, but it can also be a deceptive piece of water with no apparent surf. The water drops to depths of 70 feet or more very close to shore, which makes it attractive to boat anglers who jig wire with parachute jigs, Jig-it Eels and Hoochies right off the beach.

"You cast your lure or eel at eleven and let it drift in the current until one or two, then you retrieve it," is how George puts it, but he acknowledges that you have to read the current to adjust.

Some people fly-fish around Race Point. There was even talk of closing sections of the Outer Cape to everything but fly-fishing, which is pure nonsense, according to George.

Nowadays, the average bass taken around Race Point is 30 to 34 inches. George's biggest this year was 23 pounds, although he heard of one being taken that was 40 pounds. Twenty to twenty-five years ago, catching four or five 40s a weekend wasn't uncommon. In fact, over the years, George has taken twenty-three 50-pound bass and one over 60.

"It was November 3, 1983. I froze my ass off. It was the last trip of the year and I was using a rigged eel. That cow hit and she was boring out. I had to follow her way down the beach, and after I landed her, I kept fishing. I thought I had a big fish, and as morning approached, I could see that the fish had stretched out and it was huge. It finally weighed 61 pounds when I got it to town."

There is respect among anglers at Race Point. It was clear from all the greetings George received, many from folks he admitted he didn't know the name of, that there is more to Race Point than just good fishing, something that borders on reverence for tradition. ◄█

Illusions Of Grandeur

By Janet Messineo

When I'm fishing, especially when I'm out alone at night, I do a lot of wondering. For example: Why is it that whenever I set out to fish I am bursting with high hopes, absolutely positive that the fish will be there? I wonder, because the truth is that as I review my 20-something years of surf-casting, I have to admit that more times than not I have come home "skunked." People always say to me, "You catch lots of fish!" However, what they may not be aware of are all the hours I have put in and all the times I have come home empty-handed and forlorn because I didn't even get a little tug on the end of my line. Yes, I have caught lots and lots of fish in my life, but compared to the hours I've put in, I would say that the fish are way ahead.

I figure that there are two categories of fishermen: the recreational fishermen and the so-called "hard-core" fishermen. The first group might set out for an afternoon fishing excursion, have a great time whether they catch fish or not, call it a day and return the following week or following month to have some more fun. The second group might go out to fish on a rainy evening, stay until the sun rises and catch nothing, only to return the very next day or night, and will repeat this insanity over and over again. I've had many conversations with fellow fishermen, trying to find the word that best describes this driven behavior – "compulsive" comes pretty close.

Derby season is the time when fishing becomes hard work, and over the last couple of years I haven't had much success in having fun. The 1996 fall fishing season was very slow (to say the least), and some of my theories of why I enjoy fishing jumped out of my head and were washed away with the surf. My buddy Hawkeye says, "Fun has nothing to do with it!" I don't want to believe him because I know that at least I used to be able to maintain some sort of balance between all-or-nothing competition and having a good time. I guess Chrissie Hynde hit the nail on the head when she sang, "It's a thin line between love and hate."

Recently, I was approached by a couple of people who said that they were out to beat me in the derby this year. My stomach did a flip-flop. I haven't won any major derby prizes in almost 10 years, so I wasn't quite sure what they were talking about. On top of that, I'm having a hard enough time competing with myself, and I still have lots of "firsts" that I would like to accomplish before I'm totally satisfied, if that's even possible.

Some time ago I heard a saying that keeps running through my brain: "Once you've become a pickle, you can never go back to being a cucumber." At times I like to think of myself as a recreational fisherman, and I think that through the summer months I am just that. However, in the spring I spend a lot of time filling up my fishing deficiency left over from the winter, and from September through November I have a seemingly insatiable appetite for standing on the water's edge under a starry sky because I realize that the fish will soon begin their journey south and I will be back to my day-to-day responsibilities. In other words, I think my cucumber days are over. Yet I have also known other people who have fished all their lives and are still somehow able to stay in the cucumber category. So what exactly is it that separates recreational fishermen from the "hard-core"?

Recently I have become aware that I have illusions of grandeur each time I set out, rod in hand, although I'm not exactly sure what causes this state of mind. I know that we have all had the experience of the last cast finally attracting the fish that we have been in search of; this could be the reason why we choose to hang in there while most of the others have returned to the civilized world. Maybe it's faith; perhaps it could be optimism? What about hope? I really don't know, but I do know that I always start out excited, my mind filled with images of landing the "big one."

For example: The Illusion. It's the first night of the 1996 derby; I'm fishing with Mike Laptew. My adrenaline level is so high that I can barely breathe. I think I can pop off a 40-inch bass in the first couple of hours, switch to targeting bluefish and catch a 12-plus-pounder, relax until the sun starts to rise and then hook up to a false albacore before the weigh-in opens. I'll get a good start in a grand slam on the very first day. Illusions of Grandeur! This was the vision that I dreamed of day and night in the weeks before the derby began.

The Reality. The tide was perfect and the wind direction was in our favor; I've hammered big stripers under these same conditions. We fished for bass from a minute after midnight until about 6 a.m., catching five or six bass each, none of them over 31 inches. It was an interesting night, but a little disappointing after all the anxiety. Mike left to film the opening day at the weigh-in, and I stayed behind in search of a decent bluefish. Ah ha! I got one; I thought it could possibly go to four pounds if I got it on ice quick enough. Then I focused on getting an albie, or maybe a bonito would come by; that would make

The author gets ready for a night of fishing on East Beach, Martha's Vineyard.

my day. Oh my goodness – suddenly it was 7:45 a.m. I figured that I had better get to the weigh-in to see what was going on. No bonito and no albie, but at least I got a little blue for the first day. We all have to eat humble pie at some point, so I figured that I might as well get it over with now. I arrived at the derby headquarters at approximately 8:05. My God! They were lined up at the door with lunker bass! There was Mark Plante with a 47-pounder, Steve Amaral got a decent fish and Gorden Ditchfield had a bluefish that was almost 12 pounds! Everyone had a 40-inch to 40-pound bass, and I knew that Mike and I were all alone in my secret "hot spot." I finally swallowed my pride when the long line subsided, snuck my bluefish out of the cooler and handed it to the weighmaster. Oops – 3.69 pounds. That's under the 4-pound minimum for adults. Oh well.

But never mind; here comes another Illusion of Grandeur. Putting together the puzzle pieces starts consuming my mind once again. "I know where they got those fish," I think. "My second favorite spot! It's a nice yucky, rainy day, the wind has come around southwest, and stripers love feeding in these conditions even in the daylight hours." The passion of the chase takes over once again.

Now it's 10 a.m. and the derby is less than 12 hours old. I'm sitting on my bucket in the pouring rain on the south shore, the wind in my kisser at about 20 knots. The beach is deserted because all those fishermen who slammed the fish from midnight till six are now tucked into their warm beds, catching up on some sleep. I have started talking to myself. I think, "I'm having a good time . . . this is fun . . . I'm doing the right thing . . . the fish were here last night, so they're bound to return this afternoon . . . this is fun . . . I'm sure I'll be able to get a beauty for tonight's weigh-in . . . this is great!"

Then the hours pass, and pass some more. Not a hit! My thoughts turn for the worse. "This is ridiculous . . . this isn't fun! I'm supposed to be having fun! The derby is just over 16 hours old and I'm already nuts! I'm soaked! I'm exhausted! If I sit here all day I'll be a total waste-case for tonight's fishing . . . I'm NOT having fun! I'm going home!"

I jump into bed to catch maybe two hours of sleep before I pick up my son, Chris. I whip a dinner together, weather-band radio by my side and tide chart in hand. By the time my husband, Tristan, gets home from work, I've come up with a plan for the night. I'm out the door and I'm on a mission once again. Now I'll get that big one! Illusions of Grandeur!

I'm amazed that after fishing all night without a hit, the weary feelings disappear just as the sun starts to light the sky; the bonito and albacore fever strikes, and newfound energy carries me to my daytime perch. A tide change, a wind shift, a rising or setting sun can swiftly change my feelings of disappointment into new energy that keeps me marching toward my next (hopefully) monster catch.

This thing that I can't quite describe, the illusions of grandeur, the constantly reborn high hopes, keeps me captive all the way through to the end.

Last Day of the Derby Illusion. I get the hit that I've been waiting for, after more than 20 years of fishing. It's an incredible lunker for sure! There are 20 minutes left before the final bell rings. I've timed my travel time for this very moment. I land an amazing world-record 85-pound striper. (As the years slip by, this dream-fish keeps getting bigger and bigger.) I catch my breath and rise from my knees, after chanting, "Thank you, Lord." Adrenaline pumping, I lift this monster as if it weighs a mere 10 pounds and gently toss it into my cooler. I speed toward the weigh-in, and just 30 seconds before they hit the final bell I drag my winner to the scale. Yeah!

The Reality. I'll run downstairs and grab some coffee, throw my smelly lucky sweater on, grab those eels, jump in my buggy and head for the beach to fish the last day of the derby.

Ask me on October 19, and I'll tell you how I did. ◀━▶

Superstitions, Omens & Quirks

By Janet Messineo

Two years ago on the second day of the Martha's Vineyard Derby, I caught a 24-pound striped bass, a decent catch, after only a few casts. When I returned to my buggy and took off my waders, I noticed that I had forgotten to put my left sock on. The following morning, as I was going through my daily ritual of getting dressed to fish, I could not make myself put on that left sock.

That was it! I had found the key to having good luck! Omit that left sock and the fish will come. After about a week of having a cold left foot and no unusually spectacular fishing, I gave in and put my sock on once again.

Looking back over the years, I realize I have always worn a couple of lucky fishing sweaters that are not very attractive but helped me catch some magnificent fish. I have a purple wool sweater that is so full of holes it should have been discarded at least 10 years ago, but I can't part with it. I have a few articles of clothing that I keep in reserve, and when the fishing is really lousy for me, I pull them out of storage.

I call them the big guns. Most of them are hand-me-downs from fishermen I admire. Twelve years ago, I lost my luckiest sweater ever. I'm still not over it. It was an ugly brown turtleneck with "two bucks" on the front. Remember those sweaters? It belonged to a very dear old friend, and I caught my biggest fish and the most fish in my life wearing it.

Last fall the fishing was incredibly slow for everyone here on the Vineyard. I spent too much time alone in the dark with not even a hit. I studied my tides and wind direction, and fished live bait. My gear was in good working order and I fished areas that consistently produced fish, stripers and occasional bluefish. I knew that I had done the footwork and just had to wait. So, wait and wait and wait I did, to no avail! Although the daily weigh-in boards told me that not many fish were being caught, I couldn't stop the mental gymnastics running through my brain trying to change my situation. I never changed my clothes so many times in one fishing season, wished on so many stars, kissed eels, walked clockwise around my bucket and turned my back toward my baited rod. Who, me? Superstitious?

Shooting stars are omens for me. I believe that when I can bring to the forefront of my mind the thought of that lunker I'm pursuing before the star burns out, I will catch fish. Sometimes it works; this time it didn't, but I couldn't help trying to get a crystal-clear picture in my mind of a big bass on the end of my line before that star disappeared.

I won't even get into some of the rocks, shells and trinkets that find their way into my pockets. I guess they are called Good Luck Charms. I really know that it wasn't what I was wearing; the fish were just very scarce. Although somewhere in the back of my mind,

I'm still not sure if I just couldn't find the right combination of clothing and omens to unlock the big-fish luck door.

I've always assumed that every fisherman goes through the same rituals that I do. I just considered them part of fishing. I was chatting about some of my quirks with Stan Brown, a champion bonito fisherman from Providence, as we were standing on a jetty waiting for some fish to crash through the wall of bait that was on all sides of us.

He looked at me and said, "You're superstitious!"

I said, "No, not really!"

Later, when I had a chance to ponder our conversation, I realized he was absolutely correct. I am superstitious. As I looked back over some of my behaviors, the picture became very clear.

I've talked with numerous fishermen over the last couple of months about their habits when preparing to go fishing. I have learned that some anglers literally "just go fishing," which is hard for me to believe, but true. The majority, however, have certain rituals that must be performed before, during or while fishing. I've decided that most of these superstitious fishermen share their peculiar behaviors in a most matter-of-fact manner.

Bob Merritt, who is a familiar silhouette on the end of a jetty in the middle of the night, told me his good luck charm was his buddy, Jerry Jacobs. Jerry is not always able to join him because he's busy with a landscaping job and supporting a wife and two adorable babies. Bob is always excited when Jerry comes along because it's almost a sure thing that he will catch fish. Unfortunately, Jerry's luck isn't affected by Bob's company.

Bob Boren, a senior veteran fisherman with an extraordinary memory of fishing the Vineyard for decades, never had any tricks up his sleeve. His fishing pal, Chris Davis, had enough superstitions for the both of them. He had a certain way of lining up his gear and if Bob dared to move ever one item he was seriously told with a scowl: "Don't touch anything!"

Ed Jerome is the perpetual president of the Derby Committee. (We'll never let you retire, Ed; sorry, but we need you! Hmmm. Sounds superstitious!) It's such a heartwarmer to see him out in the weather fishing with his dad and two young sons. Eddie is one of many "hat believers." A lucky hat is a must for a great fishing night. Ed says he never wears his derby daily pins on his lucky fishing hat. He decorated another hat that he will wear around town, but won't adorn his actual fishing hat. He is also convinced that some of his rods catch fish and others stand still in the night. I share this quirk with him and always get a strong gut feeling that a particular rod will be the one that gets all the action.

David Pothier, owner of Cars Unlimited, is a key person in so many fishermen's lives. A potpourri of four-wheel-drive vehicles crowd into his shop's driveway, waiting their turns for maintenance. He understands the anxious feeling we have when the tide is right and the buggy won't get us there. He always remains calm and reassures us as we pace back and forth in his garage waiting for his expert crew to send us on our way. Now, David has a strange compulsion to dip his plug or fly into the ocean before he ties it onto his line. He explained to me why he does this, but I still don't think I quite get the reasoning. I think, if it works, don't fix it! He's got the "hat thing" and his wife Terry won't allow his fishing sweater in the house.

Mark Ward, another family man surrounded by children, each with a rod in his or her hand, said he always wears his derby pin upside down. When he's braving the rocky shores of Squibnocket and Stonewall Beach, that's how he wants to see a trophy fish come to him – belly up.

Chip Bergeron, the elusive fly-rodder who is very seldom caught in the act, would naturally wear the same hat that helped him win the nonresident bass category in 1984 with a 48-pounder. The morning of his big catch he saw a deer. That has become his omen, and I can imagine the adrenaline rush he gets when a big buck crosses his path.

Tootie Johnson is the woman I want to be when I grow up. I met Tootie last summer on Eastville Beach with her fly rod in hand. She has been fishing the Vineyard waters for about 65 years. For most of her life she was a bait slinger and a familiar sight in the middle of the night. Her contagious laugh doesn't quite overshadow the fact that she misses her walks alone in the night from Lobsterville to Dogfish Bar. She loves fly-fishing and wouldn't think of standing on the edge of the water without blue sea glass in her stripping basket. She has already landed a bonito, which is an experience that still scares me.

Her adopted dog Ringo was an omen not only for her but also for her fishing friends. Before Ringo's demise, he was known to urinate on the bait and the fishing became productive. When Tootie would get together with friends to fish, they would always say, "Please bring Ringo!"

Bob Lane, president of the Surfcasters and holder of the secret of exactly where Carl's rock is located, is infected with the "shirt thing." Not unlike my tales, he keeps a couple of hand-me-down shirts in reserve for when the going gets tough. A few years ago his good friend and fishing pal Mike Titus bought the house where Roberto Germani spent his last days. Mike found some of Roberto's flies in the house and since he was only spin-casting, he gave them to Bob. Bob hasn't dared use them for fear of losing them but always carries them in his fly pouch. Although the flies were a little tattered – a sign that they were successful fish catchers – he has tried to duplicate some of the patterns.

Steve Amaral is part of the family that has been notorious for generations as incredible fishermen. Just about everything I know about striped bass fishing I learned indirectly from the Amaral clan. Steve says he has no superstitions! He studies the wind and tides and scopes out the spots he sees as prime fish territory. I know Steve is a great fisherman and he's one of those guys I admire, but I am just dumbfounded that it can all be that simple.

No special hat! Or sweater! No spitting on Danny plugs!

Walter Lison amazed me with the comment that he doesn't have "that problem." He could be right. Those of us that have to have all these details in place can be plagued by the loss of an article of clothing.

Finally, there is Mike Laptew, the video diver who has given us a new perspective on fish behavior after thousands of years of fishing history. Mike not only has some of his own quirks but has also adopted omens from other fishermen. He had the opportunity to fish with Lou Tabory and learned that the butterfly is an omen for Lou. Last fall when

Mike was on the Vineyard to do some filming and fishing, he learned exactly how powerful the butterfly's presence can be. He was talking on the phone to his wife Donna, who had stayed at home in Rhode Island. As they were talking, Mike spotted a butterfly! He said, "Honey, a butterfly; honey, a BUTTERFLY!" At that very moment a bird swooped down and grabbed the fluttery little creature in its beak and boldly landed in Mike's full view and commenced to devour the good-luck omen! Well, doesn't it just make perfect sense that within the next 24 hours Donna called Mike with the news that their water heater and furnace had broken down and needed to be replaced. Not to mention the alternator on Mike's car broke, and when he was finally able to go fishing, there were no fish to be found.

You'll probably be able to spot some of these superstitious beach wanderers by their raggedy attire. Maybe a hat that's been worn for much longer than it was intended, a sweater that could attract critters with its aroma or pins and bangles hanging from one of the most sophisticated people in town. My son Chris and I discuss subjects like God, Santa Claus, the Tooth Fairy and the Easter Bunny. I always tell him that I believe in magic because if you don't believe in magic, it won't happen! ◄██◄

Nighttime Techniques
For The Striper Of A Lifetime

By Alan Cordts

I grew up on the New Jersey shore; my home was four blocks from the beach. I was introduced to the concept of night-fishing when I was in the seventh grade. Reading an article in *Saltwater Sportsman* magazine written by Frank Woolner about surf casting for striped bass at night, I was so impressed by the pictures of huge stripers that I decided to climb out my bedroom window (on a school night) and bicycle down to fish one of my favorite jetties. Within minutes I had buried a treble hook from a Creek Chub Surfster in my cheek, which required a trip to the hospital for a painful extraction. A little later I experienced some disciplinary pain on my rear end from my dad. My father now acknowledges that he is at least partially to blame for the surf-fishing addictions of his two older sons. We grew up in a shared bedroom with two large, mounted striped bass that he had caught just before we were born. A fish hung over each of our beds; my father recently refurbished them and they hang there still today in the Jersey homestead.

Despite this less-than-auspicious beginning, I have become a student of the night-fishing game, especially surf casting for striped bass. Recently, I've been challenged by Lake Ontario brown trout and king salmon, which are notorious night feeders. If only we could figure a little of this out in one fishing lifetime!

It is impossible to avoid fishing after dark if you expect to consistently catch large striped bass off the beaches of Southern New England, and particularly off the Cape and Martha's Vineyard. I have landed five stripers of 50 pounds or better off the beach. Every one required a headlamp for unhooking, weighing and measuring. My brother Dan has taken two surf stripers over 50 pounds, both at night. Two good friends from the Vineyard, Tom Taylor and Francis Bernard, have taken the grail, 60-pound-plus fish out of the surf at night. It's not likely that any of these fish would have been caught during the daylight hours.

When I plan for a night's hunt for striped bass on the beach, I pay close attention to the weather conditions, water conditions and, of course, the tide charts.

The weather, specifically the wind direction and wind strength, is most important, because the weather totally dictates and controls inshore water conditions. In the shallow-water domain of the surfcaster, limited as we are to the length of our casts, the water conditions need to be just right to attract and hold gamefish. Wind duration, as well as wind strength and wind direction, helps me decide which beaches I will automatically rule out or, alternatively, consider as a possible good choice.

This takes some experience as you familiarize yourself with individual locations. An example of this would be the typical fall season winds on Cape Cod and the Islands where we often have blasting southwest winds by day, changing to hard northwest winds at night. Such wind patterns over a few days will literally blow out both north and south shore beaches on the Vineyard with raging surf, chocolate-milk-colored water, and weed. This leaves almost nowhere to fish on the island, except for a few sheltered corners or east-facing beaches – not usually our first choices for big-fish hunting. When these conditions are present, I head for the Outer Cape beaches, either Nauset or beyond, where the fisherman has miles of east-facing beaches with (usually) clear, fishable water from which to choose.

Let me close my eyes and describe my idea of perfect conditions. The wind has been out of the southwest or northwest at less than 15 knots for at least four or five days, and there have been long stretches of calm wind conditions, particularly at night. All of the inshore waters are relatively calm. I do not mind night-fishing rough-water surf conditions, provided water conditions are clear to the point that I can stand knee-deep or more and see my boot foot on the bottom.

I don't like dirty water at night, especially if I'm fishing artificials. Sometimes daytime surfcasters can have banner days during avalanche surf, high wind and churned-up seas, but typically they will be skunked in calm, clear water conditions. Conversely, my experience has been that big surf/dirty water is unproductive after dark. I believe that if you must fish at night in these conditions, bottom fishing with a whole, freshly dead squid or a live eel will give you the best shot at a decent fish. But in most cases, ideal water conditions after dark are totally different than they are in the daylight.

Perfect condition number two would be a full moon or new-moon phase. During a full-moon period, I would hope for heavy cloud cover to make the night darker, as dark as possible. These moon phases, of course, develop the highest tides and strongest current flows. The big beaches of the National Seashore on the Cape and the north and south shore beaches on the Vineyard seem to fish best on the high end of the tide. However, if all other good water conditions are present (clear water and no weed), and you're having a fun, peaceful night, it's worthwhile to wade and fish around the exposed bars at low tide and then fish right through the tide cycle.

I prefer the new moon to the full-moon. During the new-moon calendar phase, look for a high tide around 3 a.m. Human nature being what it is, I guarantee you'll have less competition for prime spots if you fish these late-night high tides, and the darkness of a new moon will also help keep more fishermen in their beds than on a moonlit night.

I have experienced a few productive nights under a bright full moon, especially in the fall, but not many. You can have some spectacular nighttime fishing by the light of a full moon if bluefish are your target. For bluefish, the brighter the night is, the better your chances. But if you're seeking stripers, count on dark nights to escape pesky blues when you know they're present. If you really want to fish the blackest of nights, look for the combination of a moonless night and fog. I can assure you that striped bass love these conditions for shallow-water feeding.

Perfect condition number three: The beach I'm fishing has at least some evidence of the presence of bait. Sometimes the telltale signs of bait are subtle. One fall night, I had plugged about a mile of promising beach and was ready to walk away hitless and fishless. As a last resort, I put out an eel on a pyramid sinker. I had a hit within minutes and pulled in a large dogfish. Disgusted and tired, I was ready to go. However, the dogfish was spitting up jumbo-size sand eels – its belly was bulging with them. I cast out another eel, only to pull in another obese, bulging sand shark. I went back to plugging; I just couldn't leave the beach while this silent, biological event was taking place right in front of me.

Another hour ticked away. I changed lures repeatedly, then put on another eel and promptly caught another dogfish, just to prove to myself that nothing had changed. Finally, I caught a small striper on a plug, and then it was a bass on every cast until the sun, poking over the horizon, turned off the bite. I estimated that I had landed over 300 pounds of bass in a short time. The point I wish to make is that if you find a beach with bait present, leave only with reluctance and return often!

Be aware that not every bar or slough along the beachfront holds sand eels, one of our most common baitfish. The sandbar down the beach a hundred yards or so may be the feeding station that holds fish, rather than the huge slough that looks more promising. These honey-hole sections of beach change from year to year and sometimes after a severe storm. Some scouting is unavoidable, even along a familiar beach, and it should be done with a line in the water.

Condition number four: I am catching something, anything, such as rat blues, small stripers or even dogfish. The presence of small fish is a good indication that I'm doing things at least somewhat correctly. Not every night is going to be a winner. There are just not that many trophy fish around, compared to a few decades ago. But if I'm catching anything at all, I feel that I'm in the running for a good fish to make the trip worthwhile.

One July night in 1996 I had two nephews in tow who had just started learning to fish their home waters along the Jersey shore. We were fishing under the Gay Head cliffs, catching striper after striper, all schoolies in the 20- to 28-inch class. At the end of the tide, two good fish moved in with all the dozens of schoolies – a 23- and a 46-pounder. I still wonder what astonished my nephews more: the size of these two keepers, large by New Jersey standards and much larger than the rest of the fish they'd been catching, or my ritual of measuring, weighing and photographing the fish, then releasing them to fight another day.

When selecting lures to use at night, there's one important rule to always keep in mind: You must fish slowly. That means you should leave your fast-moving popping plugs and metal lures such as Kastmasters and Hopkins, which must be retrieved fast to avoid becoming hung up, at home. Instead, think swimming plugs, the bigger, the better. My favorites are the Danny plug and the number 40 Atom swimmers. In dead calm, clear water I will go with somewhat smaller lures like the Junior Atoms, 7-inch Rebels and large needlefish. These are the smallest lures that I will put on the end of my line. Needlefish lures are particularly effective in dark-night, crystal-clear, calm conditions. The Stan Gibbs "bottle plug" swimmer I consider a specialty lure for use in rough water or where you encounter heavy currents. It casts well and should always be in your surfbag in case you encounter in-your-face wind conditions. At night, all the plugs I've mentioned can and should be fished very slowly; this is absolutely crucial.

As far as color goes, I don't subscribe to the idea of using black plugs after dark. I want maximum visibility and that is only possible with white lures – they are all I use. Also, I remove the back trailer hook on all my three-ganghook plugs. Fish releases are easier. The plugs wag better without the third treble. Big fish always clobber their prey in the head, so the third trailing treble is unnecessary and mutilating. Save that back hook for a spare.

Other specialty lures that have worked for me on occasion are darters and skin plugs. The Stan Gibbs Darter or the hard-to-find, old-style, large Danny darter casts well into a head wind. Also, I carry a large, deep-diving Danny plug, which is really a trolling lure. This jumbo has taken some nice stripers for me out of heavy surf with an undertow; the plug digs down and stays under the heavy beach break.

At one time or another I've stuck an eelskin on every plug on the market. My favorites, though, are the number 40 Atom or a big Danny. Skin plugs are hard to cast and are probably no better than regular plugs in heavy surf or fast currents, but on dead calm, bright nights they are very special.

I'm not a fan of rubber or plastic lures for surf casting, and you won't find them in my tackle bag. Usually I'm looking for a different-size fish than these lures tend to catch. It never made sense to me, for example, to use a rubber eel when you can rig a real one and have a better bait.

Daybreak is supposedly the magic hour for all fish. Sometimes this is true in the surf. However, I seem to need a whole lot more than one hour to hunt down big striped bass. If you want to experience two to four hours of good fishing, then you'll have to find the magic tide. For the beach fisherman, this can only happen at night. Put in your time; it will come.

What Legends Are Made Of
Cape Surfcasters

By Dave Peros

Even though there have been many arguments surrounding striped bass in the matters of science, technique and other subjects, one certainty is that any bass angler around these parts who's worth his weight in salt knows the name "Cuttyhunk," and probably even has a handle on the island's history.

When Captain Bob Luce established his place in the legendary 70-pound club on September 30, 1972, by landing a 71-pounder while fishing in the area of old Chatham Inlet, he was no stranger to big bass. He had received much of his early tutelage in cow catching around Cuttyhunk.

"When I read the piece about Charlie Cinto, I couldn't believe how similar my experience was to his," Bob said. "I used to fish with Charley Haag and he was one tough son-of-a-gun. If he liked you, you were O.K., but he could be rough on folks who dropped fish. I started fishing around Cuttyhunk in 1962, I think it was, and the fishing was just fantastic. Forty-pound fish were common, and even fifties didn't turn too many heads. We fished big wooden plugs like Goo-Goo Eyes, which replaced the Creek Chubs they first used, but it was Charlie who brought wireline and jigs up to Cuttyhunk, and boy did that combination catch fish. Our goal was to catch big fish because we were competing in the Schaefer Tournament. I used to fish for the Sportsmen Unlimited Club out of Hingham. Those fish meant points for your club, and that's what we wanted."

Bob caught his first 50-pounder while fishing the waters off Cuttyhunk, but that's not where he got his start.

"I actually fished Plum Island first, and for the first two years I didn't catch a legal bass, which back then was only sixteen inches. But when I started using wire and plugs and jigs, I started bringing in big fish. I used to fish with John White, a friend of mine who is dead now. We only had one Goo-Goo Eye between us because they were so hard to come by, and we had rigged it to be used with an eelskin. John also had an eelskin rig he came up with, and when you'd catch five or six bass, everybody knew about it."

Bob started fishing the water of the Lower Cape around 1965. When he and his wife moved to East Harwich from Dorchester in 1969, he focused his attention on the productive waters of Pleasant Bay and the rips off Monomoy and Nantucket. He had figured out that by the end of June many of the big fish had left the waters around the Vineyard and Nantucket Sound and had headed for Monomoy and cooler waters to the east.

"Starting in July, things really picked up on this end of the Cape, and they'd take up residence around here and I could fish for them out of the skiff I had. Most people don't realize how much stripers are fish of habit; they return to the same waters like clockwork. Now that I help the state with tagging trips, I've seen us catch a fish one year and then catch the same fish within two days of the time we caught it the year before."

Bob minces no words when it comes to the quality of fishing he experienced from the 1960s right through the early 1980s.

"I wouldn't even want to venture a guess at how many fifty-pound fish I've caught over the years, but I remember trips where we had multiple fifties on the same day. I had all kinds of pins from Schaefer and Ashaway tournaments for fifty-pound fish; I still have them for the fifty-one and fifty-three-pounders I caught in 1967. Even as the number of smaller and medium-size fish got smaller, there were still big fish to be had. In the fall of 1982, I had a trip where we caught five fish over fifty pounds, and even as late as 1984 my wife and I caught fifteen big bass on a trip to Nantucket on November 17, including three fifties."

Despite all the big fish he has caught, and all the fish the people on his charter boat, *Striper*, have caught (Bob started chartering part time in 1978, going full time for the last six years), the 71-pounder has a special place for Bob. "I caught that fish so long ago that sometimes it's hard to remember," he said with a laugh. "That year in 1972 there were just incredible numbers of big fish in some of the holes around Chatham Inlet. The inshore groundfish boats were dressing out their fish as they were returning through the area, and I think the big fish just took up residence there. I remember we were using live pogies, and that numbers of fifties and even a few sixties were caught during those weeks. The day before, I had taken a fifty-pounder to Wally Brown to have mounted, and then the next morning I was out fishing again by myself. I was using leadcore, a treble hook and a stinger hook, and those live pogies when I had a good hit. It was early morning, about six I think, and the tide was starting to slack off when I caught that fish, and I had to put the rod down to bring it on board with the gaff. I remember thinking, 'That's a big one!' but I just kept fishing after I put it in the box. Mike Anderson and Hal Raymond were fishing near me when they saw me catch the fish. When I got back to Stage Harbor, I pulled it out to show my friends Charlie and Ray, and they couldn't believe how big it was. It wasn't until about 1:30 in the afternoon when I brought the fish to the Goose Hummock to have it weighed. Red MacFarlane weighed it in at seventy-one pounds and it measured fifty-five inches long; the affidavit says the girth was thirty-one inches, but we measured it too close to the head and I think it was bigger around than that. Even though it won the Governor's Cup that year and the Schaefer Tournament for biggest boat fish, I never sent it in to the IGFA as a record because I knew the rules about treble hooks and I think leadcore was barred, as was wire. It's funny to say it now, but after that big fish,

I kind of lost my edge for fishing; you know you're only going to catch one big fish like that in a lifetime and once I had done it, fishing wasn't quite the same. I find it more satisfying today to have other people catch when we're out in the boat; that's real exciting for me now."

Oddly enough, while the first four stripers over 70 pounds taken from waters around the Cape and Islands were taken by boat fishermen, the last member of the club was landed by Tony Stetzko Jr.

"It's hard for anybody who wasn't there in the 60s, 70s and early 80s to imagine how good fishing was around Nauset, Monomoy and the backside beaches," Tony recalls. "I remember one night when I had seven fish over fifty pounds and other people were doing the same. It was just incredible, the numbers of big fish that were around."

Like Bob, Tony explained that at certain times all of the elements came together to create fishing that was even more outstanding than the usual. It was during just such a time when Tony landed what was then the largest surf-caught rod-and-reel striper.

"In late October and early November in 1981, the fishing around Nauset was just incredible," said Tony. "I remember coming over the dunes and seeing clouds of terns so thick that the sky looked black. There were so many sand eels around that the terns hung around right into November. The regulars around Nauset were picking up fifties pretty regularly, and there were even some sixties taken, too."

As Nick Karas points out in his authoritative volume, *The Striped Bass*, "During the period 1980 to 1983, Long Island pinhookers didn't stop all the big bass from swimming to Cape Cod. Two big fish got past them, a 73-pounder taken by Anton Stetzko from the surf on Nauset Beach and a 69 1/2-pounder taken just 200 yards from the same spot a few weeks earlier by 17-year-old Stephen Petri Jr. of Lindenhurst, Long Island."

When you find out that Tony took a 61-pounder to Wally Brown to have mounted only 10 days before his 73-pounder was brought to the beach on November 3, 1981, and others had taken fish in the 50- and 60-pound class, Karas's remark about "two big fish" making it to the Cape seems a bit of an understatement.

"I wasn't even going to go fishing the night I caught my seventy-three-pounder," said Tony. "The night before, I had caught a couple of nice cod and bass over thirty pounds, but when I got home my wife told me she was going to keep working on her horse so I should go fishing and we would eat later. I called my friend Tony Chirappo; he wasn't going, but I knew that another friend, Jimmy Kostas, would be down Nauset, so I didn't hesitate to go."

After entering Nauset at the private end, he headed down to Gorilla Hole. "The tide was about halfway down and I took a cod around ten pounds there," said Tony. "Back then we would often have a nice run of cod along the beaches, and they would often hit the teasers we were using just as readily as the bass." He was using a live eel with a 7-inch black Deceiver. "When the tide was about a half-hour from low, I headed for Pochet Hole and ran into Jimmy. There was a quarter moon and the water was as calm as glass. In the third bowl down from Pochet, we saw these huge boils; there were just a few fish but they were all cows. Nobody was doing anything with them. I remember that Jimmy went up to his buggy and came back with this huge bobber with a gob of clams and threw it out there, saying that would take one."

For his part, Tony stuck with his eel and dropper. "I finally had a hit and the fish stopped, and then made this one slow run towards the edge of the opening between the two bars. It was almost like it didn't even realize at first that it was hooked. Usually I can move even a big fish, but not that one; at first I thought that maybe it had taken the dropper and become foul-hooked by the eel, but I also knew that there was a lot of weight at the end of that line. When you hear folks talk about fighting a fish for over an hour, I can't imagine it because after ten or fifteen minutes, my arm was tired. It made three runs and finally I worked it in closer where I saw it swirl and I could see a fin; I knew it was a big fish. When I got it up to the water's edge, there was no swell to help me land it and I couldn't get it over the ledge by just walking back. Finally I got it up on the beach up to about its gills and it just sank down right into the sand. I just remember how thick-looking that fish was, lying on the sand after I pulled it up. It looked more like a seal, and Jimmy agreed that it looked like one."

Tony and his friend agreed that this was a big fish, but they did not realize just how big. "While it looked big, we were catching lots of big fish and it was hard to say exactly how big it was," said Tony. "When I was dragging it up to my Blazer, I stopped for a moment and began to think that this might be even bigger than a sixty-pounder, and when I lifted it to put it in the back, I thought, 'Holy S---, what a big fish!' Even then, I went back to fishing since it was only around nine, and when I finally decided to leave and try to weigh the fish, I couldn't find my friend Mike DeSimone, who owned the Bass Run Bait & Tackle in Orleans, so I couldn't use an official scale. I went home and told my wife to come out so I could show her the cod I had caught. She wasn't too happy that I was late, but when she saw the size of that bass, she couldn't believe it. I got the bathroom scale out and weighed myself alone and then picked the fish up. It said the fish weighed eighty-six pounds, but you can't rely on that. Finally, the next day I went to Bass Run Bait & Tackle and the Goose Hummock Shop and it weighed seventy-three pounds in both places. It measured fifty-five inches and had a thirty-eight-inch girth. I caught it on seventeen-pound Stren and a Penn spinning reel, and a custom-made nine-foot fiberglass rod."

Eventually word of Tony's catch got out. "Even Channel Five sent down a helicopter with Peter Mehegan and Mary Richardson," said Tony. "It was a pretty big deal, and I'll admit that catching that fish means a lot to me. Charles Church was like a god to me, and I'd been fishing for stripers with my dad ever since I was a little kid. Catching a fish over seventy pounds was a real gift and something I'll never forget."

When Tony caught his big striper in 1981, Bob Rocchetta from Long Island had already established the all-tackle record in July of the same year with a 76-pounder taken on a live eel. Eventually Al McReynolds of New Jersey established what is currently the all-tackle standard with a 78.5-pound monster taken from one of the jetties around Atlantic City. Other than those two fish, the only other fish over 70 pounds that are documented are a 71-pounder taken in 1980, a 70 in 1987, and, the most recent member of the club, a 75.4-pound bass caught in 1992. None of which came from the waters around the Cape and Islands. That means that since Tony's 73-pounder, the last 17 years haven't seen a 70 or bigger taken from our area, which many folks consider to be the mecca of striped bass angling.

When Bob Luce talks about the waters he fishes today, you can sense the reverence he has for the rips of Monomoy and Nantucket, and his appreciation for places like Pleasant Bay and the old Chatham Inlet, while Tony Stetzko looks at his beloved backside beaches with a sense of awe and respect you can only appreciate when you talk to him. They both saw a time when big bass filled the waters they loved to fish and were fortunate enough to catch truly remarkable stripers. What they also agree on is that not only has the population of people around Cuttyhunk and the Cape changed, but so has the population of striped bass, and the amount of food they have to feed on.

Bob Luce, who has participated in tagging programs with the state Division of Marine Fisheries and other agencies for many years, has a great deal of insight into striped bass, both as a fisherman and from a scientific standpoint. His perspective is not one of panic, but instead is based on experience and reason.

"I can find plenty of fish in the thirty-pound class in the waters I fish, but for the last three years I haven't seen any forty-pounders," said Bob. "I've always believed that a forty-pound fish has to be forty-five inches or bigger, and we don't have that many around that size. If they are that long, they tend to be skinnier. There's no doubt that we have a problem with bait and the size of bass, but I can see bigger fish right around the corner. Even when the fishing was good for big fish, my friend Dennis O'Neil had a sixty-inch fish and it didn't come close in weight to the seventy-one-pounder I had. We've only learned recently, through tagging, how slowly these fish grow. You hear people say, 'We have all these thirty-four-inch fish and it will be great when they come back next year as thirty-six-inch fish,' but they don't realize that as bass get bigger, they may only grow a quarter of an inch in one year, and if food is scarce, they won't put weight on. But the fishing is still very good; people just have to be patient and understand how long it takes to grow forty- and fifty-pound fish. In August 1997, I had seven-year-old Erin Landry and her nine-year-old brother John catch IGFA small-fry world records using the fly rod. Erin's fish weighed thirty pounds and John's, twenty-eight. When people talk about how poor the fishing for so-called big fish is, I just think about those two kids hooked up at the same time and think about what it will be like in ten years or so."

In the end, every angler who has taken up striped bass fishing recently should be grateful for what we have. "Last summer there was fishing on the backside as good as it's ever been since I've been fishing it, but you have to think in terms of total numbers of fish," said Tony. "I had nights when the numbers of thirty-pound fish were incredible; you don't see many forties, and fifties or sixties are another thing altogether. But the overall quality of fishing is still very good."

Many people claim to have been around during the good old days of big bass fishing, and you hear the grumbles about "no 50s being around." Perhaps the truth is that those who complain never really experienced things as they were for fishermen like Charlie Cinto, Jim Nunes, Ed Kirker, Bob Luce and Tony Stetzko, as well as a handful of obsessed bassmen who knew what it was really like. But we can always dream of days gone by, and cross our fingers that in years to come, we will experience the stuff that legends are made of.

Rhode Island Surfmaster – Andy Lemar

By Joe Lyons

Andy Lemar...

A very respected angler remarked to me recently that, "There is a lot of local surf-fishing knowledge that has been forgotten." He then paused, and restated his comment more precisely, "Well, maybe not forgotten," he said, "but dismissed." Whether the knowledge is forgotten or dismissed is less important than the fact that, in the end, much of it will be lost.

The problem is that the most accomplished anglers are usually the most uncommunicative. Some are older, some not so old. While they understand they are part of a vital legacy, stepping from the shadows remains contrary to their nature. While they probably will never write their own stories, maybe they will let someone else. Here is the story of one of Rhode Island's Ghost Surfcasters, Andy Lemar.

Notable Catches & Awards: Three striped bass over 50 pounds. More 30s and 40s than he can remember. Winner of Jerry Sylvester Trophy (for largest surf-caught striper), Narragansett Pier Sportfishing Association, 1983. Fifteen years as Membership Chair (still serving) NPSA

Andy Lemar, still trim at 73, looks at least 10 years younger and has an easy smile. He steps out of his Jeep Cherokee, offers his hand and looks toward the darkening sky remarking, "It's a nice night tonight." Then, shaking his head, he says, "I should have picked up some eels. Point Judith is good on a night like this."

JL: What is it about fishing that has held your interest all these years?

Andy: A lot of things. Catching the fish. Being out there. I love the rocks. I love night fishing. I remember once, I was fishing with a couple of older gentlemen – this was early 80s – it was just getting dark and they left. And I thought to myself, God, I hope I never get that old. It just bothered me, and it's bothered me ever since, the fact that when you get old your balance goes and your eyesight goes, and you can't fish anymore. I'm just glad that I can still do it.

JL: So, obviously, you're still fishing.

Andy: Oh, yes. I'm fishing tonight. Starting tonight, it is going to be good. We've got a high tide around 6:30 or 7. I just love fishing in the dark; my confidence goes up 100 percent when it's dark. As opposed to, you know, day fishing. With day fishing, you're mainly after schoolies. I primarily like to fish for big fish. I have a feeling when you catch a small fish and release it, you're not doing him any good. He just might die on you. All I have to see is a little blood and that's it, I'm finished. But at night, that's when you get the bigger fish. I like to fish with eels. Have you ever heard of Gene Champlin?

JL: No.

Andy: He was a local guy. I learned eel fishing from him – with one exception. When Gene would get a hit on an eel, he would open the bail and let them run. But Gene lost fish due to them dropping the eel. So, I asked Gene if one night I could watch him. He said, "All right." So I sat on the wall at Stinky Beach and just watched him. I saw him lose a few fish – and not blues. He would get a hit and then he would say, "Aw, they dropped it." So I thought, something is just basically wrong with that.

JL: So, how do you do it?

I used to watch Bill Dance (host of a freshwater bass T.V. series) a lot. When he would get a hit on a plastic worm or something, he would lower the rod and in the same motion, set on the fish. That's how I fish eels. I get a hit, drop the rod tip, and then set.

JL: So you wait for the line to become taut, then set?

Andy: You drop the tip, and reel in while you're lowering it. Then, just as quick as you can, you set.

JL: Really?

Andy: Yup, just as quick as you can. Most of the fish are hooked right in the corner of the mouth. You

On the day after Thanksgiving in 1985, Andy caught this 51.5-pounder off the shore on Block Island.

don't miss many fish. If you wait, you get a lot of gut-hooked fish. When you get the bump, when you feel that bump, I swear, I can hear that bump in my mind's ear. That's what I love about eel fishing.

JL: You mentioned you knew Jerry Sylvester. I know he owned a tackle shop and did some guiding. He guided some celebrities too, David Niven . . . .

Andy: Clarke Gable.

JL: Yes. How did they come to seek him out?

Andy: Jerry was very well known. Jerry was a damn good fisherman. He would get a box of lures in, inspect them, and then take them out and start catching with them. He would make sure that people saw him catching and saw the plug. Within two weeks, he would sell the whole box.

JL: When did he start fishing around here?

Andy: He came during World War II, as a chauffeur for somebody, and he just stayed. I used to go to his bait shop and hang out and talk, and we got to be friends. I would write to him - he wintered in West Palm Beach – he never wrote back, but his wife, Edna, would write back for him. Then once, I stopped by to tell him I was heading back to East Providence and he asked if I wanted to watch the World Series. He had just gotten a new color TV.

So we watched the game, and then after we decided to take a ride down to the Coast Guard Restaurant parking lot before I headed home – that's where all the fishermen would hang out in those days. When I got there I could see some birds working way off in the distance, by The Clumps. So I started walking over to Jerry's car, he had spotted the birds, also. Jerry just said, I'm going to nonchalantly pull out and you meet me down there. So I calmly got in my car, and left. Nobody else had noticed.

We got there, and over the rocks he went, Jerry was like a mountain goat on rocks. So, we fished by The Clumps for a while, and we got a bunch of fish. On the way back, I started asking him questions about the Narrow River. The tide was dropping, so we walked out there. He taught me all about fishing the Narrow River that night – how to fish it, when to fish it, where the drop-off was, using the counting method.

JL: The counting method?

Andy: Yes. You make a certain cast, try to get it to the same spot. Then you let it drift and start counting, one, two, three, four, and five – you start at five. Then start reeling in. If you don't get a hit, you go to six, or seven or eight. Counting, like that.

JL: That's an interesting method.

Andy: It worked.

JL: So you'd cover all that water and you would find where the fish were holding?

Andy: Yes. The fish may be close, they may be at the drop-off, or they may be 10 yards past the drop-off, depending on where they were feeding. Once you find the spot where the fish were, you cast to the same spot, count to the same number, close the bail, let the plug drift and swing, and just when it starts vibrating in the water, they hit. Sometimes, you did not even have to start reeling in.

JL: I notice that most people, when they are fishing inlets or breachways, tend to let the plug or eel drift as far as it can, then start reeling in. They're missing a lot of water by doing it that way.

Andy: Sure.

JL: When did you feel you were at your striper-catching best? Or is that question too subjective because of the varying state of the fishery?

Andy: You're never there.

JL: No?

Andy: No. My best years, my most productive years, were over on Block Island during the 1980s. I had heard a lot about it previously to my going over there. I heard from guys on boats, "Oh gee, Block Island. Man, sometimes we have to get in so close to shore to catch the fish." And I remember, I just waffled one year, never did go. Then, the following year, I thought about it some more. I asked a number of guys if they wanted to go over. No one wanted to go. So, I went down one day, made a reservation – just for myself. I went back to Joe Mollica's shop and I told a bunch of guys I was leaving the following Tuesday and if any one wanted to go. No one wanted to go. Finally, one guy, John Snow, comes over to me and says, "I'll go with you, Andy." I said, "Look, I've got my reservation, if you are here at such and such a time we'll go. If not, I'm going anyway." So we got over there, I didn't know anybody, but there was one guy in the club who I knew was an islander, so I went over to see him. He had a combination garage/bait shop, Charlie Dodge, was his name, and there was another guy over there, he was in the club also, Billy Gavitt. And I just asked them how the fishing was. I didn't ask where. I've never felt comfortable asking people where they were catching their fish.

So John and I drove around the island, but we could not find a road to the water. Finally, we went and found Cooneymous Road (a dirt road on the island's south side). I said, "John, let's go down here." We got out, looked at the water, went back to the truck, by the time we got dressed for fishing, it was dark. John went south, toward Southwest Point, and I went north. In less than an hour after arriving, I had my first bass, on an eel. We got about four bass that first night. We didn't know what to do with the fish. At night we'd throw them on top of the truck and sleep in the truck. We had a great time. We got about 11 fish in three days, all 30- and 40-pounders. I went back again with a couple friends of mine from Ohio and we got into fish, but that was it for the year. That was the fall of 1980.

I guess the word got out because, when I went to go again, in the spring of '81, I had six vehicles in my name.

In 1982 Andy caught this 41.8-pounder in Narragansett Bay.

One day a friend comes up to me and says, "Andy, do you have a bunch of guys going over to Block Island to fish?" I said, "Yeah."

My friend said, "Are you planning to sleep in your vehicles?"

I said, "Yeah."

He says, "The police are going to be looking for you. Your name came up before the Block Island Town Council. You guys better get an apartment or something."

So we rented two apartments at The Gables, there were eleven of us, five in one apartment, five in the other, and one guy slept in his truck.

JL: What do you think of the fishery today? What are you seeing out there?

Andy: Hmm . . . It's coming back. The fish are getting bigger. There's a lot more fish, small fish, though. I recall, in all the years that I fished Block Island from the shore, I doubt whether I saw a half a dozen fish less than 15 pounds.

JL: No small fish?

Andy: No small fish, they were all usually 20 and up.

JL: Did you use needlefish at Block Island, or did you fish mostly eels?

Andy: No, I never had too much success with needlefish. I used the Redfin by Cotton Cordell. You put a little hole in it, and put 10cc of water in it.

JL: Really? 10cc?

Andy: Yes. The lip, it's plastic and an integral part of the plug, but guys would bring them through the rocks, and sometimes the lip would get broken off. Someone had given me a plug, or maybe it was one of my own, and I repaired them. So a friend of mine suggested that I should return them to the company and they would replace them. So I had maybe, 8 or 10 Redfins with broken lips that I put in a box and shipped back with a nice letter. I had a couple in there that must have leaked water. So, a few days later I got a call from a woman from this plastic-development company in Arkansas, Mary-Sue or something.

She said, "Andy, we're going to replace the lures that the lips broke off of, but what's this about 10cc?"

I said, "All the fishermen around here always put 10cc of water in the lure. I don't know who started it, but the plug seems to work a whole lot better once you put the 10cc in it."

She said, "I never heard of such a thing."

The next year, Cotton Cordell started putting out the Redfin with a red circle on the side. That meant that they were loaded with a pellet inside. I swear that was as a result of my letter.

JL: How did that plug work?

Andy: I never did like it too much. It casted well, but I think it may have been a little too heavy.

JL: Have you always fished alone?

Andy: In the 80s I fished a lot with a Providence policeman named Bobby Conn and Charlie "Tuna" Akmakjian. The three of us were inseparable for several years, but we gradually grew apart. Over the years, I've had a half a dozen partners. I've fished with a lot of different people, Art Lavalle, Art's dad, Dave Pickering, Steve McKenna – a lot of good fishermen. One night, Steve McKenna and I each got four fish in the 40-pound class on Block Island.

I go out with a girl, Rita, and we fish quite a bit together. She joined the club – that's where I met her, in the club. She and I have fished together for years. When I was working and living in East Providence, we'd fish every weekend, all night long. We would sleep in the daytime; get the eels in the evening. It was her job to get the eels.

JL: (Laughing)

Andy: She's become a good fisherwoman; she's taken bass in the 40-pound range at Block Island. I've had a boat for a while now, and we go on that quite a bit. I still surf-fish in the fall, though.

JL: Do you see a lot of guys out night fishing around here?

Andy: Not like it used to be. I've remarked about that a number of times, you just don't see guys fishing at night like you used to. A lot of nights, you don't see a soul.

JL: I've noticed it, too. The day fishing seems to be a lot more popular now. You go by spots in the day and you can't get a parking spot, but if you go at night there is nobody there.

Andy: Nobody. I like it like that. A lot of my favorite places, you can't get to anymore.

JL: What do you think makes a good fisherman?

Andy: Persistence. You start just by merely being out there. It will come to you, you know? You have to do a lot of it.

JL: Would you consider yourself a self-made fisherman, for the most part?

Andy: Mostly self-made. I never been one to ask questions or say, "Where did you get that fish?" It just bothers me. Not only that, but if people ask me where I caught a fish, I'll tell them. There are a lot of guys, you know, they won't tell you if the sun's up.

JL: Do you find that people put too much emphasis on spots? In other words, do they see spots as some kind of panacea to catching a big fish?

Andy: No. I don't think so. I've been criticized for staying in one spot too long. I figure if it isn't good here, it will be good here. I figure, the fish will be by.

JL: How many spots do you typically hit in a night?

Andy: The most I ever hit in one night is three spots.

JL: That's about what I do.

Andy: If you don't get them in three spots, forget it – try another night. I know guys that hit half a dozen spots in one night. That seems, to me, counterproductive.

JL: *How far do you range?*

Andy: I'll fish mainly the whole Rhode Island south shore and the bay. But I've fished the Cape and Block Island, of course, quite a bit.

I used to fish the Charlestown Breachway a lot but it gets crowded there. Years ago it was worse – they would have plug wars.

JL: *Plug wars?*

Andy: Yes. Guys would get mad at someone for crossing their line, so they would snag their plug and cut it off. That was before they started The Rotation. Before The Rotation, it was whoever got there first. I used to get there at high tide and wait three hours for the tide to turn just to have a good spot.

JL: *You would get to the breachway three hours before the tide turned?*

Andy: Yes. Before The Rotation, whoever got there first was king. Anyway, they did not start rotating until 1958 or so. I remember, this was in the early 50's at the Charlestown Breachway – for three

Another one of Andy's fine Block Island bass.

nights in a row, the guy to my immediate right got a 40-pounder or better, and I never got a fish. I was still learning then. One of the guys asked me to go down and gaff his fish. I had never gaffed a fish before. So I went down there, and I had my light on, there was a lot of foam in the water and I couldn't see him. So, finally, I spotted him and hit him with a nine-iron shot that put a giant hole in his side.

Well, the next day, I was talking to Jerry Sylvester about it and he said, "Was that you? I saw that fish, the guy brought it in here - it had a big hole in it!"

That was one of my most embarrassing moments.

We end our talk with Andy showing me pictures of himself with his 50-pound fish and of his NPSA tournament winner – which, oddly enough, was "only" a 47-pounder. The pictures show the Andy Lemar of 20 and 30 years ago, a big man who looks as though he could fish with the best of them. I tell Andy this, but he does not reply.

Smiling, Andy looks out the window of the Dunkin' Donuts toward Point Judith Road; no doubt he's checking for cloud cover and wind direction. After all, he's going fishing later this evening.

Fishing Clubs Of The Elizabeth Islands

By Gene Bourque

By the mid-nineteenth century, a new class of rich bankers and industrialists had emerged in the United States, many of them based in New York. Some of these men shared an interest in the outdoor life, in fishing and hunting, and were willing to pay large sums of money to pursue their hobbies. But of course, when one is used to a certain level of comfort and service, "roughing it" is a relative term. The fishing clubs that flourished on Cuttyhunk and Pasque from 1865 to the early part of this century were established to give these gentlemen and their guests a retreat from the pressures of daily life. The time they spent on the islands was filled with fishing, feasting and relaxing, with the camaraderie of others of their class. They became known as "The Millionaire's Club."

In 1864, certain members of the West Island Club in Sakonnet, Rhode Island, became increasingly dissatisfied with the rules their organization established, one of which required that the fishing "stands" had to be claimed the night before a member was to fish. This required the angler to hire a local resident to sit on his stand all night, an unacceptable expense in their view. Seven of the West Island members sailed to Cuttyhunk, liked what they saw, and in a very short time bought as much land as they could from the Slocum family and others. They formed the Cuttyhunk Fishing Association (later, Club), "incorporated for social purposes, for angling, propagating fish, and hunting." John Lynes caught the first striped bass entered in the club registry on June 18, 1864. He went on to catch fish up to 49 pounds, and once caught 33 fish in one day.

By 1865, the club had 42 members and, in a few years, was at its peak with 75 members. The original capital, $30,000, was raised by selling 75 shares at $400 each, and was used to buy land, buildings and supplies, and to hire local residents to run the club on a daily basis. Yearly dues were set at $100. Until 1882, members were not charged for the use of a room, and guests paid $3 per day.

There were many rules governing daily activities at the club. The most important pertained to the use of the fishing stands. Before the official opening of the club each year on June 15, local workmen were contracted to set out these stands, 16 in all, which were constructed of narrow planks, stanchions and ropes leading out from the shore. Planks were run from boulder to boulder, some as far as 150 feet from the beach, leading to a pair of chairs that would be used by an angler and his guest or his chummer. The chummer's job was to secure a supply of bait, usually lobster or menhaden, and begin "chumming" the water an hour or so before the sport was to fish. Lobster tails were reserved for use as bait. Rule 5 specified that if the bait was scarce, all members were to share evenly. If a fish was hooked, the chummer was responsible for gaffing and beaching the fish. A good gaffer might earn as much as $1 a fish and an exceptional fish might mean a $5 tip.

At the end of the day, all fish caught were lined up on the lawn in front of the clubhouse and it was determined if the "Big Hook" or "Little Hook" were to change hands. These prizes were property of the club but would remain in the possession of the angler landing the largest and smallest striper up to that point in the season. These symbols of yearly bragging rights were gold pins in the shape of a fishhook, inlaid with a diamond. Members and guests were required to measure, weigh and record each striper caught, regardless of size.

Striped bass weren't the only fish caught around Cuttyhunk in those days. An issue of the magazine *Sport with Rod and Gun*, published in 1883, gives this account of fishing at the club for the other predominant sport fish:

Your blue-fish has an insatiable appetite and a keen nose for a free lunch. We say this ruefully, as we reel in and put out a fresh hook to replace the one just carried away. Egad! That fellow struck like a forty pound bass and cut the line as though he carried a pair of scissors! What a game fish he is! He fights to the very last!

By today's standards, the equipment used by the surf-fishermen on Cuttyhunk in those days would seem unwieldy and primitive. Twelve- to fifteen-foot rods of greenheart or bamboo held a wooden reel, and its only drag was supplied by the angler's thumb against a piece of leather. The club members did help advance fishing tackle design, said Francis Endicott in *Sport with Rod and Gun*. "In 1865, some of the club members went to leading manufacturers of fishing line and had them develop a light, soft, pliable linen line of 30-pound test. This line became world famous and was specified and used by the best fishermen." (Until very recently, it was still possible to find dacron line in tackle shops that was labeled "Cuttyhunk.")

Fishing would start as early as 3 a.m., and the stands closest to the clubhouse were the most desirable. Club rules were very clear about the use of the stands. Rule 3 states that only the person drawing a stand by lottery shall have use of that stand the following day, but Rule 4 allows the angler to select his fishing partner if it is necessary to share a stand. The issue of guests was apparently a cause of concern among members.

Each member was allowed only one guest per visit, and the guest could not visit the club again that season. A point of contention that caused some members to break away from the Cuttyhunk Club was the unwritten law that no women were welcome at the club, forcing members to leave their wives, daughters and lady friends in boarding houses in the village or on private yachts in the harbor.

In keeping with the stated purpose of the club being formed "for social purposes," meals were an important part of the Cuttyhunk experience. Breakfast was served from 7:30 to 9, dinner at 2 and tea at 7:30. Although this appears to be a fairly light schedule, consider the menu: lobster and fresh striped bass every day, plus roasts, hams, mutton and fowl. From the club's own gardens came radishes, potatoes, tomatoes, peas, okra, eggplant, lettuce, turnips, cauliflower, carrots, squash, corn, beets, beans and peppers. Liquid refreshments were not lacking, either. Each member had his own liquor locker, which, according to original member John Lynes, was stocked with such libations as "London gin, Holland gin, 1836 and 1846 brandy, sherry, rum, rye whiskey, all kinds of wine and ale." Until room rates were raised in 1896, it was said that liquor expenditures regularly exceeded the cost of yearly dues and room fees.

Perhaps the strangest rule in the club bylaws was Rule 8, which said that every striper caught by members or visitors was assumed to be club property, and after table needs were met, the angler had the option to buy back the fish to take home. Any funds gained from this sale would be returned to the club treasury.

Captains of industry, powerful politicians, military figures of the day and leaders of financial institutions came to fish and relax at the club. Members included John Archbold, president of Standard Oil; Jay Gould, the railroad tycoon and financier; William McCormack of International

Harvester; and Hugh Auchincloss, stepfather of Jaqueline Bouvier Kennedy Onassis. Guests over the years were, among many others, Major Robert Anderson, commander of Fort Sumter at the outbreak of the Civil War; presidents Grover Cleveland and Theodore Roosevelt; railroad magnates such as J.P. Cottman and Henry Flagler; and various supreme court justices, senators and cabinet members.

Unfortunately, as the nineteenth century was coming to a close, various events began to foretell the ultimate end of the Cuttyhunk Fishing Club. Relations with the year-round populace of the island had been deteriorating for years as the club bought more and more property and sought to control seemingly all aspects of daily life. By 1888, 466 acres of the island were controlled or owned by the club, leaving only 15 acres in private hands. The club forbade farmers from gathering seaweed from shore for fertilizer, and controlled all fishing and lobstering close to shore. When islanders tried to use the famous fishing stands, the club was forced to obtain licenses from the town of Gosnold to maintain their private status, effectively keeping the locals from fishing most of the shoreline.

But the single biggest change that spelled the end of the club was a serious decline in striped bass landings. The decline began in the mid-1880s and continued into the first decade of this century. In 1865, the first full season of the club's operation, 50 members and their guests fished a total of 556 days, landing a total of 1,252 stripers. By 1906, membership had dwindled to about 25 members, and in 264 days of fishing, only one lonely striper was landed. Membership continued to drop until 1922, the last year of the club's existence, when only three members remained.

In 1921, William Wood, president of American Woolen Company and club member, purchased the remaining shares and property of the club. Mr. Wood loved Cuttyhunk and had built another house nearby, along with a small electrical plant and sewer. Mr. Wood died in 1925 and his son sold many of the houses that had been part of the club's holdings; in 1943 he sold the original clubhouse to Mr. and Mrs. Robert Moore. The Moores restored the building and furnishings and were famous for allowing visitors, curious about the old fishing club, to see the grounds, building and artifacts.

When the Cuttyhunk Fishing Association was formed in 1865, the only rule that caused debate was the unwritten one that no women would be allowed to stay at the club. A number of the members, led by John Crosby Brown, a wealthy lawyer from Philadelphia, decided that they could not accept this rule. They discovered that fishing around Pasque Island rivaled what they had found on Cuttyhunk, and between 1866 and 1869 bought the island from the Tucker family that had owned it for 170 years.

Pasque Island is located east of Cuttyhunk and Nashawena Island, and one of the prime fishing areas was (and still is) Robinsons Hole, the narrow passage between Pasque and Naushon Island. It was on this eastern end of Pasque, at Robinsons Hole, where the club built a large clubhouse, servants' quarters and other buildings.

The bylaws of the Pasque Club were similar to those of the Cuttyhunk Club (with one notable exception regarding women), and the daily routine was also very much the same. Fishing stands were run out from the beaches and among the boulders. Chummers were hired to lure in the fish, and apparently the fishing was very good. One picture from that time shows a distinguished-looking gentleman standing beside his catch, two stripers that appear to be in the 30- to 40-pound class. A stream next to the club buildings was used as a holding area for bait, primarily menhaden, but also lobsters.

Although the Pasque Club had fewer members than the Cuttyhunk Club, many guests and family members visited the island over the years. Supplies, mail and passengers were brought from New Bedford twice a week. The Pasque fishermen, like their brethren on Cuttyhunk, did not go away from the dinner table hungry, as evidenced by a typical early menu that features a choice of three fish, three meat and three entree courses, a choice of nine soups, ten vegetables, six desserts, and assorted nuts, cheeses and raisins.

Another similarity between the clubs was the assumption that they controlled all fishing and lobstering close to the islands. To enforce these rights, the Pasque Club hired a year-round resident caretaker in 1876. He received no salary but was paid a yearly stipend of $50 to fill the icehouse with ice from the island's small ponds.

John Crosby died in 1909 after serving over 40 years as club president. His son James became president, but the glory days of the club were coming to an end as membership declined, expenses rose and striped bass became scarce. James Crosby Brown Jr. acquired all remaining assets, shares and property of the club in 1923, and the club was dissolved. The Brown family used Pasque Island and the former club building for many years.

During the 1938 hurricane, many of the buildings were destroyed. The stream and marsh behind the club buildings were partially filled with sand, and the small bridge across the stream was swept away. It was said that the waves breaking on Cobbley Beach, a half-mile away, shook the whole island. The storm destroyed telegraph lines linking the island to Woods Hole, and they were never restored.

The Cuttyhunk Fishing Club influenced nearly all aspects of life on the island for over 50 years. The seasonal influx of members and their guests required a large support staff, and many islanders made a good living supplying and maintaining the club. When the club was dissolved shortly after World War I, the club property could easily have fallen into disrepair or into the hands of owners who didn't care about its rich history. Fortunately, consecutive owners William Wood, his son Cornelius, and the Moores did not fall into that category. The Moores preserved the building and grounds, retaining original furnishings, artwork and other articles from the club's heyday, even to the extent of trying to rebuild one of the original fishing stands. In 1997, the Moores sold the clubhouse property to Piero and Oriel Wood Ponzecchi. Oriel is the granddaughter of William Wood, bringing the ownership of the fishing club full circle.

The Ponzecchis have reopened the club as a bed and breakfast during the summer months, under the guidance of resident director Bonnie Veeder. Anglers can again stay and fish on the shores that were once the exclusive domain of some of the most powerful and influential men in the country. The remains of the famous stands can still be seen among the boulders, and the flagpole, topped by a striped bass, still sits on the bluff near the clubhouse. As a modern fisherman walks and casts along the rocky shore, it's easy to imagine members William Renwick and William Spence catching stripers of 64 and 56 pounds, or member William Woodhull, who caught 8 fish from 37 to 50 pounds in one day.

Boaters in Robinsons Hole can't help but notice the weathered wood-framed buildings and small lagoon on the shore of Pasque Island. These buildings are what remain of the former Pasque Island Club, including the "chummer's hall" and the farmhouse where the caretaker lived. These buildings are now owned by the Forbes family, administered by the Pasque Island Trust and are private property. To the south of the buildings is the small lagoon and anchorage. Now, as then, the fishing in Robinsons Hole and along the surrounding rocky shore is fabulous.

Striped Bass Fishing

By A. Foster Higgins

Editor's Note: The following account of fishing at the Pasque Island Club is an abridged version of a feature that appeared in Scribner's Magazine in 1889. It is perhaps the most detailed account ever published of life and fishing at the exclusive striped bass fishing clubs that dotted the southern New England coast at that time.

The Striped Bass are not migratory, being found along our coast in winter as well as summer, and in our markets at all times of the year; and one of the most potent causes of their diminution is the facility with which they are taken under the ice, by nets, spearing, etc. They are voracious feeders, entering the rivers to prey upon the "fry" of the shad, herring, and bluefish – and are particularly fond of crabs, shrimp, squids, clams, and mussels, and even lobsters, when shedding or of a sufficiently small size to be conveniently "bolted" whole. Their average weight does not exceed 20 pounds. In the Potomac, Hudson and the Connecticut Rivers the largest seldom exceed 30 to 40 pounds. The Fish Commission has for several years had a standing offer of a reward for a 60-pound fish from the Potomac, but none has yet been forthcoming. The largest Striped Bass on record was one weighing 112 pounds, taken at Orleans, Massachusetts. They are caught in large quantities by seines, wherever used, and may be captured by hook and line, either in the more robust style of heaving and hauling in the surf, or in the most dilettante style of rod and reel, and even with the artificial Fly.

"What does he weigh, Tom?"

My purpose here is to describe more particularly that mode of taking them by rod and reel, adopted by the gentlemen of the Clubs, and other anglers, at Point Judith, Narragansett, Newport, West Island, Cuttyhunk, Pasque Island, Squibnocket and other places along the coast, chosen for characteristics favorable as feeding grounds for the Striped Bass.

If we visit one of these resorts we shall see for ourselves, in what consists the fascination which draws young and old men, yachtsmen, merchants and bankers, idlers and busy men, wives and maidens, season after season, from gayer and more fashionable places, to these sober, quiet, and seemingly unattractive spots.

The home of one such fishing club is reached after a run of an hour and a half from New Bedford; and its situation and the routine of its day are perhaps sufficiently typical of all. The clubhouse and the outhouses stand prominently on a knoll, sentinelled by a lofty flagstaff, from which flies gayly the stars and stripes. The whistle of the little steamer that brings visitors advises by a series of "toots" the numbers of arriving passengers, who hurry ashore, to be welcomed most heartily by members of the Club, ladies, and children, to whom the arrival of the Boat is an "occasion," bringing twice a week letters, papers and tidings of the busy cities. It is, nevertheless, with a feeling of relief, and gracious rest, that one waves adieu to the little tug, knowing that for a period nothing is likely to disturb or annoy him from the outer world.

Learning that full tide is deemed most favorable, about 5 p.m., he will put on rough clothes; as he is sure to be more or less wet. A thoughtful member comes in bearing in his arms india rubber boots and a suit of "oilers," which he advises should be carried along as one cannot tell at what moment they will be needed. He proposes a walk to the stand, which he has drawn for the day, and hands the oilers and poles to an attendant, who, he explains, is a "chummer," or one who cuts up and prepares the bait.

After proceeding a half mile from the house and turning onto the shore we found, under the shadow of a huge, square mass of granite, halfway between the hill and water, the "chummer" busily arranging his basket, laden with menhaden packed with ice. He has a square piece of board which he places on a rock, around which are a mass of debris of menhaden bones and heads; and catching up one of these fish from his basket, he hastily scales it and cuts off the entire side close to the back bone. An incision is made lengthwise through the flesh to the skin, which enables him to double it together, skin to skin and the flesh all outside and the bait is ready – a mass of about four inches in length and weighing about two ounces. The hook, a No. 9/0, is then carefully attached to the line; the hook is furnished with a round knob on its upper end and tapers from the shank to this knob. Two half hitches are taken with the line on this taper below the knob; then the end of the line is used to make a third half hitch over the first two; the body of the line then makes a fourth

"A novel and exciting scene it is to see these loads of eager men."

over the others, and the line in one hand, the hitches are drawn tight, whilst the hook is removed by the other hand, so that when the end is cut off short, the hook will revolve without twisting the line. A good fisherman will do this himself, and when passing in his rod to get a new bait put on, will always examine the line, to see if has been chafed or injured – and if so, it must be cut off and refastened – or else he may have the pleasure of seeing a good fish lost by his line giving way at the hook at a critical moment.

One's interest is now centered on the rod, and this is seen to be short – not exceeding 8 feet in length – with large free guides and tips of german silver; sometimes of agate. Generally the rod consists of two pieces, a butt of, say, 22 inches and a tip of 5 1/2 to 6 feet – or it may be one solid bamboo rod – of size, taper and flexibility to suit fancy. The reel is usually a work of art, in which America excels all other nations. It is quite large, holding from 700 to 900 feet of line, multiplying, and will run freely one minute and a half with a twirl of the finger. The best makers strive to adjust a perfect balance between the handle and its revolution, so that the slightest pressure will stop its motion and so prevent "over running."

Following our friend's suggestion we will go out on the stand and watch his movements, and thus learn first, what is to be done, and then how to do it. He puts on his oiled trousers, to catch the drip of water which always runs off the reel to the knees and legs; and adjusts two "thumbs," fingers of crocheted wool, termed "thumb-stalls," with which pressure can be put on the reels, without experiencing the burning its rapidly revolving surface would otherwise produce.

"Tom, have you any chum ready?" to the "chummer."

"Aye, Aye, sir."

"Well throw it out." And Tom runs rapidly out on the planks, which extend out from the shore a distance of thirty to fifty feet, at which point the ends are supported by two iron stanchions embedded in one of the huge boulders there submerged. Upon the ends about three feet inside, is lashed a wooden chair, secured firmly by staples to the stand; and after making the cast, here the fisherman takes his seat. Tom throws vigorously out as far as he can all the remains of the fishes he has cut up – heads, tails, backbones and entrails – all full of oil, which soon creates on the surface of the water a "slick," and as the tide

The Fishing Stand at Cuttyhunk, Mass.

sweeps these particles out and the odor pervades the water and air, the fish are attracted. Our friend now examines his reel, and finding it is slack and the line lying loosely on it, he unreels quite a quantity, rewinding it with great care tightly and very evenly, layer by layer, until he only has an end of about two feet from the tip, to which he hangs his bait, looking firm, fresh and inviting. He now walks to the end of the stand, steps carefully in front of the chair, braces himself with his left foot on the strip clamping the two planks together, and with his right inboard toward the chair, swings the tip and bait back toward the plank. His left hand grasps the butt, his right has the thumb on the reel and fingers around the handle – then with a quick wrist and forearm movement, largely partaking of a jerk, he impels the bait outward at a slight elevation – his eyes fixed on the flying bait, his thumb barely touching the face of the reel, until he sees its flight decreasing and the bait falling; at this instant, by his thumb's pressure, he stops the revolutions of the reel, and has the satisfaction of seeing the bait fall well out into the water, and feels and sees his reel all free and the line on it firm and undisturbed. Dear reader, if you aspire to be a bass fisherman, religiously examine your reel before casting, always and in every case, and unless you see and know that it lies firmly and regularly on the reel, never hesitate, but at once unreel it and lay it on carefully; thus you will save yourself from many an impatient word and action.

At last, we have a beautiful cast, the bait has shot out at least 150 feet and fallen gently into the water, the slack has been gathered in, so that you feel the bait and know that each movement of the reel moves it slightly; and now comes in the trait of a true fisherman - patience. That kind of patience which does not lose heart, even though, for days in succession, bait after bait is cast out without return, until the fisherman feels as if he is only feeding blackfish and "cunners," with which the water abounds. Our chances this afternoon are rather slim, still there is a freshening southwest breeze, blowing from Gay Head and swash of surf begins to be heavier; but on looking over the side of the stand, the bottom with its folds and waving ribbons of yellow seaweeds is too plainly visible.

"By George! I've got him," exclaims our friend in the chair, and as we hastily look up, he is seen apparently fighting to keep his rod erect, whilst something at the other end is convulsively dragging it downward, with such jerks as threaten to part the line or break the rod. The reel is whizzing in a threatening way, and our friend has a hard time to keep his thumb on the barrel of the reel, and at the same time avoid having his knuckles rapped and torn by the rapidly revolving handle. His left, as yet, grasps the rod above the reel and forces the socket into his groin.

"Bring out that belt, Tom," he yells, and Tom comes jumping down the rocks, in one hand his gaff-hook and in the other a leather belt with a short round pocket sewed on its centre. This Tom hastily buckles around the waist of the fisherman, when, carefully shifting the pole, he places the butt in this pocket and is thus protected from possible injury, which the great leverage of the fish's pulling can easily produce. The fish, in the meantime, has succeeded in getting away, say three to four hundred feet now, and shows some hesitation. Our friend has carefully kept a pressure on the reel, whilst indulging his majesty in imaginary freedom of running – but which he begins to realize as "uncanny,"

– and as our eyes follow the slender thread of the line in its distant entry into the water, it is seen to rise, and presently with a whirl of his tail, the fish shows himself; looking then to our unskilled eyes a very monster, and as he again disappears we unhesitatingly pronounce him full six feet long.

"Oh, no," says our friend in reply, "he is not over a thirty pounder, but he is a good one – see him fight!" and the victim tugs and tugs, with a desperation born of foresight of his calamity; but in vain, and in another ten minutes he loses heart, and sheers in toward the shore, when our friend is put to all his skill to check and reel him in before he reaches a huge rock inshore for which he heads – just in time!

And now he is slowly dragged toward the stand and his beautiful color and

"By George! I've got him."

stripes are plainly seen, but he still strives by ineffectual runs, first to one side and then the other, to avert his fate; though all in vain, as Tom is now bending low down from the outer end of the plank with his sharp shining gaff-hook extended.

"A little more to the left, sir," he says, and as the fisherman inclines his pole and turns the fish's head, his gaff is extended down, under and across the fish's body; a rapid jerk upward and backward and it sinks into his silver belly. He is raised from the water, convulsively hugged by Tom, who reaches for the rod, and all of us hurry inshore to inspect and gloat over him.

"What does he weigh, Tom?" and with judicial eye Tom measures and lifts him. "I say, thirty pounds." "Well I think thirty-five," says the fisherman, the inexperienced onlooker being under the conviction that he should weigh fifty, at least, and impressed with a sense of awe – his huge mouth and head when seen for the first time.

It is now too dark to be worth while to fish longer and we are in fact a little eager to get home and exhibit our catch. So Tom puts him in the basket, covers him carefully with fresh seaweed, recklessly throws all his cut up bait for chum, and we start for the house, Tom gladly lugging his heavy basket for the glory and triumph he will have on exhibiting him. The "chummer" becomes part and parcel of his "boss," participates in all his excitements, honors and disappointments, and constitutes no small element of comfort or discord, as his temper and capacity turn out.

As we arrive at the clubhouse, windows go up, heads are thrust out, eager questioning follows, men and ladies turn out and go to the fish house to admire the beauty and guess weight. After the solemn ceremony of ascertaining his exact weight has been performed, he is carefully packed away in the ice-box, to be sent to your most valued friend, or disposed of by the club steward. It is now the judgement of connoisseurs that the flesh is improved by being kept on ice two or three days at least.

Such are the general features of this noble sport, but subject to great variation. The most remarkable catch of bass ever made at Pasque Island was with the water as clear as crystal and perfectly smooth. There happened in a school of huge bass, and they were very hungry and took bait without hesitation for over twenty-four hours after arrival; and one member comparatively inexperienced as a fisherman caught nine fish in one day aggregating 170 pounds.

Nearly, if not all bass fishermen agree in the opinion that the steam menhaden fishermen have greatly injured the bass fishing – both by depriving them of food they most eagerly seek, and also by driving them off their feeding grounds, by their huge nets. A few years ago, from the first of July to the first of November, one could reasonably expect any day to hook a large bass, at any of the noted places. Now, they can rarely be caught even where systematically chummed.

But there are many enjoyments in the surroundings. The delicious, exhilarating, health-giving air from these pure sea-waters, the soul-inspiring scenery, the varying panorama of vessels constantly moving, creates in all frequenters of these islands a real love for them. If you doubt it, come and try it.

I was once favored with a scene that indelibly printed itself on my memory. I had hooked and successfully sustained the run of a large fish, had turned him, and had warped him in, until he was within fifty feet of me; quite a heavy surf was running, of which I was availing myself to aid in bringing him in – when my "chummer" called attention to the seaweed which was running in on the line and threatened to choke up at the tip. Hardly had he spoken, when it jammed the line so that I no longer had the slightest control over the fish; the next wave moved him about ten feet in shore, and on the other side of a huge sunken boulder; and as the line became taut, although I tried all I could to extend the rod and give it play, it parted as if thread, and there I stood; stamping with vexation, utterly helpless, the heavy surf forbidding any attempt to get to him, and looking on his huge majesty rolling from side to side, nearly drowned and quite unable himself at the moment to make any exertion; but gradually he gathered power, and a sudden conviction that he was no longer a prisoner, and I had the comfort of seeing him slowly glide about, and out to sea.

My feelings were much added to, by having one of the fair sex, sitting on the bank above me watching the whole operation, and perhaps more amused at my discomfiture, than distressed by my loss.

Such are the prominent and prevailing features of the sport. The true sportsman finds his enjoyment in all the surroundings more than in the fish itself, or even its capture.

West Island Club
And The Three Sisters Of Little Compton

By Captain Charley Soares

Thousands upon thousands of reefs, ledges and boulders guard the coastline from Montauk to Maine, and few if any of these obstructions have identical signatures. After the wash rose up and curled outside my starboard rail, I sensed, then saw, another breaker forming off the port bow. Jamming the aft tiller hard a-port I idled the little bass boat between two of the hazards that formed the infamous Hopper. The person who coined the phrase "between a rock and a hard spot" wasn't likely referring to boats in tight places, but that articulation definitely pertained to my situation. The old Heathkit flasher was marking steady between 8 and 12 feet as I headed east toward The Clumps. I counted to 10 before I began a wide turn south just as the high profiles of the larger clumps loomed up large and ominous in the thick, early morning fog.

I knew exactly where I was, and that was the problem. My course should have taken me west of the lighthouse and into the mouth of the Sakonnet River, but in this area an oversight or miscalculation of just a few feet could mean the difference between safe passage and a grounding or life-threatening situation. It was less than an hour until sunrise, so I decided to tuck in close to the tall granite knobs, protected from the southeaster, and see what the false dawn or a wind shift might do to improve visibility. My handy grapnel bit into the gnarly bottom almost immediately and a short length of anchor line held me within casting distance of the little clumps. I never kill the engine when fishing in dangerous proximity to any boulder field, and this morning would be no exception.

Reaching for my trusty pliers, my hands grappled in an empty sheath and after a brief moment of panic I located the tool and discovered the reason for my current predicament. Jammed tightly between the compass bracket and the mahogany windshield was the well-worn tool that served as a third hand. The last striper had been hooked tight into the corner of the jawbone and I'd used the pliers to remove the hook. The tool tampered with the compass reading.

It was greed that got me into this predicament, but I swore it would be good judgement that would liberate me from it. I'd seen the fog creeping in, but the last fish I broke off was heavier than the combined weight of the two 20-pounders in the fish box, so I hung on under conditions that seldom ever result in satisfactory conclusions. I began casting a dead eel into the ledge that swirls just ahead of The Clumps and found a few feisty schoolies that were fooled by the dead serpent.

It's difficult to comprehend the things that go through your mind in times of stress, but as I was releasing the second fish I thought of the affluent bass fishermen who had cast lobster tails and bunker chunks to these same rocks almost 150 years ago. I could visualize their guides' (chummers) oars, held securely in callused hands, biting against the surge, holding their flat-bottomed wooden skiffs against the force of the waves.

Less than 20 minutes later I detected a cool breeze on my left cheek that indicated a favorable wind shift. With an almost imperceptible switch from east to west, the visibility improved and the rocky bastion of West Island, which protected the inner passage from breaking seas, emerged up out of the heavy, moist air.

As the fog broke and the wind shifted, the Three Sisters thrust their peaks out of the low-lying fog bank. Those fieldstone columns have survived untold hurricanes and the unforgiving fury of the Atlantic for well over 100 years. What some consider merely the ruins of the once-elegant West Island Fishing Club I view as a symbol of strength. Since the Tavares brothers took me fishing in the shadow of these columns some 40 years ago, I've been researching the history of the famous landmark. Over the years I've spoken with anyone who could provide historical or anecdotal information on one of the first groups in New England dedicated to the pursuit of striped bass.

At approximately the same time that the Cuttyhunk and Squibnocket bass clubs were assembling, a select group of wealthy individuals were in the process of forming the West Island Club. From the Newport Historical Society quarterly bulletin, published in the spring of 1977: "In December of 1864, Preston H. Hodges and others, having purchased East and West Islands, in the State of Rhode Island with all buildings and personal property thereto appertaining, formed an association for Angling and Shooting purposes and adopted and agreed to the following regulations for the government thereof." One of the regulations that came out of these dealings was to limit the membership to 30 men who were required to pay the princely sum of $1,000 each for their initiation fee.

The islands were purchased for $18,500 by the aforementioned New York residents,

The Three Sisters. The three stone columns are all that remain of what was once an outpost of six buildings erected on West Island for the purpose of providing shelter and comfort to wealthy fishermen. The club was founded in 1864, opened its first season in 1865 and closed at the end of the 1906 season. The high bluff in the left background is the sheer cliff on the west side that rises some 40 feet above the surface.

but contrary to popular belief, this was not the first bass club or year-round habitation of West Island. In previous conversations with old salts who related stories passed on to them by their parents and grandparents, it was learned that both East and West islands were the year-round residences of two families of full-time commercial fishermen until 1853. On or about that time, the islands passed into the hands of a group of Fall River, Massachusetts, entrepreneurs who were men of means who also had a keen interest in the striper fishing this location had become famous for. When the West Island syndicate took title of the islands in 1864, there was already a modest hotel building erected by the former owners on the site.

During the winter of 1864 and into the spring of 1865, West Island was abuzz with carpenters and local laborers in preparation for the club's first season. By the time the club officially opened in June of 1865, the wharf had been repaired, skiffs had been built and refitted and the former hotel was converted to serve as the temporary West Island Clubhouse. In a photo dated about 1900 there appears to be five or six well-maintained buildings on the island, but it is doubtful any of these were completed for the 1865 opener in time for the arrival of trophy bass in June of that first year.

In numerous conversations and interviews with the older gents and historians who visited the trap houses at Sakonnet Point, the general consensus was that the buildings were not completed during the cold and rough winter of the first year, but that new buildings and renovations were constructed over a longer period of time. The historians I refer to were in their late 70s, with one gent in his 80s, at the time of our conversations in the early 1960s. This would put their fathers and grandfathers, who they affirmed worked for the West Island Club, in a time frame to be on hand for the beginning and end of that golden era of striped bass fishing.

My sources indicated that there was not a great deal of historical information on the club in Little Compton (although there was a great deal of anecdotal information from individuals whose family members were employed there) because there were no local members. And most of the members opted to sail to the club from Newport or the dock near the Fall River line rather than make the long and uncomfortable overland journey to Little Compton via carriage or wagon.

The club proved to be a tremendous benefit to the local economy. Fishermen, farmers and all types of tradesmen found work in the construction of new buildings, improvements in the docks, and the building and rebuilding of the all-important bass stands. Local farms were the source of fresh food and vegetables until the thick, rich soil on the island was tilled and began providing fresh vegetables for the members. One of the provisions in the club's constitution was that it was founded for the purpose of angling and shooting, but no one was aware of, and there was never any official mention of, gunning taking place on the island. The only hunting that would have been available at that time would have been pass shooting for sea ducks in the very early spring and late fall, and the prospect of members accustomed to dining on the finest of foods eating sea-duck breast appears to be remote.

Also in the employ of these captains of industry were cooks, chummers, maids, boat builders and skippers to ferry them to and from their boats and the mainland. I was told that the Vanderbilt yacht often lay at anchor in the lee of East Island, protected from the southwest winds. Whenever the yacht lay at anchor, there were numerous trips made by its tender and the small fleet of skiffs berthed at the club, hauling supplies from the markets of New York and Europe to provision the club's larder.

West Island was countrified when compared to Vanderbilt's Breakers, that formidable building visible just across the Sakonnet, but West Island was a refuge for the giants of Wall Street and U.S. Supreme Court justices, as well as senators and numerous persons of high rank. Such notables as Rensselaer, Payne, Charles Tiffany of the famous jewelry store of the same name, along with secretaries of state, the head of the New York Bar Association and presidents Chester A. Arthur and Grover Cleveland, sought out this rustic comfort and the opportunity to angle for the prized striped bass.

Elsewhere along the striper coast, just a short while later, other men of means were in the process of forming their own bass clubs at Cuttyhunk, Squibnocket and Pasque Island. Although the membership at West Island was limited to 30 members, it was doubtful, due to time restrictions and (early on) the limited accommodations, that more than half of them were ever there at the same time in the early years. The members who were accustomed to the very best the world had to offer were more than willing to make sacrifices for the opportunity to angle for the revered seven-striped fish.

In the early years the club prospered, with every conceivable luxury and accommodation shipped in to make life on the "rock" quite comfortable. One of the bylaws specifically stated that members' wives could accompany them on trips to the island. What that implied, at least to me, was that no other female company would be sanctioned. A few of the members who rankled at the fact that women were allowed, left to form their own clubs along the south side of the Elizabeth Islands and off the west side of the Vineyard, but that is another story.

One bit of anecdotal information I obtained from the Sakonnet elders was that the month of June served as a barometer for the coming season. If the month of June started off with good catches, the attendance at the club was heavy throughout the season. While there are numerous locations from which a fisherman could cast to stripers, it was the bass stands that enabled them to cast their baits farther out into the Hopper and reach the washes of the nearby reefs and ledges, which were the preferred locations. With only a limited number of bass stands, the men gathered after a sumptuous dinner and cocktails to roll the dice on the velvet of the pool table to cast for stands for the following day's fishing. While some locations were better than others, there were no mediocre places to fish for bass at West Island.

The club was in operation from 1865 until it closed at the end of the 1906 season, a span of 42 years. Anyone who doubts that fishing for striped bass was first and foremost in the members' inclinations need only research the meticulous records of their catches to determine that the rise and fall of the striped bass population was responsible for the formation and eventual demise of this unique organization. During that first year of the club's operation, members must have been in high spirits now that they were finally able to fish from the boulders of their solitary ocean retreat. The first season was by no means a banner year, but the meticulous records of the steward listed each and every striper, along with all the pertinent details associated with the catch.

From the log of the West Island Club: "September 11, 1866. Wind northwest, cold as the Devil. Water calm, a perfect level. Fished faithfully, caught two bass. Slipped upon the rocks and wet my —."

During the first season 832 stripers up to 25 pounds were caught, but by 1869 the count was down to 536 stripers landed for that year. The record year was 1874 when 2,406 stripers to 32 pounds added up to a total weight of 11,356 pounds. The euphoria over the record-breaking year was tempered the following season with 713 stripers to 44 pounds, less than a third of the previous year's catch. For the 10-year period from 1876 to 1885 the numbers of fish fluctuated from a high of 957 bass in 1876 to a low of just 173 bass in 1881. The total of only 22 bass brought to gaff for the entire 1886 season must have been devastating for some, but optimistic fishermen were rewarded with a catch of 735 bass to 50 pounds the following season. From that time forward it was obvious the striped bass resource was in decline. In 1893 there were just 28 bass to 50 pounds recorded for that season, then 23 bass to 47 pounds in 1895.

Fishing was still mediocre but leveled off until back-to-back seasons of 11 and 28 stripers respectively in 1904 and 1905. The golden era of striped bass fishing on West Island was about to expire. During the last few years most of the members stayed away, with only four intrepid fishermen visiting the island in its last years of existence. In 1906 there were only 8 striped bass to 22 pounds caught, and the majority of the members agreed it was time to sell their interest in their club.

Although the West Island Club closed at a time when bass were in severe decline, there were entries in their ledger that spoke of very different times. The largest striper was recorded by Philo T. Ruggles and weighed in at 64 pounds. I believe Mr. Ruggles was a member of the same family that Ruggles Avenue in Newport is named for. The intrepid Mr. Ruggles set another club record on August 20, 1872, when he caught 87 stripers from 2 to 9 pounds in a single day. On August 2, 1866, members reported a huge school of big bass seen in very clear water; one was estimated to be in the 100-pound class.

A report in the log for June 25, 1871, is again of clear water and a catch of 11 stripers for a total weight of 208 pounds, which included a 52- and a 56-pounder:

"June 25, 1871. No sea. Water so clear that nearly every fish was seen as he took the bait. Water alive all day with large bass. Had there been a good sea a very large catch would have been certain (sic)."

On July 7, 1876, P. T. Ruggles was once again "high hook," landing a 55-pound bass that measured 50 inches long with a 28-inch girth. During the 42 years that records of the club were kept, there were 11 stripers in the 50-pound class weighed, with 57 pounds the heaviest. Only two 60s were captured, the 64-pound bass caught in 1877 and the other a 60-pound trophy in 1894.

The club did not open for the 1907 fishing season and was put in charge of a caretaker until it was finally sold to Joseph Wainwright, one of the four members who returned for the last season in 1906. The club that members purchased for $18,500 in 1864 and invested thousands of dollars in was sold for $7,500. The new owner set about restoring the buildings, boats and grounds to their former condition, enjoying the comforts and seclusion he had come to appreciate at West Island.

Upon Wainwright's death in 1917, West Island was inherited by his two sons, but without full-time occupation, vandalism and the elements took their toll. The family donated the islands to the Episcopal Diocese of Rhode Island, from which they soon passed on to other parties. Vandals set fire to the buildings in 1929, and the stark columns you see today are all that remain.

In 1983 Jesse Lloyd O'Connor assigned both West and East islands to the Sakonnet Preservation Society, which owns it to this day.

This jumbled expanse of granite is much like others along our shores between Maine and Long Island, but this particular location was not selected by chance. It was the lure of big stripers that attracted millionaires and mill workers to cast into the white water that swirled around the foundation of this austere-looking ridge of granite. Once you've fooled a trophy striper here, then managed to extract it from this concentration of boulders and reefs, the craving to return grows stronger and your response is not so much a fishing trip as a pilgrimage to an extraordinary historical landmark.

Over the past four decades I've made numerous trips to West Island, and although on many occasions I fished alone, I never felt lonely. I have never cast a plug or trolled a lure in the shadow of the Sisters when I did not feel the presence of the kindred spirits who angled here before my time in a place I can't help but believe God created for striped bass.

After years of habitation by some of the wealthiest and most famous men of their time, West Island has returned to its natural state, where gulls, cormorants and other seabirds return to roost. The only thing that hasn't changed is the annual migration of stripers. In lean years and times of plenty they return to the rocks where the Sound washes over the submerged reefs and boulders and up against the resilient stone base of the island, where presidents once cast lines out toward the lair of the revered striper. The Three Sisters are remnants of a time when farmers rubbed elbows with millionaires, and these rugged pillars form the steeple of a shrine where fishermen from all walks of life still come to worship at the altar of the striped bass. ◄█▶

Credits...

The following people and organizations were extremely helpful in my research, which covers a period from approximately 1960 through this past winter. I only wish I knew the names of so many of the individuals I interviewed through introductions of other historians who provided factual and anecdotal information about the club. My sincere apologies to any persons, organizations or lenders of written material I may have omitted.

Special thanks to the staff and members of the Newport Historical Society, the Little Compton Historical Society, Fall River Historical Society, Carl and Carolyn Haffenreffer, Carlton Brownell and Mike and Richard F. Rogers. Valuable information was also obtained from Nate Atwater, Carl Wilcox of the F.N. Wilcox Trap Company, Barney Wordell, Charles Roshina and the old-timers we visited at the trap house at Sakonnet Point in Little Compton, Rhode Island. Thanks to Louie Waite; the booklet *Newport History, The West Island Club* by Nicholas B. Wainwright; the Little Compton town clerk and tax department; and our friend, the Little Compton weather lady, Inger Ormston, for all her valuable leads.

The Crosby Striper

By Captain David DeCastro

W hat's in a name? Boat manufacturers give their products, and sometimes their entire product line, names meant to conjure up a certain image in the prospective buyer's mind. Names like Mako, Marlin, Blackfin and Cobia, for example, evoke the idea of power and agility, characteristics found in these fish. Other boat names are chosen to represent characteristics the prospective buyer may see (or wish to see) in himself such as Intrepid, Contender, Salty Dog or Commander.

In 1947 Wilton Crosby of Osterville, Massachusetts, designed a handsome and very functional 24-foot sport-fishing craft aimed at the growing numbers of striped bass fishing enthusiasts of that postwar era. He named his creation, quite simply, "Striper," and a legend was born.

The Striper featured many of the characteristics of bass boats of that era. She was heavily constructed, with white oak frames, keel and stringers, and was planked with the finest Philippine mahogany. The hull had a hard chine and a full keel to provide stability, good tracking underway and protection for the propeller and rudder. The Striper's large cockpit made the boat an excellent fishing platform.

Most of the earliest bass boats had no cabin, and the few that did had only a small cuddy cabin used mainly for storage. The Striper design was a departure from this concept of the fishing machine distilled to its essence because it had a trunk cabin with two spacious bunks, a head under one of the bunks, a small galley and about five and a half feet of head room. The Striper had bridged the gap between hard-core fishing boats and family cruisers and made striped bass fishing a true family affair. When you go aboard a Striper for the first time, you will be amazed at how much space there is in both the cockpit and the cabin for a boat just 24 feet long and 8 feet, 9 inches wide.

The Crosby Striper is one of those timeless designs that will never go out of style and will always be the mark of a discriminating and knowledgeable boater.

Crosby continued to build the Striper out of wood for over three decades, and they were all built to order, as they are today, so no two Stripers are exactly alike. By the early 1980s the craftsmen at Crosby had to follow market demand and advancing technology and start building the Striper in fiberglass. To reproduce the Striper as faithfully as possible, they used a recently constructed wood Striper as a plug from which they made a mold. The mold was so accurate that the first hulls to be made in the mold actually showed the grain of the wood from the plug boat. People who saw the first fiberglass Crosby Striper at the boat shows were convinced that the boat was made from wood. Needless to say, none of the boat's good sea-keeping qualities were lost in the transition from wood to fiberglass.

The first Stripers were powered by a single Chrysler Crown six-cylinder gasoline engine. By the late 1950s the 120-horsepower Palmer gasoline engine was standard power. High-speed lightweight diesel engines would not be available until the late 1970s. About the same time that the Stripers began to be built from fiberglass, diesel engines came on the market that were suitable for powering boats in this size and performance range. The first diesel-powered Striper had a 100-horsepower Westerbeke diesel engine. More powerful engines were soon to follow. The most recently built Stripers are powered by either the 4-cylinder turbocharged Yanmar diesel or the Volvo TAMD 41, both producing 210 horsepower. Either of these engines will push the Striper along at 20 knots at a fuel consumption rate of around 3 to 4 gallons per hour. The 70-gallon fuel capacity will give the boat a 300-mile cruising range with a healthy reserve. A 230-horsepower, 4.3-liter V-6 gasoline engine is also available that will give the boat similar performance, the trade-off being lower initial cost for shorter service life of the gasoline engine.

It was no accident that the Striper was a perfect fit for fishing the waters of New England. The Crosby Yacht Yard started building boats in 1850, and by the time the first Striper hit the water nearly 100 years later, they were already famous for the many custom boats they had built. They began building the Wianno Senior one-design sailboat in 1914 and continue to so today. Wianno Seniors are very popular on Cape Cod,

This photograph came from the 1958 Crosby Striper brochure. Even though the Striper was conceived more than half a century ago, its real-world performance still surpasses that of the vast majority of boats in its size range.

and numerous families have kept the same boat for many generations. President John F. Kennedy's sailboat on display at the Kennedy Memorial Library is a Wianno Senior and it is still maintained by the Crosby Yard. The Striper hasn't yet achieved the same status as the Wianno as far as collectibility, but many Stripers stay in the family for generations, as well. Like Wianno owners, many Striper owners bring their boats back to the Crosby Yacht Yard each winter for storage and maintenance.

In 1962 the Crosby Yacht Yard displayed their latest Striper at the prestigious New York Boat Show, where it was a smashing success. This boat was then purchased by a Cape Cod gentleman who had served as a U.S. naval officer in World War II. He loved the boat and kept it for the rest of his life. After he passed away about eight years ago, his children inherited the boat. They knew how much he loved that boat, so to honor his memory, they brought the boat back to the Crosby Yard for a complete restoration. For the next eight years, the family enjoyed the use of the boat and meticulously cared for it. This Striper was perhaps the best-maintained wooden example in existence. But tragedy struck when this past December the storage shed where this boat and many others were stored burned to the ground. The beautiful boat was destroyed, along with many other craft, including 20 irreplaceable Wianno Seniors.

Crosby Stripers continue to be very popular fishing and "picnic" boats in use around Cape Cod and the Islands, but some Stripers have had unusual careers. J. Gregory Wheeler, a wooden boat builder from Marshfield, undertook the restoration of a 1957 vintage Striper during the winter of 1986-87. The boat had been stored out of the water at the Hingham Shipyard for many years and was in rough shape. When the boat arrived at Greg's shop, you could still see the faded Metropolitan District Commission emblem on the sides of the hull, with the words "Harbor Patrol" barely visible next to the emblem! Greg finished the restoration in 1987 and returned the boat to her very proud owner and civilian life.

These are not boats for the casual, first-time boat owner. The typical Striper owner is an experienced hand and in many cases has moved into a Striper after owning a larger boat. In the course of my research for this article, I had a conversation with Larry Zalis, a lawyer from Barnstable who owned and fished extensively from a Crosby Striper. Larry is a very experienced boater and serious angler, who is a licensed captain and an accredited marine surveyor. He owned a 1984 model, powered by a 100-horsepower diesel engine. He kept the boat in Centerville and fished all over Nantucket Sound, all around Martha's Vineyard and Nantucket and the rips of Monomoy Island for stripers, bluefish, fluke and sea bass. In his opinion the Crosby Striper is the best rough-water boat he has ever fished from. One of the many boats he owned prior to the Crosby Striper was a Tripp Angler, another bass boat with a reputation for seaworthiness. It is fair to say that he is in a position to offer a valid comparison.

As testamonial to this, one day Larry and his brother were heading out of West Bay to go fishing in 25-knot winds, and there was a large beam-sea running. Most boats under these conditions would be rolling onto their beam ends and would be very hard to control. Larry related how the Striper simply rose up over the oncoming waves and

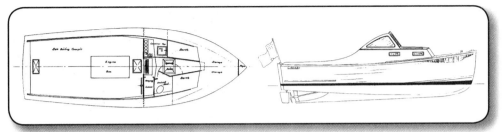

A true fisherman's craft that still offers creature comforts; there are few other boats that look so much at home in the waters of New England.

settled into the next trough without listing more than a few degrees, maintaining cruising speed all the while. Strong southwesterly winds and strong opposing tides can make Nantucket Sound a nasty place at times, and these are the conditions the Striper was designed to handle with ease.

Even though Larry didn't purchase his Striper brand-new from Crosby, he was very impressed with the support they gave him whenever he had any questions about the boat. Larry ranges far and wide from his home port in search of fish, and he told me that the 14-knot cruising speed of his Striper was just a little too slow for his liking so he sold the boat after hundreds of enjoyable hours fishing aboard her. He was quick to add that when he is ready to purchase another boat, it would be another Striper with the more powerful 200-horsepower diesel engine and the optional stern controls.

If you are looking to purchase a Crosby Striper, it is very unlikely you will find one for sale in the classified adds of most periodicals. Stripers are in high demand and they don't stay on the market very long. Your best source for used Stripers is the Crosby Yacht Yard brokerage. They will also be more than happy to build a brand-new one for you, equipped just about any way you can imagine. The joiner work and finish from the Crosby Yacht Yard are outstanding. When I asked how they achieved such a fine finish on their brightwork, Greg Eagan, Crosby president, told me it was a trade secret and left it at that!

The Crosby Striper is one of those timeless designs that will never go out of style and will always be the mark of a discriminating and knowledgeable boater. Even though the Striper was conceived more than half a century ago, its real world performance still surpasses that of the vast majority of boats in its size range. A true fisherman's craft that still offers creature comforts, there are few other boats that look so much at home in the waters of New England. ◄██►

Cuttyhunk Bass Boats
Captain Jim Nunes And The *Rudy J.*

By Dave Peros

When I was a senior in high school, my parents bought me a copy of Frank Woolner's *Modern Saltwater Sport Fishing*. As someone who knew of Mr. Woolner's reputation as editor-in-chief of *Saltwater Sportsman* magazine when it was still a fishing magazine devoted to the shorebound, moderate-income angler and, therefore, of great value to a young fishing nut such as myself, I regarded this gift of Mr. Woolner's work as a treasure. I spent hours poring over its pages, enthralled by his unique way of speaking and the evident saltiness of someone who had been there when it truly was "the good old days."

As someone who spent much of his life growing up on Cape Cod, where his fishing was pretty much limited to beaches he could reach by foot or bike, there was always mention in the history of Cape fishing a spot that held almost mythic proportions in my imagination: Cuttyhunk. From the tale of Charles Church's 73-pounder in 1913 to the trophy that Charlie Cinto caught in 1967, which tipped the scales at exactly the same number, this island was the place of legends. Cuttyhunk was synonymous with big fish and big water, and it remains that way today.

Mr. Woolner's book was filled with references to Cuttyhunk, as any reputable book should be if it even mentions the history of striped bass. But it was a picture of Captain Bob Smith's MacKenzie – Gray Cuttyhunk bass boat that caught my attention. I studied that picture for the longest time, burning every detail into my memory: the large swimming plugs hanging along the inside of the gunwales, the casting rods in vertical holders, the tillers fore and aft, the engine box amidships and the pile of big stripers along the port side of the deck.

As a kid, one of our neighbors in Popponesset, Mr. Bellavance, had a big, wide-open boat that I like to romance about today. Even though it was only a plywood hull, it still had the big engine box and the wide-open deck that I saw later in the photo of Captain Smith's *Susan B.* Mr. Bellavance's boat wasn't fast and it wasn't necessarily pretty compared to the boats we have today, but it was a fishing boat, and even though I only got to go out once or twice on it, I still think about it today and imagine what happened to it. Back then I thought of it as a Cuttyhunk bass boat, one of the finest kind.

Though Mr. Bellavance's boat was a seaworthy craft, I know now that she was no Cuttyhunker. Over the years, I have become more and more familiar with the term "Cuttyhunk bass boat" and have had the opportunity to meet people who know quite a bit about them, including Ed Koskella. Despite everything I had learned over the years, it was last winter and spring that I received my first proper schooling in Cuttyhunk bass fishing boats – and I emphasize the term "fishing." Captain John Christian, whom I had known for several years as the only charter captain out of the Falmouth area who specializes in fishing the Elizabeth Islands, hooked me up with Captain Jim Nunes, the last of the full-time charter captains who still bases his operation out of Cuttyhunk.

Getting the chance to meet and talk to Captain Nunes was a very big deal to me since Cuttyhunkers are notoriously reticent, and the captains who make a living chasing striped bass around the island are even more so.

During our conversations, Captain Nunes told about his experiences with Captain Bob Smith, whose boat I had imagined working Sow and Pigs when I first saw that photo of the *Susan B*. Captain Nunes had gone to high school with Charlie Tilton Jr., whose family had lived on Cuttyhunk for generations. Just as they do today, Cuttyhunkers have a school that takes their children through grade eight and then they make arrangements to send them to a mainland high school. In Charlie Jr.'s case, that meant Dartmouth High School, and there he became buddies with Jim Nunes. They remain best friends to this day.

During his high school years, Jim spent his summers with Charlie, Jr. out on Cuttyhunk and "we used to sit out on the docks and watch the charter captains come in: Bob Smith, Coot Hall, Bob Tilton, Lloyd Bosworth, Nat Gifford, Frank Sabatowski, Charlie Haag, A. P. Tilton, Carlton Veeder and Charlie's dad, Charlie Sr. That was probably when there were more Cuttyhunk captains working the area full time than at any other. It was really special being able to spend time on Cuttyhunk and I really came to love the island."

For the Cuttyhunk captains of that time, the MacKenzie-Gray bass boat and versions made by other builders were the end result of an evolution that started with wooden skiffs that Bob Tilton and Coot Hall used. As Captain Nunes recalls, those Dodge skiffs were about 16 to 18 feet long, and while they were strong boats, they were also very wet.

Eventually, Ernie MacKenzie came up with a hull design that would set the standard for boats that were used to work the waters around Cuttyhunk and the rest of the Elizabeths, as well as other spots where big water required a boat that had the right feel where rips and currents roared.

As Ed Koskella wrote in a story in *On The Water*, "At that time, the stripers were abundant and the sport fishery was vibrant. *Ginger* was a response to the demand for a strong, buoyant and stable vessel to work the rips and rocks of the reefs where the fish fed. Ernie, or Mac as all those who knew him called him, built the first Cuttyhunker in Marion, Massachusetts. She was lapstrake over sawn white oak frames, all bolted and riveted together in a method of traditional boat building that was both pragmatic and beautiful."

It was 1944 when Ernie MacKenzie built *Ginger,* and when you look at a picture of her today, it's apparent what he had in mind when building her. With plenty of freeboard and a V-hull that was brought to much less of a dead rise in the stern than in modern fiberglass boats, the MacKenzie

design pushed and moved water out of its way in a manner that you have to see and feel to appreciate. Unlike designs that carry much of the flare of their bow all the way to the stern, Cuttyhunk bass boats were meant to sit deeply and comfortably in heavy seas, without all of the rolling and twitching that you see in contemporary hulls, especially those built in glass. As Captain Nunes likes to describe it, "When I run the *Rudy J.* in heavy seas, she goes right through and sits right, while those glass boats are bobbing about like corks." The heavy keel and incredibly strong system of ribs, battens and 1-inch thick planking allowed the Cuttyhunk bass boat to absorb unforeseen meetings with the reefs and boulders that dot the Elizabeths and other favored fishing grounds such as Devil's Bridge and Gay Head, most of which would rip out the bottoms of your average boat, or at least split its seams wide open.

Even though Captain Nunes became quite familiar during his years on Cuttyhunk with the bass boat design that was favored by the charter-boat skippers, the economic realities of being a young man just starting out in the 1950s saw him own two other boats before moving up to the *Rudy J.* A Jafco skiff was first, and later on came a Silverton, both wide-open plywood hulls with inboard power. Eventually, Captain Nunes did some chartering out of the Silverton, "which was a good boat for tossing eel rigs, which is how we used to fish back then. I will tell you this: Even though I trusted those boats and had fished with Charlie's father a number of times out on the Pigs, it wasn't for two or three years before I tried fishing there by myself. I see guys nowadays who go charging out there with no idea of what they're doing and they don't have the proper respect for the area."

There are more and more anglers fishing the rips around the Elizabeth Islands by anchoring and chunking, a method that allows an angler to get away with less of a boat. But that type of fishing was anathema to the Cuttyhunk captains Nunes knew, and he regards it the same way; for them, fishing meant casting, drifting and trolling. Captain Nunes knew that when he elected to become a full-time charter captain, he needed a hull made for holding steady and secure in a rip line while lines were played out, and drifts were set up and down in currents running deep and strong.

Nunes was plenty familiar with Captain Smith and the *Susan B.*, regarding him as a mentor.

"I'll tell you, Bob Smith was one tough fisherman. He taught me almost everything I knew about fishing back then, not because he told me, but because he talked about fishing and I listened. People always insisted on asking those old Cuttyhunkers questions, but I kept my mouth shut and my ears open and picked things up. And fishing with Charlie's father was also an education in itself; he'd take us out when he didn't have a charter and that really helped."

Nunes certainly admired the MacKenzie design, which eventually became more familiar as the MacKenzie-Gray Cuttyhunk bass boat after Ernie MacKenzie hooked up with Al Gray for the second time in the 1960s, when they formed MacKenzie Gray Boat Company in Taunton. Still, it was another bass boat owned by Captain Lloyd Bosworth that caught Nunes' eye and would eventually lead him to become skipper of the *Rudy J.*

The boat that Lloyd Bosworth brought to Cuttyhunk was built by Enoch Winslow. Jim Nunes knew he had to have one.

"It was all teak on top and even though that proved to be impractical in terms of upkeep with all of the hard fishing he did, Lloyd Bosworth never had a bad word to say about that boat. Eventually, Lloyd sold it to Walter Ketchum and had Mr. Winslow build another one for him. After a while, Walter sold Lloyd's old boat to Charlie Tilton Sr., who was Lloyd's father-in-law. In 1966 when I decided to take up chartering full time, I went to see Mr. Winslow himself."

Already in his 80s when Nunes looked him up, Winslow was working out of a little garage in Mattapoisett that once served as a printing press, and Nunes recalls "it had really low ceilings. He had this little office and he had a hull already started when I went to see him. He had started it out as a cabin cruiser, but it was still a bare hull and Mr. Winslow decided to sell it to me."

Of course, as a proper Cuttyhunk captain of the time, Nunes had no use for cabins or any of the other ancillary equipment that eventually adorned what folks lump together as Cuttyhunk bass boats. There would be no windshields, forward rails, steering wheels or canvas; no, what Jim Nunes wanted was the wide-open boat that he had grown to cherish, with only a spray rail at the aft end of the forward deck, an inboard engine and box, and tillers fore and aft.

Still, there was the matter of money, and when Nunes asked how much, Mr. Winslow replied, "'Jimmy, I'm going to guess around $5,000 or $5,500'. And I said, 'O.K., go ahead.' There was no contract and all of this was done on a handshake. I gave him a deposit and over time I kept paying him as I got the money. I remember when we were finished and he delivered the boat, Mr. Winslow gave me $400 or $500 back and said, 'Jimmy, it ended up costing less than I thought, so here's some of your money back.' That's the kind of man Mr. Winslow was."

With the hull almost completed, Nunes pitched in and helped Mr. Winslow with setting the deck planking and finishing the rest of the interior, but Nunes laughs and says, "When it came to finishing that boat, I was as rough as they come. Mr. Winslow could do more with just the most basic hand tools than these guys today can do with all of their fancy power equipment. I remember when I was trying to set the kick rail along the inside of the gunwale where it meets the deck and I was cussing because I couldn't get it right. Mr. Winslow said, 'What's the matter, Jimmy?' and he came over and told me to hold it in place. Then he took a pencil and ran it along the deck, took the rail over to a bench and cut it along the scribe marks he had made, and it fit perfectly, as if it had been made for there."

Even after the boat was launched in Mattapoisett and Captain Nunes proudly ran her over to her berth on Cuttyhunk, Mr. Winslow wasn't through with the *Rudy J.*: "When I got it to Cuttyhunk and let the hull swell up, there was still a leak around the transom. I called Mr. Winslow and told him I'd bring it back to Mattapoisett, but he insisted on coming over and he did, with his tool box in hand. I ran her up on a beach and she sat there on her keel and Mr. Winslow found that he had left out two fasteners. Well, he fixed it right there and when I asked him how much I owed him, he said, 'Jimmy, you don't owe me nothing,' and that was that."

The Cuttyhunk designs are well known for their ability to move through the water rather than banging about, and as Koskella pointed out, "Two factors probably contribute to this. One is the fact they were built of naturally buoyant materials with strong vibration and sound attenuating qualities. The bottom also absorbed water into its pores as the season progressed. This accumulated weight down low adds tremendously to their stability."

Every year when the *Rudy J.* is moved off its crib and relaunched, Captain Nunes lets it sit at its dock in Padanaram to allow its bottom to swell, but as he carefully points out, "Even after a couple of weeks, you won't find more than a tablespoon of water in the hull." Whatever water is needed to swell things tight is kept at a minimum and even then it becomes part of the *Rudy J.*'s sweet ride.

While Lloyd Bosworth's boat was outfitted with hardware that he made himself, Captain Nunes made due with fittings he was able to buy at local marine stores. However, when it came to purchasing power for the *Rudy J.*, he went right to the source.

"Back then, all the Cuttyhunkers got their motors from Art Gell in Somerset. I went to see him, told him what I wanted, and he said, 'O.K., no problem.' It was that simple. We used straight 6 Crusaders and I made sure I had all the spare parts for it since they were hard to come by on the island, and you always wanted to make sure you could get your motor running if you wanted to go fishing. I had two heads and I'd swap one for the other every year. Eventually, planing them down made them too thin, so I repowered with a Chevy 308, which is a small V-8. Peter Chase bought the old Crusader and, from what I hear, it's still running."

At 24 1/2 feet long with an 8 1/2-foot beam at the stern, the *Rudy J.* weighs just over 6,000 pounds. Her transom is 31 inches from waterline to the top rail, and she has a full 4- to 5-inch oak keel running down from the bow to where the flare of the skeg that protects the prop begins. Fully loaded, the *Rudy J.* draws about 18 inches aft. With the 308 V-8, she cruises at 2,600 r.p.m., which makes about 14 knots. Her top end is 4,400 r.p.m., but Captain Nunes clearly points out that "she isn't built for speed. In fact, if you run her too hard, she has a tendency to wobble. She works with the water rather than trying to fly over the top of it."

Like many of the other Cuttyhunk captains, Jim Nunes had named his bass boat after a family member. Bob Smith had named his after his daughter Susan, and Charlie Tilton Sr. named his Dorsal, Jr. after his wife Doris, daughter Sally and son Charlie Jr. The *Rudy J.* was named after Jim's father, Rudolph Joseph Nunes.

"My father was my best friend in the world; I owe so much to him. We were close to buying a boat together when he died, and there was no question in my mind what I would call the boat Enoch Wilson built for me."

Despite the affection Captain Nunes had for the *Rudy J.*, he, like most charter captains, eventually turned his eyes toward a bigger boat. Years later, in 1978, he purchased a 26-foot Fortier. With the emergence of fiberglass boat building in the 70s, many takeoffs on the Cuttyhunk bass boat, molded in glass, came on the market. There were boats like Dyers, which were always glass, while boat builders like Brownell moved more slowly into the new material, but the boat that caught the eye of many a bass boat faithful was the one made by Roger Fortier and his son, Ronnie. As Captain Nunes pointed out, "Roger and Ronnie are the most honest people you'd want to meet in the boat-building business. The Fortiers became very popular and it took over a year for me to get my new boat. Even today, while other boat builders cut down on their quality once their boats get popular, the Fortiers still make their boats as well or even better than when they started."

Eventually, as much as Captain Nunes liked his Fortier, which he also named the *Rudy J.*, he soon came to a realization: she wasn't the old *Rudy J.* Captain Nunes began his quest to get the *Rudy J.* back, but her owner could not be swayed to sell for some time.

When Captain Nunes finally realized his dream of owning the Rudy J. again, he found that "in another year or two, you could have taken a match to her. Even if you take the best care of a wooden boat, the bottom gets tender after about thirty years and you're looking at replanking her. In this case, the Rudy J. was in horrible shape and she needed a lot of work."

The man that Captain Nunes turned to in undertaking this task was Chris Gray, the son of Al Gray, who was Ernie MacKenzie's partner all those years ago. Chris had to strip the bottom entirely and check out the oak ribs to make sure they were all sound, eventually finding that two needed replacement. Chris also added a beam that he ran down the interior over the keel area that helped stiffen the *Rudy J.* even more.

From there it was a matter of replanking the bottom with new mahogany using silicone brass fasteners. Captain Nunes also decided that the old plank deck and batten interiors of the gunwales needed upgrading, so they stripped the interior out and replaced the deck and interior walls with plywood, covered over on all sides with fiberglass. He also thought of replacing the two 25-gallon fuel tanks he keeps in the transom with one tank underneath the deck, but decided that the *Rudy J.* was designed for the weight as it was distributed originally. There also wasn't a pressing need for more fuel capacity, since on 28 to 30 gallons "I can go from Padanaram to the Pigs and then over to Gay Head, back over to Quicks, and make the return trip to drop off a party at Padanaram."

"Chris has those same kinds of skills that people like Enoch Wilson did," Jim explained. "He's the best damn wooden boat builder I know of today. He can really work with his hands and it was really something to see the *Rudy J.* looking like she did when Mr. Winslow built her." Nunes also admitted that the bottom replacement and interior upgrade cost almost three times as much as the original *Rudy J.* did.

While many people cite the issue of upkeep as a major reason for buying a fiberglass boat, Captain Nunes is convinced that "if you keep an old wooden boat up, there's not much more maintenance than fiberglass. When I pull her in the fall, I lightly sand the bottom and put on a thin coat of bottom paint. In the spring, I put another coat of bottom paint on and paint the rest of the hull. Then I put her in the water and let her swell up and paint the inside. It takes about six or seven good days for me to complete the work, and if I have any problems during the season, I take care of them right away."

Captain Nunes puts about 2,000 hours a season on the *Rudy J.* "I used to put a new engine in every three years, but with the new Chevy I don't have to do that. I do change the belts and hoses every season and I know how to handle any repairs that come around while I'm out on Cuttyhunk, unless it requires major machinery. I know the sound of that engine so well that I run it by ear; I can tell you exactly what the r.p.m. are by the sound it makes. I always fish her from the rear tiller and very rarely even run her from the front tiller. She doesn't sound the same from up there. And I would never have any boat other than one that had a tiller because you have total control at all times."

In the long run, Captain Jim Nunes acknowledged that "there's a certain nostalgia about having a wooden Cuttyhunk bass boat that is built specifically for fishing, like the old-timers used when I was younger. I don't know what it is; they look so nice and I love to just look at them. There's a club that comes down here and they all own MacKenzies, of all shapes and sizes. It's great to see all of those MacKenzies because they're wooden, but I still like the wide-open ones the best."

Captain Nunes particularity about old Cuttyhunk bass boats was most clearly brought out to me when I ran a picture of a contemporary fiberglass version all gussied up in an article that I wrote about him last year. Guys in the coffee shop in Padanaram kidded him a bit and he gave me heck about my indiscretion, although in a manner more akin to a teacher telling a student who he believes should know better.

Captain Nunes' proudly points out that "all these years I've never had to turn around in the Rudy J. I've gone through some bad stuff before, but when other folks have had to give in, we've made it out to go fishing. I know that if she pounds it's because I've headed her into the seas wrong. Just this fall when I brought her back to Padanaram to pull her for the season, there were seven- to eight-footers and I had to go over to Mishaum Point to swing around and come in, something I haven't had to do before. Still, I wouldn't have wanted to be in any other boat and that's the truth."

The Moon In June
– Myth Or Magic?

By Captain Charley Soares

B ooking a June moon trip with a topnotch Cuttyhunk skipper has always been about as likely as drawing the inside face card for a royal straight flush. It didn't happen often and when it did, it was usually the result of someone else's misfortune. Famous Cuttyhunk guides seldom if ever advertised trips, at least not for June, because those dates were never available. The same fares that fished the "Moon In June" in 1959 booked the exact time slots for the 1960s years in advance, many paying a premium for the probability of hooking up with a record linesider.

I fished that very same June moon in my own boat but never in the traditional manner of dragging a huge swimming plug on wire along the wave-washed boulders that form Sow and Pigs Reef because it was too dangerous. Certainly the jagged boulders lurking just below or breaking the surface were a problem, but they were nothing akin to being rammed or driven onto the rip by the guides. This was their domain, and they were ferociously custodial about protecting it from trespassers. If that sounds like an embellishment, just ask Charlie Cinto, who captured the first modern-day 73-pound striper, or Jay Vee, who caught numerous 50s on the Pigs. Anyone who fished with Sabby, Smitty or Haag understood the dangers to anyone who intended to troll a plug along what the guides considered their private domain. The competition between the guides was so intense that if you happened to witness the way they acted toward and treated one another, you'd have understood what they might administer to an interloper. There were some huge bass hooked, landed and lost during the brief window of the June full moon, but larger stripers were caught during the remainder of the season under little if any moonlight.

This 30-pound bass was caught in less than four feet of water on a pitch-black night. If there were a moon the fish would not have moved in this close to the shallows.

You could ask 20 prominent striper fishermen and receive 20 different answers as to why the June moon was always considered so advantageous. However, for this piece I'll provide my personal observations along with that of some individuals who broke the magic 60-pound barrier, as well as some of the most famous of all the Cuttyhunk guides, including one who initially tried to run me off the island. After he suspended his efforts to drive me onto the rocks and ram me, I ran an errand for him and he actually began to treat me civilly, even confiding in me after I became his personal gofor between Cuttyhunk and the mainland.

May has always been one of the most productive months for catching trophy bass in relatively shallow inland waterways, where they follow the scent of the spawning herring up into the head of rivers and salt marshes. June is when the big spawners arrive off the coast of Rhode Island and Massachusetts, stopping to feed at Block Island and Cuttyhunk before moving farther eastward on their spring migration. Even if I could have arranged for a trip with one of the famed Cuttyhunk skippers, I would never have been able to afford it. It wasn't that you had to be a high roller to fish the June moon, but it was usually businessmen or perhaps an ironworker like Charlie Cinto who banked all of his vacation and overtime earnings to finance his trips.

One of our bass club members owned a Brownell bass boat, as well as a lucrative business, but he was usually too busy to use his own boat. He sold the boat and began booking charters with the top Cuttyhunk skippers, and he informed me that he came out way ahead financially and enjoyed the fishing a lot more with a lot fewer headaches over the problems associated with owning a wooden boat. Over the years I've learned there is only one thing worse than not having a boat, and that's owning a boat and not having the time to use it. This businessman was a sharpie, and he learned a great deal about fishing with the best of the best, but he never overcame his fear of fishing nights on his own. He referred to my little inboard bass boat as a "catcher" because she was very quiet and left a tiny footprint. One late afternoon, when he and a fellow entrepreneur came alongside to jig a tidal rip, their loud V-8 bass boat with underwater exhaust spooked the fish while my quiet little rig moved among the schools catching doubles on every pass.

After that episode he made several trips with me jigging that rip where we caught stripers from 3 to 30 pounds. But the big trip would be a three-day June moon trip to Cuttyhunk that he and his buddy had booked with one of the legendary guides a year in advance. This guy was no rookie – during a June moon trip he fished several years before, he counted nine 50-pound-plus bass unloaded from six island charter boats; one was his own 55-pounder. In previous years he had won three of our club's tourneys with bass of 56, 55 and 53 pounds, all caught during the celebrated moon. But this year was different.

They fished the early evening of the night before the full moon, jigging up bass from 12 to 20 pounds until the sun set and the action quit. That night they fished the famous rip at Sow and Pigs and did not catch a single heavy bass, while another charter boat fished Gay Head and recorded a solitary 30-pounder under the moonlight. Every morning before the sun came up they had fast and furious fishing, wire-lining bass from schoolies to the mid-20-pound class. But on their three-day stay, they did not catch a trophy while the moon shone or much of anything after daylight or moonrise. Most sports treated to that kind of action would say they had experienced great fishing, yet these men were spoiled. Past outings had raised unrealistically high expectations, even for those days when 40-pound bass were common and there was almost always a 50 and an occasional 60 brought to the scales.

The 28-pounder brought back to our weigh station was his largest fish, and it was evident he was extremely disappointed. Meanwhile during that same period, we fished every evening into the nighttime and caught stripers from 14 to 33 pounds. Completely unbeknownst to us, the men who we believed were "slaying" the bass were not privy to the same type of action.

The more affluent members so accustomed to owning bragging rights to fantastic catches could not believe they were bested by a couple of kids fishing from a tiny bass boat in their own back yard. It wasn't until the weighmaster read the affidavits and current standings at the club meeting, along with our standings in R.J. Schaefer Fishing Contest, that they came to grasp the reality of the situation. The point is, there was more at work there than just being with a famous guide at a legendary rip while the full moon shone in June.

Then there were the times when I had no doubt about the effect of the June moon. Three days after another June full moon the same gentleman was aboard my boat and we were fishing the waters off Westport Harbor. We took three bass to 22 pounds before sunset when the fish turned off. We fished all the way west to Sakonnet Point, then turned back, fishing every piece of productive habitat without so much as a sniff. Later that night, as we made the turn toward the harbor to call it quits, a piece of the moon slipped over the horizon casting a pale white glow on the water. I moved out to a shallow boulder field, and on the third cast my deckmate was into a heavy fish. The moon began to climb into the ebony night sky, turning the seascape from black to pale light. By the time we ran out of live eels there were nine big linesiders lying on either side of the motor box. For years I'd been trying to determine the effect of celestial events and tides, and the value of stealth, but there was no doubt in my mind that there were fish present that night, perhaps in many of the places we'd tried, and the appearance of that moon turned them on.

Is the June moon really worthy of all the hype it receives? In my opinion, probably not.

This bass fell for a white plug on a moonlit night. We use light colors for bright nights and dark colors for moonless nights.

While June has always been a very good month for my clients and me, I scored a 58-pound 8-ounce striper on a dark July night and gaffed a 60 during that month for a mate during the dark period of the new moon. Despite the success I've enjoyed in June and July, it's been the periods around the September and October moons that have been the most productive for me.

There are advantages and disadvantages to fishing various phases of the moon, no matter the month, and they are amplified by full-and new-moon periods. If there are less experienced anglers on board, the experienced fisherman comes to realize that the stronger currents usually result in a certain amount of tension in those who are not as comfortable as we who work striper habitat in the darkness of a new moon. Fishing at night is certainly not for everyone. The familiar daytime shoreline is an alien place after sunset when ranges disappear and judging distances becomes more difficult. The once-familiar passage through the clumps or boulders disappears and all there is in front of you is a wall of rocks and white water. Good electronics certainly help, but my bass routes do not contain a single location where a straight course will take me from the fishing grounds to the harbor, so familiarity with numerous ranges and highly developed night vision are imperative.

From a fishing perspective, perhaps the most difficult problem to overcome when there is no moonlight is glowing phosphorescence, which can make 20-pound-test line look like a brilliant hawser being drawn through the water, and a slow-moving plug takes on the appearance of a glowing miniature submarine. Fire in the water does not make it impossible to catch fish, it just takes more patience and skill to present your baits in a natural fashion.

One old-timer who was generous with his counsel referred to the new moon as the "black moon." We learned to catch fishing during these black periods by being extremely quiet and employing the highest degree of stealth. If you've fished during these times you may have had the experience of finding a school of fish and watching what appeared to be luminescent flashes streaking in all directions. Those are schools of predators looking for any trace of forage moving and creating even the slightest bit of light. Late one very dark night I eased the boat into a cove along Ocean Drive in Newport and we were greeted with a brilliant light show as a huge school of stripers scattered. The bass had been working over a large concentration of forage fish they had pushed up against the beach. After cutting the engine and waiting for things to quiet down, we drifted among the fish, which we could see by the trails they left in their wakes. We began picking out fish and casting eels in front of them. That night we caught fish on almost every cast because we allowed the eels to sink without any retrieve and the bass attacked them with a vengeance. Had we cast the eels and begun retrieving, the lures and lines would have lit up like comets and the bass would have shied from them. That night I understood what is meant by "shooting fish in a barrel."

When we returned to the dock, the four other boats that left the harbor with us had returned and the anglers complained they had no luck except just before dusk because the fire in the water made fishing impossible. In order to be successful you have to adjust your tactics to the conditions. Just because there is no moonlight does not mean predators don't or won't eat; they just change their tactics and you must do the same to consistently catch fish.

Look at any calendar or the *Eldridge Tide and Pilot Book* and you will discover there are not many nights when there isn't at least some moonlight. Over the years we've caught trophy bass during the full moon and gaffed stripers up to 60 pounds in the inky darkness of the black moon. There are some very good skippers out there, some known for their consistent production and others for their tenacity and integrity. Captain Fred Bowman of Bottom Line Charters is famous for both. In 2002 he guided his parties to two 50s and six 40s, all in the month of June. In 2001 it was five 50s and a like number of 40s, but here's the kicker: the majority of these fish came in the daytime hours. Three of my own 50s have come during the daytime, two of them on eels and one on an umbrella rig at 11:30 in the morning. My recent research resulted in twenty-seven 50-pound-plus stripers that I could verify for the 2002 season, and guess what? Not a single one was landed on the night of the full moon.

The days and nights around the moon in June have always been one of the most productive periods to land a trophy or record fish, no question about it. Just don't fall for the idea that it is the only time to take a trophy striper. ◄▬

Trolling Etiquette And Other Considerations

By Captain Mike Hogan

Saltwater sport fishing is a passion for many, hobby for some, an excuse to be on the water for others and a source of income for a few. Regardless of where your classification may fall, it is very easy to get hooked on the excitement of landing a trophy-size bass or experiencing the thrill of a deviously hard-fighting bluefish. More and more anglers join the fishing ranks each year in their pursuit of fishing adventures. Unfortunately, living in New England affords us only so many months of decent boating weather. Therefore, it can be guaranteed that many anglers will make it a priority to hit popular fishing destinations on beautiful summer mornings, especially on weekends. But as with circling through a parking lot during the holiday season, tensions heat up when countless boats are fishing the same area.

Many of us spend a lot of time and consideration thinking about how and where to catch trophy fish. However, due to increased inshore fishing traffic, boat rage has been cropping up more and more in recent years. Thus, it is important to think about how we can fish with a little more emphasis on etiquette. The season is simply too short to have a day ruined by confrontations with others due to inadvertent crowding, wasteful techniques and the misunderstanding of certain fishing scenarios.

Although this year's summer season has passed, it is perhaps a good time to stop and look at a few basic principles of inshore fishing etiquette for gamefish in our area. After all, there are only a finite amount of "hot spots" out there; we should work as a team so that we all return to the docks with smiles.

Picture a beautiful Saturday morning in June as you arrive at your targeted fishing destination. Perhaps you're fishing along one of Wasque's many rips, just southeast of Martha's Vineyard. You notice that the conditions are perfect. A nice rip has formed and terns swoop down periodically, grabbing at small squid pushed to the surface by large striped bass. With two wire lines rigged for jigging recently let out, you slowly sidle up to the rip. As you swing from left to right several yards in front of the first wave, you hook up! Suddenly, the other rod goes down, too. You watch proudly some moments later as two nice keepers swing over the gunwales.

As you set out the lines again, you turn the boat and reposition back to your favorite nook on the rip. However, this time you're not alone. Another boat has arrived and is fishing in "your spot"! He is also hooking up. Reluctant to lose the spot, the new boat continues to hover in front of the rip. You even notice a bass "surfing" behind the boat, as the force of the tide pulling against the fish brings it to the surface. Short of bringing your vessel to ramming speed, you are stuck until he moves off.

Crowding is perhaps the quickest way to upset your fishing neighbor. One might also go so far as to say that crowding is the most frequently practiced etiquette violation. Unfortunately, people sometimes forget that the water doesn't belong to just one boat. Though it is nice to have free rein in an area, there are indeed times when fishermen have no choice but to cooperate with each other in close quarters.

In the "rip hog" scenario described above, issues arose because two boats were unable to fish on one particular portion of the rip. However, it was indeed possible for these two boats to fish successfully and in harmony. The solution could have been found by creating a circular trolling pattern, allowing each angler an equal opportunity to share the excellent fishing. (The circular trolling pattern also works well in other tight areas such as sandbars, boulder fields, channels, wrecks and over holes.) While fishing a rip, many boats often slide back and forth from left to right against the tide, allowing their lures to hang along the edge and through the rip itself. Rotation will allow a few boats to troll effectively until fish are hooked or the sequence allows another boat to move in. It is easy to do, and not much fishing time is lost. An example of this method is shown below:

In a trolling rotation, the lead boat hovers against the tide in front of the rip until hooked up or after a reasonable amount of time slides away so another boat can slip in. In either event, the lead boat should veer off the spot, allowing others to move in. The size of the general area will dictate how many boats can fish. Concentration is required in all close-quarter situations. It is easy to inadvertently cut another boat off when focusing on the task at hand, catching fish. Be mindful of others. Don't be a rip hog!

How do you know when you are too close to somebody? The generally accepted rule of thumb is that if you have to restrict distance while casting to avoid another boat, you're too close. Although this guideline may be applicable in many situations, it may not be entirely practical on a busy morning. On the other hand, if you are able to politely lean over and ask for a little Grey Poupon, you are definitely too close. Use your best judgment here and make sure you're considerate of others. If you accidentally cut somebody off or approach too closely, an apologetic wave goes a long way. It is important to remember that everybody makes mistakes. There is no need to fly off the handle if you are on the receiving end of an error. After all, experiencing a fun day of fishing on the water is our goal.

When approaching a spot, do so with courtesy, reducing your speed significantly before arriving. Slow down at least 100 yards outside the group of boats. Once on scene, the next step is to assess the situation. What methods are people using to catch fish? Are boats trolling, drifting or at anchor? Which way is the tide running? Where is the wind coming from? Are fish on top or down deep? It is essential to ask yourself these questions before you begin.

Try to understand the methods people are using to catch fish. If there is an informal pattern, follow it. Trolling against the general flow will make fishing difficult for everybody. Do not let out so much line that it is difficult for another angler to judge how far back your lures are. Generally speaking, much more than 130 feet of line is unnecessary unless you are fishing with wire in very deep water with strong currents. An angler experienced in the art of trolling also knows not to cut directly in front of another boat so that it has to stop in order to avoid running over lines. The same holds true when passing from behind.

In certain situations, you might need to adjust your game plan a little. For example, picture arriving at Quicks Hole, along the Elizabeth Islands, and after asking yourself the above questions, you notice a group of boats at anchor just behind the green can where you intended to fish. It would be a bad idea to let lines out and start trolling in the same area, according to your original plan. (Silly as it may sound, this happens enough so that it's worth mentioning.) If you're committed to trolling, try to find structure in the immediate area rather than trying to weave your way around your neighbors. Not only is this an easy way to create tangles, you can also be disturbing the school of fish that boats are focused on - certainly not your quickest route to making new friends.

When all else fails, one might decide that, "When in Rome, do as the Romans." If this is the case, approaching a group of boats at anchor with the intent of doing it yourself requires similar forethought to the conditions described above. Approach from the upwind or up-tide side. Once in position, discreetely release your anchor, allowing out enough line to fall into your desired location ahead or alongside of the existing boats. Anchoring too closely beside or behind another boat is considered poor etiquette, as you will be sitting above where another is trying to fish. The courteous angler will be mindful of the lay of the existing fishermen at anchor and not crowd another's space.

Similar principles hold true for approaching boats that are drift-fishing. Enter where boats are beginning their drift. Avoid stopping to fish directly ahead of somebody who is up-tide or upwind as you might interfere with his fishing. In certain situations, boats drift at different speeds. It is always considered courteous to approach drifting boats from upwind or up-tide. This will also help you avoid a collision course with others who may be drifting at different speeds.

Excitement and adrenaline often get the best of people when fish start breaking. Etiquette can go right out the window. I personally experienced this last August when the bonito first arrived in Vineyard Sound. Due to the numerous reports pointing to Hedge Fence, just south of East Chop, there were so many boats in the area it seemed like we were at the blessing of the fleet.

After about a half-hour of trolling small deep-running plugs, fish started appearing with the tide. Although scattered in small groups, the bonito meant business, jumping clear out of the water and busting furiously. Unfortunately, my fishing neighbors meant business, too. Each time the school started jumping, boats would rush at the fish, seemingly at full throttle. I wasn't sure what was going to happen once they actually got there. To this day I chuckle whenever I picture the vision of four bows all pointing at each other, forming a circle, with only one or two fish left to actually jump. No casts were made, as there wasn't room to do so.

Aside from the obvious difficulties associated with many boats chasing fish around in a haphazard manner, the fish will grow wary, resulting in scattered fish that are less excited by what you have to offer. When chasing breaking fish, remember that they are usually on the move. Anticipate where they are heading and try to intercept them. Plowing into the school kills the fishing for everyone and will result in a significant etiquette violation if you directly ruin an opportunity for someone else.

Avoid the throttle-and-cast madness by studying the general movements of breaking fish as you analyze the wind and tide direction around structure. Often, it is easy to discern a predictable pattern. Once you can make a reasonable guess, hold tight in the "fish zone" and only modest repositioning will be required as they reappear. Though this technique requires a certain degree of self-control, it can pay off. The ability to predict where fish will move next results in easier fishing, increased hookups and less frustration.

It's very easy to become frustrated with others on the water who seemingly lack consideration of the fishing community. A motor vessel pushing a barge while making its way through a channel while you try to fish is an annoyance that may sound familiar. But as we all know, we all have certain rules of the road to follow. In places where large craft pass through a major channel, often with strong tides, specific rules of the road must be followed. By fishing in highly traversed areas, you acknowledge certain challenges. Contending with a large wake here and there and moving out of the way are examples. Etiquette here means keeping a watchful eye for general traffic in order to quickly move out of the way. If you find yourself getting agitated while fishing in or near a busy right-of-way, it is time to move. Life is too short to have a day of fishing ruined. Experienced anglers only fish in high-traffic zones during off-peak times when general boat traffic is minimal.

Approaching an area: Approach an area slowly as you assess the situation. Ask yourself the following questions: What are the conditions like? Are boats trolling, drifting or at anchor? Be courteous of those who are already fishing. Try to go with the flow rather than disrupt the group.

Always follow the general rules of the road: When traffic increases, boats will inevitably cross paths. Two very important rules to remember while fishing: 1) Boats over your right bow have right-of-way. Make your change of course and give way well ahead of time, don't wait until the last possible moment. 2) When approaching another boat head on, pass it with your port side facing its port side.

Hooked fish: Always yield to an angler with a fish on, even if it means reeling in your lines.

Arriving and leaving the fishing grounds: Tread lightly. Come and go slowly. Always allow at least 100 yards for a comfort zone. Boats zipping every which way can put down the fish.

Rigging: What is everybody else doing? Try not to use excessive rigging that will easily tangle with others. Remember that too much line out will make it hard for others to anticipate when it is safe to turn.

Courteous clearance: Try not to crowd another angler so that it is difficult for him to maneuver.

Very small areas: Leave very small areas to first-comers. There are indeed some spots that are too small for more than one boat at a time. Usually this will be in a shallow water area.

Replace lost gear: Accidents do happen. In addition to your apology, always offer replacement of equipment if a mishap is your fault. Understand when it is someone else's mishap.

Working structure with many boats: Don't be a rip hog! Form a circular pattern in order to share a small area. Often, more than one boat can fish a defined area.

Breaking fish: Avoid crashing through breaking fish, as this will push them down. Try anticipating their movements in order to intercept the school.

Be aware of your boating environment, and practice common sense and good manners. In stepping down from my soapbox, I hope I have left behind some general thoughts and considerations that are useful. Tight lines everyone! ◄━

The End

If you would like to learn more about fishing in New England, check out these other fine books published by *On The Water*.

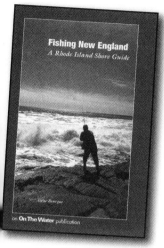 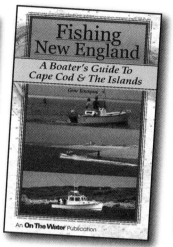 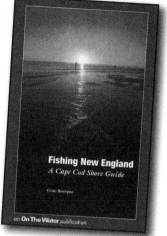

| **Fishing New England – A Rhode Island Shore Guide** | **Fishing New England – A Boater's Guide To Cape Cod & The Islands** | **Fishing New England – A Cape Cod Shore Guide** |

Rhode Island is the smallest state in the union, but with 384 miles of tidal shoreline, the saltwater fishing possibilities are almost endless. *Fishing New England, A Rhode Island Shore Guide* lists over 50 shore-fishing locations for everyone from those with families and small children to the dedicated surfcaster. Where and when to fish each spot, along with detailed maps, driving directions and access information, is included. Local experts provide additional background on techniques, history and fishing strategy.

Rock piles and rips, shallow sand flats and estuaries, the waters around Cape Cod, Martha's Vineyard, Nantucket and the Elizabeth Islands offer a wealth of possibilities to the angler. Whether you prefer bouncing bait along the bottom for fluke or scup, want to tangle with feisty bluefish or striped bass or have set your sights on the ultimate prize in these legendary waters, bluefin tuna, this book will tell you where to start your quest. You'll also learn some of the techniques used by local experts to take trophy fish and even find a few of their special spots not found on any chart. *Fishing New England - A Boater's Guide To Cape Cod & The Islands* will put you on the fish!

For the first time, anglers have a comprehensive guide to shore-fishing locations along one of the most productive and scenic fishing destinations in the world, Cape Cod, Massachusetts. From the Cape Cod Canal to Provincetown, *Fishing New England, A Cape Cod Shore Guide* profiles over 40 spots, including information on when and where to fish them, detailed maps and directions, and sidebars on techniques and the rich history of sport fishing on the Cape.

On The Water, LLC • Falmouth, MA • www.OnTheWater.com